THE LEGAL WORD BOOK

Compiled by
Frank S. Gordon and Thomas M.S. Hemnes

 Houghton Mifflin • Boston

A Uniform System of Citation, Twelfth Edition, copyright © 1976 by The Columbia Law Review, The Harvard Law Review Association, The University of Pennsylvania Law Review, and The Yale Law Journal.

All correspondence and inquiries should be directed to
Dictionary and Reference Division, Houghton Mifflin Company
Two Park Street, Boston, MA 02107

Library of Congress Cataloging in Publication Data
Gordon, Frank S., 1952-
The legal word book.
    1. Law — Terms and phrases. I. Hemnes, Thomas M.S.,
1948- joint author. II. Title.
KF156.G6   340.1'4   78-6000
ISBN 0-395-26662-9

CONTENTS

HOW TO USE THIS BOOK

The Legal Word Book has been prepared in order to fill the long-standing need for an adequate, convenient speller of terms used in the legal profession and for a quick-reference guide to the preparation of legal forms, documents, and citations.

Twenty thousand terms are listed in alphabetical order and in the clearest and most useful possible way. Many of the entries included are in common usage, but each has a specific legal meaning or use. Information is provided on how to spell the words, how to divide them into syllables, and which syllables are stressed when the words are pronounced.

The Legal Word Book contains a comprehensive list of abbreviations that includes those for court reports and law journals. Directories — with addresses — are provided for the Federal court system, for embassies and consulates of the United States, and for the counties and county seats of the states of the United States. Also entered are sections on forms of address, proofreaders' marks, and Roman numerals; a perpetual calendar; postal abbreviations; and telephone area codes for many cities in the United States and other countries.

ORDER OF ENTRIES

The list of entries is given in strict alphabetical order for quick and easy access.

Each entry appears in the form in which it is most commonly used, for example, the plural of a noun (*reprisals; consular courts*), the present participle of a verb (*charging lien*), and so on; some words are entered in both the singular and the plural (*damage; damages*).

Series of multiword phrases sharing a common element — be it first, middle, or last — are listed under the key word in the following style:

> bill
>   — for a new tri′al
>   — in na′ture of a — of re·view′
>   sup′ple·men′tal —

> ab i·ni′ti·o′
>   — mun′di′

In such a series the dash functions as a sort of ditto mark and indicates that the key word or phrase (in the cases above, the word *bill* and the phrase *ab initio*) is repeated in each subsequent phrase in place of the dash: *bill for a new trial, bill in nature of a bill of review,* and *supplemental bill; ab initio mundi.*

In some phrases the same key word functions in more than one part of speech. In such cases the key word of the main entry is followed by a part-of-speech label (*n.*, noun; *v.*, verb; *adv.*, adverb; and *adj.*, adjective), and each phrase is entered under the part of speech to which it belongs:

> hon′or *v.*
> hon′or *n.*
>   — courts
>   of′fice of —

Sometimes the key word has both a capitalized form and a lower-case form. Phrases are entered under the appropriate main-entry form:

court	Court
civ′il —	— of Ad′mi·ral·ty
crim′i·nal —	Su·preme′ Ju·di′cial —
— of ap·peals′	Su·preme′ — of Er′rors

These would be written *civil court, criminal court, court of appeals; Court of Admiralty, Supreme Judicial Court,* and *Supreme Court of Errors.*

DIVISION OF WORDS

The Legal Word Book shows how words may correctly be divided into syllables. With the exception of law French and a few foreign words not yet assimilated into the language, all words have been analyzed and divided according to the same criteria applied in *The American Dictionary of the English Language,* a recognized authority on words, and in *The Word Book* (Houghton Mifflin Company, 1976), a speller presenting a list of the most commonly used words in the English language and a useful adjunct to *The Legal Word Book.* Law Latin terms have been included in this system of division because they are part of the legal lexicon of native speakers of English and are pronounced accordingly.

Divisions are shown by means of a centered dot, an accent mark, or a hyphen:

pac′tum   blue′-sky′ law   cur′so·ry ex·am′i·na′tion

STRESS

In this book syllables that are stressed when a word is pronounced are indicated. Two different stress marks are used; the first, a boldface stress, indicates the syllable that has the primary stress in the word:

as′signs   hin′der and de·lay′

The second mark, a lighter stress, indicates syllables that are pronounced with less stress than those marked with a primary stress but with a stronger stress than unmarked syllables:

de·fam′a·cast′   co·ju′di·ces′   heir′ship′

At times stress shifts when a word is used in a different part of speech:

pur′port′ *n.*   rec′ord *n.*
pur·port′ *v.*   re·cord′ *v.*

Forms given are identified by the applicable part-of-speech label in italics.

VARIANTS

Variant, or alternate, spellings of a word are given after the preferred spelling form and appear as follows:

as·size′ *or* as·sise′   en·dorse′ *or* in·dorse′

ab·ac′tion
a·ban′don
a·ban′do·nee′
a·ban′don·ment
ab an·ti′quo′
a·bat′a·ble nui′sance
a·bate′
a·bate′ment
a·ba′tor
ab′bey
ab′bot
ab·bre′vi·a′tions
ab·bre′vi·a′tors
ab·broch′ment *or*
 ab·broach′ment
ab′di·ca′tion
ab·duc′tion
a·bear′ance
a·bet′
a·bet′tor
a·bey′ance
a·bide′
a·bil′i·ty
ab i·ni′ti·o′
 — mun′di′
ab′ju·ra′tion
ab·jure′
a′ble sea′man
ab′le·gate
a·bode′
a·bol′ish
ab′o·li′tion
a·bor′ti·fa′cient
a·bor′tion
a·bor′tion·ist
a·bor′tus
a·bout′
a·bove′

a·bridge′
a·bridg′ment
a·broach′ment *or*
 a·broach′ment
a·broad′
ab′ro·gate′
ab′ro·ga′tion
ab·scond′
ab′sence
ab′sent
ab′sen·tee′
ab′so·lute′
ab′so·lute′ly
ab′so·lu′tion
ab′so·lut′ism
ab·solve′
abs′que
ab·sten′tion
ab′stract′ *n.*
ab·stract′ *v.*
ab·strac′tion
ab·surd′i·ty
a·buse′
a·bu′sive
a·but′
a·but′ments
a·but′tals
a·but′ter
ac′a·deme′
a·cad′e·my
ac·cel′er·a′tion
ac·cept′
ac·cept′ance
ac·cep′tor
ac·cess′
ac·ces′sion
ac·ces′so·ry
ac′ci·dent
ac′ci·den′tal
ac·com′mo·da′tion
 — en·dors′er
 — mak′er
 — par′ty

ac·com′pa·ny
ac·com′plice
ac·cord′ *v.*
ac·cord′ *n.*
 — and sat′is·fac′-
 tion
ac·cor′dance
ac·cor′dant
ac·couche·ment′
ac·count′
 — book
ac·count′a·ble
ac·count′ant
ac·count′ing
ac·counts
 — pay′a·ble
 — re·ceiv′a·ble
ac·cred′it
ac·cre′tion
ac·cru′al ba′sis
ac·crue′
ac·cru′ing
ac·cu′mu·la′tions
ac·cu′mu·la′tive
ac′cu·sa′tion
ac·cu′sa·to′ry part
ac·cuse′
ac·cused′
ac·cus′er
ac·cus′tomed
ac·knowl′edge
ac·knowl′edg·ment
ac′o·lyte′
a′cre
a·cross′
act
ac·quaint′ed
ac·quest′
ac′qui·esce′
ac′qui·es′cence
 — in pais
 — of God
ac·quire′

ac′qui·si′tion
ac·quit′
ac·quit′tal
ac·quit′tance
ac·quit′ted
act′ing
ac′tion
   — for mon′ey had
     and re·ceived′
   — in per·so′nam, in
     rem
   — qua′si′ in rem
   — to qui′et ti′tle
ac′tion·a·ble
ac′tive
ac·tiv′i·ty
ac′tor
ac′tu·al
ac′tum
ac′tus
ad cul′pam
ad dam′num
a·dapt′ed
add
ad·den′dum
ad·dict′ v.
ad′dict n.
ad di′em
ad·di′tion
ad·di′tion·al
   — in·sured′
ad·di′tur
ad′dled
ad·dress′
ad·duce′
a·deem′
a·demp′tion
ad′e·quate
ad·her′ence
ad·her′ing
ad·he′sion
ad hoc
ad hom′i·nem

ad in′fi·ni′tum
ad′i·po′ce·re′
ad′i·ra′tus
ad′it
ad′i·tus
ad·ja′cent
ad′jec·tive law
ad·join′ing
ad·journ′
ad·journ′ment
ad·judge′
ad·ju′di·cate′
ad·ju′di·ca′tion
ad·junct′
ad·ju·ra′tion
ad·just′
ad·just′er
ad·just′ment
ad·ju·tant gen′er·al
ad·leg′i·a′re′
ad li′tem
ad·meas′ure·ment
ad·min′is·ter
ad·min′is·tra′tion
ad·min′is·tra′tive
ad·min′is·tra′tor
   — de bo′nis non
ad·min′is·tra′trix
ad′mi·ral
ad′mi·ral·ty
ad·mis′si·ble
ad·mis′sion
ad·mis′sions
ad·mit′
ad·mit′tance
ad·mix′ture
ad·mon′ish
ad′mo·ni′tion
a·do′be
ad′o·les′cence
a·dopt′
a·dop′tion
ad pro′se·quen′dum

ad quem
ad rec′tum
ad re′spon·den′dum
a·drift′
a·dult′
a·dul′ter·a′tion
a·dul′ter·y
ad va·len′ti·am
ad va·lo′rem
ad·vance′
ad·vance′ment
ad·vanc′es
ad·van′tage
ad′ven·ti′tious
ad·ven′ture
ad·ven′tur·er
ad′ver·sar′y
   — pro·ceed′ing
ad·verse′
   — in′ter·est
   — par′ty
   — pos·ses′sion
ad′ver·tise′
ad′ver·tise′ment
ad·vice′
ad·vise′
ad·vised′
ad·vis′ed·ly
ad·vise′ment
ad·vi′so·ry
   — o·pin′ion
ad′vo·ca·cy
ad′vo·cate′ v.
ad′vo·cate n.
aer′o·drome′
aer′o·naut′
aer′o·plane′
aer′o·stat′ics
aes·thet′ic
af·fair′
af·fairs′
af·fect′
af·fec′tion

af·fec′tus
af·feer′
af·fi′ance
af·fi′ant
af′fi·da′re′
af′fi·da′vit
— of serv′ice
af·fil′i·ate′
af·fil′i·a′tion
af·fin′i·ty
af·firm′
af·firm′ance
af·firm′ant
af′fir·ma′tion
— of fact
af·firm′a·tive
— ac′tion
— de·fense′
— proof
— re·lief′
af·fix′
af·fix′ing
af·flic′tion
af·fray′
af·freight′ment
af·front′
a·fore′said′
a·fore′thought′
a for′ti·o′ri′
af′ter
af′ter–ac·quired′
— ti′tle
af′ter–born child
af′ter–dis·cov′ered
— ev′i·dence
af′ter sight
af′ter·math′
af′ter·noon′
af′ter·thought′
af′ter·ward
af′ter·wards
a·gainst′
a·gal′ma

age
a′gen·cy
— cou′pled with
in′ter·est
a′gent
a′ger
ag′gra·vat′ed as·-
sault′
ag′gra·vat′ing
ag′gra·va′tion
ag′gre·gate′
ag′gre·gates′
ag′gre·ga′tion
ag·gres′sor
ag·grieved′
— par′ty
a·gi′o′
a·gi·o′tage
a·gist′
a·gist′er
a·gist′ers
a·gist′ment
a·gis′tor
ag′i·ta′tor
ag·no′men
ag·nom′i·na′tion
ag′o·ny
a·graph′i·a
a·grar′i·an
— laws
a·grar′i·um
a·gree′
a·greed′
— case
— or′der
— state′ment of
facts
a·gree′ment
— not to be per·-
formed′ with·in′
a year
a·gre·er′
ag′ri·cul′tur·al

— lien
ag′ri·cul′ture
aid *n*.
aid *v*.
— and a·bet′
— and as·sist′
— and com′fort
aid′er
— and a·bet′tor
aids
ail′ment
air
— cours′es
air′-con·di′tion
air′craft′
air′plane′
air′port′
air′ship′
air′way′
a·journ′ment *or* a·-
journe′ment
a·kin′
al′co·hol′ic bev′er·-
age
al′co·hol′ism
al′der·man
a′le·a·to′ry con′-
tract′
a′li·a
a′li·a·men′ta
a′li·as
— dic′tus
— ex′e·cu′tion
— sub·poe′na
— sum′mons
— tax war′rant
— writ
— writ of ex′e·-
cu′tion
al′i·bi′
a′li·en
— a·mi′ *or* a·my′
— and se·di′tion laws

— friend
al'ien·a·ble
al'ien·age
al'ien·ate'
al'ien·a'tion
— of af·fec'tions
al'ien·ee'
al'ien·ism
al'ien·ist
al'ien·or'
a·lign'ment
a·like'
al'i·men·ta
al'i·mo'ny
al'i·quot'
al'i·ter
a'li·un'de'
ev'i·dence —
— rule
a·live
all
— and sin'gu·lar
— faults
— fours
All-A·mer'i·can
al'le·ga'tion
— of fact
al·lege'
al·leged'
al·le'giance
al'le·gi·a're'
al'ley
al·li'ance
al·li'sion
al'lo·ca·ble
al'lo·cate'
al'lo·ca'tion
al'lo·ca'tur'
al·lo·cu'tion
al·lo'di·al
al'lo·graph'
al·longe'
al'lo·path'ic prac'-

tice
al·lot'
al·lot'ment
al·lot'tee'
al·low'
al·low'ance
— pen·den'te' li'te'
al'loy'
al·lu'vi·o' ma'ris
al·lu'vi·on
al'ly
al'ma·nac'
al'ma·ri'a
alms
alms'house'
a·lone'
a·long'
al'so
al'ter
al'ter·a'tion
al'ter·ca'tion
al'ter e'go
al'ter·nat
al'ter·nate' v.
al'ter·nate n.
al·ter'na·tive
— plead'ing
— re·lief'
— re·main'ders
a·lum'nus
a·mal'ga·ma'tion
am·bas'sa·dor
am'bi·dex'ter
am'bi·gu'i·ty
— up·on' the fac'-
tum
am'bit
am·blot'ic
am'bu·lance
— chas'er
— chas'ing
am'bu·la·to'ry
am'bush'

a·me'lio·rat'ing
waste
a·me'lio·ra'tions
a·me'na·ble
a·mend'
a·mend'ment
a·mends'
a·men'i·ty
a men'sa et tho'ro'
a·merce
a·merce'ment
A·mer'i·can
A·mer'i·can Bar
As·so'ci·a'tion
a·mi' or a·my'
am'i·ca·ble
a·mi'cus cu'ri·ae'
am·ne'si·a
am'nes·ty
a·mong'
am'or·ti·za'tion
am'or·tize'
a·mo'tion
a·mount'
— in con'tro·ver'sy
— in dis·pute'
a·muse'ment
an'aes·the'si·a or
an'es·the'si·a
an'a·graph'
a·nal'o·gous
a·nal'o·gy
an·aph'ro·dis'i·a
an'ar·chist
an'ar·chy
a·nath'e·ma
a·nath'e·ma·tize'
an'ces'tor
an·ces'tral
an'chor
an'chor·age
an'cient
— deed

— doc′u·ments
— lights
— wa′ter·course′
— writ′ings
an′cients
an′cil·lar′y
— ad·min′is·tra′tion
— at·tach′ment
— ju′ris·dic′tion
— pro·ceed′ing
— re·ceiv′er
an′eu·rysm *or*
  an′eu·rism
a·new′
an′ga·ry
  right of —
an′ger
an·gi′na pec′to·ris
an′gling
an′guish
an′i·mal
an′i·mus
— fu·ran′di′
— tes·tan′di′
an′nals
an′nex
an′nex·a′tion
an′ni·ver′sa·ry
an′no′ Dom′i·ni′
an′no·ta′tion
an·nounced′
an·noy′ance
an′nu·al
— as·say′
— de·pre′ci·a′tion
an′nu·al·ly
an·nu′i·tant
an·nu′i·ty
an·nul′
an·nul′ment
a·nom′a·lous
a·non′y·mous
an′swer

an′te·ce′dent
an′te·date′
an·ten′na
an′te·nup′tial
— con′tract′
— set′tle·ments
an′thra·co′sis
an′thrax′
an′thro·pom′e·try
an′ti·trust′ acts
an·tic′i·pa′tion
an·tic′i·pa·to′ry
  breach of con′-
  tract′
an·tig′ra·phy
an·tin′o·my
a pais
a·part′ment
a′pex′
a·pha′si·a
a·pho′ni·a
ap′o·ge′an tides
ap′o·plex′y
a·pos′ta·cy *or*
  a·pos′ta·sy
a poste′ri·o′ri
a·pos′tles
a·poth′e·car′y
ap·pa·ra′tus
ap·par′el
ap·par′ent
— a′gen·cy
— au·thor′i·ty
— dan′ger
ap·peal′
— bond
— in for′ma pau′-
  per·is
ap·pealed′
ap·pear′
— of rec′ord
ap·pear′ance
ap·pel′lant

ap·pel′late
— court
— ju′ris·dic′tion
ap′pel·lee′
ap·pend′
ap·pend′age
ap·pen′dant
ap·pen′dix
ap′per·tain′
ap′per·tain′ing
ap·pli′ance
ap′pli·ca·ble
ap′pli·cant
ap′pli·ca′tion
ap·ply′
ap·point′
ap·point′ee′
ap·point′ment
ap·poin′tor
ap·por′tion
ap·por′tion·ment
ap·prais′al
ap·praise′
ap·praise′ment
ap·prais′er
ap·pre′cia·ble
ap·pre′ci·ate′
ap·pre′ci·a′tion in
  val′ue
ap′pre·hend′
ap′pre·hen′sion
ap·pren′tice
ap·pren′tice·ship′
ap·proach′
  right of —
ap·proach′es
ap·pro′pri·ate *adj.*
ap·pro′pri·ate′ *v.*
ap·pro′pri·a′tion
— bill
ap·pro′pri·a′tor
ap·prov′al
ap·prove′

ap·prove′ment
ap·prov′er
ap·prox′i·mate′
ap·prox′i·ma′tion
ap·pur′te·nance
ap·pur′te·nant
a·prax′i·a
à pren′dre
a pri·o′ri
apt
a quo
ar′a·ble land
ar′bi·ter
ar′bi·trage′
ar·bit′ra·ment
ar′bi·trar′i·ly
ar′bi·trar′i·ness
ar′bi·trar′y
ar′bi·tra′tion
— clause
ar′bi·tra′tor
ar′bor
arch·bish′op
arch·dea′con
ar′che·type′
ar′chi·tect′
ar′chives′
ar′chi·vist
ar′e·a
ar′e·a·way′
a·rere′
ar′gu·en·do′
ar′gu·ment
ar′gu·men′ta·tive
a·rise′
ar′is·toc′ra·cy
arm of the sea
armed
ar′mi·stice
ar′mor·y
arms
ar′my
a·round′

ar·raign′
ar·raign′ment
ar·range′ment
ar·ray′
ar·rear′ages
ar·rears′
ar·rest′
— of judg′ment
ar·ri′val
ar·rive′
ar′ro·ga′tion
ar′se·nals
ar′son
art
prior —
words of —
ar·te′sian well
ar′ti·cle
ar′ti·cled clerk
ar′ti·cles
— of a·gree′ment
— of as·so′ci·a′-
tion
— of faith
— of im·peach′-
ment
— of in·cor′po·ra′-
tion
— of part′ner·ship′
ar′ti·fice
ar·tif′i·cer
ar′ti·fi′cial
— pre·sump′tions
ar′ti·fi′cial·ly
ar′ti·san
as a·gainst′
as be·tween′
as is
as per
as such
as·cend′
as·cen′dants
as·cent′

as′cer·tain′
ask
as′pect′
as·per′sions
as′phalt′
as·phyx′i·a
as·phyx′i·a′tion
as′pi·rin
as′por·ta′tion
as·sas′si·na′tion
as·sault′
— with in·tent′ to
com·mit′ man′-
slaugh′ter
— with in·tent′ to
com·mit′ mur′der
— with in·tent′ to
com·mit′ rape
— with in·tent′ to
com·mit′ rob′-
ber·y
as·say′
— of′fice
as·say′er
as·sem′blage
as·sem′ble
as·sem′bly
un·law′ful —
as·sent′
as·sert′
as·sess′
as·sessed′
— val′u·a′tion
as·sess′ment
— dis′trict
— la′bor
— list
— pe′ri·od
— roll
as·ses′sor
as′sets′
as′sev·er·a′tion
as·sign′

as·sign′a·bil′i·ty
as·sign′a·ble
as·sign·ee′
  — for the ben′e·fit
    of cred′i·tors
as·sign′ment
as·sign·or′
as·signs′
as·sist′
as·sis′tance
  — of coun′sel
as·sis′tant
as·size′ *or* as·sise′
as·siz′es *or* as·sis′es
as·so′ci·ate′
as·so′ci·a′tion
as·sume′
as·sump′sit
  — for mon′ey had
    and re′ceived
  — on quan′tum
    me·ru′it
as·sump′tion
  — of in·debt′ed·-
    ness
  — of risk
as·sur′ance
as·sure′
as·sured′
as·tip′u·la′tion
a·sy′lum
at arm′s length
at bar
a te′ner·is an′nis
a terme
a′the·ist
at large
at law
at′om·ize′
a·tro′cious as·sault′
  and bat′ter·y
a·troc′i·ty
at′ro·pine′

at·tach′
at′ta·ché′
at·tached′
at·tach′ing cred′i·tor
at·tach′ment
  — ex′e·cu′tion
at·tain′
at·tain′der
at·tempt′
at·ten′dant *n.*
at·ten′dant *adj.*
  — terms
at·ten′tion
at·test′
at′tes·ta′tion
  — clause
  — of will
at·test′ed cop′y
at·test′ing wit′ness
at·tes′tor
at·torn′
at′tor·na′re′
at·tor′ney
  — at law
  — gen′er·al
  — in fact
  letter of —
  — of rec′ord
  power of —
at·tor′ney′s lien
at·tor′ney·ship′
at·trac′tive nui′-
  sance doc′trine
au be·soin′
auc′tion
auc′tion·eer′
au′di·ence
au′dit
au′di·ta quer′e·la
au′di·tor
aug′men·ta′tion
aunt
au·then′tic

au·then′ti·ca′tion
au′thor
au·thor′i·ties
au·thor′i·ty
  ap·par′ent —
  ex·press′ —
  gen′er·al —
  im·plied′ —
au′thor·ize′
au′to-op′tic ev′i·-
  dence
au·toc′ra·cy
au′to·graph′
au′to·graph′ic
au′to·mat′ic
au·tom′a·tism
au′to·mo·bile′
au·ton′o·my
au′top′sy
au·top′tic prof′er·-
  ence
au′tre
  — droit
  — vie
aux·il′ia·ry
a·vail′a·ble
a·vails′
av′e·nue′
a·ver′
av′er·age
a·ver′ment
a′vi·a′tion
a vin′cu·lo mat′ri·-
  mo′ni·i′
a·vo·cat′
av′o·ca′tion
a·void′
a·void′a·ble con′se·-
  quenc·es
a·void′ance
av′oir·du·pois′
a·vouch′er
a·vow′

a·vow'al
a·vow'ry
a·vul'sion
a·wait'
a·ward'
ax'i·om

B

bach'e·lor
back
  — tax'es
back'ing
back'-seat' driv'er
back'ward·a'tion *or*
  back'a·da'tion
back'ward
  for'ward and — at
    sea
back'wards
back'wa'ter
bad
  — debt
  — faith
  — mo'tive
  — ti'tle
badge
  — of fraud
bag
bag'gage
  — car
bail *v*.
bail *n*.
  — bond
bail'a·ble
  — ac'tion
  — of·fense'
  — proc'ess
bail'ee'
bail'iff

bail'i·wick'
bail'ment
  ac'tu·al —
  con·struc'tive —
  — for hire
  — for mu'tu·al
    ben'e·fit
  gra·tu'i·tous —
  in·vol'un·tar'y —
  — lease
bail'or
bait
bak'er
bak'er·y
bal'ance
  net —
  — of con·ven'ience
  — of pow'er
  — sheet
bal'co·nies
bale
bal'last
bal'la·stage'
bal·loon'
  — mort'gage
bal'lot
  — box
ban
ba·nal'
ba·nal'i·ty
banc
ban'dit
bane
ban'ish·ment
ban'is·ter and rail'-
  ing
bank
  — ac·count'
  — check
  — draft
  joint-stock —
  — note
  sav'ings —

bank'a·ble pa'per
bank'book'
bank'er
bank'er's
  — ac·cept'ance
  — lien
  — note
bank'ing
  — hours
bank'rupt'
  — law
bank'rupt·cy
  ad·ju'di·ca'tion of —
  — pro·ceed'ings
  vol'un·tar'y —
ban'ner
bar
  — as·so'ci·a'tion
bar'ba·rous
bar'ber
bare
  — or mere li'cen·-
    see'
  — pat'ent li'cense
  — trus·tee'
bar'gain
  — and sale
bar'gain·ee'
bar'gain·or'
barge
bark
barn
Barn'ard's Inn
bar'on
bar'on·et
bar'o·ny
bar'ra·tor *or* bar'-
  re·tor
bar'ra·trous
bar'ra·try *or*
  bar're·try
barred
bar'rel

bar'ren·ness
bar'ri·cade'
bar'ri·er
bar'ris·ter
bar'ter
bas'al frac'ture
base
based
  — up·on'
base'ball'
base'ment
ba'ses'
bas'es
ba·sil'i·ca
ba'sin
ba'sis
bas'tard
bas'tard·ize'
bas'tard·y
  — proc'ess'
bat'tel
bat'ter·y
baux'ite'
bawd
bawd'y·house'
bay
bay'gall'
bay'ou
bay win'dow
beach
bea'con
bea'con·age
bea'dle
bear
  — arms
  — in'ter·est
bear'er
bear'ers
bear'ing date
beast
beat
be·come'
bed

bed'ding
bede'house'
bed'el
bed'lam
beef
beer
be·get'
beg'gar
be·gin'
be·got'ten
be·gun'
be·half'
be·hav'ior
be·hoof'
be·lief'
bel·lig'er·en·cy
bel·lig'er·ents
bel'lum
be·long'
be·long'ings
be·low'
bench
  — war'rant
ben'e·fice
ben'e·fi'cial
  — en·joy'ment
  — es·tate'
  — in'ter·est
  — or be·nev'o·lent
    as·so'ci·a'tion
  — pow'er
  — use
ben'e·fi'ci·ar·y
  change of —
  — heir
ben'e·fit
  — of bar'gain rule
  — of coun'sel
  — of dis·cus'sion
be·nev'o·lence
be·nev'o·lent
  — as·so'ci·a'tions
  — cor'po·ra'tion

  — so·ci'e·ty
be·queath'
be·quest'
berm bank
ber'ton
be·seech'
be·sot'
bes'se·mer·iz'ing
best
  — ev'i·dence
bes'ti·al'i·ty
be·stow'
bet
be·tray'al
be·troth'al
be·trothed'
be·troth'ment
bet'ter·ment
  — acts
bev'er·age
be·yond' a rea'-
  son·a·ble doubt
bi'as
Bi'ble
bi·cam'er·al sys'tem
bid
  — in
  — off
  upset —
bid'der
bid'dings
  — com·pet'i·tive
biel'brief'
bi·en'ni·al·ly
biens
big'a·my
big'ot
bi·lan'
bi·lat'er·al con'tract'
bil'boes
bilged
bill
  cross —

— for a new tri′al
— for fore·clo′-
  sure
— for fraud
— in aid of ex′e·-
  cu′tion
— in na′ture of a —
  of re·view′
— in na′ture of a —
  of re·viv′or
— in na′ture of a
  sup′ple·men′tal —
— in na′ture of
  in′ter·plead′er
— o·blig′a·to′ry
— of ad·ven′ture
— of at·tain′der
— of con·form′i·ty
— of costs
— of cred′it
— of debt
— of dis·cov′er·y
— of en′try
— of ex·cep′tions
— of ex·change′
— of gross ad·ven′-
  ture
— of health
— of in·dict′ment
— of in′for·ma′-
  tion
— of in′ter·plead′-
  er
— of lad′ing
— of par·tic′u·lars
— of peace
— of re·view′
— of re·viv′or
— of re·viv′or and
  sup′ple·ment
— of rights
— of sale
— of sight
— pay′a·ble

— pe′nal
pri·vate —
— qui′a tim′et
— re·ceiv′a·ble
— sin′gle
sup′ple·men′tal —
— to car′ry a de·-
  cree′ in′to ex′e·-
  cu′tion
— to per·pet′u·ate′
  tes′ti·mo′ny
— to qui′et pos·-
  ses′sion and ti′tle
— to sus·pend′ a
  de·cree′
— to take tes′ti·-
  mo′ny de be′ne′
  es′se′
bill′board′
bil′let
bil′liard ta′bles
bil′ly
bi′me·tal′lic
bi·met′al·lism
bind
— out
bind′er
bind′ing
— in·struc′tion
— o′ver
bi·par′tite′
birth
bis
bish′op
bi·tu′men
bi·tu′mi·nous coal
black a′cre and
  white a′cre
black′jack′
black′list′
black′mail′
black′smith′ shop
blanc seign
blank

— ac·cept′ance
— en·dorse′ment
blan′ket
— pol′i·cy
blanks
blas′phe·my
blast′ing
bleach′ers
blees
blend′ed price
ble′ta
blind
— car
— cor′ner
— nail′ing
— wag′on
blind′craft′
block
— book sys′tem
— book′ing
— hol′er
— of sur′veys′
block to block rule
block·ade′
block′age
— rule
block′head′
blood
blood′hounds′
bludg′eon
blue
— laws
— notes
blue′-sky′ law
bluff
blum′ba
blun′der
blun′der·buss′
board
— meas′ure
— of al′der·men
— of di·rec′tors
— of ed′u·ca′tion
— of med′i·cal ex·-

am'in·ers
— of trade
board'er
board'ing house
boat
boat'a·ble
boat'ing
boat'swain
bob'tail' driv'er
bob'tailed ca·boose'
bob'tails'
bod'i·ly
bod'y
  — cor'po·rate
  — ex'e·cu'tion
  — heirs
  — of a coun'ty
  — of an in'stru··
    ment
  — of laws
  — of the of·fense'
  — pol'i·tic
boil'ar·y
boil'er
bolt
bolt'ing
bo·na' *pl. n.*
bo·na' *adj.*
  — fi'de'
  — fi'des'
bo·nan'za
bond
  — and mort'gage
  claim —
  cor'po·rate —
  — cred'i·tor
  — for deed
  forth'com·ing —
  — for ti'tle
  gen'er·al mort'-
    gage —
  in'come' —
  in·dem'ni·ty —
  — is'sue

li'a·bil'i·ty —
Lloyd's —
mu·nic'i·pal —
— of in·debt'ed·-
  ness
re·liv'er·y —
sim'ple —
sin'gle —
straw —
— with sure'ty
bond'age
bond'ed
  — in·debt'ed·ness
  — ware'house'
bonds'man
bon'i·fi·ca'tion
bo'nus
  — stock
bon'y
boo'dle
bood'ling
book
  — ac·count'
  — debt
  — of o·rig'i·nal en'-
    tries
  — val'ue
booked
book'ing con'tract'
book'mak'er
book'mak'ing
books of ac·count'
boom
boom'age
boot'ing-corn' *or*
  bot'ing-corn'
boot'leg'ger
boot'leg'ging
boo'ty
booze
born
  — a·live'
  — out of wed'-
    lock'

bor'ough
bor·ras'ca
bor'row
bor'row·er
bor'row·ings
both
bot'tle
bot'tom land
bot'tom·ry
bot'u·lism
bought
  — and sold notes
boul'e·vard'
bound
bound'a·ry
bound'ers
bounds
boun'ty
bour·geois'
bourse
bo'vine
boy'cott'
Boyd rule
brake
branch
  — of the sea
  — pi'lot
brand
brand'ing
brawl
breach
  — of close
  — of con'tract'
  — of cov'e·nant
  — of du'ty
  — of prom'ise
  — of the peace
  — of trust
  — of war'ran·ty
break
  — and take
break'ing
  — bulk
breath

breath'ing
breed
breth'ren
breve
bre·vet'
bre'vi·a
bre'vi·ate *n.*
bre'vi·ate' *v.*
brew'er
bribe
brib'er·y
Bride'well
bridge
— mas'ters
brief
— of ti'tle
brief'ly
brine
bring
— a·bout'
— suit
bring'ing er'ror
broad in·ter'pre·ta'-
tion
bro·cage'
bro'ken
bro'ker
bro'ker·age
— con'tract'
broth'el
broth'er
broth'er-in-law'
brought
— to tri'al
bru'tum ful'men
buck'et·ing
bud'get
buff'er
buf·fet'
bug'ger·y
build
build'er
build'ing

— and loan as·so'-
ci·a'tion
— lien
— per'mit
— site
bulk
— sales acts
bull
bul'le·tin
bul'lion
— fund
bum·bail'iff
bun'co' game
bun'dle
buoy
bur'den of proof
bu'reau
bu·reauc'ra·cy
burg *or* burgh
bur'gage
— hold'ing
— ten'ure
bur'gess
bur'glar
bur·glar'i·ous·ly
bur'glar·y
— in the first de·-
gree'
bur'go·mas'ter
burh
bur'i·al
burk'ing
burk'ism
bur'law courts
bur·lesque'
burn
bur·ro'chi·um
bur'sa
bur'sar
bur·sar'i·a
bur'y·ing ground
bush'el
busi'ness

— a'gent
— cor'po·ra'tion
— en'ter·prise'
— hours
— loss'es
— name
— trust
butch'er
butt
but'tals
butte
but'ted
— and bound'ed
butts
— and bounds
buy
— in
buy'er
buy'ing
— long
— ti'tles
by'-bid'der
by'-bid'ding
by law
by'law' men
by'laws'
by'-pass'ing
by rea'son of
by'stand'er
by vir'tue of

C

ca·bal'
cab'al·lar'i·a
ca·ban'a
cab'a·ret
cab'i·net
— coun'cil
ca'ble

— trans·fer′
cab′o·tage
ca·dav′er
ca·dav′er·ous
ca′de·re′
ca′det
ca′dit
ca·du′ca′ry
cae′ter·or·um
cae′ter·us
ca·fé′
ca·hoots′
cal′a·boose′
ca·lam′i·ty
cal′cu·late′
cal′cu·lat′ed
cal′en·dar
call
call′a·ble
— bonds
call′ers
call′ing
— an e·lec′tion
— the dock′et
— the ju′ry
— to tes′ti·fy′
ca·lum′ni·a
cal′um·ny
cam′er·a
cam′ou·flage′
camp
cam·paign′
cam′pa·nar′i·um
cam′pa·ni′le′
camp′ers
ca·nal′
can′cel
can′cel·la′tion
can′di·date′
can′on
ca·non′i·cal
— dis′a·bil′i·ty
can′on·ist

can′tel *or* can′tle
can′tred
can′vass
can′vass·er
ca′pa·ble
ca·pac′i·ty
ca′pax′ do′li′
cape
ca′pi·as
— ad com′pu·tan′-
dum
— ad pro′se·quen′-
dum
— ad re′spon·den′-
dum
— ad sat′is·fac′i-
en′dum
— ex′ten·di′ fa′ci·as
— in with′er·nam′
— pro fi′ne′
— ut′la·ga′tum
cap′i·a·tur′ pro
fi′ne′
cap′i·ta
per —
cap′i·tal *n.*
cap′i·tal *adj.*
— as′sets′
— case *or* crime
— ex·pen′di·ture
— gains
— im·pair′ment
— in·crease′
— in·vest′ment
— out′lay′
— pun′ish·ment
— re·cov′er·y
— stock
— stock tax
— sur′plus
cap′i·tal·ist
cap′i·tal·i·za′tion
meth′od

cap′i·tal·ize′
cap′i·ta′tim
cap′i·ta′tion tax
ca·pit′u·la′tion
cap′tain
cap′ta′tor
cap′tion
cap′tives
cap′tor
cap′ture
cap′ut
car′at
car·ca′num
car·ca′tus
car′cel·age
car′cer
car′di·nal
care′less
care′less·ly
car′go
Car′lisle ta′bles
car′nal
— a·buse′
— knowl′edge
car′nal·i·ter
car′nal·ly knew
car′riage
car′ri·cle *or*
car′ra·cle
car′ri·er
car′ri·er's lien
car′ry
— a mem′ber
— an e·lec′tion
— costs
— on trade or
busi′ness
car′ry·ing a·way′
cart
— bote
car′ta
carte blanche
car·tel′

car'tu·lar'y
car'u·cate
case
— law
— sys'tem
case'ment
cash
— ac·count'
— book
— con'tract'
— dis'count'
— mar'ket val'ue
— note
— price
— sale
— sur·ren'der val'ue
— val'ue
cash·ier'
cash·iered'
cash·ier's' check
cas'ing-head' gas
cas'ket
cas·sa're'
cast
— a·way'
cast'a·way'
cas'ti·ga·to'ry
cast'ing vote
cas'u·al
— em·ploy'ment
— pau'per
— poor
cas'u·al·ty
ca'sus
— bel'li'
— foe'de·ris
— for·tu'i·tus
— o·mis'sus
cat'al·la
cat'als
ca·tas'tro·phe
catch'ings
catch'land'

catch'poll'
ca·the'dral
cat'tle
— gate
— pass
— range
— rus'tling
cat'tle·guard
Cau·ca'sian
cau'cus
cau'sa
— list
— mor'tis
— pat'et
— prox'i·ma
— re·mot'a
— si·ne' qua non
— tur'pis
cau'sa·tor
cause *v.*
— suit to be
brought
cause *n.*
— books
— list
— of ac'tion
— of in'ju·ry
Causes Cé·lèbres'
cause'way'
cau'tion
cau'tion·ar'y
— judg'ment
cau'tious
ca've·at'
— ac'tor
— emp'tor'
— to will
— ven'di·tor'
— vi'a·tor'
ca've·a'tor
ca·ve're'
cease
cede

cel·a'tion
cel'i·ba·cy
cem'e·ter'y
cen·si·taire'
cen'sive
cen'sor·ship
cen'sure
cen'sus
— re'ga'lis
cent
cen'tal
cen'te·na
cen'ter
cen·time'
cen'tral·i·za'tion
cen'tu·ry
ceorl
ce'pi
ce'pit
— et ab·dux'it
— et as'por·ta'vit
— in a'li·o' lo'co'
ce'ra *or* ce're
— im·pres'sa
cer'tain
cer'tain·ty
cer·tif'i·cate
— of pub'lic con-
ven'ience and
ne·ces'si·ty
— of reg'is·try
— of stock
cer'ti·fied'
— check
— cop'y
— pub'lic ac·count'-
ant
cer'ti·fy'
cer'ti·o·ra'ri
ces·sa're'
ces'sion
— of goods
cess'ment

ces'sor
ces·tui'
— que trust
— que use
— que vie
ces·tuy'
chace
chace'a·ble
chac'er
chain of ti'tle
chair'man
chal'dron, chal'-
    dern, or chal'der
chal'lenge v.
chal'lenge n.
— for cause
gen'er·al —
per·emp'to·ry —
prin'ci·pal —
— prop'ter af·fec'-
    tum
— prop'ter de·fec'-
    tum
— prop'ter de·lic'-
    tum
— prop'ter ho·no'-
    ris re·spec'tum
— to the ar'ray
— to the fa'vor
— to the pan'el
— to the poll
cham'ber
— of com'merce
— sur'veys'
cham'ber·lain
cham'bers
cham'fer
cha·motte'
cham'per·tor
cham'per·tous
cham'per·ty
cham'pi·on
chance

chance'-med'ley
chan'cel·lor
chan'cer
chan'cer·y
change
chan'nel
chap'el
chap'er·on'
chap'lain
chap'ter
char'ac·ter
charge v.
charge n.
— and dis'charge'
gen'er·al —
— off
spe'cial —
charge sheet
charge'a·ble
charg'es
charg'ing lien
char'i·ta·ble
— be·quest'
— cor'po·ra'tion
— in'sti·tu'tion
— or'gan·i·za'tion
— trust
char'i·ty
char'la·tan
chart
char'ta
char'ter v.
char'ter n.
— boat
— par'ty
char'ter·er
char'ter·house'
cha·rue'
chase
chas'sis
chaste
— char'ac·ter
chas'ti·ty

chat'tel
— mort'gage
— real
real —
chaud'-med'ley
chauf'feur
cheat
cheat'ers
check v.
check n.
cash·ier's' —
check'book'
check'-off sys'tem
check'-roll'
cheque
Cher'o·kee' Na'tion
che'vage
chi·cane'
Chick'a·saw' Na'-
    tion
chief
— judge
— jus'tice
— mag'is·trate'
ten'ant in —
child
post'hu·mous —
qua·si' post'hu·-
    mous —
chil'dren
child's part
chill'ing a sale
chi·rop'o·dist
chi·rop'o·dy
chi'ro·prac'tic
chi'ro·prac'tor
chiv'al·ry
choate lien
chops
chose
— in ac'tion
— in pos·ses'sion
cho'sen free'-

hold'ers
Chris'tian
— name
Chris'ti·an'i·ty
chron'ic
church
— prop'er·ty
— war'dens
churl
cic'a·trix'
ci'der
ci'pher
cir'ca
cir'cuit
— courts
— courts of ap·-
peals'
— judge
— jus'tice
cir·cu'i·ty of ac'tion
cir'cu·lar
— let'ter of cred'it
— notes
cir'cu·la'ted
cir'cu·la'tion
cir·cum'fer·en'tial
cir'cum·stanc'es
cir'cum·stan'tial
ev'i·dence
cir'cum·ven'tion
cir'cus
cis'ta
ci·ta'tion
— of au·thor'i·ties
cite
cit'i·zen
cit'i·zen·ship'
cit'y
— coun'cil
— e·lec'tion
civ'ic
civ'il
— ac'tion

— dam'age acts
— en·force'ment
pro·ceed'ing
— in'for·ma'tion
— in'quest
— li'a·bil'i·ty
— nui'sance
— ob'li·ga'tion
— of'fice
— of'fi·cer
— rights
— serv'ice
— side
— town'ship'
ci·vil'ian
ci'vi·lis
civ'i·li·za'tion
Civ'il Law
claim n.
claim v.
— ac·crued'
— and de'liv'er·y
— bond
— in eq'ui·ty
— of own'er·ship',
right, and ti'tle
— prop'er·ty bond
claim'ant
clam'or
clan·des'tine
class
— ac'tion
— gift
— rep're·sen·ta'tion
clas'si·fi·ca'tion
— of risks
clas'si·fied'
clas'si·fy'
clause
clau'sum
— fre'git
clean
— bill of lad'ing

— hands
clear
— and con·vinc'ing
proof
— and pres'ent
dan'ger
— an·nu'i·ty
— chance
— days
— ev'i·dence
— proof
— ti'tle
— val'ue
clear'ance
clear'ing
— ti'tle
clear'ing-house'
clear'ings
clear'ly
— er·ro'ne·ous
cler'gy
cler'gy·man
cler'i·cal
— er'ror
— mis·pri'sion
cler'i·cus
— mer·ca'ti'
— pa·ro'chi·a'lis
clerk
— of ar·raigns'
— of as·size'
— of court
— of en·roll'ments
— of in·dict'ments
— of rec'ords and
writs
— of seats
— of the crown in
chan'cer·y
— of the house of
com'mons
— of the mar'ket
— of the par'lia·-

ments
— of the peace
— of the pet'ty bag
— of the priv'y seal
— of the sig'net
— of the ta'ble
  clerks
clerk'ship'
cli'ent
cli'en·te'la
Clif'ford's Inn
clipped sov'er·eign·-
  ty
clo'ere
close v.
close n.
close adj.
— cor'po·ra'tion
— jail ex'e·cu'tion
closed
— shop
— shop con'tract'
close-hauled
clo'ture
cloud on ti'tle
clough
club
club law
clutch
clyp'e·us or
  clip'e·us
coach
co'ad·ju'tor
co'ad·min'is·tra'tor
co'ad·ven'tur·er
co'a·li'tion
co'as·sign·ee'
coast v.
coast n.
— guard
— wa'ters
coast'er
coast'ing

— trade
coast'wise'
cock'bill'
cock'et
cock'pit'
code
— ci·vil'
— d'in·struc·tion'
  cri·mi·nelle'
— noir
— pé·nal'
Code
— Na·po·lé·on'
— of Jus·tin'i·an
— of Mil'i·tar'y
  Jus'tice
co'dex
— Gre·go'ri·a'nus
— Her·mog'e·ni·a'-
  nus
— Ju'ris Ca·non'i·-
  ci'
— Jus·tin'i·a'ne·us
— Re·pet'i·tae'
  Prae·lec'ti·o'nis
— The·o·do'si·a'nus
— Vet'us
cod'i·cil
cod'i·fi·ca'tion
co·emp'tion
co·e'qual
co·erce'
co·er'cion
co'ex·ec'u·tor
cof'fer·er of the
  queen's house'-
  hold'
cog'nates'
cog·ni'ti·o'
cog·ni'ti·o·nes'
cog·ni'ti·o'ni·bus
  mit·ten'dis
cog'ni·za·ble

cog'ni·zance
cog·ni·zee'
cog'ni·zor
cog·no'men
cog·no'vit
— ac'ti·o'nem
co·hab'it
co·hab'i·ta'tion
Co'han Rule
co·heir'
co·heir'ess
coif
coin
coin'age
co'in·sur'ance
co'i·tus
co·ju'di·ces'
Coke's in'sti·tutes'
cold blood
co·li'ber·tus
col·laps'i·ble cor'-
  po·ra'tion
col·lat'er·al
— at·tack'
— es·top'pel
— facts
— im·peach'ment
— in·her'i·tance tax
— kins'men
— line
— prom'ise
— se·cu'ri·ty
— un'der·tak'ing
col·la'tion
col·la'ti·o'ne'
  he·rem'i·ta'gi·i'
col·la'ti·o' sig·no'-
  rum
col·lect'
— on de·liv'er·y
col·lect'i·ble
col·lec'tive
— bar'gain·ing

— bar'gain·ing
a·gree'ment
— la'bor
a·gree'ment
col·lec'tor
col·leg'a·tar'y
col'lege
col·le'gi·a
col·lide'
col'lier·y
col·li'sion
col·lo·ca'tion
col·lo'qui·um
col·lu'sion
col·lu'sive ac'tion
colne
col'o·ny
col'or
— of au·thor'i·ty
— of law
— of of'fice
— of ti'tle
col'or·a·ble
— claim
col'ored
col'pic·es
colt
com'bar·ones'
com'bat
com'bi·na'tion
— in re·straint' of
trade
com·bus'ti·o'
co'mes'
comes and de·fends'
com'fort
com'i·ta'tus
co'mi·tes'
co'mi·tis'sa
co'mi·ti'va
com'i·ty
com'ma
com·mand'

com·mand'er in
chief
com·mand'er·y
com·mand'ment
com·mence'
com·mence'ment of
a dec'la·ra'tion
com'ment'
— up·on' the ev'i-
dence
com'merce
— a·mong' the
states
do·mes'tic —
for'eign —
in'ter·na'tion·al —
in'ter·state' —
in'tra·state' —
— with for'eign
na'tions
— with In'di·an
tribes
com·mer'ci·a bel'li'
com·mer'cial
— court
— es·tab'lish·ment
— frus·tra'tion
— law
— let'ter of cred'it
— pa'per
com·min'gle
com·mis'sion
— mer'chant
— of an·tic'i·pa'-
tion
— of ap·praise'-
ment and sale
— of ar·ray'
— of as·size'
— of un·liv'er·y
com·mis'sioned of'-
fi·cers
com·mis'sion·er

Com·mis'sion·er of
Pat'ents and
Trade'marks
com·mis'sions
com·mit'
com·mit'ment
com·mit'tee
com'mo·da'tum
com·mod'i·ties
com·mod'i·ty
com'mon
— ap·pen'dant
— ap·pur'te·nant
— at large
— bench
— en'e·my doc'trine
— hu·man'i·ty doc'-
trine
— in gross
— law
— nui'sance
— of dig'ging
— of es·to'vers
— of pis'ca·ry
— of shack
— of tur'ba·ry
— pleas
— re·cov'er·y
— sans nom·bre'
com'mon·a·ble
com'mon·al·ty
com'mon·ance
com'mon·ers
com'mon-law'
— ac'tion
— as·sign'ments
— cheat
— con·tempt'
— courts
— crime
— ju'ris·dic'tion
— lar'ce·ny
— lien

— mar'riage
— mort'gage
— pro·ce'dure acts
— rem'e·dy
— trade'mark'
— wife
com'mons
Com'mons
— House of
com'mon·wealth'
com'mo·ran·cy
com'mo·rant
com'mo·ri·en'tes'
com'morth' *or*
   com'orth'
com'mote'
com·mo'tion
com·mune'
com·mu'ne'
   — con·cil'i·um
   — concilium reg'ni'
   — pla'ci·tum
   — vin'cu·lum
com'mu'ni·a
   — pla'ci·ta
com·mu'ni' cus·to'-
   di·a
com·mu'ni·cate'
com·mu'ni·ca'tion
   con'fi·den'tial —
   priv'i·leged —
com·mu'ni·bus an'-
   nis
com·mu'nis
   — rix'a·trix'
   — scrip'tur·a
   — sti'pes'
com'mu·nism
com'mu·nist
Com'mu·nist
com'mu·ni'tas
   reg'ni' Ang'li·ae'
com·mu'ni·ty

— prop'er·ty
com'mu·ta'tion
com'pact' *n.*
com·pact' *adj.*
com·pan'age
Com·pan'ion of the
   Gar'ter
com·pan'ions
com'pa·ny
   joint'-stock' —
   lim'it·ed —
   pub'lic —
com·par'a·tive
   — neg'li·gence
   — rec'ti·tude'
com'pass·ing
com·pat'i·bil'i·ty
com·pel'
com·pen'di·um
com·pen'sa·ble
   — in'ju·ry
com'pen·sa'ti·o'
   crim'i·nis
com·pen·sa'tion
com·pen'sa·to'ry
   dam'ag·es
com·pe'ru·it ad di'-
   em
com·pete'
com'pe·ten·cy
com'pe·tent
   — au·thor'i·ty
   — ev'i·dence
   — court
   — wit'ness
com'pe·ti'tion
com·pet'i·tive
   — bid'ding
com·pet'i·tors
com'pil·a'tion
com·pile'
com·piled' stat'utes
com·plain'ant

com·plaint'
com·plete'
com·plet'ed
com·ple'tion
com'pli·cat'ed
com'plice
com·ply'
com'pos men'tis
com'pos su'i'
com·pos'ite work
com'po·si'tion
   — deed
   — in bank'rupt·cy
   — of mat'ter
com·pound' *v.*
com·pound' *n.*
com·pound' *adj.*
   — in'ter·est
   — lar'ce·ny
com·pound'er
com·pound'ing a
   fel'o·ny
com'print'
com·prise'
com'pro·mise'
   — verdict
   of'fer of —
comp·trol'ler
com·pul'sa
com·pul'sion
com·pul'so·ry *n.*
com·pul'so·ry *adj.*
   — ar'bi·tra'tion
   — non'suit'
   — proc'ess'
   — sale or pur'-
   chase
com'pur·ga·tor
com'pu·ta'tion
com'pu·tus
con·ceal'
con·cealed'
con·ceal'ers

con·ceal'ment
con·cep'tion
con·cern'
con·cerned'
con·cern'ing
con·cert'ed ac'tion
con·ces'si'
con·ces'si·o'
con·ces'sion
con·ces'sit sol've·re'
con·ces'sor
con·ces'sum
con·ces'sus
con·cil'i·ab'u·lum
con·cil'i·a'tion
con·cil'i·um
— re'gis
con'ci·o·na'tor
con·clude'
con·clud'ed
con·clu'sion
— of fact
— of law
con·clu'sive
— ev'i·dence
con'cord'
con·cor'dat'
con·cor'di·a
con'cu·bar'i·a
con·cu'be·ant
con·cu'bi·nage
con'cu·bine'
con·cur'
con·cur'rence
con·cur'rent
— ju'ris·dic'tion
— liens
— pow'er
con·cur'so'
con·demn'
con'dem·na'tion
con·dic'ti·o'
— cer'ti'

— ex le'ge'
— in deb'i·ta'ti'
— re'i' fur·ti'vae'
— si'ne' cau'sa
con·di'ti·o'
con·di'tion
af·firm'a·tive —
cas'u·al —
con·sis'tent —
cop'u·la'tive —
de·pend'ent —
dis·junc'tive —
dis·solv'ing —
— en fait
es·tate' on —
ex·press' —
im·plied' —
im·pos'si·ble —
— in deed
in'de·pend'ent —
— in fact
— in law
mixed —
mu'tu·al —
neg'a·tive —
— of sale
pos'si·ble —
po'tes·ta'tive —
prec'e·dent —
re·pug'nant —
res'o·lu·to'ry —
sin'gle —
sub'se·quent —
sus·pen'sive —
con·di'tion·al
— en·dorse'ment
con'do·min'i·um
con'do·na'tion
con·done'
con·duce'
con·duct' v.
con'duct' n.
— es·top'pel by —

cone and key
con·fec'ti·o'
con·fed'er·a·cy
con·fed'er·a'tion
con'fer·ence
con·fess'
con·fes'si·o'
con·fes'sion
— and a·void'ance
— of de·fense'
— of judg'ment
con·fes'so'
bill tak'en pro —
con·fes'sor
con·fide'
con'fi·dence
— game
con·fi·den'tial
— com·mu'ni·ca'-
tions
— re·la'tion
con·fine'ment
con·firm'
con'fir·ma'ti·o'
— char·ta'rum
— cres'cens'
— di·min'u·ens'
— per·fi'ci·ens'
con'fir·ma'tion
— of sale
con'firm·ee'
con·firm'or
con·fis'ca·ble
con·fis·ca're'
con·fis·cate'
con·fis'ca·tee'
con·fis·ca'tion
— acts
— cases
con·fis'ca·to'ry
— rates
con'fisk'
con·fi'tens' re'us

con'flict of laws
con'flict·ing ev'i-
   dence
Con·form'i·ty
   — Act
   — stat'ute
con·frai·rie'
con'freres
con'fron·ta'tion
con·fu'sion
con·fute'
con'ge·a·ble
con'gre·gate'
con'gre·ga'tion
con'gress
con'gress·man
con·jec'ti·o'
con·jec'ture
con·joint' rob'ber·y
con·joints'
con·ju·dex'
con'ju·gal
   — rights
con·junc'tim
   — et di·vi'sim
con·junc'tive
con'ju·ra'ti·o'
con'ju·ra'tion
con'jur·a'tor
con·nect'
con·nect'ed
con·nec'tion
con·niv'ance
con·nive'
con'quer·or
con'quest
con'ques·tor
con·qui·si'ti·o'
con'san·guin'i·ty
   — lin'e·al and col-
     lat'er·al
con'science
   — of the court

con'sci·en'tious ob-·
   jec'tor
con·scrip'tion
con·se·crate'
con·sec'u·tive
con·sen'su·al
   — con'tract'
   — mar'riage
con·sen'sus ad
   i'dem
con·sent'
   — de·cree'
   — ex·press' —
   — im·plied' —
   — judg'ment
con'se·quence
con·ser'va·tor
con·serve'
con·sid'er
con·sid'er·a·ble
con·si'de·ra'ti·o' cu'-
   ri·ae'
con·sid'er·a'tion
   con·cur'rent —
   con·tin'u·ing —
   ex'e·cut'ed —
   ex'ec·u·to'ry —
   ex·press' —
   fail'ure of —
   fair and val'u·a-
     ble —
   fair —
   good —
   gra·tu'i·tous —
   il·le'gal —
   im·plied' —
   im·pos'si·ble —
   in·ad'e·quate —
   le'gal —
   nom'i·nal —
   past —
   pe·cu'ni·ar'y —
   suf·fi'cient —

   val'u·a·ble —
   want of —
con·sid'er·a'tur
con·sid'ered
con'sign'
con'sign·ee'
con·sign'ment
con·sign'or
con·si'li·um
con·si'mi·li' ca'su'
con·sist'
con·sist'ent
con·sist'ing
con·sis'tor
con'so·la'tion
con·sol'i·date'
con·sol'i·da'tion of
   ben'e·fic·es
con·sol'i·da'tions of
   cor'por·a'tions
con·sor'ti·um
con'sort·ship'
con·spic'u·ous
con'spir'a·cy
con'spi·ra'ti·o·ne'
con·spir'a·tors
con·spire'
con'sta·ble
con'sta·ble·wick'
con·stab'u·la'ri·us
con'stant
con'stant·ly
con'stat'
con·sta'te'
con·stit'u·ent
con'sti·tut'ed au-·
   thor'i·ties
con'sti·tu'tion
con'sti·tu'tion·al
   — al·cal'de'
   — con·ven'tion
   — court
   — law

— of'fi·cer
— right
con·straint'
con·struct'
con·struc'tion
con·struc'tive
— as·sent'
— au·thor'i·ty
— e·vic'tion
strict and lib'er·al —
— tak'ing
con·strue'
con'stu·prate'
con'sue·tu'di·nes
con'sue·tu·din'i·bus
et ser·vi'ci·is
con'su·e'tu·do'
— An'gli·ca'na
— cu'ri·ae'
con'sul
con'su·lar courts
con·sul'tar·y re··
sponse'
con'sul·ta'tion
con·sum'er
con·sum'mate *adj.*
— lien
con'sum·mate' *v.*
con'sum·ma'tion
con·sump'tion
con·tan'go'
con·temn'er
con'tem·plate'
con'tem·pla'tion
— of bank'rupt·cy
— of death
— of in·sol'ven·cy
con·tempt'
— of court
con·ten'tious
con·tent'ment
con'tents
con·ter'mi·nous

con·test' *v.*
con·test' *n.*
con·test'ed e·lec'tion
con'text'
Con'ti·nen'tal Con'-
gress
con·tin'gen·cy
— with dou'ble as'-
pect'
con·tin'gent
— claim
— es·tate', in'ter··
est *or* right
— fund
— li'a·bil'i·ty
con·tin'u·ance
con·tin'u·an'do'
con·tin'u·ing
con·tin'u·ous
— ad·verse' use
con·tin'u·ous·ly
con'tra
— bo'nos mo'res'
— for'mam col·la'-
ti·o'nis
— for'mam do'ni'
— for'mam feof·fa'-
men·ti'
— for'mam stat'u·ti'
— jus com·mu'ne'
— leg'em ter'rae'
— om'nes' gen'tes'
— pa'cem
— pro'fe·ren'tem
— va'di·um et pleg'-
i·um
— ver'i·ta'tem lex
nun'quam al'i··
quid' per'mit·tit
con'tra·band'
con'tract'
con·di'tion·al —
es·top'pel by —

spe'cial —
un·con'scion·a·ble —
u·su'ri·ous —
writ'ten —
con'tracts'
ex'e·cut'ed and
ex·ec'u·to'ry —
ex·press' and
im·plied' —
joint and sev'er·al —
qua'si' —
con·trac'tion
con'trac'tor
con·trac'tu·al ob'li·-
ga'tion
con·tra·dict'
con·tra·dic'tion in
terms
con·tra·fac'ti·o'
con·tra·li·ga'ti·o'
con·tra·man·da'ti·o'
con·tra·man·da'tum
con·tra·pla'ci·tum
con·tra·pos·i'ti·o'
còn'tra'ry
— to the ev'i·dence
— to law
con·tra·ven'ing eq'-
ui·ty
con·tra·ven'tion
con·trec·ta'ti·o'
con·trib'ute
con·tri·bu'tion
con·trib'u·to'ry *n.*
con·trib'u·to'ry *adj.*
— neg'li·gence
con·trol'
con·trol'ler
con·trol'ment
con'trov·er
con'tro·ver'sy
con'tro·vert'
con'tu·mace' cap'i··

en'do
con·tu·ma·cy
con·tu·max'
con·tu·me·ly
con·tuse'
con·tu'sion
co'nu·sance
co'nu·sant
co'nu·see'
co'nu·sor
con·va·les'cence
con·ven'a·ble
con·vene'
con·ven'ience and
   ne·ces'si·ty
con·ven'ient
con'vent
con·ven'ti·cle
con·ven'tion
con·ven'tion·al
con'ven·ti·o'ne'
con·ven'tions
con·ven'tu·als
con'ver·sant
con'ver·san'tes
con'ver·sa'tion
con'verse'
con·ver'sion
  con·struc'tive —
  di·rect' —
  fraud'u·lent —
con·vey'
con·vey'ance
con·vey'anc·er
con·vey'anc·ing
con·vict' v.
con'vict' n.
con·vict'ed
con·vic'tion
con·vinc'ing proof
con·viv'i·um
con·vo·ca'tion
con'voy'

co·ob'li·gor'
co·op'er·ate'
co·op'er·a'tion
co·op'er·ti·o'
co·op'er·tum
co·op'er·tu·ra
co·op'er·tus
co'-op·ta'tion
co·or'di·nate'
co·par'ce·nar'y
co·part'ner
co·part'ner·ship'
cope
cope'man or copes'-
  man
copes'mate'
cop'pa
cop'pice
cop'ro·la'li·a
copse
cop'u·la
cop'u·la'tive term
cop'y
cop'y·hold'
cop'y·right'
Cop'y·right' Act
co'ram
  — dom'i·no' reg'e'
  — ip'so' reg'e'
  — no'bis
  — non ju'di·ce'
  — pa·ri'bus
  — sec'ta·tor'i·bus
  — vo'bis
cord
co're·spond'ent
corn
corn'age
cor'ner
cor·net'
co·ro'di·o' ha·ben'-
  do'
co·ro'di·um

cor'o·dy
cor'ol·lar'y
co·ro'na
  — ma'la
co·ro·na're'
cor'o·na'tion
cor'o·ner
cor'o·ner's
  — court
  — in'quest'
cor'po·ral
  — pun'ish·ment
cor'po·rate
  — al'ter e'go
  — bod'y
  — bonds
  — fran'chise'
  — name
  — pur'pose
cor'po·ra'tion
  busi'ness —
  — de fac'to'
  — de ju're'
  joint'-stock' —
  mi'gra·to'ry —
  qua'si' pub'lic —
cor'po·ra'tions
  ag·gre'gate and
    sole —
  close and o'pen —
  do·mes'tic and for'-
    eign —
  ec·cle'si·as'ti·cal and
    lay —
  el'ee·mos'y·nar'y
    and
    civ'il —
  mu·nic'i·pal —
  pub'lic and pri'-
    vate —
  pub'lic-serv'ice —
  qua'si' —
  sub·sid'i·ar'y and

par′ent —
cor′po·ra′tor
cor·po′re·al
 — her′e·dit′a·ments
 — prop′er·ty
corps dip·lo·ma·-
 tique′
corpse
cor′pus
 — cum cau′sa
 — de·lic′ti′
 — ju′ris
 — can·o·ni′ci′
 — ci·vil′is
cor·rect′ at·test′
cor·rec′tion
cor·rec′tor of the
 sta′ple
cor·rel′a·tive
cor′res·pond′ence
cor′res·pond′ent
cor·rob′o·rate′
cor·rob′o·rat′ing ev′-
 i·dence′
cor·rob′o·ra′tive ev′-
 i·dence
cor·rupt′
Cor·rupt′ Prac′tic·es
 Act
cor·rup′tion
cor·rupt′ly
corse′let
corse′-pres′ent
cor′tex′
cor′tis
cos′en·age, cos′in·-
 age, or cous′in·-
 age
cos′en·ing
cosh′er·ing
cost
 — bond
co-stip′u·la′tor-cost′-

plus′ con′tract
costs
 bill of —
 bond for —
 cer·tif′i·cate for —
 dou′ble —
 — of col·lec′tion
 se·cu′ri·ty for —
co-sure′ties
cot·ag′i·um
cot·ar′i·us
co·ten′an·cy
co′te·rie
cotes′wold′
cot′land
cot′seth·la
cot′seth·land
cot′set·us
cot′tage
cot′ti·er ten′an·cy
cot′ton
cot·u′chans
couch′ant
couch′er or courch′-
 er
coun′cil
 com′mon —
 priv′y —
coun′sel
coun′sel·or or
 coun′sel·lor
count v.
count n.
 spe′cial —
count′-out′
coun′te·nance
count′er n.
coun′ter adj.
coun′ter·claim′
coun′ter·feit
coun′ter·feit·er
coun′ter·fe′sance
coun′ter·mand′

coun′ter·part′
coun′ter-rolls′
coun′ter·sign′
coun′ter·vail′
coun′ter·vail′ing
 eq′ui·ty
coun′tors
coun′try
counts
 com′mon —
coun′ty
 — seat
cou′pled with an
 in′ter·est
cou′pons
course
 — of bus′i·ness
 — of em·ploy′ment
court
 — a·bove′
 — be·low′
 civ′il —
 crim′i·nal —
 de fac′to′ —
 — en banc
 eq′ui·ty —
 full —
 — in bank
 in·fe′ri·or —
 law —
 — of ap·peals′
 — of bank′rupt·cy
 — of chan′cer·y
 — of claims
 — of com′mon
 pleas
 — of com′pe·tent
 ju′ris·dic′tion
 — of cus′toms and
 pat′ent ap·peals′
 — of eq′ui·ty
 — of er′ror
 — of ex·cheq′uer

— of first in'stance
— of law
— of lim'it·ed ju'ris-dic'tion
— of ni'si' pri'us
— of pro'bate'
— of rec'ord
— of star cham'ber
— of the cor'o·ner
pro'bate' —
su·pe'ri·or —
Court
  High — of Ad'mi·-ral·ty
  — of Ad'mi·ral·ty
  His Maj'es·ty's — of Ap·peal'
  Su·preme' Ju·di'·cial —
  Su·preme' — of Er'-rors
court'-bar'on
court'-hand'
court'house'
court'-leet'
court'-mar'tial
courts
  — of ap·peals'
  — of as·size' and ni'si' pri'us
court'yard'
cous'in
  first —
  quar'ter —
  sec'ond —
co·ve·na·ble'
cov'e·nant
  ab'so·lute' —
  af·firm'a·tive —
  — a·gainst' en·cum'-branc·es
  aux·il'ia·ry —
  col·lat'er·al —

con·cur'rent —
con·di'tion·al —
con·tin'u·ing —
de·clar'a·to'ry —
de·pend'ent —
dis·junc'tive —
ex'e·cut·ed —
ex·ec'u·to'ry —
ex·press' —
— for fur'ther as·-sur'ance
— for qui'et as·-sur'ance
— for ti'tle
full —
gen'er·al —
im·plied' —
in'de·pend'ent —
— in gross
in·her'ent —
in·tran'si·tive —
joint —
mu'tu·al —
neg'a·tive —
— not to sue
o·blig'a·to'ry —
— of non'claim'
— of right to con·-vey'
— of sei'zin *or* sei'-sin
— of war'ran·ty
per'son·al —
prin'ci·pal —
real —
— run'ning with land
— run'ning with ti'tle
sep'a·rate —
sev'er·al —
spe·cif'ic —
— to con·vey'

— to re·new'
— to stand seized *or* seised
tran'si·tive —
u'su·al —
cov'e·nan·tee'
cov'e·nan'tor
cov'er
cov'ert
cov'er·ture
cov'in
cov'i·nous
cow'ard·ice
coz'en *or* cos'en
craft
cran'age
cra'ven
cra'zy
cre·ate'
cre·den'tials
cred'i·bil'i·ty
cred'i·ble
  — per'son
  — wit'ness
cred'it
  bill of —
  let'ter of —
  line of —
  per'son·al —
cred'it·ed
cred'i·tor
  at·tach'ing —
  — ben'e·fi'ci·ar'y
  cer·tif'i·cate' —
  ex'e·cu'tion —
  gen'er·al —
  judg'ment —
  pe·ti'tion·ing —
  prin'ci·pal —
  se·cured' —
  sub'se·quent —
  war'rant —
cred'i·tors' bill *or*

suit
cred′its
  mu′tu·al —
creed
cre·ma′tion
cre·pus′cu·lum
crest
cre′tin·ism
cri′er
cri·ez′ la peez
crime
  com′mon law —
  — a·gainst′ na′ture
  — a·gainst′ the
    oth′er
  — ma′la in se
  — ma′la pro·hib′-
    i·ta
  high —
  in′fa·mous —
  qua′si′ —
  stat′u·to′ry —
cri′men
  — fal′si
  — lae′sae′ maj′-
    es·ta′tis
crim′i·nal *n.*
crim′i·nal *adj.*
  — con′ver·sa′tion
  — in′for·ma′tion
  — in·tent′
  — mal′ver·sa′tion
crim′i·nal·ist
crim′i·nate′
crim′i·nol′o·gy
crimp
crip′pling
crit′i·cism
cro′ci·a
croft
crois′es
croi′teir
crook

crook′ed
crop′per
cross
  — ac′tion
  — claim
  — de·mand′
  — er′rors
  — sale
crossed check
cross′-ex·am′i·na′-
  tion
cross′ing
crowd
crown
  — cas′es
  — cas′es re·served′
  — court
  — debts
  — lands
  — law
  — of′fice
  — of′fice in chan′-
    cer·y
  — pa′per
  — side
  — so·lic′i·tor
croy
cru·ce′ sig·na′ti′
cru′el and un·u′su·al
  pun′ish·ment
cru′el·ty
cruise
cry de pais *or* cri
  de pais
cry′er
cryp′ta
cuck′old
cui bo′no′
cul·a′gi·um
cul de sac
cul′pa
cul′pa·bil′is
cul′pa·ble

cul′prit
cul′ti·vate′
cul′ti·vat′ed
cul′ti·va′tor
cul·tu′ra
cul′vert·age
cum cop′u·la
cum o′ne·re′
cum tes′ta·men′to′
  an·nex′o′
cu′mu·la′tive
  — ev′i·dence
cun′ni·lin′gus
cun′tey-cun′tey
cu′ra
cu′rate
cur′a·tive
cu·ra′tor
cu·ra′tor·ship′
cu·ra·trix′
cure
  — by ver′dict
cur′few
cu′ri·a
  — ad′vi·sa′ri′ vult
  — bar′on·is *or* bar′-
    on·um
  — co′mi·ta′tus
  — cur′sus aq′uae′
  — do′mi·ni′
  — mag′na
  — ma·jo′ris
  — mil′i·tum
  — pa·la′ti·i′
  — pe′dis pul′ver·i-
    za′ti′
  — pen′ti·ci·a′rum
  — per·so′nae′
  — re′gis
cur′ing ti′tle
cur′nock′
cur′ren·cy
cur′rent

— ac·count'
— debt fund rule
— ex·pens'es
— funds
— li'a·bil'i·ties
— main'te·nance
— mon'ey
— ob'li·ga'tions
— price
— rate of wag'es
— rev'e·nues
— val'ue
— wag'es
— year
cur·ric'u·lum
cur'rit qua·tu'or
  pe'di·bus
curs'ing
cur'si'tor bar'on
cur'si·tors
cur'so'
cur'sor
cur'so·ry ex·am'i··
  na'tion
cur·tail'
cur'te·sy
— con·sum'mate
— in·i'ti·ate
Cur'teyn'
cur'ti·lage
cur·ti'les' ter'rae'
cur·til'li·um
cur'tis
cus·to'des
cus·to'di·a le'gis
cus·to'di·am lease
cus'to·dy
cus'tom
— du'ties
cus'tom·house'
— bro'ker
cus'tom·ar'i·ly
cus'tom·ar'y

— dis'patch
— es·tates'
— free'hold'
— serv'ic·es
— ten'ants
cus'tom·er
cus'toms
— court
cus'tos
— bre'vi·um
— fe·ra'rum
— hor're·i' re'gi·i'
— ma'ris
— mo'rum
— pla'ci·to'rum co·
  ro'nae'
— ro'tu·lo'rum
— ter'rae'
cus·tu'ma
— an·ti'qua si've'
  mag'na
— par'va et no'va
cuth'red
cut'purse'
cut'ter of the
  tal'lies
cy'ne·bot
cy'ne·bote'
cy'ne·gild'
cy'-pres'
cy·rog'ra·phar'i·us
cy·rog'ra·phum
czar

D

dac'ty·log'ra·phy
dag'ger
dai'ly
  av'er·age — bal'-

ance
— bal'ances
dair'y
dale and sale
dam
dam'age
— fea'sant *or* fai'-
  sant
— to per'son
dam'age–cleer'
dam'aged
dam'ag·es
ac'tu·al —
com·pen'sa·to'ry —
con'se·quen'tial —
ex·em'pla·ry —
gen'er·al —
— ir·rep'a·ra·ble
liq'ui·dat'ed — and
  pen'al·ties
nom'i·nal —
pe·cu'ni·ar'y —
prox'i·mate —
re·mote' —
spe'cial —
spec'u·la·tive —
— ul'tra
un·liq'ui·dat'ed —
dame
damn
dam'na
dam·na'tus
dam·ni·fi·ca'tion
dam'ni·fy'
dam'num
— abs'que' in·ju'-
  ri·a
— fa·ta'le'
Dane'gelt' *or* Dane'-
  geld'
Dane'lage'
dan'ger
dan·ger'i·a

dan'ger·ous
  — per se
dan'ism
dap'i·fer
dar·raign'
dar·rein'
  — con·tin'u·ance
  — pre·sent'ment
dash
da'ta
date
  — of in'ju·ry
  — of is'sue
da'tive
da'tum
daugh'ter
daugh'ter–in–law'
dau·phin'
day
  — cer'tain
  — in court
day'book'
dayer'i·a
day'light'
day'-rule' *or* day'-writ'
days
  — in bank
  — of grace
days'man
day'time'
day'were'
dea'con
dead'-born'
dead freight
dead let'ter
dead let'ters
dead'ly weap'on
  — per se
dead'man'
dead man's part
  — stat'ute
dead'-pledge'

deaf and dumb
deal
deal'er
deal'ers' talk
deal'ings
dean
death
  — du'ty
  nat'ur·al —
  pre·sump'tive —
  — trap
  — war'rant
  — watch
death'bed'
  — deed
deaths'man
de ban'co'
de·bas'ing
de·bauch'
de·bauch'er·y
de be'ne' es'se
de·ben'ture
  — in·den'ture
  — stock
deb'et
  — et det'i·net
  — et sol'et
  — si'ne' bre've'
de bi·en' et de mal
de bi·ens' le mort
deb'it
deb'i·tor
deb'i·trix'
deb'i·tum
  — si'ne' bre'vi'
de bo'no' et ma'lo'
debt
  an·ces'tral —
  judg'ment —
  le'gal —
  liq'uid —
debt'ee'
debt'or

debt'or's sum'mons
Dec'a·logue'
de·ca·na'tus
de·ca'ni·a
de·ca'nus
de·cap'i·ta'tion
de·cease'
de·ceased'
de·ce'dent
de·ceit
de·cen'a·ry *or* de·cen'na·ry
de'cen·cy
de·cen'na
de·cep'tion
de·ces'sus
de·cide'
dec'i·ma'tion
de·cime'
de·ci'sion
  — on mer'its
de·clar'ant
dec'la·ra'tion
  — a·gainst' in'ter·est
  — in chief
  — of div'i·dend
  — of home'stead'
  — of in·ten'tion
  — of right
  — of trust
  — of war
  dy'ing —
  self'-serv'ing —
Dec'la·ra'tion
  — of In'de·pend'ence
  — of Lon'don
  — of Par'is
  — of St. Pe'ters·burg'
de·clar'a·tor of trust
de·clar'a·to'ry
  — ac'tion

— de·cree′
— judg′ment
— stat′ute′
de·clare′
de clau′so′ frac′to′
de·clin′a·to′ry
— ex·cep′tions
— plea
de·cline′
de·col·la′ti·o′
de co·mon′ droit
de′com·posed′
de con·sil′i·o′ *or*
  con·cil′i·o′
— cu′ri·ae′
dec′o·rate′
dec′o·ra′tor
de cor′po·re′ com′-
  i·ta′tus
de′coy′
de·cree′
con·sent′ —
de·fi′cien·cy —
— ni′si′
— of dis′tri·bu′tion
— of in·sol′ven·cy
— of nul′li·ty
— pro con·fes′so′
de·crep′it
de·cre′tal
— or′der
de·crown′ing
de·cry′
de cu′jus
de cur′su′
de′di′
ded′i·cate′
ded′i·ca′tion
de di′e′ in di′em
ded′i·mus po′tes·ta′-
  tem
de·di′tion
de do′lo′ ma′lo′

de do′nis
de·duct′i·ble
de·duc′tion
— for new
deed
es·top′pel by —
— for a nom′i·nal
  sum
gra·tu′i·tous —
— in fee
— in·dent′ed
— in·den′ture
— of cov′e·nant
— of gift
— of re·lease′
— of sep′a·ra′tion
— of trust
— poll
— to lead uses
deem
deem′sters
de·face′
de fac′to′
— con′tract′
— gov′ern·ment
— in′te·gra′tion
— seg′re·ga′tion
de faire é·chelle′
de′fal·ca′tion
de·falk′
de·fam′a·cast′
def′a·ma′tion
de·fam′a·to′ry
— per quod
— per se
de·fault′
de·fea′sance
de·fea′si·ble
— fee
— ti′tle
de·fea′sive
de·feat′
de′fect′

— of par′ties
— of sub′stance
de·fec′tive
— ti′tle
de·fec′tus
de·fend′
de·fend′ant
— in error
de·fen′da·re′
de·fen′de·mus
de·fend′er
de′fen·er·a′tion
de·fense′
af·firm′a·tive —
eq′ui·ta·ble —
le′gal —
pre′ter·mit′ted —
real —
de′fen·si′va
de·fen′so′
de·fer′
de·ferred′
— life an·nu′i·ties
— pay′ments
— sen′tence
— stock
de·fi′ance
de·fi′cien·cy
— bill
def′i·cit
de·file′
de·file′ment
de·fine′
def′i·nite
defi·ni′ti·o′
def′i·ni′tion
de·fin′i·tive
de·flect′
def′lo·ra′tion
de·force′
de·force′ment
de·for′ci·ant
de·form′i·ty

de·fos'sion
de·fraud'
de'fraud·a'tion
de·funct'
de fur'to'
de·gas'ter
deg'ra·da'tion
de·grad'ing
de gra'ti·a
de·gree'
de·horn'er
de·hors'
de·hy'drate'
De'i' gra'ti·a
de in'cre·men'to'
de in·ju'ri·a
de ju'di·ci'is
de ju're'
de lat'e·re'
de'la'tor
de'la·tu'ra
de·lay'
del bi·en' es·tre'
del cre'de·re'
de·lec'tus
  per·so'nae'
del'e·gate'
del'e·gates'
  the high court of —
del'e·ga'tion
de·lete'
del'e·te'ri·ous
delf
de·lib'e·rate' v.
de·lib'e·rate adj.
de·lib'e·rate·ly
de·lib'e·ra'tion
del'i·ca·tes'sen
de·lict'
de·lic'tu·al fault
de·lic'tum
de·lim'it
de·lim'i·ta'tion

de·lin'quen·cy
de·lin'quent n.
de·lin'quent adj.
  — child
  — ju've·nile
  — tax'es
de·lir'i·um
  — fe·brile'
  — tre'mens
de·liv'er·ance
de·liv'er·y
  ab'so·lute' and con-
    di'tion·al —
  ac'tu·al and con-
    struc'tive —
  — bond
  — order
  sec'ond —
  sym·bol'ic —
de·lu'sion
de·main'
de ma'lo'
de·mand' v.
de·mand' n.
  cross —
  — in re·con·ven'-
    tion
  — note
  on —
de·mand'ant
de·man'dress
de·mean'or
de·mens'
de·ment'ed
de·men·te·nant' en
  a·vant'
de·men'ti·a
  — prae'cox'
de·mesne'
  — lands
  — lands of the
    crown
de·mesn'i·al

dem'i
de min'i·mus non
  cu'rat lex
dem'i-sangue' or
  dem'y-sangue'
de·mise' v.
de·mise' n.
  — and re'de·mise'
  — of the crown
  single —
de·mi'si'
de·mis'si·o'
de·mo'bil·i·za'tion
de·moc'ra·cy
dem'o·crat'ic
de·mol'ish
de·mon'e·ti·za'tion
dem'on·strate'
dem'on·stra'ti·o'
dem'on·stra'tion
de·mon'stra·tive
  — ev'i·dence
  — leg'a·cy
de·mo'tion
de·mur'
de·mur'ra·ble
de·mur'rage
de·mur'rant
de·mur'rer
  — book
  gen'er·al —
  — o're' ten'us
  pa·rol' —
  speak'ing —
  spe'cial —
  — to ev'i·dence
  — to in'ter·rog'a-
    to'ries
dem'y-sanke'
den
den and strond
de·nar'i·ate'
de·nar'i·i'

— de ca·ri·ta'te'
— Pe'tri
de·nar'i·us
— de'i'
— ter'tius com'i·-
ta'tus
de·ni'al
gen'e·ral —
spe·cif'ic —
den·ier'
den'i·za'tion
den·ize'
den'i·zen
de·nom'i·na'tion
de·nom'i·na'tion·al
de·nounce'
de·nounce'ment
de no'vo'
den·shir'ing of land
den'ti·frice
den'tist
den'tis·try
de·nu'mer·a'tion
de·nun'ci·a'tion
de·nun'ti·a'ti·o'
de·ny'
de'o·dand'
de of·fi'ce'
deor hedge
de·part'
de·part'ment
de·par'ture
de·pas'ture
de·pec'u·la'tion
de·pen'da·ble
de·pend'ence
de·pend'en·cy
de·pend'ent n.
de·pend'ent adj.
— con·di'tions
— con'tract'
— cov'e·nant
— prom'ise

— rel'a·tive rev'o·-
ca'tion
de·pend'ing
de·pe'sas
de pla·ci'to'
de·plet'a·ble ec'o·-
nom'ic in'ter·est
de·plete'
de·ple'tion
de'po·lym'er·i·za'-
tion
de·po'nent
de·pop'u·la'ti·o' a·-
gro'rum
de·pop'u·la'tion
de'por·ta'tion
de·pose'
de·pos'it v.
de·pos'it n.
— ac·count'
— com'pa·ny
— of ti'tle deeds
— slip
de·pos'i·tar'y
dep'o·si'tion
— de be'ne' es'se
de·pos'i·tor
de·pos'i·to'ry
de·pos'i·tum
de'pot
de prae·sen'ti'
de·prave'
de·praved' mind
de'pre·ci·a'tion
— re·serve'
dep're·da'tion
de·pres'sion
dep'ri·va'tion
de·prive'
de qui'bus
de quo
dep'u·tize'
dep'u·ty

de·raign'
de·rail'er
de·rail'ment
de·range'ment
der'e·lict
qua'si' —
der'e·lic'tion
de ri·en' cul·pa·ble'
de·riv'a·tive
— ac'tion
— con·vey'ances
de·rive'
de·rived'
der'o·ga'tion
de·rog'a·to'ry clause
de sa vie
de·scend'
de·scend'ant
de·scend'er
de·scend'i·ble
de·scent'
— cast
col·lat'er·al line
of —
di·rect' line of —
line of —
ma·ter'nal line of —
pa·ter'nal line of —
de·scribe'
de·scrip'ti·o' per·so'-
nae'
de·scrip'tion
de·scrip'tive
des'e·crate'
de·sert'
de·sert'er
de·ser'tion
de·serv'ing
des'ic·cate'
de·sign'
des'ig·nate'
des'ig·nat'ing pe·ti'-
tion

des′ig·na′tion
des′ig·na′ti·o′ per·-
  so′nae′
de·signed′
de·sign′ed·ly
de·sire′
de·siste′ment
de son tort
des·patch′es
des′per·ate
  — debt
de·spite′
de·spi′tus
de·spoil′
des′pon·sa′tion
des′pot
des′pot·ism
des·ren′a·ble
des′ti·na′tion
  — du père de fa-
    mille′
des′ti·tute′
de·stroy′
de·struc′tion
de·tail′
de·tain′
de·tain′er
de·tain′ment
de·tec′tion
de·tec′tive
de·tec′tor
de·ten′tion
de·ter′
de·te′ri·o·ra′tion
de·ter′mi·na·ble
de·ter′mi·nate
  — ob′li·ga′tion
de·ter′mi·na′tion
  — of will
de·ter′mine
de·tin′et
de·tin′ue
  — of goods in frank

    mar′riage
de·tin′u·it
de′tour′
de·tourne′ment
de·trac′tion
det′ri·ment
de u′na par′te′
deu′ter·og′a·my
dev′as·ta′tion
de′vas·ta′vit
de·vel′op
de·vel′oped wa′ter
de·vest′
de′vi·a′tion
de·vice′
dev′il·ling
de·vis′a·ble
de·vise′
  con·di′tion·al —
  con·tin′gent —
  ex·ec′u·to′ry —
  gen′er·al —
  lapsed —
  re·sid′u·ar′y —
  spe·cif′ic —
  vest′ed —
de·vi·see′
de·vi′sor
dev′o·lu′tion
dev′o·lu′tive ap·-
  peal′
de·volve′
de·vul′can·ize′
de·vy′
dex′tras da′re′
di·ac′o·nate
di·ac′o·nus
di·ag·no′sis
di·ag′o·nal
di′a·lec′tics
di·al′lage
di·a·nat′ic
di·ar′i·um

di′a·ther′my
di′a·tim
di′ca
dice
di co·lon′na
dic′ta
dic′tate′
dic·ta′tion
dic′ta·tor
dic·ta′tor·ship′ of
  pro′le·tar′i·at
dic·to′res′
dic′tum
  o·bi′ter —
  sim′plex′ —
die *n*.
die *v*.
  — with·out′ is′sue
di′e·i′ dic′ti·o′
di′em clau′sit ex·-
  tre′mum
di′es
  — a·mo′ris
  — a quo
  — ce′dit
  — com·mu′nes in
    ban′co
  — Do·min′i·cus
  — ex·cres′cens′
  — gra′ti·ae′
  — in′ter·ci′si′
  — ju·rid′i·cus
  — le·git′i·mus
  — mar′chi·ae′
  — non ju·rid′i·cus
  — pa′cis
  — so·lar′is
  — so′lis
  — u·til′es′
di′es′ da′tus
  — in ban′co
  — par′ti·bus
  — pre′ce par′ti·um

di'et
di·e'ta
Dieu Son acte
dif·fa'ce·re'
dif'fer·ence
dif'fi·cult'
dif'for·ci·a're'
dif·fuse'
dig'a·ma *or* dig'a·my
di'gest'
di'ges'ta
Di'gests'
dig'ging
dig'ni·tar'y
dig'ni·ty
di·ju'di·ca'tion
dike
dik'ing
di·lap'i·da'tion
dil'a·to'ry
  — de·fense'
  — ex·cep'tions
  — pleas
dil'i·gence
  due —
  ex·traor'di·nar'y —
  great —
  high —
  low —
  nec'es·sar y —
  or'di·nar'y —
  rea'son·a·ble —
  slight —
  spe'cial —
dil'i·gent
dime
di·min'ished re·
  spon'si·bil'i·ty
  doc'trine
dim'i·nu'tion
di·mi'si'
di·mi'sit
dim'is·so'ry let'ters

di·nar'chy
di·ner'o'
di·oc'e·san
  — courts
  — mis'sion
di'o·cese
di·oi·chi'a
dip
di·plo'ma
di·plo'ma·cy
dip'lo·mat'ics
dip'so·ma'ni·a
dip'so·ma'ni·ac'
dip'tych
dip'tych·a
di·rect' *v.*
di·rect' *adj.*
  — at·tack'
  — cause
  — ev'i·dence
  — ex'am·i·na'tion
  — in'ju·ry
  — in'ter·est
  — loss
  — pay'ment
  — tax
di·rec'tion
di·rect'ly
di·rec'tor
Di·rec'tor of the
  Mint
di·rec'tors
di·rec'to·ry
  — stat'ute
  — trust
dirt
dis'a·bil'i·ty
  tem'po·rar'y —
  to'tal —
dis·a'ble
dis·a'bling stat'utes
dis·ad·vo'ca·re'
dis·af·firm'

dis·af·firm'ance
dis·af·for'est
dis·a·gree'ment
dis·alt'
dis·al·low'
dis·ap·pro·pri·a'tion
dis·ap·prove'
di·sas'ter
dis·a·vow'
dis·bar'
dis·bo·ca'ti·o'
dis·burse'ments
dis·charge'
dis'ci·pline
dis·claim'er
dis·close'
dis·clo'sure
dis·com'mon
dis'con·tin'u·ance
  — of an es·tate'
dis'con·tin'u·ous
dis'con·ven'a·ble
dis'count'
  — bro'ker
dis·cov'er
dis·cov'ert
dis·cov'er·y
dis·cred'it
dis·creet'ly
dis·crep'an·cy
dis·crete'ly
dis·cre'tion
dis·cre'tion·ar'y
  — dam'ag·es
  — pow'er
  — trusts
dis·crim'i·na'tion
dis·cus'sion
dis·ease'
dis·en·tail'ing deed
dis·fig'ure·ment
dis·fran'chise'
dis·fran'chise'ment

dis·gav'el
dis·grace'
dis·grad'ing
dis·guise'
dis·her'i·tor
dis·hon'es·ty
dis·hon'or
dis·in·car'cer·ate'
dis·in·fect'ed
dis·in·her'i·tance
dis·in·ter'
dis·in'ter·est·ed
— wit'ness
dis·junc'tive
— al'le·ga'tion
— term
dis·lo·ca'tion
dis·loy'al
dismes
dis·miss'
dis·miss'al
— a·greed'
— com'pen·sa'tion
— with prej'u·dice
— with·out' prej'u·-
  dice
dis·missed'
— for want of
  eq'ui·ty
dis·mort'gage
dis·or'der
dis·or'der·ly
— con'duct'
— house
— per'sons
dis·par'a·ga'ti·o'
dis·par'a·ga'tion
dis·par'age
dis·par'age·ment
dis·patch' or
  des·patch'
dis·pau'per
dis·pel'
dis·pen'sa·ry

dis'pen·sa'tion
dis·pense'
dis·place'
dis·play'
dis·pos'a·ble
  por'tion
dis·po'sàl
dis·pose' of
dis·pos'ing
— ca·pac'i·ty
— mind
dis'po·si'tion
dis·pos'i·tive facts
dis'pos·sess'
dis'pos·ses'sion
dis·prove'
dis·pun'ish·a·ble
dis·put'a·ble
  pre·sump'tion
dis·pute'
dis·qual'i·fy'
dis·rate'
dis're·gard'
dis're·pair'
dis're·pute'
dis·sec'tion
dis·seise'
dis'sei·see'
dis'sei·sin
dis·sei'si·trix'
dis·sei'si'tus
dis·sei'sor
dis·sei'so·ress
dis·sem'ble
dis·sent'
dis·sent'er
dis·sent'ers
dis'sig·na're'
dis'so·lute'
dis'so·lu'tion
— of par'lia·ment
dis·solve'
dis·solv'ing bond
dis·suade'

dis'tance
dis·till'
dis·till'er
dis·till'er·y
dis·tinct'
dis·tinc'tive·ly
dis·tin'guish
dis·tort'
dis·tract'ed per'son
dis·trac'tion rule
dis·train'
dis·train'er or
  dis·trai'nor
dis·traint'
dis·tress'
— and dan'ger
— in'fin·ite
sec'ond —
— war'rant
writ of grand —
dis·trib'ute
dis·trib'u·tee'
dis'tri·bu'tion
dis·trib'u·tive
— jus'tice
— share
dis'trict
— at·tor'ney
— clerk
— court
— judge
— par'ish·es
— reg'is·try
Dis'trict of
  Co·lum'bi·a
dis·trin'gas
dis·trin'ge·re'
dis·turb'
dis·turb'ance
— of peace
dis·turb'er
ditch
ditch'ing, dik'ing,
  or til'ing

di·verge'
di'vers
di·ver'sion
di·ver'si·ty
  — of cit'i·zen·ship'
di·vert'
dives
di·vest'
di·ves'ti·tive fact
di·vide'
div'i·dend'
  — ad·di'tion
  cu'mu·la'tive —
  ex —
  ex·traor'di·nar'y —
  liq'ui·da'tion —
  pre·ferred' —
  scrip —
  stock —
div'i·den'da
di·vine' right of
  kings
di·vis'i·ble
  — con'tract'
  — of·fense'
di·vi'sion
  — of o·pin'ion
di·vi'sion·al courts
di·vorce'
  — a men'sa et
    tho'ro'
  — a vin·cu'lo'
    mat'ri·mo'ni·i'
  for'eign —
  lim'it·ed —
  — suit
di·vulge'
doc'i·ma'si·a
  pul·mo'num
dock *v.*
dock *n.*
  — war'rant
dock'age
dock'et

dock'-mas'ter
doc'tor
doc'tri·nal in·ter'-
  pre·ta'tion
doc'trine
doc'u·ment
  for'eign —
  pub'lic —
doc'u·ments
  an'cient —
  ju·di'cial —
doc'u·men'ta·ry
  — ev'i·dence
dog'-draw'
dog'ger
dog'ma
do'ing busi'ness
doit'kin *or* doit
dole
do'lus
  — bo'nus
  — ma'lus
do'main
dom'bec' *or*
  dom'boc'
dome
Dome'-Book'
Domes'day'
Domes'day' Book
domes'men
do·mes'tic *n.*
do·mes'tic *adj.*
  — an'i·mals
  — courts
  — pur'pos·es
  — ser'vant
do·mes'ti·cat'ed
do·mes'ti·cus
dom'i·cile'
  change of —
  com·mer'cial —
  de fac'to' —
  do·mes'tic —
  e·lect'ed —

  for'eign —
  mat'ri·mo'ni·al —
  — of choice
  — of cor'po·ra'tion
  — of or'i·gin
  — of suc·ces'sion
dom'i·ciled'
dom'i·cil'i·ar'y
  — ad·min'is·tra'tion
dom'i·cil'i·ate'
dom'i·nate'
do·min'i·cum
do·min'ion
do'mi·nus li'tis
do'mus
Do'mus
  — De'i'
  — Pro·ce'rum
do·na·tar'i·us
do·na'ti·o'
  — in'ter vi'vos'
  — mor'tis cau'sa
  — prop'ter
    nup'ti·as'
do·na'tion
  — lands
don'a·tive trust
do'na'tor
don'a·to'ri·us
don'a·to'ry
done
do'nec'
do'nee'
do'nis, stat'ute de
do'nor
doom
Dooms'day Book
dope
dor'mant
  — claim
  — ex'e·cu'tion
  — judg'ment
  — part'ner
dor'mi·to'ry

dor′sum
dor′ture
dos·si·er′
dot
do′tage
do′tal
  — prop′er·ty
do·ta′tion
dote *v.*
do′te *n.*
do′tis ad·min′is·tra′-
  ti·o′
do′tis·sa
dou′ble
  — as·sess′ment
  — a·dul′ter·y
  — costs
  — cred′i·tor
  — dam′ag·es
  — ea′gle
  — en′try
  — fine
  — flem′ish bond
  — glaz′ing
  — house
  — in·sur′ance
  — jeop′ard·y
  — pat′ent·ing
  — re·cov′er·y
  — rent
  — tax·a′tion
  — tax rule
  — use
  — val′ue
  — vouch′er
  — waste
  — will
dou′bles
doubt
doubt′ful ti′tle
doun
dove
dow′a·ble

dow′a·ger
  — queen
dow′er
  — by com′mon law
  — by cus′tom
  — de la plus belle
  — ex as·sen′su′
    pat′ris
  — un′de′ ni′hil
    hab′et
dowle stones
dow′ment
down′ward course
dow′ress
dow′ry
Doyle rule
doze
doz′en peers
drach′ma
dra·co′ni·an laws
dra′co re′gis
draff
draft
drafts′man
drag
Dra′go doctrine
drain
drain′age dis′trict
dram
  — shop
  — shop act
dra′ma
dra·mat′ic com′po·-
  si′tion
dra·mat′ic work
draught
draw *n.*
draw *v.*
draw′back′
draw·ee′
draw′er
draw′ing
draw′latch′es

dray′age
dredge
dreit′-dreit′
drench′es *or*
  dreng′es
dren′gage
dress′ing
dri′er
drift *v.*
drift *n.*
drifts of the for′est
drift′-stuff′
drift′way′
drill and com·plete′
  a well
drilled
drill′ing in
drink′ing shop
drip
drive *n.*
drive *v.*
driv′er
driv′ing
droit
  — close
  — com′mon
  — cou·tu·mi·er′
  — d'ac·ces·sion′
  — d'ac·crois·se·-
    ment′
  — d'au·baine′
  — de de·trac·tion′
  — de suite
  — in′ter·na′tion·al
  — mar·i·time′
  — na·tu·rel′
droit′-droit′
droits
  — ci·vils′
  — of ad·mir′al·ty
droi·tu′ral
drop let′ter
drov′er's pass

drown
drug
drug′gist
drug′store′
drunk
drunk′en·ness
dry
— check
— dock
— ex·change′
— mort′gage
— nat′u·ral gas
— oil
— trust
du′al na′tion·al′i·ty
du′ar·chy′
du′bi·tans
du′bi·tan′te′
du′bi·ta·tur′
du′bi·ta′vit
duc′at
du′ces′ te′cum′
— li′cet lan·gui′dus
duch′y
— court of
Lan·cas′ter
duck′ing stool
due
— and prop′er care
— and rea·son′a·ble
care
— bill
— care
— com′pen·sa′tion
— con·sid′e·ra′tion
— course hold′er
— course of law
— date
— dil′i·gence
— in′flu·ence
— no′tice
— post′ing
— proc′ess′ of law

— proof
— re·gard′
du′el
du′el·ing
du·el′lum
dues
Duke of York's
laws
du·loc′ra·cy
du′ly
— qual′i·fied′
dum
— so′la
dumb′-bid′ding
dum·mo′do′
dum′my *n.*
dum′my *adj.*
— di·rec′tor
dump
dump′ing
dun
dun′geon
dun′nage
du′o·dec′i·ma
ma′nus
du′o·de′na
— ma·nu′
du′o·de′num
du′plex′
— house
— que′re·la
— val′or
mar′i·ta′gi·i′
du′pli·cate′ *v.*
du′pli·cate *n.*
— will
du′pli·ca′tum jus
du·plic′i·tous
— ap·peal′
du·plic′i·ty
du′ra·ble lease
du′ran·te′
— ab·sen′ti·a

— mi·no′re′ ae·ta′te′
— vi·du·i·ta′te′
— vir′gin·i·ta′te′
— vi′ta
du·ra′tion
du·ress′
— of goods
— of im·pris′on-
ment
— per mi′nas
du·res′sor
Dur′ham rule
dur′ing
— good be·hav′ior
Dutch lot′ter·y
du′ties
— of de·trac′tion
— on im′ports′
du′ty
ju·di′cial —
le′gal —
— of ton′nage
— of wa′ter
dwell
dwell′ing house *or*
dwell′ing place
dy′ing
— dec′la·ra′tion
— with·out′ is′sue
dyke reed *or* dyke
reeve
dy′nas·ty
dys′pa·reu′ni·a
dys·pep′si·a

E

each
— and eve′ry
ea′gle

earl
earl'dom
Earl Mar'shal of
    Eng'land
ear'mark'
earn
earned in'come'
earn'er
ear'nest
    — mon'ey
earn'ing
    — ca·pac'i·ty
    — pow'er
earn'ings
    gross —
    net —
    sur'plus —
earth
ear'-wit'ness
ease
ease'ment
    af·firm'a·tive —
    ap·par'ent —
    ap·pur'te·nant —
    — by pre·scrip'tion
    con·tin'u·ing —
    dis'con·tin'u·ing —
    eq'ui·ta·ble —
    im·plied' —
    — in gross
    in'ter·mit'tent —
    neg'a·tive —
    — of ac'cess'
    — of con·ven'ience
    — of ne·ces'si·ty
    pri'vate —
    pub'lic —
    qua'si' —
    re·cip'ro·cal
        neg'a·tive —
    sec'on·dar'y —
east
East'er

— dues
— of'fer·ings
— term
east'er·ly
eat'ing house
eaves
eaves'drop'ping
eb'ba
ebb and flow
e·bri'e·ty
ec'cen·tric'i·ty
ec'chy·mo'sis
ec·cle'si·as'tic
ec·cle'si·as'ti·cal
    — au·thor'i·ties
    — com·mis'sion·ers
    — coun'cil
    — courts
    — ju'ris·dic'tion
    — law
    — mat'ter
ech'o·la'li·a
ec·lec'tic
    — prac'tice
e·con'o·miz'er
e·con'o·my
e con'tra
e con·ver'so'
ec'u·men'i·cal
edge
    — lease
e'dict'
E'dicts of
    Jus·tin'i·an
e·di'tion
ed'i·tor
ed'i·tus
ed'u·cate'
ed'u·ca'tion
ed'u·ca'tion·al
    in'sti·tu'tion
ef·fect'
ef·fect'ing loan

ef·fec'tive pro·cur'-
    ing cause
ef·fects'
ef·fi'cient
    — cause
    — in'ter·ven'ing
        cause
ef'fi·gy
ef'flux'
ef·flux'ion of time
ef'fort
ef·frac'tion
ef·frac'tor
e'go
e'gress
eire or eyre
eis'ne'
ei'ther
e·ject'
e·jec'ta
e·jec'tion
e·jec'ti·o·ne'
    — cus·to'di·ae'
    — fir'mae'
e·ject'ment
e·jec'tor
e·jec'tum
e'ju·ra'tion
e·jus'dem gen'e·ris
e·las'tic
eld'est
e·lect'ed
e·lec'tion
    — au'di·tors
    es·top'pel by —
    — re·turns'
e·lec'tive
    — fran'chise'
    — of'fice
e·lec'tor
e·lec'tor·al
    — col'lege
    — com·mis'sion

e·lec'tric'i·ty
e·lec'tro·car'di·og'-
　ra·phy
e·lec'tro·cute'
e·lec'tro·cu'tion
e·lec'trol'y·sis
el'ee·mos'y·nar'y
　— cor'po·ra'tion
e·le'git
el'e·ment
el'e·ments
el'e·va'tor
el'i·gi·bil'i·ty
el'i·gi·ble
e·lim'i·na'tion
e'lin·gua'tion
e·li'sors
el·lip'sis
e·loign'ment
e'lon·ga'ta
e'lon·ga'tus
e'lon·ga'vit
e·lope'ment
else'where'
e·man'ci·pa'tion
E·man'ci·pa'tion
　Proc'la·ma'tion
em·bar'go
em'bas·sage
em'bas·sy
em·bez'zle·ment
em'ble·ments
em'bo·lism
em'bo·lus
em·brac'er·y
e·men'da
e·men'dals
e·merge'
e·mer'gen·cy
em'i·grant
em'i·gra'tion
em'i·nence
em'i·nent do·main'

em'is·sar'y
e·mis'sion
e·mit'
e·mol'u·ment
em'per·or
em'pire'
em·pir'ic
em·pir'i·cal
em·plead'
em·ploy'
em·ployed'
em·ploy'ee
em·ploy'er
em·ploy'ers'
　li'a·bil'i·ty acts
em·ploy'ment
em·po'ri·um
em·pow'er
em'pre·sa'ri·os
emp'tor'
en·a'ble
en·a'bling
　— act
　— pow'er
en·act'
en·act'ing clause
en banc
en·bre·ver'
en·ceinte'
en·close'
en·clos'ure
en·cour'age
en·croach'
en·croach'ment
en·cum'ber
en·cum'brance
en·cum'branc·er
en·deav'or
en de·meure'
en·den'zie or
　en·den'i·zen
en'do·car·di'tis
en·dorse' or

in·dorse'
en'dors·ee' or
　in'dors·ee'
en·dorse'ment or
　in·dorse'ment
　ac·com'mo·da'-
　　tion —
　blank —
　con·di'tion·al —
　full —
　ir·reg'u·lar —
　prop'er —
　qual'i·fied' —
　reg'u·lar —
　re·stric'tive —
　spe'cial —
en·dors'er or
　in·dors'er
en·dow'
en·dow'ment
　— pol'i·cy
end to end
en·dur'ance
en'e·my
　pub'lic —
en fait'
en·feoff'
en·feoff'ment
en·force'
en·force'a·ble
en·fran'chise'
en·fran'chise'ment
　— of cop'y·holds'
en·gage'
en·gaged' in
　com'merce
en·gage'ment
en·gen'der
en'gine
en'gi·neer'
en'gi·neer'ing
en·grav'ing
en gros

en·gross'
en·gross'er
en·gross'ing
en·hanced'
en·hér·i·tance'
e·ni'ti·a pars
en·join'
en·joy'
en·joy'ment
   ad·verse' —
   qui'et —
en·large'
en·larg·er' l'es·tate'
en·larg'ing
en·list'ment
en masse'
en mort mayne
e·nor'mous
en o'wel main
en·roll'
en·roll'ment
   — of ves'sels
en route
en·seal'
en·serv'er
ens le'gis
en·sue'
en·tail'
en·tailed'
en·tail'ment
en·tend'ment
en'ter
en·ter·ceur'
en·ter·ing
   — judg'ments
en'ter·prise'
en'ter·tain'ment
en·thu'si·asts'
en·tice'
en·tire'
   — blood
   — con'tract'
en·tire'ty

en·ti'tle
en'ti·ty
en'trails'
en'trance
en·trap'
en·trap'ment
en·treat'y
en·tre·bat'
en'tre·pôt
en'try
   — ad com·mu'nem
    le'gum
   — by court
   for'ci·ble —
   — of judg'ment
   pre-emp'tion —
   writ of —
en'try·man
e·nu'mer·at'ed
e·nu'mer·a'tors
en·ure'
en·vel'op
en've·lope'
en ven'tre sa mère
en vie
en'voy'
en'zyme'
e'o'
   — di'e'
   — in·stan'ti'
   — in·tu'i·tu'
   — lo'ci'
   — nom'i·ne'
ep'i·dem'ic
ep'i·lep'sy
e·piph'y·sis
e·pis'co·pa·cy
E·pis'co·pa'li·an
e·pis'co·pate
e·pis'to·la
e·pis'to·lae'
e plu'ri·bus u'num
ep'och

e'qual
   — pro·tec'tion of
    the laws
e·qual'i·ty
e·qual'i·za'tion
e'qual·ize'
e'qual·ly di·vid'ed
e'qui·lib'ri·um
e'qui·nox'
e·quip'
e·quip'ment
eq'ui·ta·ble
   — ac'tion
   — as·sign'ment
   — con·ver'sion
   — de·fense'
   — doc'trine of
    ap·prox'i·ma'tion
   — e·lec'tion
   — es·top'pel
   — ex'e·cu'tion
   — liens
   — rate of in'ter·est
   — re·coup'ment
   — re·scis'sion
eq·ui'tas' se'qui-·
   tur' le'gem
eq'ui·ty
   coun'ter·vail'ing —
   courts of —
   — fol'lows the law
   — ju'ris·dic'tion
   — ju'ris·pru'dence
   nat'u·ral —
   — of re·demp'tion
   per'fect —
   — term
e·quiv'a·lent
e·quiv'o·cal
e·ra'sure
e·rect'
e·rec'tion
er'got

e·ro'sion
er'rant
　— wa'ter
er·ra'ta
er·ra'tum
er·ro'ne·ous
er'ror
　— ap·par'ent of
　　rec'ord
　— case
　— co'ram' no'bis
　— coram vo'bis
harm'ful —
harm'less —
　— in fact
　— in law
　— in vac'u·o'
　— no'mi·nus
　— of fact
　— of law
re·vers'i·ble —
writ of —
er'rors
as·sign'ment of —
cross —
　— ex·cept'ed
es'ca·la'tor clause
es·cape'
　— way
es·cheat'
es·chea'tor
Es·co·be'do rule
es'crow
es'ne·cy
es·pou'sals
es'quire'
es·sar'ter'
es·sar'tum
es'sence
　— of the con'tract'
es·sen'tial
es·sen'tial·ly
es·soin'

es·tab'lish
es·tab'lish·ment
es·tate'
ab'so·lute' —
　— at suf'fer·ance
　— at will
　— by e·le'git
　— by en·tire'ty
　— by pur'chase
　— by stat'ute mer'-
　　chant
　— by statute sta'ple
　— by the cur'te·sy
　— by the en·tire'ty
con·di'tion·al —
con·tin'gent —
ex'e·cut'ed —
ex'ec·u·to'ry —
executory de·-
　vise' —
executory re·main'-
　der —
fast —
　— for life
　— for years
　— from pe'ri·od to
　　pe'ri·od
　— from year to year
　— in com'mon
　— in co·par'ce·nar'y
　— in dow'er
　— in ex·pec'tan·cy
　— in fee sim'ple
　— in fee tail
　— in joint ten'an·cy
　— in lands
　— in re·main'der
　— in re·ver'sion
　— less than free'-
　　hold'
　— of freehold
　— of in·her'i·tance
　— on con·di'tion·al

lim'i·ta'tion
　— on limitation
　— pur au'tre vie
qual'i·fied' —
qua'si' — tail
real —
　— sub'ject to a
　　con·di'tion·al
　　lim'i·ta'tion
　— tail
　— tax
　— up·on' con·di'tion
　— upon condition
　　ex·pressed'
　— upon condition
　　im·plied'
vest'ed —
es·tates' of the
　realm
es'ti·mate'
es'ti·mat'ed cost
es·top'
es·top'pel
es·top'pel a·gainst'
　es·top'pel
es·to'vers
es·tray'
es·treat'
es·trepe'
es·trepe'ment
es'tu·ar'y
et
et al'i·i' è con'tra
et al'i·us
et al'lo·ca'tur'
et cet'er·a *or* et
　caet'er·a
eth'i·cal
eth'ics
etch'ing
et non
et sic
et ux'or'

eu·no·my
eu′nuch
eu′tha·na′si·a
e·va′si·o′
e·va′sion
e·va′sive
eve
e′ven
e′ven·ing
e·vent′
eve′ry
e·vict′
e·vic′tion
ev′i·dence
— of debt
— prop′er
ev′i·dent
ev′i·den′ti·ar·y
— facts
ev′i·dent·ly
e′vil
ev′o·ca′tion
ev′o·lu′tion
e·volved′
ew′age
ex
ex·ac′tion
ex al′ter·a par′te′
ex·am′en
ex·am′i·na′tion
ex·am′in·er
ex·am′in·ers
ex·an′nu·al roll
ex bo′nis
ex ca·the′dra
ex cau′sa
Ex′cel·len·cy
ex·cept′
ex·cept′ing
ex·cep′ti·o′
ex·cep′tion
— en masse
ex·cess′

— in·sur′ance
ex·cess′es
ex·ces′sive
— bail
ex·ces′sive·ly
ex·change′
ex·changed′
ex·cheq′uer
ex·cise′
— law
ex·clu′sion
ex·clu′sive
— a′gen·cy
— ju′ris·dic′tion
— of in′ter·est and
  costs
— own′er·ship′
— pos·ses′sion
— rem′e·dy
ex·clu′sive·ly
ex co·lo′re′
ex con′trac′tu′
ex′cul·pate′
ex′cul·pa′tion
ex·cul′pa·to′ry
— clause
ex cu′ri·a
ex·cus′a·ble
— as·sault′
— hom′i·cide′
— ne·glect′
ex·cus′a·tor′
ex·cuse′
ex de·fec′tu′
  san′gui·nis
ex de·lic′to′
ex div′i·dend
ex do·lo′ ma′lo′
— non o·ri′tur′
  ac′ti·o′
ex′e·cute′
ex′e·cut′ed
— con·sid′er·a′tion

— fine
— note
ex′e·cu′tion
— cred′i·tor
— lien
— of in′stru·ment
— sale
ex′e·cu′ti·o·ne′
  fa′ci·en′da
ex′e·cu′tion·er
ex·ec′u·tive
— a′gen·cy
— ca·pac′i·ty
ex·ec′u·tor
— named in will
— trus·tee′
ex·ec′u·to′ry
— con·sid′er·a′tion
— in′ter·ests
— lim′i·ta′tion
— proc′ess′
ex·ec′u·tress
ex·ec′u·trix′
ex·em′plar′
ex·em′pli·fi·ca′tion
ex·em′pli′ gra′ti·a
ex·empt′
ex·emp′tion
— laws
words of —
ex·empts′
ex′er·cise′
— of judg′ment
— of ju·di′cial
  dis·cre′tion
ex′er·cised′
  do·min′ion
ex′er·cis′ing an
  op′tion
ex fac′to′
ex gra′ti·a
ex·haus′tion of
  ad·min′is·tra′tive

rem'e·dies
ex·hib'e·re'
ex·hib'it
ex·hib'i·tant
ex·hib'it·ed
ex'hi·bi'tion
ex'hu·ma'tion
ex hy·poth'e·si'
ex'i·gence
ex'i·gen·cy
— of a bond
— of a writ
ex'i·gen'dar'y
ex'i·gent
— list
ex'i·gi·ble
— debt
ex'i·gi' fa'ci·as'
ex'ile'
ex in·dus'tri·a
ex·ist'
ex·is'tence
ex·ist'ing
— claim
— cred'i·tors
— debt
— use
ex'it
— wound
ex le'ge'
ex le'gi·bus
ex lo·ca'to'
ex ma'le·fi'ci·o'
ex ma·li'ti·a
ex me'ro' mo'to'
ex mo'ra
ex mu·tu'o'
ex ni·hi'lo' ni'hil fit
ex of·fi'ci·o'
ex·on'er·ate'
ex·on'er·a'tion
ex·or'bi·tant
ex par'te'

— ma·ter'na
— pa·ter'na
ex·pa'tri·a'tion
ex·pect'
ex·pect'an·cy
— of life
ex·pect'ant
— es·tates'
— heir
— right
ex'pec·ta'tion of life
ex·pect'ed
ex·pe'di·en·cy
ex·pe'di·ent
ex·ped'i·ment
ex·ped'i·ta'tion
ex'pe·dite'
ex'pe·dit'er
ex'pe·di'tion
ex'pe·di'tious
ex·pel'
ex·pend'
ex·pen'de·re'
ex·pen'di·tors
ex·pen'di·ture
ex·pense'
ex·pens'es of
ad·min'is·tra'tion
ex·pe'ri·ence
ex·per'i·ment
ex·per'i·men'tal
tes'ti·mo'ny
ex'pert'
— ev'i·dence
— wit'ness·es
ex'pi·ra'tion
ex·pire'
ex·plic'it
ex'ploi·ta'tion
ex'plo·ra'tion
ex·plo'sion
ex·plo'sive
ex·port' *v.*

ex'port *n.*
ex'por·ta'tion
ex·pose'
ex'po·si'tion
ex·pos'i·to'ry
stat'ute
ex post fac'to'
ex post facto law
ex·po'sure
ex·press'
— ab'ro·ga'tion
— ac'tive trust
— as·sump'sit
— au·thor'i·ty
— re·pub'li·ca'tion
ex·pressed'
ex·pres'si·o' u·ni'us
est ex·clu'si·o'
al·ter'i·us
ex·press'ly
ex·pro'pri·a'tion
ex pro'pri·o'
— mo'tu'
— vi·go're'
ex·pul'sion
ex·punge'
ex'pur·ga'tion
ex'pur·ga'tor
ex re·la'ti·o'ne'
ex tem'po·re'
ex·tend'
ex·tend'ed
ex·tend'ing
ex·ten'sion
— of note
ex·ten'sive
ex·tent'
— in aid
— in chief
ex·ten'u·ate'
ex·ten'u·at'ing
cir'cum·stanc'es
ex·ten'u·a'tion

ex·te'ri·or
ex·ter'nal
— vi'o·lent and
ac'ci·den'tal
means
ex·ter'ri·to'ri·al'i·ty
ex tes'ta·men'to'
ex·tinct'
ex·tin'guish
ex·tin'guish·ment
— of com'mon
— of cop'y·hold'
— of debts
— of leg'a·cy
— of lien
— of rent
— of ways
ex'tir·pa'tion
ex·tor'sive·ly
ex·tort'
ex·tor'tion
ex'tra
— al·low'ance
— com·mer'ci·a
— com'pen·sa'tion
— feo'dum
— ju'di·ci'um
— jus
— le'gem
— serv'ic·es
— ter'ri·to'ri·um
— vi'am
— vir'es'
ex·tract' v.
ex'tract' n.
ex'tra·di'tion
ex'tra·do'tal
prop'er·ty
ex'tra·haz'ard·ous
ex'tra·ju·di'cial
ex'tra·ju·di'cial·ly
ex'tra·lat'er·al right
ex'tra·mu'ral

ex·tra'ne·ous
— ev'i·dence
— of·fense'
ex·traor'di·nar'y
ex'tra·pa·ro'chi·al
ex'tra·ter·ri·to'ri-·
al'i·ty
ex·treme'
— and re·peat'ed
cru'el·ty
— cru'el·ty
ex·tre'mis
ex·trem'i·ty
ex·trin'sic
— am'bi·gu'i·ty
— ev'i·dence
ex·u·la're'
ex u'na par'te'
ex vol'un·ta'te'
ey
eye'wit'ness
ey'ott or ey'ot
eyre

F

fab'ric
— lands
fab'ri·ca
fab'ri·ca're'
fab'ri·cate'
fab'ri·cat'ed
ev'i·dence
fab'ri·cat'ing
fab'ri·ca'tion
face
— a·mount'
— of in'stru·ment
— of pol'i·cy
— val'ue

fa'cial dis·fig'ure-·
ment
fa'ci·as'
fa'ci·en'do'
fa'cies'
fac'ile
fa·cil'i·tate'
fa·cil'i·ties
fa·cil'i·ty
fac'ing
fac·sim'i·le
— pro'bate'
fact
fac'ta
fac'to'
— et an'i·mo'
fac'tor
fac'tor·age
fac'tor·ing
fac'to·riz'ing
proc'ess'
fac'tors' acts
fac'to·ry
facts
fac'tum
— ju·rid'i·cum
— pro'bans
fac'ul·ta'tive
com'pen·sa'tion
fac'ul·ties
fac'ul·ty
faed'er-feoh'
fag'got
fail
fail'ure
— of con·sid'er·a'-
tion
— of ev'i·dence
— of is'sue
— of proof
— of ti'tle
faint ac'tion
fair n.

fair *adj.*
— a·bridg′ment
— and eq′ui·ta·ble
— and equitable
　　val′ue
— and fea′si·ble
— and full e·quiv′-
　　a·lent for loss
— and im·par′tial
　　ju′ry
— and impartial
　　tri′al
— and prop′er
　　le′gal
　　as·sess′ment
— and rea′son·a·ble
　　com′pen·sa′tion
— and reasonable
　　mar′ket val′ue
— and reasonable
　　value
— and val′u·a·ble
　　con·sid′er·a′tion
— cash mar′ket
　　val′ue
— cash val′ue
— com′ment
— com′pe·ti′tion
— con·sid′er·a′tion
— e·quiv′a·lent
— mar′ket val′ue
— on its face
— plead′er
— pre·pon′der·ance
— price
— re·turn′ on
　　in·vest′ment
— tri′al
— us′age
— val′u·a′tion
— val′ue
fair′ly
fair′way′

fait
— ac·com·pli′
— en·rolle′
faith
faith′ful
faith′ful·ly
fai·tours′
fake
fak′er
fa′kir
fal′ang
fal·ca′re′
fald′stool′
fall *v.*
fall *n.*
— of land
fall′ing
fal·lo′pi·an tube
fal′low
— land
fal′lum
fal·sa′re′
fal·sa′ri·us *or*
　　fal·ca′ri·ous
false
— ac′tion
— and fraud′u·lent
— and mis·lead′ing
　　state′ment
— an′swer
— ar·rest′
— char′ac·ter
— checks
— claim
— dem′on·stra′tion
— en′try
— mak′ing
— or fraud′u·lent
　　claim
— per′son·a′tion
— pre′tens′es
— rec′ord
— rep′re·sen·ta′tion

— re·turn′
— state′ment
— swear′ing
— to′ken
— ver′dict
— weights
— wit′ness
— words
false′hood′
false′ly
— im·per′son·ate′
— make
fal′si·fi·ca′tion
fal′si·fy′
fal′si·fy′ing
— a judg′ment
— a rec′ord
fal′si·ty
fal′so·nar′i·us
fal′sus
fal′sus in u′no′,
　　fal′sus in
　　om′ni·bus
fa′ma
fam′a·cide′
fa·mil′i·a
fa·mil′iar
fa·mil′i·ar′i·ty
fam′i·ly
— car doc′trine
— ex·pens′es
— pur′pose
　　doc′trine
— serv′ice rule
fa·nat′ic
fan′ci·ful trade name
far′del of land
fard′ing-deal′
fare
far′leu′
far′ley
farm *v.*
farm *n.*

— let
farm'er
farm'ing
farm'-to'-mar'ket
  roads
far'o'
far'ri·er
far'thing
— of land
far'vand'
fas
fas'cism
fas'cist
fast bill of
  ex·cep'tions
fast day
fa'tal
— er'rors
— in'ju·ry
— var'i·ance
fa'ther
fa'ther-in-law'
fath'om
fa·tu'a mu'li·er'
fa·tu'i·tas'
fa'tum
fat'u·ous
fa·tu'um ju·dic'i·um
fa·tu'us
fau'bourg'
fau'ces' ter'rae'
fault
fau'tor
faux
fa'vor
feal
feal'ty
fear
fea'sance
fea'sant
fea'si·ble
fea'sor
feasts

fe'ci·al law
fed'er·al
— com'mon law
— courts
— gov'ern·ment
— in'stru·men·tal'-
  i·ty
— ques'tion
Fed'er·al Trade
  Com·mis'sion
Federalist, The
fed'er·ate'
fed'er·at'ed
fed'er·a'tion
fee
— farm
— farm rent
— sim'ple
— tail
feed
feigned
— ac·com'plice
— ac'tion
— dis·eas'es
— is'sue
fe·lag'us
fele
fel·la'ti·o'
fel·la'tion
fel'low
— heir
— rule
— ser'vant
fe'lo de se
fel'on
fe·lo'ni·a
fe·lo'ni·ce'
fe·lo'ni·ous
— as·sault'
— hom'i·cide'
fe·lo'ni·ous·ly
fel'o·ny
  com·pound'ing of —

  mis·pri'sion of —
  re·duc'i·ble —
fel'o·ny-mur'der rule
fe'male
feme *or* femme
— cov'ert
— sole
— sole trad'er
fem'i·cide'
fem'i·nine
femme
— coul·eur' lib·re'
fe·na'ti·o'
fence *v.*
fence *n.*
— coun'ty
— month
fenc'ing pat'ents
fend'er
fen'er·a'tion
Fe·ni'an
feod
feod'al
— ac'tions
feo'dum
feoff'ment
— to us'es
feof'for
feo·na'ti·o'
fer'ae'
— bes'ti·ae'
— na·tu'rae'
fer·del'la ter'rae'
fer'i·a
ferme
fer'men·ta'tion
fer'ment'ed liq'uors
fer'mo·ry
fer·ra'tor
fer'ri·age
fer'rum
fer'ry
fer'ry·boat'

fer′ry·man
fes′ta in cap′pis
fest′ing man′
fest′ing·pen′ny
fes′tum
fe′ti·cide′
fet′ters
feud
feu′dal
— courts
— law
— sys′tem
feu′dal·ism
feu′dal·ize′
feu′dar·y
feud′bote′
feu′dum
— an′ti·qu′um
— a·per′tum
— fran′cum
— hau′ber·ti′cum
— im′pro·pri′um
— in·di′vi·du′um
— lai′cum′
— li·gi′um
— ma·ter′num
— mil·i·ta′re′
— no′bi·le′
— no′vum
— no′vum ut
an′ti·qu′um
— pa·ter′num
— pro·pri′um
— tal′li·a′tum
few
fi·an·cer′
fi′at′
— jus′ti·ti′a
— justitia, ru′at
coe′lum
— ut pet′i·tur′
fi′aunt′
fic′tion

— of law
fic·ti′tious
— ac′tion
— name
— pay·ee′
— per′son
— plain′tiff
— prom′ise
fi′de·i′-com′mis·sar′y
fi·del′i·tas′
fi·del′i·ty bond
fi′des′
bo′na —
ma′la —
u·ber′ri·ma —
fi·du′cial
fi·du′ci·ar′y
— ca·pac′i·ty
— con′tract′
— heir
— re·la′tion
fief
— ten′ant
field
— book
fight
fig′ures
fil′a·cer
fi·la′re′
filch′ing
file *n.*
file *v.*
— wrap′per
es·top′pel
fil′i·ate′
fil′i·a′tion
— pro·ceed′ing
fil′i·us
— nul′li·us
— pop′u·li′
fill
fil′ly
fi′lum

— aq′uae′
— for′est·ae′
— vi′ae′
fi′nal
— de·ci′sion
— dis′po·si′tion
— set′tle·ment
fi′nance′ charge
fi·nanc′es
fi·nan′cial
— worth
fin′an·cier′
find
find′er
find′er's fee
find′ing
— of fact
fine *v.*
fine *n.*
— for al′ien·a′tion
— force
fi′nem fa′ce·re′
fines le roy
fin′ger
fin′ger·prints′
fi′nis
fi·ni′ti·o′
fird′fare′
fird′wite′
fire
— door
— es·cape′
— ex′it
— in·sur′ance
— wall
fire′arm′
fire′bug′
fire′fight′er
fire′man
fire′proof′
fire′wood′
fire′works′
fir′kin

firm
  — name
fir'ma
fir·ma'ri·us
firm'ly
first
  — blush
  — class
  — de'vi·see'
  — fruits
  — heir
  — im·pres'sion
first'-de·gree' burn
first in, first out rule
fisc
fis'cal
  — year
fish'er·y
fit
fix
  — up
fixed
  — as'set'
  — cap'i·tal
  — in·debt'ed·ness
  — li'a·bil'i·ties
fix'ing bail
fix'ture
fla'co'
flag
fla'grans
  — bel'lum
fla'grant
  — ne·ces'si·ty
fla·gran'te'
  — bel'lo'
  — de·lic'to'
flash check
flat'ter·y
flee from jus'tice
fleet
Fle'ta
flight

flim'flam'
float
float'a·ble
float'ing
  — cap'i·tal
  — debt
flog'ging
flood
floor
  — plan
  — plan fi·nanc'ing
  — plan'ning
floored
flor'in
flot'ag·es
flo·ter'i·al dis'trict
flot'sam *or* flot'san
flour'ish
flow'age
flow'ing
flume
flu'vi·us
flux'us
fly'ma
foal
fod'der
foe'ner·a'tion
foe'ti·cide'
foe'tus
fol'ge·re'
fol'gers
fo'li·o'
fol'low
fol'lows the
  prop'er·ty
foot
  — a'cre
  — front'age rule
foot'prints'
for ac·count' of
For'a·ker act
for·bar·rer'
for·bear'ance

for cause
force
  — ma·jes·ture'
  — ma·jeure'
forced
  — heirs
  — sale
forc'es
for'ci·ble
  — de·tain'er
  — en'try
  — tres'pass
for col·lec'tion
fore·close'
fore·clos'ure
fore'hand' rent
for'eign
  — ex·change'
  — judg'ment
  — ju'ris·dic'tion
for'eign·er
fore'man
fo·ren'sic
  — med'i·cine
fore·see'a·bil'i·ty
fore'shore'
fore'sight'
for'est
for'est·age
fore·stall'
fore·stall'er
fore·stall'ing
for'es·tar'i·us
for'est·er
for'feit
for'feit·a·ble
for'fei·ture'
forge
forg'er·y
fo'ris
fo'ris·fac'tu·ra
fo'ris·fa'mi·li·a're'
fo'ris·fa·mil'i·at'ed

fo'ris·fa·mil'i·a'tus
fo'ris·ju'di·ca'ti·o'
fo'ris·ju'di·ca'tus
for·ju·rer'
form
for'ma
   — pau'per·is
for'mal
for·mal'i·ties
for·mal'i·ty
for·ma'ta bre'vi·a
formed
   — ac'tion
   — de·sign'
for'me·don'
forms of ac'tion
for'mu·la
for'mu·lae'
for'ni·ca'tion
for'nix
for·swear'
for·taxed'
forth'com'ing
forth'with'
for'ti·o·ri'
for·tuit'
for·tu'i·tous
   — e·vent'
for·tu'i·ty
for'tune
fo'rum
   — ac'tus
   — con'sci·en'ti·ae'
   — con'ten·ti·o'sum
   — con·trac'tus
   — con·ven'i·ens'
   — do·mes'ti·cum
   — do·mi·cil'i·i'
   — ec'cle·si·as'ti·cum
   — li'ge·an'ti·ae' re'i'
   — non con·ven'i·ens'
   — o·rig'i·nis
   — re'gi·um

   — re'i'
   — rei gest'ae'
   — rei sit'ae'
   — sec'u·la're'
for val'ue re·ceived'
for'ward
for'ward·er
for'ward·ing
for'wards
fos·sa'tum
fosse way *or* fosse
fos'ter·age
fos'ter·ing
fos'ter·land'
fos'ter par'ent
found
foun·da'tion
found'ed
found'er
found'ers' shares
found'ling
four cor'ners
Four'teenth'
   A·mend'ment
foy
frac'ti·o'
frac'tion
frac'tion·al
frag·men'ta
frame'-up'
framed
franc
fran'chise'
fran'cus
   — ban'cus
   — ten'ens'
frank
   — al·moigne'
   — chase
   — fee
   — ferm
   — fold
   — mar'riage

   — pledge
   — ten'ant
   — ten'e·ment
fra·ter'nal
   — ben'e·fit
      as·so'ci·a'tion
   — in·sur'ance
fra·ter'ni·ty
frat'ri·age
frat'ri·cide'
fraud
   ac'tu·al—
   con·struc'tive—
   — in fact
   — in law
   — in trea'ty
fraud'u·lent
   — al'ien·a'tion
   — con·ceal'ment
   — con·ver'sion
   — con·vey'ance
   — pref'er·enc·es
   — rep're·sen·ta'tion
   — con·vey'anc·es
   stat'utes of or
      a·gainst' — con·-
      vey'anc·es
fray
frec'tum
free
   — and clear
   — and e'qual
   — bench
   — bord
   — en'ter·prise'
   — en'try, e'gress,
      and re'gress
   — on board
free'dom
   — of re·lig'ion
   — of speech and of
      the press
free'hold'

free'hold'er
free'man
free'man's roll
freight
— book'ing
— car
— train
freight'er
French'man
frend'wite'
fre·net'i·cus
freo'ling
fre'quent *adj.*
fre·quent' *v.*
fre·quent'er
fres'ca
fresh
— dis·seis'in
— pur·suit'
fresh'et
fre'tum
fri'ars
friend
— of the court
friend'ly
— fire
— suit
fri·gid'i·ty
frisk
friv'o·lous
from time to time
front'-foot' rule
front'age
front'ag·er
fron·tier'
front'ing and
a·but'ting
fruc'tus
— in·dus'tri·a'les'
fruit
— of crime
frus·tra'tion
fu'gam fe'cit

fu·ga'tor
fu'gi·ta'tion
fu'gi·tive
— from jus'tice
— of·fend'ers
full
— age
— an'swer
— blood
— court
— cous'in
— cov'e·nants
— de·fense'
— faith and cred'it
— proof
func'tion
func'tion·al
de·pre'ci·a'tion
func'tion·ar'y
fund *v.*
fund *n.*
re·volv'ing —
sink'ing —
fun'da·men'tal
— er'ror
— law
fun·da'mus
fun'da·tor
fun'di' pub'li·ci'
fu·ne'ral
fun'gi·ble
fur
fu·ran'di' an'i·mus
fu'ri·o'sus
fur'long'
fur'lough
fur'nish
fur'ni·ture
fu'ror' bre'vis
fur'ther
— con·sid'er·a'tion
fur'ther·ance
fur'tive

fur'tum
— man'i·fes'tum
fus'tis
fu'ture
— ac·quired'
prop'er·ty
— es·tate'
— in'ter·ests
fu'tures
fu·tu'ri'

G

gab'el
gaf'ol
gain
gain'age
gain'er·y
gain'ful
— em·ploy'ment
— oc'cu·pa'tion
gale
gal'lon
gal'lows
gam'ble
gam'bler
game
— laws
— of chance
game'keep'er
gam'ing
gang'ster
gante'lope
gaol
gaol'er
ga·rage'
gar'ble
gard'e·in
gar'den
gar'di·a'nus

ga·rene'
gar'nish
gar'nish·ee'
gar'nish·ment
gar'nish·or
gar'ri·son
gar·rot'ing
gar'ter
garth
gas'o·line'
gast
gas·tel'
gas·tine'
gate
gauge
gauge'a·tor
gaug'er
gav'el
gav'el·kind'
gav'el·ler
gav'el·man
ga·zette'
ge·boc'ced
geld
geld'a·ble
geld'ing
gelt
ge·mot'
ge'ne·al'o·gy
gene'arch'
gen'er·al
— as·sign'ment for
    ben'e·fit of
    cred'i·tors
— as·sump'sit
— be·quest'
— cir'cu·la'tion
— court
— es·tate'
— ex·cep'tion
— ex·ec'u·tor
— fee con·di'tion·al
— ju'ris·dic'tion

— law
— lien
— pow'er of
    ap·point'ment
Gen'er·al As·sem'-
    bly
gen'er·a'tion
gens
gen'tes'
gen·til'es'
gen'tle·man
gen'tle·wo'man
gen'u·ine
ge'nus
ge'rens'
Ger'man
ger·mane'
ger·ma'nus
ger'ry·man'der
ger·sume'
ges·ta'tion
ges'tum
gib'bet
gift
— cau'sa mor'tis
— in'ter vi'vos'
— o'ver
— to a class
gif'ta aq'uae'
gild
gin men
gi·ran'te
gise·ment'
gis·er'
gise'tak'er
gist
gist tak'ers
give
— and be·queath'
— no'tice
giv'er
glean'ing
gle'ba

glid'ing
globe doc'trine
gloss
glos'sa
gob
go'ing
— and com'ing rule
— con'cern
— price
— through the bar
— val'ue
gold bond
gold'smiths' notes
gon'or·rhe'a
good
— and law'ful men
— and val'id
— be·hav'ior
— cause
— con·sid'er·a'tion
— faith
— rec'ord ti'tle
— re·pute'
— Sa·mar'i·tan
    doc'trine
— ti'tle
— will
goods
— and chat'tels
— sold and
    de·liv'ered
goods, wares, and
    mer'chan·dise'
gov'ern
gov'ern·ment
— de fac'to'
— de ju're'
fed'er·al —
lo'cal —
gov'ern·ment'al
— im·mu'ni·ty
gov'er·nor
grab'bots

grace
　days of —
　— pe′ri·od
grade v.
grade n.
　— cross′ing
grad′ed of·fense′
grad′u·ate′ v.
grad′u·ate n.
gra′dus
graft
grain
　— rent
grain′age
gram′mar school
gramme
grand n.
grand adj.
　— days
　— re·mon′strance
grand′child′
grand′fa′ther
　— clause
grand′moth′er
grand′stand′ play
grange
　— cas′es
gran′ge·ar′i·us
grant
　— and de·mise′
　— and to freight let
　— of per′son·al
　　prop′er·ty
　— to uses
grant, bar′gain, and
　sell
gran·tee′
gran′tor
gran′tor's lien
grat′i·fi·ca′tion
gra′tis
　— dic′tum
gra·tu′i·tous

— al·low′ance
— guest
— li′cen·see′
— pas′sen·ger
gra·tu′i·ty
gra·va′men
grave
grav′el pit
grav′en dock
grave′yard′
gra′vis
Gray's Inn
great
great′-
　grand′chil′dren
green′back′
Gre·gor′i·an code
gre′mi·um
gres·sume′
greve
griev′ance
grieved
griev′ous
griff
groat
gro′cer
grog′shop′
gross
　— in·ad′e·qua·cy
　— in′come′
　— pre′mi·um
　— prof′it
　— weight
grosse·ment′
ground
　— of ac′tion
guar′an·tee′
　— stock
guar′an·tor
guar′an·ty v.
guar′an·ty n.
　— fund
guard′age

guard′i·an
　— ad li′tem
　do·mes′tic —
　— for nur′ture
　gen′er·al —
　— in soc′age
　nat′ur·al —
　tes′ta·men′tar′y —
guard′i·an·ship′
guer·pi′ or guer·py′
guest
gui·don′ de la mer
guild
guild′hall′
　— sit′tings
guil′lo·tine′
guilt
guilt′y
guin′ea
gut′ter
gy′nar·chy
gy′ne·coc′ra·cy
gy′ne·col′o·gist
gy′ne·col′o·gy
gy·ra′tion
gyves

H

ha′be·as cor′pus
　— ad de·lib′er·an′-
　　dum et re·cip′-
　　i·en′dum
　— ad fac′i·en′dum
　　et re·cip′i·en′dum
　— ad pro′se·quen′-
　　dum
　— ad
　　re′spon·den′dum
　— ad sat′is·fac′i·-

en'dum
— ad sub'jic·i·en'-
   dum
— ad tes'ti·fi·-
   can'dum
— cum cau'sa
ha·ben'dum
— et ten·en'dum
ha·ben'tes'
  hom'i·nes'
hab'il·is
hab'it
— and re·pute'
hab'i·tan·cy
ha·bi·tant'
hab'i·ta'tion
ha·bit'u·al
— crim'i·nal
— drunk'ard
ha·bit'u·al·ly
ha'ble
ha'ci·en'da
hack stand
hack'ney
— car'riag·es
haec est fi·na'lis
  con·cor'di·a
haer'es'
— de fac'to'
— in'sti·tu'tus
— le·git'i·mus
— rec'tus
haer'e·ta're'
haf'ne'
half
— blood
— broth'er
— dol'lar
— ea'gle
— sec'tion
— sis'ter
— year
half'-tim'er

ha'li·mas
hall
hall'mark'
hall'age
hal·lu'ci·na'tion
ham'let
ham'mer
han'a·per-of'fice
hand *n.*
— mon'ey
hand *v.*
— down
hand'bill'
hand'bor'ow
hand'cuffs'
han'dle
hand'sale'
hand'sel
hand'writ'ing
han'dy·man'
hang
hanged, drawn,
  and quar'tered
hang'ing
hang'man
hanse
Han'se·at'ic
Hanse Towns
hans'grave'
hap
hap'pi·ness
har'bin·ger
har'bor
hard
— cas'es
— of hear'ing
hard'pan'
hard'ship'
har'i·ot
har·mon'ic plane
har'mo·nize'
har'mo·ny
har'ness

har'ri·ott
har'vest·ing
has'pa
hatch
hatch'way'
haugh
haul
haul'age
haut che·min'
haut es·tret'
have and hold
ha'ven
hawk'er
hawk'ing
hay in stack
hay'-bote'
haz'ard
haz'ard·ous
head
— mon'ey
— of a fam'i·ly
— of wa'ter
head'land'
head'-note'
head'right'
heal'er
health
  bill of —
  board of —
health'y
hear'ing
— de no'vo'
  fair —
  fi'nal —
  pre·lim'i·nar'y —
  un·fair' —
hear'say'
hearth
heat'
— of pas'sion
— pros·tra'tion
— stroke
heave to

He′brew
hedge
hedge′-bote′
hedge′-priest′
hedg′ing
heed′less
heel′er
he·gem′o·ny
heif′er
heir
— ap·par′ent
— at law
— ben′e·fi′ci·ar′y
— by a·dop′tion
— by cus′tom
— by de·vise′
— col·lat′er·al
— con·ven′tion·al
— ex·pec′tant
forced —
— gen′er·al
ir·reg′u·lar —
le′gal —
lin′e·al —
male —
— of the blood
— of the body
— pre·sump′tive
right —
— spe′cial
heir′dom
heir′ess
heir′looms′
heirs
— and as·signs′
bod′i·ly —
joint —
law′ful —
le·git′i·mate —
nat′ur·al —
heir′ship′
— mov′a·bles
held

helm
hem′i·ple′gi·a
hence′forth′
hench′man
Hep′burn Act
hep′tar′chy
her′ald
her′ald·ry
herb′age
her′ben·ger *or*
har′bin·ger
herd
herd′er
here·af′ter
her′e·dit′a·ments
cor·po′re·al —
in·cor·po′re·al —
he·red′i·tar′y
— dis·ease′
— suc·ces′sion
he·red′i·ty
her′e·sy
here′to·fore′
her′i·ot
her′is·cin′di·um
her′i·ta·ble
— bond
— ju′ris·dic′tions
— ob′li·ga′tion
her·maph′ro·dite′
her′me·neu′tics
Her·mog′e·ni·an
Code
her′ni·a
her′us
he who seeks
eq′ui·ty must do
eq′ui·ty
hide and gain
hi′er·ar′chy
high
— de·gree′ of care
and dil′i·gence

high′bind′er
high′er and low′er
scale
high′est
— de·gree′ of care
— proved val′ue
High′ness
high′way′
pub′lic —
— rob′ber·y
high′way′man
hig′ler
hi′jack′er *or*
high′jack′er
hin′der and de·lay′
hire
hir′er
hir′ing
His Ex′cel·len·cy
His Hon′or
hith′er·to′
hoast′men
hob′bit
hoc
hog
hogs′head′
hold
hold′er
— in due course
hold′ing
— com′pa·ny
hol′i·day′
holm
hol′o·graph′
hom′age
— ju′ry
— liege
hom′ag·er
ho′ma·gi′um
— lig′i·um
— red′de·re′
home
— of′fice

— port
— rule
home'stall'
home'stead'
— ex·emp'tion laws
hom'i·ci'dal
hom'i·cide'
   — by mis'ad·ven'-
     ture
   — by ne·ces'si·ty
   cul'pa·ble —
   ex·cus'a·ble —
   fe·lo'ni·ous —
   jus'ti·fi'a·ble —
   neg'li·gent —
   — per in'for·tu'-
     ni·um
   — se de'fen·den'do'
ho'mi·cid'i·um
ho'mi·na'ti·o'
homme
ho'mo'
   — li'ber
   — Ro·ma'nus
hon'es·te' vi'veʹre'
hon'es·tus
hon'or v.
hon'or n.
   — courts
   of'fice of —
hon'or·a·ble
   — dis'charge'
hon'o·rar'i·um
hon'or·ar'y
hook'land'
hope
ho'ra
hor'i·zon'tal price'-
   fix'ing con'tracts'
horn'book'
hors
   — pris
horse

— guards
horse'pow'er
hos'pi·tal
hos'pi·ta·li·za'tion
hos'pi·tal·lers
hos'pi·ta'tor
hos·pit'i·a
hos·pit'i·cide'
hos·pit'i·um
host
hos'tage
hos'ti·cide'
hos'tile
   — em·bar'go
   — fire
   — pos·ses'sion
   — wit'ness
hos·til'i·ty
hos'tler
hotch'pot'
ho·tel'
hough
hour
house
   bawd'y —
   board'ing —
   — burn'ing
   du'plex' —
   dwell'ing —
   man'sion —
   — of cor·rec'tion
   — of ill fame
   — of ref'uge
   — of wor'ship
   pub'lic —
   tip'pling —
House
   In'ner —
   — of Com'mons
   — of Del'e·gates'
   — of Keys
   — of Lords
   — of Rep're·sen'-

   ta·tives
   Out'er —
house'age
house'-bote'
house'break'ing
house'hold'
   — stuff
house'hold'er
house'keep'er
hov'el
howgh
hoy
hoy'man
huck'ster
hue and cry
hu'i'
huis
huis·se'ri·um
huis·si·ers'
hulks
hull
hu·man'i·tar'i·an
   doc'trine
hun'dred
   — court
hun'dred·ors
hun'dred·weight'
hung ju'ry
hun'ger
hunt'ing
hur'dle
hur'ri·cane'
hurt
hus'band
   — and wife
hus'band·man
hus'band·ry
hush mon'ey
hust'ings
hy'brid
hy'giene'
hyp·not'ic drugs
hyp'no·tism

hy·pos′ta·sis
hy·poth′e·ca
hy·poth′e·cate′
hy·poth′e·ca′tion
— bond
hy·poth′e·sis
hy′po·thet′i·cal
ques′tion
hys′ter·ec′to·my
hys·ter′i·a
hys′ter·ot′o·my

I

i′bi·dem′
i′dem′
— so′nans
idem per idem
i·den′ti·cal
i·den′ti·fi·ca′tion
i·den′ti·ty
id′e·o′
ides
id est
id′i·o·cy
id′i·o·path′ic
— dis·ease′
— in·san′i·ty
id′i·ot
id·o′ne·us
ig′no·min′y
ig′no·ra′mus
ig′no·rance
ig′no·ran′ti·a
— fac′ti′ ex·cu′sat
— le′gis nem′i·nem
excusat
ig′no·ra′ti·o′
e·len′chi′
ig·nore′

ik′bal′
— da′wa′
ik′rah′
ik′rar′
— na′ma′
ill
— fame
il·le′gal
il′le·gal′i·ty
il′le·git′i·ma·cy
il′le·git′i·mate
il·lev′i·a·ble
il·lic′it
il·lic′i·te′
il·lit′er·ate
ill′ness
il·loc′a·ble
il′lud
il·lu′sion
il·lu′so·ry
— ap·point′ment
— prom′ise
il·lus′tri·ous
im·ag′ine
im′be·cil′i·ty
im′i·ta′tion
im′ma·te′ri·al
— a·ver′ment
— var′i·ance
im·me′di·ate
— cause
— de·scent′
im·me′di·ate·ly
im′me·mo′ri·al
— pos·ses′sion
— us′age
im′mi·gra′tion
im′mi·nent
— dan′ger
im·mod′er·ate
im·mor′al
im′mor·al′i·ty
im·mov′a·bles

im·mu′ni·ty
im·pair′
im·pair′ing the
ob′li·ga′tion of
con′tracts′
im·pan′el
im·parl′
im·par′lance
im·par′tial
— ju′ry
im·peach′
im·peach′ment
ar′ti·cles of —
col·lat′er·al —
— of an·nu′i·ty
— of waste
— of wit′ness
im·pech′i·a′re′
im·pede′
im·pe′di·ens′
im·ped′i·ments
im·per′a·tive
im·per′fect
im·per′ti·nence
im·per′ti·nent
im·pig′no·ra′tion
im·pla′ci·ta′re′
im·plead′
im·plead′ed
im′ple·ments
im′pli·ca′ta
im′pli·ca′tion
im·plied′
im·por·ta′tion
im·port′ed
im′ports′
im′por·tu′ni·ty
im·pose′
im′po·si′tion
im·pos′si·bil′i·ty
im′posts′
im′po·tence
im·pound′

im'pre·scrip'ti·bil'i·ty
im'pre·scrip'ti·ble
  rights
im·pres'sion
  case of first —
im·press'ment
im·prest' mon'ey
im'pre·ti'a·bil'is
im'pri·ma'tur
im·pris'on
im·pris'on·ment
im·pris'ti'
im·prob'a·ble
im·prop'er
im·prove'
im·proved'
im·prove'ment
im·prove'ments
im·prov'i·dence
im·prov'i·dent·ly
im'pulse'
im·pu'ni·ty
im·put'ed
  — knowl'edge
  — neg'li·gence
  — no'tice
in·ad'e·quate
  — con·sid'er·a'tion
  — dam'ag·es
  — price
  — rem'e·dy at law
in'ad·mis'si·ble
in ad·ver'sum
in'ad·ver'tence
in·al'ien·a·ble
in a'li·o' lo'co'
in am·big'u·o'
in a·per'ta lu'ce'
in a·pic'i·bus ju'ris
in ar·tic'u·lo'
  — mor'tis
in·au'gu·ra'tion
in au'tre droit

in ban'co'
in be'ing
in cam'er·a
in'ca·pac'i·ty
in cap'i·ta
in cap'i·te'
in·car'cer·a'tion
in·cen'di·ar'y
in·cep'tion
in·cert'ae'
  per·so'nae'
in'cest'
in·ces'tu·o'si'
in'char·ta're'
in chief
in·cho'ate
  — dow'er
  — in'stru·ment
  — in'ter·est
  — lien
  — right
in'ci·dent
in·cin'er·a'tion
in·cite'
in'ci·vi'le'
in·civ'ism
in·close'
in·closed' lands
in·clo'sure
  — acts
in·clude'
in·clu'si·o' u'ni·us
  est ex·clu'si·o'
  al·ter'i·us
in·clu'sive
  — sur'vey'
in·co'las
  dom'i·cil'i·um
  fa'cit
in'come'
  — tax
  — tax de·fi'cien·cy
in com·men'dam'

in com'mon
in com·mu'ni'
in'com·mu'ni·ca'tion
in'com·mut'a·ble
in'com·pat'i·bil'i·ty
in'com·pat'i·ble
in·com'pe·tence
in·com'pe·ten·cy
in·com'pe·tent
  ev'i·dence
in'con·clu'sive
in con·junc'tion with
in'con·sis'tent
in'con·test'a·bil'i·ty
in·con'ti·nence
in'con·ti·nen'ti'
in'con·ven'ience
in·co'po·li'tus
in·cor'po·ra'mus
in·cor'po·rate'
in·cor'po·ra'tion
in cor'po·re'
in'cor·po're·al
  — chat'tels
  — her'e·dit'a·ments
  — prop'er·ty
in·cor'ri·gi·ble
in'cor·rupt'i·ble
in·crease'
  af'fi·da'vit of —
  costs of —
in'cre·ment
in'cre·men'tum
in·crim'i·nate'
in·crim'i·nat'ing
  — ad·mis'sion
  — cir'cum·stance'
in·crim'i·na·to'ry
  state'ment
in·croach'ment
in·cul'pate'
in·cul'pa·to'ry
in·cum'bent

in·cum′ber
in·cum′branc·es
  cov′e·nant
    a·gainst′ —
in·cum′branc·er
in·cur′
in·cur′a·ble dis·ease′
in·cur′ra·men′tum
in cus·to′di·a le′gis
in′de′
in·deb′i·ta′tus
  as·sump′sit —
in·debt′ed·ness
in·de′cen·cy
  pub′lic —
in·de′cent
  — as·sault′
  — ex′hi·bi′tion
  — ex·po′sure
  — lib′er·ties
  — pub′li·ca′tions
in′de·feas′i·ble
in·def′i·nite
  — fail′ure of is′sue
  — leg′a·cy
in de·lic′to′
in·dem′ni·fy′
in·dem′ni·tee′
in·dem′ni·tor
in·dem′ni·ty
  — bond
  — con′tract′
in′dent′ *n.*
in·dent′ *v.*
in·den′ture
in′de·pend′ence
in′de·pend′ent
  — con′trac′tor
  — cov′e·nant
in′de·ter′mi·nate
  — ob′li·ga′tion
  — sen′tence
in′dex′

  — an′i·mi′ ser′mo′
In′di·an
  — dep′re·da′tions
    acts
  — res′er·va′tion
  — ti′tle
  — tribe
in′di·ca′tion
in·dic′a·tive
  ev′i·dence
in′di·ca′vit
in·di′ci·a
in·di′ci·um
in·dict′
in·dict′a·ble
in·dict′ed
in′dic·tee′
in·dic′ti·o′
in·dict′ment
in·dic′tor
in di′em
in·dif′fer·ent
in′di·gent
  — in·sane′ per′son
in·dig′ni·ty
in′di·rect′
  — at·tack′
  — ev′i·dence
  — tax
in′dis·pen′sa·ble
  — ev′i·dence
  — par′ties
in′dis·tan′ter′
in′di·vid′u·al
  — as′sets′
  — debts
  — sys′tem of
    lo·ca′tion
in′di·vid′u·al·ly
in′di·vis′i·ble
in′di·vi′sum
in do·min′i·co′
in·dorse′

in′dors·ee′
  — in due course
in·dorse′ment
  ac·com′mo·da′-
    tion —
  blank —
  con·di′tion·al —
  full —
  ir·reg′u·lar —
  prop′er —
  qual′i·fied′ —
  reg′u·lar —
  re·stric′tive —
  spe′cial —
  special — of writ
in·dors′er
in dor′so′
in du′bi·o′
in·du′bi·ta·ble proof
in·duce′
in·duce′ment
in·du′ci·ae′
in·duct′
in·duc′ti·o′
in·duc′tion
in·dul′gence
in du′plo′
in·dus′tri·al
in′dus·try
in·e′bri·ate
in′ef·fi′cien·cy
in·el′i·gi·bil′i·ty
in·el′i·gi·ble
in′es·cap′a·ble per′il
in es′se
in est de ju′re
in ev′i·dence
in·ev′i·ta·ble
  — ac′ci·dent
in ex·cam′bi·o′
in ex′e·cu′tion and
  pur·su′ance of
in ex′i·tu′

in ex·ten'so'
in ex·trem'is
in fa'ci·e' cu'ri·ae'
in fa'ci·en'do'
in fact
in fac'to'
in·fa'mi·a
in'fa·mous
  — crime
  — pun'ish·ment
in'fa·my
in'fan·cy
in'fans
in'fant
in·fan'ti·cide'
in fa·vo'rem
  — lib'er·ta'tus
  — vi'tae'
in·fec'tion
in fe·o'do'
in·feoff'ment
in'fer·ence
in'fer·ence on
  in'fer·ence
in'fer·en'tial
  — facts
in·fe'ri·or
  — court
in'feu·da'tion
in'fi·del
in'fi·de'lis
in fi'e·ri'
in fi'ne'
in·firm'
in·fir'ma·tive
  — con·sid'er·a'tion
  — fact
  — hy·poth'e·sis
in·fir'mi·ty
in'flu·ence
in·for'mal
in'for·mal'i·ty
in for'ma pau'per·is

in'for·ma'tion
  crim'i·nal —
  — in the na'ture of
    a quo war'ran·to'
  — of in·tru'sion
in'for·ma'tus non
  sum
in·form'er
in fo'ro'
  — con'sci·en'ti·ae'
  — con'ten·ti·o'so'
in'fra
  — ae·ta'tem'
  — an'nos' nu·bil'es'
  — an'num
  — annum luc'tus
  — bra'chi·a
  — civ'i·ta'tem
  — dig'ni·ta'tem
    cu'ri·ae'
  — fu·ro'rem
  — hos·pit'i·um
  — ju'ris·dic'ti·o'-
    nem
  — me'tas'
  — prae·sid'i·a
  — qua'tu·or' ma'ri·a
  — quatuor
    pa·ri'e·tes'
  — reg'num
in·frac'tion
in·fringe'ment
  con·trib'u·to'ry —
  — of cop'y·right'
  — of pat'ent
  — of trade'mark'
in·fring'er
in'fu·ga're'
in·fu'sion
in fu'tu·ro'
in gen'e·re'
in·ge'ni·um
in'ge·nu'i·tas'

in'ge·nu'i·ty
in·gen'u·us
in·grat'i·tude'
in gre'mi·o' le'gis
in'gress'
in gross
in'gros·sa'tor
in·gross'ing
in'gui·nal
in·hab'it
in·hab'i·tant
in hac par'te'
in haec ver'ba
in·here'
in·her'ent
  — pow'er
  — pow'ers of a
    court
in·her'ent·ly
  dan'ger·ous
in·her'e·trix'
in·her'it
in·her'it·a·ble blood
in·her'i·tance
  — act
  es·tate' of —
  — tax
in hoc
in·hu'man treat'ment
in i'is·dem' ter'mi·nis
in in'di·vid'u·o'
in in'fi·ni'tum
in in'i·ti·o'
in in·teg'rum
in in·vid'i·um
in in·vi'tum
in·i'tial
  — car'ri·er
in·i'ti·ate'
in·i'ti·a·tive
In'i·ur'col·leg'ui'a
in·junc'tion
  fi'nal —

in·ter·loc′u·to′ry —
man′da·to′ry —
per′ma·nent —
per·pet′u·al —
pre·lim′i·nar′y —
pre·ven′tive —
pro·vi′sion·al —
spe′cial —
tem′po·rar′y —
in′jure
in ju′re′
— al·ter′i·us
— pro′pri·o′
in·ju′ri·a
— abs′que dam′no′
— non ex·cu′sat
in·ju′ri·am
— non prae·sum′-
i·tur′
in·ju′ri·ous words
in′ju·ry
ir·rep′a·ra·ble —
per′son·al —
in·jus′tice
in jus vo·ca′re′
in kind
in′la·ga′tion
in′land′ adv.
in′land adj.
— bill of ex·change′
— nav′i·ga′tion
— trade
— wa′ters
in·law′
in law
in lec′to′ mor·ta′li′
in lieu of
in lim′i·ne′
in li′tem
in lo′co′
— pa·ren′tis
in ma·jo′rem
cau′te·lam′

in ma′lam par′tem
in′mate′
in max′i·ma
po·ten′ti·a
min′i·ma li·cen′ti·a
in me′di·as′ res
in med′i·co′
in mis′er·i·cor′di·a
in mi′ti·o′ri′ sen′su′
in mo′dum as·si′sae′
in mo′ra′
in mor′tu·a ma′nu′
inn
in·nav′i·ga·bil′i·ty
in·nav′i·ga·ble
in′ner
— bar′ris·ter
— house
inn′ings
inn′keep′er
in′no·cence
in′no·cent
in·nom′i·nate
— con′tracts′
in no′tis
in′no·va′tion
Inns of Chan′cer·y
Inns of Court
in nu·bi′bus
in′nu·en′do
in′quest′
cor′o·ner′s —
— of lu′na·cy
— of of′fice
— of sher′iffs
in nul′li·us bo′nis
in o′di·um
spo′li·a·to′ris
in om′ni·bus
in pais
es·top′pel —
in pa′ri′ cau′sa
— de·lic′to′

— ma·te′ri·a
in pa′ti·en′do′
in pec′to·re′ ju′di·cis
in pe·jo′rem par′tem
in per′pe·tu′i·ty
in per′son
in per·so′nam, in
rem
in ple′na vi′ta
in ple′no′ lu′mi·ne′
in pos′se
in po·tes′ta·te′
pa·ren′tis
in prae·sen′ti′
in pren′der
in pri′mis
in prin·cip′i·o′
in promp′tu′
in pro′pri·a
per·so′na
in′qui·si′tion
— of lu′na·cy
in·quis′i·tor
in re
in re′bus
in re·gard′ to
in rem
judg′ment —
qua′si′ —
in ren′der
in re′rum na·tu′ra
in·sane′
in·san′i·ty
cho·re′ic —
con·gen′i·tal —
id′i·o·path′ic —
le′gal —
ma·ni′a·cal-
de·pres′sive —
pel·lag′rous —
pol′y·neu·rit′ic —
pu·er′per·al —
syph′i·lit′ic —

trau·mat′ic —
in·scrip′tion
in′se·cure′
in·sen′si·ble
in sep·a·ra′li′
in·sig′ni·a
in sim′i·li′ ma·te′ri·a
in′sim·ul
in·sin′u·a′tion
in′so·la′tion
in sol′i·do′
in sol′i·dum
in so′lo′
in·sol′ven·cy
in·sol′vent
in spe′cie′
in·spect′
in·spec′tion
in·spec′tor
in·spec′tor·ship′,
  deed of
in·stall′
in′stal·la′tion
in·stall′ments
in′stance
  — court
in′stant
in′stan·ta′ne·ous
in′stant·er
in′stant·ly
in′star
in sta′tu′ quo
in′sti·gate′
in′sti·ga′tion
in′stir·pa′re′
in stir′pes′
in′sti·tute′
in′sti·tut′ed
  ex·ec′u·tor
In′sti·tutes′
  — of Gai′us
  — of Jus·tin′i·an
  — of Lord Coke

in′sti·tu′tion
in′sti·tu′ti·o·nes′
in·struct′
in·struc′tion
  per·emp′to·ry —
in′stru·ment
  — of ap·peal′
  — of ev′i·dence
in′stru·men′ta
in′stru·men′tal
in′stru·men·tal′i·ty
  rule
in′sub·or′di·na′tion
in sub·sid′i·um
in′suf·fi′cien·cy
  — of ev′i·dence to
    sup·port′ ver′dict
in′su·la
in′su·late′
in·su′per
in·sur′a·ble
  — in′ter·est
in·sur′ance
  ac′ci·dent —
  — ad·just′er
  — a′gent
  as·sess′ment life —
    pol′i·cy
  au′to·mo·bile′ —
  — bro′ker
  bur′gla·ry —
  cas′u·al·ty —
  com·mer′cial —
  — com·mis′sion·er
  — com′pa·ny
  em·ploy′ers′ —
  em·ploy′er′s
    li′a·bil′i·ty —
  fi·del′i·ty —
  fire —
  fra·ter′nal —
  guar′an·ty —
  in·dem′ni·ty —

in·dus′tri·al —
li′a·bil′i·ty —
life —
live′stock′ —
ma·rine′ —
mo′tor ve′hi·cle —
mu′tu·al —
old line life —
plate glass —
  — pol′i·cy
  — pre′mi·um
steam boil′er —
term —
ti′tle —
tor·na′do —
  — trust
in·sure′
in·sured′
in·sur′er
in·sur′gent
in′sur·rec′tion
in′takes′
in·tan′gi·ble
  — as′set′
  — prop′er·ty
in tan′tum
in′te·ger
in′te·grat′ed
in′te·gra′tion
  de fac′to′ —
  de ju′re′ —
in·teg′ri·ty
in·tel′li·gi·bil′i·ty
in·tem′per·ance
in·tend′
in·tend′ant
in·tend′ed wife
in·tend′ment of law
in·tent′
in·ten′ti·o′ cae′ca′
  ma′la′
in·ten′tion
in·ten′tion·al

in'ter
in'ter a'li·a
in'ter a'li·os'
in'ter a'pi·ces' ju'ris
in'ter bra'chi·a
in'ter·cep'tion
in'ter·change'a·bly
in'ter·com'mon
in'ter·com·mun'ing
in'ter con·ju'ges'
in'ter con·junc'tas
  per·so'nas
in'ter·course'
in'ter·dict'
in'ter·dic'tion
  — of fire and wa'ter
in'ter·es'se
  pro — su'o'
  — ter'mi·ni'
in'ter·est
  com'pound —
  joint —
  le'gal —
  sim'ple —
  — up·on' —
in'ter·fere'
in'ter·fer'ence
in'ter·im
  — com·mit'ti·tur'
  — cu·ra'tor
  — or'der
  — re·ceipt'
in'ter·in·sur'ance
in'ter·lin'e·a'tion
in'ter·loc'u·tor
in'ter·loc'u·to'ry
in'ter·lop'ers
in'ter·mar'riage
in'ter·med'dle
in'ter·me'di·ar'y
in'ter·me'di·ate
in ter'mi·nis
  ter'mi·nan'ti·bus

in'ter·mit'tent
  ease'ment
in'ter·mix'ture
in'tern'
in·ter'nal
In·ter'nal Rev'e·nue
  Serv'ice
in'ter·na'tion·al
  — court of jus'tice
  — law
in'ter pa'res'
in'ter par'tes'
in'ter·pel'late
in'ter·plea'
in'ter·plead'er
in·ter'po·late'
in·ter'po·la'tion
in·ter·po·si'tion
in·ter'pret
in·ter'pre·ta'tion
  close —
  lib'er·al —
  strict —
in·ter'pret·er
in'ter re·ga'lia
in'ter·reg'num
in'ter·rog'a·to'ries
in ter·ro'rem
  — pop'u·li'
in'ter·rup'tion
in'ter·sec'tion
in'ter se, in'ter
  se'se'
in'ter·state'
  — com'merce
in'ter·ven'ing
  — act
  — a'gen·cy
  — cause
  — dam'ag·es
  — force
in'ter·ve'nor
in'ter·ven'tion

in'ter vi'rum et
  ux'o·rem
in'ter vi'vos'
in·tes'ta·ble
in·tes'ta·cy
in·tes'tate'
  — suc·ces'sion
in tes'ti·mo'ni·um
in'ti·ma·cy
in'ti·mate adj.
in'ti·mate' v.
in'ti·ma'tion
in·tim'i·da'tion
in·tol'er·a·ble
in to'to'
in·tox'i·cat'ed
in·tox'i·cat'ing
  liq'uor
in·tox'i·ca'tion
in'tox·im'e·ter
in'tra
in tra·jec'tu'
in'tra·lim'i·nal
in'tra·mu'ral
in tran'si·tu'
in'tra pa·ri·et'es'
in'tra·state'
in'tra vi'res'
in·trin'sic ev'i·dence
in'tro·duc'tion
in·trud'er
in·tru'sion
in·trust'
in'un·da'tion
in·ure'
in·ure'ment
in ut·ro'que' ju're'
in vac'u·o'
in vad'i·o'
in·val'id
in·va'sion
in·vent'
in·ven'tion

in·ven'tor
in'ven·to'ry
in ven'tre sa mère
in·ven'tus
in·vest'
in·ves'ti·ga'tion
in·ves'ti·tive fact
in·ves'ti·ture'
in·vest'ment
in vin·cu'lis
in·vi'o·la·bil'i·ty
in'vi·ta'tion
in·vite'
in·vit'ee'
in'voice'
in·vol'un·ta'ry
    — man'slaugh'ter
    — ser'vi·tude'
i·o'ta
ip'se'
ip'se' dix'it
ip'so' fac'to'
ip'so' ju're'
ir·ra'tion·al
ir·re·cus'a·ble
ir·reg'u·lar
ir·reg'u·lar'i·ty
ir·rel'e·van'cy
ir·rel'e·vant
ir're·mov'a·bil'i·ty
ir're·ple'vi·a·ble
ir're·sis'ti·ble
    — force
    — im'pulse'
ir·rev'o·ca·ble
ir'ri·ga'tion
ir'ri·tant
is'land
i'so·late'
is'su·a·ble
is'sue *v.*
is'sue *n.*
    col·lat'er·al —

    — in fact
    — in law
    ul'ti·mate —
is'sues and prof'its
i'tem
i'tem·ize'
i·tin'er·ant
    — ped'dling
    — ven'dor
its
it's

J

jac'ti·ta'tion
jac·ti'vus
jac'tus
jail
jail'er *or* jail'or
jan'i·tor
ja'nus-faced'
Ja'son clause
jay'walk'ing
jeo'faile'
jeop'ard·y
jerk
jet'sam
jet'ti·son
jet'ty
jew'el
jew'el·ry
jit'ney
job'ber
John Doe
join
join'der
    — in de·mur'rer
    — in is'sue
    — in plead'ing
    — of ac'tions

    — of er'ror
    — of is'sue
    — of of'fens·es
    — of par'ties
joint
    — ac·count'
    — ac'tion
    — and sev'er·al
    — au'thor·ship'
    — cause of ac'tion
    — debt'ors
    — en'ter·prise'
    — es·tate'
    — fea'sors in pa'ri'
        de·lic'to'
    — li'a·bil'i·ty
    — lives
    — neg'li·gence
    — of·fense'
    — pol'i·cy
    — stock in·sur'ance
        com'pa·ny
    — tort
    — ven'ture
joint'ist
joint'ly
    — and sev'er·al·ly
join'tress *or*
   join'tu·ress
join'ture
jok'er
jos'tle
jou·ir'
jour
    — en banc
jour'nal
jour'ney
jour'ney·man
jour'neys ac·count'
ju'dex'
judge
    — ad'vo·cate
    — ad'vo·cate

gen′er·al
— de fac′to′
— or′di·nar′y
— pro tem′po·re′
judge′-made law
judg′ment *or*
judge′ment
— cred′i·tor
— debt
— debt′or
de·fault′ —
de·fi′cien·cy —
dor′mant —
es·top′pel by —
fi′nal —
— in per·so′nam
— in rem
— in re·trax′it
— in′ter par′tes′
— lien
mon′ey —
— on mer′its
per′son·al —
ju′di·ca·to′ries
ju′di·ca·ture′
— acts
ju′di·ces′
ju·di′cial
— act
— ac′tion
— cir′cuit
— cog′ni·zance
— com′i·ty
— cy pres
— dic′tum
— no′tice
— o·pin′ion
ju·di′ci·ar′y
— act
ju·di′cious·ly
ju·dic′i·um
— cap·i·ta′le′

— De′i′
juge de paix
jump bail
jun′ior
— cred′i·tor
— ex′e·cu′tion
— lien
— right
junk′shop′
jun′ta *or* jun′to
ju′ra
ju·ra′re′
ju′rat′
ju·ra′tion
ju·ra′tor
ju′rats′
ju′re′
— bel′li′
— ci·vil′i′
— gen·ti′um
— ux·or′is
ju·rid′i·cal
— day
ju′ris
— pos·i·ti′vi′
— pri·va′ti′
— pub′li·ci′
— ut′rum′
ju′ris·con′sult′
jur′is·con·sul′tus
ju′ris·dic′tion
— in per·so′nam
— in rem
ju′ris·dic′tion·al
— a·mount′
— facts
ju′ris·pru′dence
ju′rist
ju·ris′tic
ju′ror
— des′ig·nate
ju′ry

— box
fair and im·par′tial—
grand —
— list
— of good and
law′ful men
pet′it —
— proc′ess′
— wheel
ju′ry·man
ju′ry·wom′an
jus
— ab′sti·nen′di′
— a·bu·ten′di′
— ac′cres·cen′di′
— bel′li′
— can′o·ni′cum
— ci′vi·le′
— com·mu′ne′
— co·ro′nae′
— cu′ri·al′i·ta′tis
— da′re′
— di·ce′re′
— dis′po·nen′di′
— dis′tra·hen′di′
— div′i·den′di′
— du′pli·ca′tum
— fal·can′di′
— gen′ti·um
— glad′i·i′
— hab·en′di′
— hae·red′i·ta′tis
— in′cog·ni′tum
— in′di·vid′u·um
— in per·so′nam
— in re
— in re a′li·e′na
— in re prop′ri·a
— le·git·i′mum
— mar′i·ti′
— na·tu′rae′
— na·tu·ra′le′

— nav'i·gan'di'
— non scrip'tum
— per·so·na'rum
— pos'ses·si·o'nis
— pos'si·den'di'
— pri·va'tum
— pro·pri'e·ta'tis
— pub·li'cum
— quaes'i·tum
— re'cu·per·an'di'
— re'rum
— san·gui'nis
— scrip'tum
— so'li'
— spa'ti·an'di'
— stric'tum
— ter'ti·i'
— u·ten'di'
just
— com'pen·sa'tion
jus'tice v.
jus'tice n.
— of the peace
jus'tic·es
— of as·size'
— of gaol de·liv'er·y
— of ni'si' pri'us
— of o'yer and
ter'min·er
— of the hun'dred
— of the pa·vil'ion
— of the quo'rum
— of trail'-bas'ton
jus'tice·ship'
jus'ti·ci'a·ble
— con'tro·ver'sy
jus'ti·cies'
jus'ti·fi'a·ble
jus'ti·fi·ca'tion
jus'ti·fi·ca'tors
jus'ti·fied'
just'ness

ju've·nile'
— de·lin'quent
jux'ta
— ra'tam'
jux'ta·po·si'tion

K

ka·ha'kai'
ka·ha'wai'
kai'a
keep n.
keep v.
— house
keep'er
— of the for'est
— of the great seal
— of the king's
con'science
— of the priv'y seal
— of the touch
keep'ing
— books
— term
— the peace
kelp'-shore'
kent'lage
kerf
kernes
key'age
key'us
kid'der
kid'nap·ping or kid'-
nap·ing
kil'der·kin
kill'ing by
mis'ad·ven'ture
kin
kind

kin'dred
king'dom
king'-geld'
king's
— ad'vo·cate
— bench
— cham'bers
— cor'o·ner and
at·tor'ney
— coun'sel
— proc'tor
— re·mem'branc·er
kings'-at-arms'
kins'folk'
kins'man
kins'wom'an
kin'tal or kin'tle
kint'lidge
kiss'ing the book
klep'to·ma'ni·a
knack'er
knave
knave'ship'
knight
knight'hood'
knight-mar'shal
knights
— bach'e·lors
— ban'ner·et
— of St. Mi'chael
and St. George
— of St. Pat'rick
— of the Bath
— of the Cham'ber
— of the Gar'ter
— of the post
— of the shire
— of the this'tle
— serv'ice
knock down
know all men
know'ing·ly

— and will'ful·ly
knowl'edge
known
    — heirs
Ko'ran
ko·shu·ba'
ku·le'an·a
kyth

L

la'bel
la'bor
    — dis·pute'
    — or'gan·i·za'tion
    — sep'a·ra'tion
    — un'ion
la'bor·er
la'bor·ers, statutes
    of
La'cey Act
lach'es
    es·top'pel by —
lack of
    ju'ris·dic'tion
lac'ta
la·cu'na
la'cus
lad'en in bulk
lad'ing, bill of
la'dy-court'
lage
    — day
lage'-man'
la'ge·na
lahl'slit'
la'i·ty
Lam'beth de·gree'
lame duck
land

— cer'tif·i·cate
— cop
— court
— de·part'ment
— farm
— gab'el
gen'er·al — of'fice
— grant
— pat'ent
— rev'e·nues
seat'ed —
— tax
— ten'ant
— wait'er
— war'rant
land'ed
    — es·tate' or
       prop'er·ty
    — es·tates' court
    — pro·pri'e·tor
    — se·cur'i·ties
land'grave'
land'ing
land'locked'
land'lord'
land'-poor'
land'-reeve'
    — and ten'ant
land'lord`s war'rant
land'mark'
lands
    ac·com'mo·da'-
       tion —
    boun'ty —
    cer·tif'i·cate —
    — claus'es con'sol·-
       i·da'tion acts
    crown —
    de·mesne' —
    do·na'tion —
    fab'ric —
    farm —
    tide —

lands, ten'e·ments,
    and
    her'e·dit'a·ments
lan'guage
lap'i·da'tion
lap'page
lapse v.
lapse n.
    — pat'ent
lapsed
    — de·vise'
    — leg'a·cy
    — pol'i·cy
lar'board
lar'ce·nous
    — in·tent'
lar'ce·ny
    com'mon-law' —
    com'pound —
    — by bail·ee'
    con·struc'tive —
    — from the per'son
    grand —
    mixed —
    pet'it —
    sim'ple —
las·civ'i·ous
    — car'riage
    — co·hab'i·ta'tion
last
    — an'te·ce'dent rule
    — clear chance
    — re·sort'
    — will
la'tent
    — deed
    — de'fect'
    — eq'ui·ty
lat'er·al
    — rail'road'
    — sup·port'
lat·ro'ci·na'tion
lat·ro'cin·y

lau'dum
launce'gay'
launch
lau're·ate
lau'rels
law
— ar'bi·trar'y
— charges
— court of ap·peals'
— en·force'ment
   of'fi·cer
— French
— Lat'in
— list
— lords
— mar'tial
— mer'chant
— of ev'i·dence
— of na'tions
— of na'ture
— of the case
— of the land
— re·ports'
Law Day
law'ful
— age
— au·thor'i·ties
— cause
— dam'ag·es
— de·pend'ents
— dis'charge'
— en'try
— goods
— heirs
— is'sue
— rep're·sen'ta·tives
law'less
— man
laws
— of the sev'er·al
   states
— of war
law'suit'

law'yer
lay n.
— days
— sys'tem
lay adj.
— cor'po·ra'tion
— fee
— judge
— peo'ple
lay v.
— dam'ages
— off
— out
laye
lay'ing the ven'ue
lay'man
lay'off'
lay'out'
lay'stall'
le roi or le roy
lea or ley
lead'ing
— a use
— case
— coun'sel
— ques'tion
league
leak'age
le·al'
lé·alte'
lean
leap year
learn
learn'ed
learn'ing
lease
lease'hold'
lé·aute'
leave v.
— and li'cense
— no is'sue
leave n.
— of ab'sence

— of court
— to de·fend'
lec'tur·er
ledg'er
— book
leet
leets
leg'a·cy
ab'so·lute' —
ac·cu'mu·la'tive —
ad·di'tion·al —
al'ter·nate —
con·di'tion·al —
con·tin'gent —
cu'mu·la'tive —
de·mon'stra·tive —
— du'ty
gen'er·al —
in·def'i·nite —
lapsed —
mo'dal —
pe·cu'ni·ar'y —
re·sid'u·ar'y —
spe'cial —
spe·cif'ic —
— tax
trust —
u'ni·ver'sal —
le'gal
— a·cu'men
— age
— as'sets
— ca·pac'i·ty to sue
— cap'i·tal
— cause
— con·clu'sion
— cru'el·ty
— de·pend'ent
— det'ri·ment
— dis·trib'u·tees'
— du'ty
— en'ti·ty
— es·top'pel

— eth′ics
— ev′i·dence
— ex·cuse′
— fraud
— heirs
— hol′i·day
— in′ju·ry
— in·san′i·ty
— in′ter·est
— in·vest′ment
— is′sue
— jeop′ard·y
— li′a·bil′i·ty
— mal′ice
— name
— neg′li·gence
— no′tice
— ob′li·ga′tion
— per′son·al
  rep′re·sen′ta·tive
— pos·ses′sor
— prej′u·dice
— pre·sump′tion
— priv′i·ty
— pro·ceed′ing
— rate of in′ter·est
— rep′re·sen′ta·tive
— re·scis′sion
— re·serve′
— res′i·dence
— right
— strike
— sub′di·vi′sions
— sub′ro·ga′tion
— ti′tle
— u′su·fruct′
— vot′er
— will′ful·ness
le·ga′lis ho′mo′
le·gal′i·ty
le′gal·i·za′tion
le′gal·ize′
le′gal·ized′

nui′sance
le′gal·ly
— a·dopt′ed
— com·mit′ted
— com′pe·tent
— con′sti·tut′ed
  court
— suf·fi′cient
  ev′i·dence
— sufficient ten′der
le′gal·ness
le·ga′re′
leg′a·tar′y
leg′a·tee′
le·ga′tion
le·ga′tor
leg′a·to′ry
le′gem
leg′is·late′
leg′is·la′tion
leg′is·la′tive
— act
— courts
— de·part′ment
— ex·pens′es
— func′tion
— of′fi·cer
— pow′er
leg′is·la′tor
leg′is·la′ture
le·git′i·ma·cy
le·git′i·mate′ v.
le·git′i·mate adj.
le·git′i·ma′tion
le·git′i·me′
le·git′i·mus
le′git vel non?
lend
lend′er
lend′ing mon′ey or
  cred′it
les′ing or leas′ing
le′sion

les′sa
les·see′
less′er of·fense′
les′sor
— of the plain′tiff
lest
let n.
let v.
— in
le′thal
— weap′on
let′ter
— book
— car′ri·er
— mis′sive
— of cre′dence
— of ex·change′
— of li′cense
— of marque
— of re·call′
let′ters
— of ab′so·lu′tion
— of ad·min′is·tra′-
  tion
— of guard′i·an·-
  ship′
— of re·quest′
— ro′ga·to′ry
— tes′ta·men′ta·ry
let′ting
— out
le·vant′ et
cou·chant′
lev′ee
— dis′trict
lev′i·a·ble
Le·vit′i·cal de·grees′
lev′i·ty
lev′y
eq′ui·ta·ble —
lewd
— and las·civ′i·ous
  co·hab′i·ta′tion

— house
lewd′ness
lex
   — ag·rar′i·a
   — a·mis′sa
   — An·gli′ae′
   — a·pos′ta·ta
   — ap·par′ens′
   — a·quil′i·a
   — bar′ba·ra
   — Bre·ho′ni·a
   — com·mis·so′ri·a
   — com·mu′nis
   — do′mi·cil′i·i′
   — fo′ri′
   — ju′di·ci·a′lis
   — lo′ci′
   — loci ac′tus
   — loci
     ce′le·bra′ti·o′nis
   — loci con·trac′tus
   — loci de·lic′tus
   — loci do′mi·cil′i·i′
   — loci re′i′ si′tae′
   — loci so·lu′ti·o′nis
   — ma′ni·fes′ta
   — mer′ca·to′ri·a
   — na′tu·ra′le′
   — non co′git ad
     im′pos·si·bil′i·a
   — non cu′rat de
     min′i·mis
   — Ro·ma′na
   — sac·ra′men·ta′lis
   — si′tus
   — ta′li·o′nis
   — ter′rae′
ley
li′a·bil′i·ty
   — for dam′ag·es
   — in·sur′ance
   lim′it·ed —
   per′son·al —

sec′on·dar′y —
   strict —
li′a·ble
li′bel *v.*
li′bel *n.*
   — of re·view′
li′bel·ant
li′bel·lee′
li′bel·ous
   — per quod
   — per se
li′ber
lib′er·al
   strict and — con·-
     struc′tion in·ter′-
     pre·ta′tion
lib′er·ate′
lib′er·a′tion
lib′er·ti·cide′
lib′er·ties
lib′er·ty
   civ′il —
   nat′ur·al —
   — of a port
   — of con′science
   — of con′tract′
   — of speech
   — of the globe
   — of the press
   — of the rules
   per′son·al —
   po·lit′i·cal —
   re·lig′ious —
   — to hold pleas
li′bra
   — pen′sa
li′brar′y
li′cense
   — cas′es
   ex·clu′sive —
   ex′e·cut′ed —
   ex·ec′u·to′ry —
   ex·press′ —

im·plied′ —
   — in am′or·ti·za′tion
li′censed vict′ual
li′cen·see′
   — by in′vi·ta′tion
   — by per·mis′sion
li′cens·ing acts
li·cen′tious·ness
li′cet
lick′ing of thumbs
lie *n.*
   — de·tec′tor
lie *v.*
   — in grant
   — in liv′er·y
   — in wait
   — to
liege
   — hom′age
   — lord
liege′man
lien
   — ac·count′
   — cred′i·tor
lien·ee′
lien′or
lieu
   — lands
   — tax
lieu·ten′ant
   — colo′nel
   — com·mand′er
   — gen′er·al
   — gov′er·nor
life
   — an·nu′i·ty
   — es·tate′
   — in be′ing
   — in·sur′ance
   — or limb
   — peer′age
   — ta′bles
life′hold′

life′land′
li·ga′re′
lige′ance
light′house′
— board
light′ship′
light′er·age
lights
li·gi′us
like
— ben′e·fits
— char′ac·ter
like′li·hood′
like′ly
like′wise′
limb
lim′it
lim′i·ta′tion
col·lat′er·al —
con·di′tion·al —
con·tin′gent —
— in law
— o′ver
spe′cial —
— ti′tle
ti′tle by —
words of —
lim′i·ted
— ad·min′is·tra′tion
— ap·peal′
— guar′an·ty
— ju′ris·dic′tion
— li′a·bil′i·ty
— pow′er of
ap·point′ment
— pub′li·ca′tion
Lin′coln's Inn
lin′e·a
— ob·li′qua
— rec′ta
lin′e·age
lin′e·al
— con′san·guin′i·ty

— le·scent′
— heir
— war′ran·ty
lines and cor′ners
liq′ui·date′
liq′ui·dat′ed
— ac·count′
— claim
— dam′ag·es
— debt
— de·mand′
liq′ui·dat′ing
— dis′tri·bu′tion
— part′ner
liq′ui·da′tion
— div′i·dend
— tax′a·ble
liq′ui·da′tor
liq′uid debt
liq′uor
— deal′er
— shop
lis
— al′i·bi′ pen′dens′
— mo′ta
— pen′dens′
li′te′ pen·den′te′
li′ter *or* li′tre
li′te·ra
li′te·rae′
— hu·ma′ni·o′res′
— mor·tu′ae′
lit′er·al
— con′tract′
lit′er·ar′y
— com′po·si′tion
— prop′er·ty
lit′er·ate
lit′i·gant
lit′i·gate′
lit′i·ga′tion
li·ti′gious
li′tre

lit′tor·al
Lit′vi·nov
As·sign′ment
liv′er·y
— con·vey′ance
— of sei′sin
— of′fice
— sta′ble
liv′er·y·man
lives in be′ing
live′stock′
— in·sur′ance
live stor′age
liv′ing
— a·part′
— in a·dul′ter·y
— in o′pen and
no·to′ri·ous
adultery
— sep′ar·ate and
a·part′
— to·geth′er
— with hus′band
Lloyd's
— bonds
— in·sur′ance
load′ing
load line
loan
— as·so′ci·a′tion
— cer·tif′i·cates
— for ex·change′
— for use
gra·tu′i·tous —
— so·ci′e·ties
loaned em·ploy·ee′
lob′by·ing
lob′by·ist
lo′cal
— ac′tions
— af·fairs′
— a′gent
— and spe′cial

leg'is·la'tion
— as·sess'ment
— chat'tel
— im·prove'ment
— law
— op'tion
— prej'u·dice
lo·cal'i·ty
lo'cate'
lo'cat'ed
lo·ca'tion
loc'a·tive calls
lo'ca'tor
locked
lock'out'
lock'up' house
lo'co·mo'tive
lo'co' pa·ren'tis
lo'cus
— con·trac'tus
— de·lic'ti'
— in quo
— poen'i·ten'ti·ae'
— re'git ac'tum
— re'i' si'tae'
— stan'di'
lode
lode'man *or*
loads'man
lodg'er
lodg'ing house
lodg'ings
log'book'
log'ging
log'ic
log'i·cal
— rel'e·van·cy
loi'ter
Lom'bards'
Lon'don Lloyds
long
— ac·count'
— ton

lon·gev'i·ty pay
Long Par'lia·ment
long'shore·man
look and lis'ten
look'out'
lord
— ad'vo·cate
— and vas'sal
— chief bar'on
— chief jus'tice
— high chan'cel·lor
— high stew'ard
— high treas'ur·er
— in gross
— jus'tice clerk
— keep'er
— lieu·ten'ant
— may'or
— may'or's court
— of a man'or
— or'di·nar'y
— par'a·mount'
— priv'y seal
— war'den of
Cinque Ports
lords
— ap·pel'lants
— com·mis'sion·ers
— jus'tic·es of
ap·peal'
— march'ers
— of ap·peal'
— of appeal in
or'di·nar'y
— of er·ec'tion
— of par'lia·ment
— or·dain'ers
— spir'i·tu·al
— tem'po·ral
lord'ship'
lost prop'er·ty
lot'ter·y
low wa'ter

low'-wa'ter mark
loy'al
loy'al·ty
lu'cra·tive
lu'cre
lug'gage
lum'ber
lu'men
lu'mi·na
lu'mi·na're'
lump'ing sale
lump sum
lump'-sum'
— pay'ment
— set'tle·ment
lu'na·cy
lu'nar
— month
lu'na·tic
lur'gu·la·ry
ly'ing
— by
— in fran'chise'
— in grant
— in wait
lynch law

mace
— bear'er
mace'-proof'
mach'i·na'tion
ma·chine'
ma·chin'er·y
made known
mad'man'
mad'ness
Mad Par'lia·ment
ma·gis'ter

mag′is·te′ri·al
  — pre′cinct
mag′is·tra·cy
mag′is·trate′
mag′is·trate's court
Mag′na Char′ta *or*
  Mag′na Car′ta
mag′na cul′pa
maid′en
  — as·size′
mail
  — mat′ter
mail′a·ble
maim
main
  — chan′nel
main-à-main′
main′ly
main′per·na·ble
main′prise
main·tain′
main·tained′
main·tain′or
main′te·nance
  — as·sess′ment
maî′tre
maj′es·ty
ma′jor
  — and mi′nor fault
    rule
  — gen′er·al
ma·jo′ra re·ga′li·a
ma·jor′i·ty
  — of stock′hold′ers
  — rule
  — vote
make
  — a con′tract′
  — an as·sign′ment
  — an a·ward′
  — de·fault′
mak′er
mak′ing law

mal
  — grée
ma′la′
  — fi′des′
  — in se
  — prax′is
  — pro·hib′i·ta
mal′ad·min′is·tra′tion
mal′con′duct
mal′e·dic′tion
mal′e·fac′tion
mal′e·fac′tor
mal·fea′sance
mal′ice
  ac′tu·al —
  — a·fore′thought′
  con·struc′tive —
  ex·press′ —
  gen′er·al —
  im·plied′ —
  — in fact
  — in law
  le′gal —
  par·tic′u·lar —
  pre′con·ceived′ —
  pre·med′i·tat′ed —
  — pre′pense′
  spe′cial —
  u′ni·ver′sal —
ma·li′cious
  — a·ban′don·ment
  — a·buse′ of le′gal
    proc′ess′
  — ac′cu·sa′tion
  — act
  — ar·rest′
  — in′ju·ry
  — kill′ing
  — mis′chief
  — mo′tive
  — pros′e·cu′tion
  — tres′pass
  — use of proc′ess′

ma·li′cious·ly
ma·li′cious·ness
ma·lin′ger
mal′le·a·ble
ma′lo′ a′ni·mo′
ma′lo′ gra′to′
ma′lo′ sen′su′
mal·prac′tice
mal·treat′ment
ma′lum
  — in se
  — pro·hib′i·tum
man′a·cles
man′age
man′age·ment
man′ag·er
man′ag·ing a′gent
manche pres′ent
man′ci·pate′
man·da′mus
man′da·tar′y
man′date′
man′da·to′ry *n.*
man′da·to′ry *adj.*
  — in·junc′tion
man·da′vi′ bal′li·vo′
ma′ni·a
  — a po′tu′
  — fa·nat′i·ca
  fit of —
  hom′i·ci′dal —
  — tra·si·tor′i·a
man′hood′
man′i·fest′
  — law
man′i·fes′to
man′kind′
man′ner
  — and form
man′ning
man of straw
man′or
ma·no′ri·al

manse
man′sion
  — house
man′slaugh′ter
  in·vol′un·ta′ry —
  mis′de·mean′or —
  vol′un·ta′ry —
man′steal′ing
man·tic′u·late′
man′traps′
man′u·al
  — de·liv′er·y
  — gift
  — la′bor
  — rates
man′u·fac′to′ry
man′u·fac′ture
man′u·fac′tur·er
man′u·fac′tur·ers
  li′a·bil′i·ty
  doc′trine
man′u·mis′sion
ma′nu′ o′pe·ra
ma·nu·re′
man′u·script′
mar′a·thon′
ma·raud′er
march′es
ma·re′
  — clau′sum
  — li′be·rum
mar·e′schal
ma·ret′tum
mar′gin
  — of prof′it
mar′gin·al
  — note
  — street
mar′i·jua′na
ma·ri·na′ri·us
ma·rine′
  — belt
  — car′ri·er

— con′tract′
— in·sur′ance
— in′ter·est
— league
— risk
Ma·rine′ Corps
mar′i·ner
mar′i·schal
mar′i·tal
  — co·er′cion
  — fourth
  — por′tion
  — rights and du′ties
mar′i·time′
  — belt
  — cause
  — con′tract′
  — court
  — in′ter·est
  — ju′ris·dic′tion
  — law
  — lien
  — loan
  — prof′it
  — serv′ice
  — state
  — tort
mar′i·tus
mark
marke′pen′ny
mar′ket
  — geld
  — o·vert′
  — price
  — val′ue
mar′ket·a·ble
  — ti′tle
marks′man
Mar′kush′ doc′trine
marque, law of
marque and
  re·pri′sal, let′ters
  of

mar′quis *or*
  mar′quess
mar′riage
  — bro′ker·age
  — cer′e·mo′ny
  — cer·tif′i·cate′
  — con·sid′er·a′tion
  — li′cense
  — no′tice book
  — per ver′ba de
    prae·sen′ti′
  — por′tion
  — prom′ise
  — set′tle·ment
mar′shal
  — of the queen's
    bench
mar′shal·ing
  — as′sets′
  — liens
  — rem′e·dies
  — se·cu′ri·ties
mar′tial law
mar′tin·mas′
mas′o·chism
Ma′son-Dix′on line
mas′sa
Mas′sa·chu′setts
  — rule
  — trust
Mass′es
mass pick′et·ing
mass strike
mast
  — sell′ing
mas′ter
  — and ser′vant
  — at com′mon law
  — in chan′cer·y
  — in lu′na·cy
  — of a ship
  — of the crown
    of′fice

— of the fac'ul·ties
— of the horse
— of the mint
— of the ord'nance
— of the rolls
spec'ial —
tax'ing —
mate
ma·te'ri·a
ma·te'ri·al
  — al'le·ga'tion
  — al'ter·a'tion
  — ev'i·dence
  — fact
ma·te'ri·al·man
ma·ter'nal
  — line
  — prop'er·ty
ma·ter'na ma·ter'nis
ma·ter'ni·ty
math'e·mat'i·cal
  ev'i·dence
mat'i·ma
mat'ri·cide'
ma·tric'u·la
ma·tric'u·late'
mat'ri·mo'ni·al
  — ac'tion
  — caus'es
  — co·hab'i·ta'tion
  — dom'i·cile'
  — res
mat'ri·mo'ny
ma'trix
ma'tron
mat'ter
  — in con'tro·ver'sy
  — in deed
  — in is'sue
  — in pais
  — of course
  — of fact
  — of form

— of law
— of rec'ord
— of sub'stance
ma·ture'
ma·tur'i·ty
max'im
max'i·mum
may'hem'
may'hem·a'vit
mayn
mayn·o·ver'
may'or
may'or·al'ty
may'or·ess
may'or's court
mead'ow
mean
  — low'er low tide
  — low tide
  — re·serve'
me·an'der
  — lines
mean'ing
means
meas'ure
  — of dam'ag·es
  — of val'ue
meas'ur·er
meas'ur·ing mon'ey
me·chan'ic
me·chan'i·cal
  — arm
  — e·quiv'a·lent
  — move'ment
  — proc'ess'
  — skill
me·chan'ic's lien
me'di·a
  con'clu·den'di'
me'di·ate'
  — da'tum
  — de·scent'
  — pow'ers

— tes'ti·mo'ny
me'di·a'tion
me'di·a'tor
me'di·a'tors of
  ques'tions
med'i·cal
  — ev'i·dence
  — ju'ris·pru'dence
  — serv'ic·es
med'i·cine
  — chest
  fo·ren'sic —
med'i·co'le'gal
Med'i·ter·ra'ne·an
  pass'port'
med·le'tum
med'ley
meet'ing
  — of minds
meg'a·lo·ma'ni·a
mei'lic·ke sys'tem
mein'dre age
mel'an·cho'li·a
me'li·or'
me'lio·ra'tions
mem'ber
  — of con'gress
  — of par'lia·ment
mem'ber·ship'
  cor'po·ra'tion
mem'brum
mem'o·ran'dum
  — ar'ti·cles
  — check
  — clause
  — in er'ror
  — of al'ter·a'tion
  — of as·so'ci·a'tion
  — sale
mem'o·ri'ter'
mem'o·ri·za'tion
mem'o·ry
  le'gal —

men'ace
me·ni·al
men of straw
mens
  — le'gis
  — leg'is·la·to'ris
  — re'a
  — tes'ta·to'ris in
    tes'ta·men'tis
    spec·tan'da est
men'sa
  — et tho'ro'
men·sa'li·a
men'sis
men'sor
men'tal
  — al'ien·a'tion
  — an'guish
  — ca·pac'i·ty
  — com'pe·tence
  — cru'el·ty
  — de'fect
  — in'ca·pac'i·ty
  — in·com'pe·ten·cy
  — res'er·va'tion
men'te' cap'tus
men·ti'ri'
men'ti·ti'on
mer'ca·ble
mer'can·tant
mer'can·tile'
  — a'gen·cies
  — law
  — pa'per
  — part'ner·ship'
mer'cat
mer·ca·tive
mer·ca'tum
mer·ca·ture
mer'ce·dar'y
Mer'cen lage
mer'chan·dise'
mer'chant

com·mis'sion —
  law —
  — sea'man
  stat'ute —
mer'chant·a·bil'i·ty
mer'chant·a·ble
  — ti'tle
mer'chant·man
mer'ci·a·ment
Mer'ci·an law
mer'cy
mère
mere
  — li'cen·see'
  — mo'tion
  — right
  — stone
mere'ly
mer'e·tri'cious
merg'er
  con·glom'er·ate —
  hor'i·zon'tal —
  ver'ti·cal —
mer'i·to'ri·ous
  — cause of ac'tion
  — con·sid'er·a'tion
  — de·fense'
mer'its
mer'it sys'tem
mese
mes·nal'ty *or*
  mes·nal'i·ty
mesne
  — as·sign'ment
  — en·cum'brance
  — lord
  writ of —
mes'sage
mes'sen·ger
mes'suage
mes·ti'zo
me'ta
me·tab'o·lism

me·tach'ro'nism
me·tal'lic
me'ter *or* me'tre
metes and bounds
meth'od
meth'o·ma'ni·a
me'tre
met'ric sys'tem
me·trop'o·lis
met'ro·pol'i·tan
me'tus
Mich'ael·mas
  — term
mich'el·ge'mote'
mich'el-syn'oth *or*
  mich'el-syn'od
mid'-chan'nel
mid'dle
  — line of main
    chan'nel
  — of the riv'er
  — term
  — thread
mid'dle·man'
mid'ship'man
Mid'sum'mer Day
mid'way'
mid'wife'
mile
mile'age
mile'stones'
mil'i·tar'y
  — forc'es
  — gov'ern·ment
  — ju'ris·dic'tion
  — law
  — serv'ice
mi·li'tia
mi·li'tia·men
mill
  — pow'er
  — priv'i·lege
  — run

— site
milled mon'ey
mill'ing in tran'sit
min'a·ble
mind
mind and mem'o·ry
mine
min'er
min'er·al *n.*
min'er·al *adj.*
— deed
— dis'trict
— lands
— lease
— lode
— right
— roy'al·ty
— ser'vi·tude'
min'i·mum
— wage
min'ing
— claim
— com'pan·ies
— dis'trict
— lease
— lo·ca'tion
— part'ner·ship'
— rent
min'is·ter
min'is·te'ri·al
— act
— du'ty
— of'fice
— of'fi·cer
— pow'er
— trust
min'is·ters plen'i-
po·ten'ti·ar'y
min'is·try
mi'nor
mi·nor'i·ty
mint
— mark

— mas'ter
mint'age
mi'nus
min'ute
— book
min'utes
Miranda rule
mir'ror
mis'ad·ven'ture
mis'al·lege'
mis'ap·pli·ca'tion
mis'ap·pro'pri·a'tion
mis·be·hav'ior
mis·brand'ing
mis·car'riage
— of jus'tice
mis·cast'ing
mis·ce·ge·na'tion
mis·charge'
mis'chief
mis·cog'ni·zant
mis·con'duct
mis·con·tin'u·ance
mis·cre·ant
mis·date'
mis·de·liv'er·y
mis·de·mean'ant
mis·de·mean'or
mis·de·scrip'tion
mis·di·rec'tion
mise
— mon'ey
mis'e·re·re'
mis·er·i·cor'di·a
mis·fea'sance
mis·for'tune
mis·join'der
mis·lead'ing
mis·no'mer
mis·plead'ing
mis·pri'sion
neg'a·tive —
— of fel'o·ny

— of trea'son
pos'i·tive —
mis·read'ing
mis·re·cit'al
mis'rep·re·sen·ta'tion
false —
fraud'u·lent —
in'no·cent —
ma·ter'i·al —
neg'li·gent —
mis'sion·ar'ies
mis'sions
mis'sives
mis·take'
mu'tu·al —
— of fact
— of law
Mis'ter
Mis'tress *or*
mis'tress
mis·tri'al
mis·us'er
mit'i·gat'ing
cir'cum·stanc'es
mit'i·ga'tion
— of dam'ag·es
mit·ter'
mit'ti·mus
mixed
— es·tate'
— in·sur'ance
com'pa·ny
— laws
— ques'tion of law
and fact
— ques'tions
— sub'jects of
prop'er·ty
mix'tion
M'Nagh'ten rule
mob
mob'bing and
ri'ot·ing

mo·bil′i·a
mock
mo′dal leg′a·cy
mode
mod′el
mod′er·ate *adj.*
mod′er·ate′ *v.*
mod′er·a′tor
mod′i·fi·ca′tion
mod′i·fy′
mo′do′ et for′ma′
mo′dus
   — hab′i·lis
   — va·can′di′
moe′ble
moer′da
moi′e·ty
mo′les·ta′tion
Mol·mu′tian laws
mo·men′tum
mon′a·chism
mon′ar·chy
mon·e′ta
mon·e·ta′gi·um
mon′e·tar′y
mon′ey
   — bill
   — claims
   — de·mand′
   — had and
     re·ceived′
   — of a·dieu′
mon′ey·chang′er
mon′ey or′der
mon′ey-or′der
   of′fice
mon′ger
mon′i·ment
mo·ni′tion
mon′i·to′ry
mo·noc′ra·cy
mon′o·crat′
mo·nog′a·my

mon′o·gram′
mon′o·graph′
mo·nom′a·chy
mon′o·ma′ni·a
mon′o·po′li·um
mo·nop′o·ly
mon′ster
mon·strans′ de
   droit
month
mon′u·ment
moon′shine′
moor
moor′age
moor′ing
moot *n.*
moot *adj.*
   — court
   — hall
   — hill
   — man
moot′ing
mor′al
   — ac′tions
   — cer′tain·ty
   — con·sid′er·a′tion
   — du·ress′
   — ev′i·dence
   — fraud
   — haz′ard
   — in·san′i·ty
   — law
   — ob′li·ga′tion
   — tur′pi·tude′
mor′a·to′ri·um
mor′a·tur′ in le′ge′
more or less
more·o′ver
Mor′mon
mo′ron′
mor′phi·no·ma′ni·a
   or mor′phin·ism
Mor′ris plan

com′pa·ny
mors
mort
mor′tal
mor·tal′i·ty
   — ta′bles
mort′gage
   chat′tel —
   con·ven′tion·al —
   eq′ui·ta·ble —
   first —
   first — bonds
   gen′er·al —
   ju·di′cial —
   le′gal —
   — of goods
   pur′chase-mon′ey —
   sec′ond —
   tac′it —
   Welsh —
mort′ga·gee′
   — in pos·ses′sion
mort′ga·gor′
mor′ti·fi·ca′tion
mor′tis cau′sa
mort′main′
   — acts
mor′tu·ar′y
   — ta′bles
mor·tu′us
most fa′vored
   na′tion clause
mote
moth′er-in-law′
mo′tion
mo′tive
mo′tor·cy′cle
mo′tor ve′hi·cle
mount′ings
mourn′ing
mouth of riv′er
mov′a·ble
   — es·tate′

— free'hold'
mov'a·bles
move
move'ment
mov'ent *or* mov'ant
mov'ing pa'pers
muf'fler
mu·lat'to
mulct
mule
mu·li·er'
— puis·né'
mu'li·er·a'tus
mul'ta
mul'ti·far'i·ous·ness
mul'ti·par'tite'
mul'ti·ple
mul'ti·plic'i·ty
— of ac'tions
— of suits
mul'ti·tude'
mum'mi·fi·ca'tion
mu·nic'i·pal
— ac'tion
— af·fairs'
— aid
— au·thor'i·ties
— bonds
— char'ter
— claims
— cor'po·ra'tion
— corporation de
fac'to'
— courts
— dom'i·cile'
— e·lec'tion
— func'tion
— gov'ern·ment
— iaw
— lien
— of'fi·cer
— or'di·nance

— pur'pos·es
qua'si' —
— se·cu'ri·ties
— tax·a'tion
— war'rants
mu·nic'i·pal'i·ty
mu'ni·ments
mu·ni'tions
mu'ral mon'u·ments
mur'der
fel'o·ny —
first-de·gree' —
— in the first
de·gree'
— in the sec'ond
degree
sec'ond-de·gree' —
— with mal'ice
a·fore'thought'
mur'drum
mu·se'um
mus'ter
— mas'ter
— book
— roll
mu·ta'tion
— of li'bel
mu·ta'tis mu·tan'dis
mute
mu'ti·la'tion
mu'ti·nous
mu'ti·ny
mu'tu·al
— af·fray'
— ben'e·fit
as·so'ci·a'tion
— re·lief'
as·so'ci·a'tion
— re·serve'
com'pa·ny
— sav'ings bank
— wills

mu'tu·al'i·ty
mu'tu·ar'y
mu·tu'um

N

na·if'
na'ked
name
— and arms clause
name'ly
narr and cog·no'vit
law
nar'ra·tive
nar'ra·tor
na'tion
na'tion·al
na'tion·al'i·ty
na'tive
na·tu'ra bre·vi'um
nat'u·ral
— af·fec'tion
— law
— life
nat'u·ral-born'
sub'ject
nat'u·ral·i·za'tion
nat'u·ra·lize'
nat'u·ra·lized'
cit'i·zen
nau·fra'gi·um
naught
nau'ti·cal
— as·ses'sors
— mile
na'val
— base
— courts
— courts'-mar'tial

— law
— of'fi·cer
nav'i·ga'ble
— riv'er or stream
— wa'ters
nav'i·gate'
nav'i·ga'tion
— ser'vi·tude'
na'vy
— bills
— de·part'ment
neap tide
neat cat'tle
ne·ca'tion
nec'es·sa'ries
nec'es·sa'ry
— in'fer·ence
ne·ces'si·tous
cir'cum·stanc'es
ne·ces'si·ty
ne·croph'i·lism
need'ful
need'less
need'y
ne ex'e·at'
— bond
neg'a·tive
— a·ver'ment
— con·di'tion
— preg'nant
ne·glect'
ne·glect'ed mi'nor
neg'li·gence
ac'tion·a·ble —
col·lat'er·al —
com·par'a·tive —
con·cur'rent —
con·trib'u·tor'y —
crim'i·nal —
cul'pa·ble —
de·grees' of —
gross —

haz'ard·ous —
le'gal —
or'di·nar'y —
pas'sive —
— per se
slight —
sub'se·quent —
wan'ton —
— will'ful
neg'li·gent
— es·cape'
— of·fense'
neg'li·gent·ly
ne·go'tia·bil'i·ty
ne·go'tia·ble
— in·stru'ments
ne·go'ti·ate'
ne·go'ti·a'tion
ne'gro
neigh'bor
neigh'bor·hood'
ne'mo'
neph'ew
nep'o·tism
ner'vous·ness
net
— as'sets'
— bal'ance
— earn'ings
— es·tate'
— in'come'
— lev'el an'nu·al
pre'mi·um
— loss
— pre'mi·um
— price
— pro'ceeds'
— prof'its
— rev'e·nues'
— sin'gle pre'mi·um
— ton'nage
— val'ue

— weight
— worth
neu'tral
neu·tral'i·ty
— laws
new
— and use'ful
— as'sets'
— as·sign'ment
— cause of ac'tion
— for old
— mat'ter
— style
— tri'al
New'gate'
New Inn
new'ly dis·cov'ered
ev'i·dence
news'pa'per
next
— de·vi·see'
— e·ven'tu·al
es·tate'
— of kin
— pres'en·ta'tion
nick'name'
nid'er·ling,
nid'er·ing, *or*
nith'ing
niece
ni·ent'
night mag'is·trate'
ni'hil
— di'cit
— est
— ha'bet
ni'hil·ist
nil
— de'bet
nim'mer
ni'si' pri'us
no·bil'i·ty

no'cent
nol'le pro·se'qui'
no'lo' con·ten'de·re'
no'men
  — ju'ris
nom'i·nal
  — cap'i·tal
  — con·sid'er·a'tion
  — dam'ag·es
  — de·fen'dant
  — part'ner
  — par'ty
  — plain'tiff
nom'i·nate' v.
nom'i·nate adj.
  — con'tracts'
nom'i·nat'ing and
  re·duc'ing
nom'i·na'tion
  — pa'per
nom'i·nee'
non
  — as·sump'sit
  — ce'pit
  — com'pos men'tis
  — est fac'tum
  — ob·stan'te'
  — obstante
    ve·re·dic'to'
  — o·mit'tas
  — pros
non'a·bil'i·ty
non'ac·cep'tance
non·ac'cess'
non·ad·mis'sion
non'age
non'an·ces'tral
  es·tate'
non'ap·par'ent
  ease'ment
non'ap·pear'ance
non·as·sess'a·ble
non·bail'a·ble

non·can'cel·a·ble
non'claim'
non'com·bat'ant
non'com·mis'sioned
non'com·pet'i·tive
  traf'fic
non'con·form'ing
  uses
non'con·form'ist
non'con·test'a·ble
non'con·tin'u·ous
  ease'ment
non·cu'mu·la'tive
  div'i·dends
non'de·liv'er·y
non'de·script'
non'de·tach'a·ble
  fa·cil'i·ties
non'di·rec'tion
non'dis·clo'sure
non'e·nu'mer·at'ed
  day
non·fea'sance
non·for'feit·a·ble
non·func'tion·al
non·in'ter·course'
non·in'ter·ven'tion
  will
non·is'su·a·ble pleas
non·join'der
non·ju'rors
non·lev'i·a·ble
non·mail'a·ble
non·med'i·cal
  pol'i·cy
non·mer'chant·a·ble
  ti'tle
non·nav'i·ga·ble
non·ne·go'tia·ble
non·oc'cu·pa'tion·al
non·pay'ment
non'per·form'ance
non·prof'it

non·res'i·dence
non·res'i·dent
non·sane'
  — mem'o·ry
non'sense'
non·suit'
non·us'er
non·waiv'er
  a·gree'ment
nor'mal·ly
Nor'man French
nos'trum
no'ta
no·tar'i·al
  — will
no'ta·ry pub'lic
no·ta'tion
note v.
note n.
  — of hand
notes
not ex·ceed'ing
not guilt'y
no'tice
  a·ver'ment of —
  im·me'di·ate —
  — in lieu of serv'ice
  ju·di'cial —
  — of ap·pear'ance
  — of judg'ment
  — of lis pen'dens'
  — of mo'tion
  per'son·al —
  pre·sump'tive —
  pub'lic —
  rea'son·a·ble —
  — to ad·mit'
  — to plead
  — to quit
no'ti·fy'
not'ing
not to be
  per·formed'

with·in' one year
no'to·ri'e'ty
no·to'ri·ous
— in·sol'ven·cy
— pos·ses'sion
not trans·fer'a·ble
no·va'tion
nov'el
— as·sign'ment
— dis·sei'sin
No·vel'lae'
Con'sti·tu'ti·o'nes'
Nov'els
nov'el·ty
no'vus ho'mo'
nox'ious
nu'da
— pa'ti·en'ti·a
— pos·ses'si·o'
nude
— con'tract'
— mat'ter
— pact
nu'dum pac'tum
nu'ga·to'ry
nui'sance
a·bate'ment of a —
ac'tion·a·ble —
— at law
com'mon —
con·tin'u·ing —
— in fact
— per ac·ci'dens'
per'ma·nent —
— per se
nul
— ti'el rec'ord
null
nul'la bo'na
nul'li·ty
— of mar'riage
nul'li·us fil'i·us
num'bers game

nun'ci·o'
nunc pro tunc
nun'cu·pate'
nun'cu·pa'tive will
nup'tial
nur'ture
nyc·them'er·on'
nym'pho·ma'ni·a

oath
as·ser'to·ry —
cor'po·ral —
— ex of·fi'ci·o'
ex'tra·ju·di'cial —
false —
— in li'tem
ju·di'cial —
— of al·le'giance
of·fi'cial —
poor debt'or's —
prom'is·so'ry —
pur'ga·to·ry —
qual'i·fied' —
sol'emn —
sup'ple·to'ry —
vol'un·tar'y —
o·be'di·ence
o'bit
— si'ne' pro'le'
o'bit·er
— dic'tum
ob·ject' v.
ob'ject n.
ob·jec'tion
ob'jects of a pow'er
ob'late'
— rolls
ob·la'ti'

ob·la'tion
ob'li·gate'
ob'li·ga'ti·o'
ob'li·ga'tion
ab'so·lute' —
ac·ces'so·ry —
al·ter'na·tive —
con·di'tion·al —
con·junc'tive —
con·trac'tu·al —
de·ter'mi·nate —
di·vis'i·ble —
ex·press' —
her'i·ta·ble —
im·plied' —
in'de·ter'mi·nate —
in'di·vis'i·ble —
joint —
mor'al —
— of a con'tract'
pe'nal —
per'son·al —
pri'ma'ry —
prim'i·tive —
prin'ci·pal —
real —
sec'on·da'ry —
sev'er·al —
sim'ple —
sin'gle —
sol'i·dar'y —
o·blig'a·to'ry
— pact
— writ'ing
ob'li·gee'
ob'li·gor'
o·blit'er·a'tion
o·bliv'i·on
o·bliv'i·ous
ob'lo·quy
ob·nox'ious
ob·rep'tion
ob·scene'

ob·scen′i·ty
ob·scure′
ob·serve′
ob·sig′na·to′ry
ob′so·les′cence
ob′so·les′cent
ob′so·lete′
ob·stan′te′
ob·stet′rics
ob′sti·nate
ob·stric′tion
ob·struct′
ob·struct′ing
  — an of′fi·cer
  — jus′tice
  — proc′ess′
ob·struc′tion
  — to nav′i·ga′tion
ob·tain′
ob·ven′tion
ob′vi·ous
  — dan′ger
  — risk
oc·ca′sion
oc′cu·pan·cy
oc′cu·pant
oc′cu·pa′tion
oc′cu·pa′tion·al
  — dis·ease′
oc′cu·pa′tive
oc′cu·pi′er
oc′cu·py′
oc′cu·py′ing
  claim′ant
oc·cur′
oc·cur′rence
o′cean
oc′tave
oc′u·list
odd lot
  — doc′trine
o′di·ous

o′di·um
of coun′sel
of course
of·fend′er
of·fense′
  con·tin′u·ing —
  crim′i·nal —
  qua′si′ —
of·fen′sive
  — lan′guage
  — weap′on
of′fer v.
of′fer n.
  — of com′pro·mise′
of′fer·ings
of′fice
  min′is·te′ri·al —
  po·lit′i·cal —
  prin′ci·pal —
  pub′lic —
  state —
of′fi·cer
  — de fac′to′
  — de ju′re′
  war′rant —
of·fi′cial n.
of·fi′cial adj.
  — mis·con′duct
of·fi′cial·ty
of·fi′cious will
of force
off′set′
off′spring′
of grace
of rec′ord
of right
of the blood
O·ler′on, laws of
ol′i·gar′chy
ol′i·gop′o·ly
ol′o·graph′
ol′o·graph′ic

tes′ta·ment
O·lym′pi·ad′
om′buds·man
o·mis′sion
o·mit′tance
om′ni·bus′
  — bill
om′ni·um
on ac·count′
  — of whom it may
    con·cern′
on all fours
on call
on de·fault′
on de·mand′
one per′son, one
  vote
on′er·ous
  — cause
  — con′tract′
  — deed
  — gift
  — ti′tle
on file
on or a·bout′
on or be·fore′
on stand
on the per′son
o′nus
  — pro·ban′di′
o′pen
  — a judg′ment
  — a rule
  — bulk
  — the plead′ings
o′pen-end′
  a·gree′ment
o′pen·ing
  — state′ment of
    coun′sel
o′pen·tide′
op′er·a n.

o'pe·ra *pl. n.*
op'er·ate'
op'er·a'tion
op'er·a·tive
  — part
  — words
ope'tide'
oph'thal·mol'o·gist
o·pin'ion
  con·cur'ring —
  dis·sent'ing —
  — ev'i·dence
  per cu'ri·am —
o'pi·um
op·pos'er
op'po·site
  — par'ty
op'po·si'tion
op·pres'sion
op·pres'sor
op·pro'bri·um
op·ti'cian
op'ti·ma·cy
op'tion
op'tion·al writ
op·tom'e·trist
op·tom'e·try
o'pus
o'ral
  — con'tract'
  — ev'i·dence
  — plead'ing
Or'ange·men
or'a·tor
or'a·trix'
or·ba'tion
or·dain'
or·dain'ers
or·deal'
or'der
  charg'ing —
  de·cre'tal —

fi'nal —
in'ter·loc'u·to'ry —
mon'ey —
  — ni'si'
  — of dis·charge'
  — of fil'i·a'tion
  — of re·viv'or
re·strain'ing —
speak'ing —
stop —
or'der·ly
or'ders
  — of the day
or'di·nance
or'di·nar'y *n.*
or'di·nar'y *adj.*
  — course of
    busi'ness
or'di·na'tion
ore'-leave'
or·gan'ic
  — act
  — law
or'gan·ize'
o·rig'i·nal
  — bill
  — in·ven'tor
  — ju'ris·dic'tion
  — writ
or'phan
or'phan·age
  — part
or'phans' court
or'tho·pe'dist
os·ten'si·ble
  — a'gen·cy
  — au·thor'i·ty
  — part'ner
os'te·o·path'
os'te·op'a·thy
Os'wald's law
oth'er·wise'

ought
oust
oust'er
ou·ster'
  — le main
  — le mer
out'age
out'-bound'a·ries
out'build'ing
out'cast'
out'crop'
out'er bar
out'fit'
out'go'
out'house'
out'law'
out'lawed'
out'law'ry
out'line'
out'lot'
out of court
out of pock'et rule
out'part·ers
out'rage'
out'rid'ers
out'right'
out·side'
out·stand'ing
  — and o'pen
    ac·count'
o'ver·charge'
o'ver·come'
o'ver·draft'
o'ver·draw'
o'ver·due'
o'ver·haul' *v.*
o'ver·haul' *n.*
o'ver·head' *adj. & n.*
o'ver·head' *adv.*
o'ver·in·sur'ance
o'ver·load' *v.*
o'ver·load' *n.*

o'ver·ly'ing right
o'ver·rate'
o'ver·reach'ing
  clause
o'ver·ride'
o'ver·rid'ing
  roy'al·ty
o'ver·rule'
o'vers
o·vert'
— act
— word
o'ver·take'
o'ver·time'
— wage
o'ver·ture
owe
ow'el·ty
— of ex·change'
— of par·ti'tion
— of serv'ic·es
ow'ing
own
owned by
own'er
  eq'ui·ta·ble —
  gen'er·al and
    ben'e·fi'cial —
  joint —
  le'gal —
  part —
  real —
  rec'ord —
  re·put'ed —
  ri·par'i·an —
  sole and un'con-·
    di'tion·al —
  spe'cial —
own'er·ship'
o'yer
— and ter'min·er
o'yez'

P

pa·ca're'
pace
pac'i·fi·ca'tion
pac'i·fist
pack'age
pack'er
pact
— de non
  a·li·en·an'do
nude —
o·blig'a·to'ry —
pac'tum
— de non
  a·li·en·an'do
nu'dum —
pad'dock
pa·go'da
pais *or* pays
pa·la'gi·um
palm off
palm'ing off
  doc'trine
palm'is·try
pal'pa·ble
pam'phlet
pan'der
pan'der·er
pan·dox'a·tor
pan'el
pan·ier'
pan'nel·la'tion
pan'to·mime'
pa'per
  ac·com'mo·da'-
    tion —
  — block·ade'
  com·mer'cial —

— hang'ings
— mon'ey
par
par'age *or*
  par·a'gi·um
par'a·graph'
par'al·lel'
pa·ral'y·sis
par'a·mount'
  — eq'ui·ty
  — ti'tle
par'a·noi'a
par'aph
par'a·pher·na'lia
pa·ra'tum ha'be·o'
par'cel
par'cels
par'ce·nar'y
par'cen·er
parch'ment
par'don
  ab'so·lute' —
  con·di'tion·al —
  ex·ec'u·tive —
  full —
  gen'er·al —
  par'tial —
  un'con·di'tion·al —
par'don·ers
par'ens'
  — pa'tri·ae'
par'ent
par'ent·age
par·en'te·la
pa·ren'the·sis
pa·ren'ti·cide'
pa'res'
pa'ri'
  — cau'sa
  — de·lic'to
  — ma·te'ri·a
  — mu'tu·el

— pas'su
par'ish
pa·rish'ion·ers
par'i·ty
pa'ri·um ju·di'ci·um
park'ing
park'way'
par'lia·ment
par'lia·men'ta·ry
— law
pa·ro'chi·al
pa·rol'
— a·gree'ment
— ev'i·dence
— ev'i·dence rule
pa·role'
pa·rols' de ley
par'ri·cide'
pars
— re'a
par'son
par'son·age
par'tial
— ac·count'
— av'er·age
— de·pend'en·cy
— e·vic'tion
— ev'i·dence
— in·san'i·ty
— loss
— pay'ment
— ver'dict
par'ti·ble lands
par·tic'i·pate'
par·tic'u·lar
par·tic'u·lar'i·ty
par·tic'u·lars
— of sale
par'ties
— and priv'ies
— in in'ter·est
par·ti'tion

— of a suc·ces'sion
part'ner
dor'mant —
liq'ui·dat'ing —
nom'i·nal —
os·ten'si·ble —
qua·si' —
se'cret —
si'lent —
sleep'ing —
sol'vent —
spe'cial —
sur·viv'ing —
part'ner·ship'
— as'sets'
— at will
com·mer'cial —
— debt
gen'er·al —
lim'it·ed —
— in com'men·dam
trad'ing —
par'ty n.
— ag·grieved'
— in'jured
real —
real — in in'ter·est
— to be charged
par'ty adj.
— ju'ry
— struc'ture
— wall
pas'sage
pass'book'
pas'sen·ger
pas'sim
pass'ing tick'et
pas'sion
pas'sive
pass'port'
pas'ture
pat'ent adj.

— am'bi·gu'i·ty
— de'fect'
let'ters —
— writ
pat'ent n.
— bill of'fice
de·sign' —
land —
— of'fice
— of pre·ced'ence
pi'o·neer' —
plant —
re·is'sued —
— right
— right deal'er
— rolls
pat'ent·a·ble
pat'ent·ee'
pa'ter
— pa'tri·ae'
pa'ter·fa·mil'i·as
pa·ter'nal
— line
— pow'er
— prop'er·ty
pa·ter'ni·ty
pa·thol'o·gy
pa·tib'u·lar'y
pa·tib'u·lat'ed
pa'ti·ens'
pa'tient
pa'tri·a
pa'tri·arch'
pat'ri·cide'
pat'ri·mo'ny
pa·trol'man
pa'tron
pa'tron·age
pa'tron·ize'
pau'per
pawn
pawn'bro'ker

pawn·ee′
pawn′or
pax re′gis
pay′a·ble
— af′ter sight
— on de·mand′
pay·ee′
pay′er
pay′ment
— into court
part —
par′tial —
vol′un·tar′y —
peace
— and qui′e·tude′
ar′ti·cles of the —
bill of —
breach of —
con·ser′va·tor of
the —
jus′tice of the —
— of′fi·cers
pub′lic —
peace′a·ble
pec′u·la′tion
pe·cu′liar
pe·cu′ni·a
pe·cu′ni·ar′y
— ben′e·fits
— caus′es
— con·di′tion
— loss
ped′dler
ped′er·as′ty
pe·des′tri·an
ped′i·gree′
peer′age
peer′ess
peers
pe′nal
— ac′tion
— bill
— bond

— clause
— laws
— ser′vi·tude′
— stat′utes
— sum
pen′al·ty
pen′den·cy
pen′dens′
pen′dent ju′ris·dic′-
tion
pen·den′te′ li′te′
pend′ing
pen′e·tra′tion
pen′i·ten′tia·ry
pen′sion
pen′sion·er
pe′on·age
peo′ple
per
per·am′bu·la′tion
per and post
per an′num
per au′tre vie′
per cap′i·ta
per·ceiv′a·ble risk
per cent or
per·cent′
per·cep′tion
perch
per′co·late′
per′co·lat′ing
wa′ters
per cu′ri·am
per·di′da
per di′em
per·du′ra·ble
per·emp′tion
per·emp′to·ry
— chal′lenge
— day
— ex·cep′tions
— pa′per
— un′der·tak′ing

per′fect
— at′tes·ta′tion
clause
per′fi·dy
per·form′
per for′mam do′ni′
per·form′ance
part —
spe·cif′ic —
per frau′dem
per′il
per′ils
— of the lakes
— of the sea
per in·dus′tri·um
per in·for·tu′ni·um
pe′ri·od
pe′ri·od′i·cal
pe·riph′ra·sis
per′ish
per′ish·a·ble
— com·mod′i·ty
— goods
per′ju·ry
per′ma·nent
— a·bode′
— dis′a·bil′i·ty
— em·ploy′ment
per mis′ad·ven′ture
per·mis′sion
per·mis′sions
per·mis′sive
— use
— waste
per·mit′ v.
per′mit n.
per mit·ter′ le droit
per mit·ter′ l′es·tate′
per′mu·ta′tion
per my et per tout
per′nan·cy
per′pe·tra′tor
per·pet′u·al

per'pe·tu'i·ty
per proc'u·ra'tion
per'qui·sites
per quod
per se
per'son
per·so'na
per'son·a·ble
per'son·al
— ef·fects'
— law
— li'a·bil'i·ty
per'son·al·ty
per'son·ate'
per stir'pes'
per·suade'
per·sua'sion
per·tain'
per'ti·nent
per to'tam cu'ri·am
per tout et non per
    my
per'tur·ba'tion
per·verse'
per year
Pe'ter's pence
pet'it
pe·tite' as·size'
pe·ti'ti·o' prin·cip'i·i'
pe·ti'tion
— de droit
— in bank'rupt·cy
pe·ti'tion·er
pe·ti'tion·ing
    cred'i·tor
pet'i·to'ry ac'tion
pet'ti·fog'ger
pet'ty
— bag of'fice
— of'fi·cers
phar'ma·cist
phar'ma·cy
phle·bi'tis

pho·tog'ra·pher
pho·tog'ra·phy
phy'la·sist
phys'i·cal
— de·pre'ci·a'tion
— dis'a·bil'i·ty
— fact
— im·pos'si·bil'i·ty
— in'ca·pac'i·ty
— in'ju·ry
— ne·ces'si·ty
phy·si'cian
phys'i·o·ther'a·py
pi'a·cle
pick'et
pick'et·ing
    peace'a·ble —
    un·law'ful —
pick'pock'et
piece work
pie·pou'dre *or* pie'-
    pow'der
pier
pil'fer
pil'fer·age
pil'fer·er
pil'lage
pil'lo·ry
pi'lot·age
— au·thor'i·ties
pimp
pi'o·neer' pat'ent
pi'ra·cy
pi'rate
pi·rat'i·cal·ly
pis'ca·ry
pis'tol
pit'tance
plac'ard
place
— of con'tract'
— of de·liv'er·y
— of em·ploy'ment

plac'er
— claim
— lo·ca'tion
pla'cit
pla'ci·ta ju'ris
pla'ci·tum
pla'gia·rism
pla'gia·rist
pla'gia·ry
plague
plaint
plain'tiff
— in er'ror
    use —
plan·ta'tion
plat
plea
    af·firm'a·tive —
    a·nom'a·lous —
    bad —
    com'mon —
    coun'ter —
    dil'a·to·ry —
    dou'ble —
    false —
    for'eign —
— in a·bate'ment
— in bar
— in dis·charge'
    neg'a·tive —
— of con·fes'sion
    and a·void'ance
— of guilt'y
— of no'lo'
    con·ten'de·re
— of re·lease'
    per·emp'to·ry —
— side
    spe'cial —
    spe'cial — in bar
plead
— is'su·a·bly
— o'ver

— to the mer'its
plead'ed
plead'er
  spe'cial —
plead'ing
  ar·tic'u·lat'ed —
  dou'ble —
  spe'cial —
plead'ings
ple·be'ian
pleb'i·scite'
ple·da·ble'
pledge
pledg·ee'
pledg'er·y
pledg'es
pledg'or
ple'na·ry
  — con·fes'sion
  — suit
ple'ne'
plen'i·po·ten'ti·ar'y
ple'vin
plight
plot
plot'tage
plumb'er
plun'der
plun'der·age
plu·ral'i·ty
poach
poach'ing
point
  — re·served'
poi'son
po'lar star rule
po·lice'
  — court
  — mag'is·trate'
  — of'fi·cer
  — pow'er
  — reg'u·la'tions
  — su'per·vi'sion

pol'i·cy
  blan'ket —
  en·dow'ment —
  float'ing —
  in'ter·est —
  — loan
  mixed —
  — of in·sur'ance
  o'pen —
  paid'up' —
  pub'lic —
  time —
  val'ued —
  voy'age —
  wa'ger —
po·lit'i·cal
  — par'ty
  — ques'tions
  — rights
pol'i·tics
pol'i·ty
poll
  — money
  — tax
poll'ing the ju'ry
polls
pol·lute'
po·lyg'a·my
pool'ing
  — as'sets'
  — con'tracts'
poor
  — law
  — rate
poor'-law' board
pop'er·y
pop'u·lace
por'no·graph'ic
por·rect'ing
port
  — charg'es
  — dues
  for'eign —

home —
  — of de·liv'er·y
  — of de·par'ture
  — of des'ti·na'tion
  — of dis·charge'
  — of en'try
  — risk
  — toll
por'ter
por'ter·age
por'tion
pos'i·tive
  — ev'i·dence
  — law
  — wrong
po·si·ti'vi' ju'ris
pos'se
pos·sess'
pos·sessed'
pos·ses'sion
  ac'tu·al —
  ad·verse' —
  chose in —
  civ'il —
  con·struc'tive —
  cor·po're·al —
  de·riv'a·tive —
  es·tate' in —
  ex·clu'sive —
  hos'tile —
  na'ked —
  nat'u·ral —
  o'pen —
  peace'a·ble —
  ped'al —
  scram'bling —
  u'ni·ty of —
  va'cant —
pos·ses'sion is
  nine'-tenths' of
  the law
pos·ses'sor
  — bo'na fide

— ma'la fide
pos·ses'so·ry
  — ac'tion
  — claim
  — judg'ment
  — lien
pos'si·bil'i·ty
  bare —
  — cou'pled with an
    in'ter·est
  na'ked —
  — of re·vert'er
  — on a —
pos'si·ble
post
  — di'em
  — dis·sei'sin
  — ex·change'
  — fac'to'
  — hac
  — na'tus
  — notes
  — o'bit
  — of'fice
  — roads
  — ter'mi·num
post'age
  — stamp
post'al
  — cur'ren·cy
  — sav'ings
    de·pos'i·to'ries
post'date'
post'dat'ed check
pos·te'ri·or'i·ty
pos·ter'i·ty
post'hu·mous
  — child
  — work
post'man
post'mark'
post'mas'ter
post'mas'ter

gen'er·al
post'-mor'tem
post·nup'tial
  — set'tle·ment
post·pone'
po'ta·ble
po'ten·tate'
po·ten'tial
pound
pow'er
  ap·pen'dant —
  ap·pur'te·nant —
  — cou'pled with an
    in'ter·est
  ex·clu'sive —
  ex·ec'u·tive —
  na'ked —
  — of ap·point'ment
  — of at·tor'ney
  — of dis·po·si'tion
  — of rev'o·ca'tion
  — of sale
  — of vis'i·ta'tion
pow'ers
  col·lat'er·al —
  gen'er·al and
    spe'cial —
  general and special
    — in trust
  im·plied' —
  — in gross
  in·her'ent —
  min'is·te'ri·al —
prac'ti·ca·ble
prac'ti·ca·bly
prac'ti·cal
prac'tice
  — of law
  — of med'i·cine
prac'tic·es
prac·ti'tion·er
prae'ci·pe'
prae'di·al

prae·to'ri·an law
prae·var'i·ca·tor'
prag·mat'ic
prai'rie
prax'is
prayer
pre'am·ble
pre·au'di·ence
pre·car'i·ous
  — cir'cum·stanc'es
  — loan
  — pos·ses'sion
  — right
  — trade
prec'a·to'ry
  — trust
  — words
pre·cau'tion
pre'ced·ence
pre'ced·en'cy
prec'e·dent
  — con·di'tion
prec'e·dents sub
  si·len'ti·o'
pre·ced'ing
pre'ce·par'ti·um
pre'cept'
pre'cinct
pre'ci·pe'
pre·cip'i·ta'tion
pre·cise'
pre·clude'
pre'cog·ni'tion
pre·con'tract'
pred'e·ces'sor
pre'di·al
  — ser'vi·tude'
pred'i·cate' *v.*
pred'i·cate *n.* & *adj.*
pre·dom'i·nant
pre-emp'tion
pre-emp'tion·er
pre'fect'

pre·fer′
pref′er·ence
pre·ferred′
— debt
— div′i·dend′
— stock
preg′nan·cy
preg′nant neg′a·tive
prej′u·dice
without —
prej′u·di′cial er′ror
prel′ate
pre·lim′i·nar′y
pre·med′i·tate′
pre·med′i·tat′ed
de·sign′
pre·med′i·tat′ed·ly
pre·med′i·ta′tion
pre·mier′
pre·mier′ ser′jeant,
the queen's
prem′is·es
pre′mi·um
pren·der′ or
pren′dre
prep′a·ra′tion
pre·pare′
pre·pense′
pre·pon′der·ance
pre·rog′a·tive
pres
pres′by·ter
Pres′by·te′ri·an·ism
pre·scrib′a·ble
pre·scribe′
pre·scrip′tion
cor′po·ra′tions by —
pres′ence
— of an of′fic·er
— of the court
— of the tes′ta′tor
pre·sent′ v.
pres′ent n.

pres′ent adj.
— con·vey′ance
— en·joy′ment
— es·tate′
— in′ter·est
— time
— use
pres′en·ta′tion
pre·sen′ta·tive
ad·vow′son
pre·sent′er
pres′ent·ly
pre·sent′ment
pres′ents
pres′er·va′tion
pre·serve′
pre·side′
pres′i·dent
— judge
— of the coun′cil
pres′i·den′tial
e·lec′tors
President of the
U·nit′ed States
pre·sid′ing judge
press′ing sea′men
pre·sum′a·bly
pre·sume′
pre·sump′ti·o′
pre·sump′tion
ir′re·but′ta·ble —
— of in′no·cence
— of sur·vi′vor·ship′
re·but′ta·ble —
pre·sump′tive
— ev′i·dence
pre·tend′
prête-nom′
pre′tens′es
false —
pre′ter le′gal
pre′ter·mit′
pre′ter·mit′ted heir

pre′text′
pre′ti·um
— af′fec·ti·o′nis
— pe′ric·u′li′
pre·vail′
pre·vail′ing
— par′ty
— pric′es
pre·var′i·ca′tion
pre·vent′
pre·ven′tion
pre·ven′tive jus′tice
pre′vi·ous
— ques′tion
pre′vi·ous·ly
price
— cur′rent
— dis·crim′i·na′tion
— ex·pect′an·cy
pri′ma fa′cie′
— case
— ev′i·dence
pri′mage
pri′ma·ry
— al′le·ga′tion
— dis·pos′al of the
soil
— ev′i·dence
— pow′ers
— pur′pose
pri′mate′
prime
prime min′is·ter
pri·mer′
prim′er
— fine
— sei′sin
prim′i·tive
ob′li·ga′tion
pri′mo·gen′i·ture
prince
Prince of Wales
Prin′cess Roy′al

prin'ci·pal *adj*.
prin'ci·pal *n*.
  — of the house
  un'dis·closed' —
  vice —
prin'ci·ple
print
print'ing
pri'or *n*.
  — pe'tens'
  — tem·po're'
    po'ti·or'
pri'or *adj*.
  — cred'i·tor
  — lien
pri'o·ri' pe·ten'ti'
pri·or'i·ty
prise
pris'on
  — bounds
  — breach
  — break'ing
pris'on·er
  — at the bar
  — of war
pri'va·cy, right of
pri'vate
  — bill of'fice
  — ex·am'i·na'tion
  — in'ter·na'tion·al
    law
  — law
  — per'son
  — street
pri'va·teer'
pri·va'tion
priv'ies
priv'i·lege
  — ab'so·lute'
  — from ar·rest'
  — of tran'sit
  qual'i·fied' —
  real —

spe'cial —
  — tax
  writ of —
priv'i·leged
  — com·mu'ni·-
    ca'tions
  — cop'y·holds'
  — debts
  — ves'sel
priv'i·leg·es and
  im·mu'ni·ties
priv'i·ty
  — of blood
  — of con'tract'
  — of es·tate'
  — or knowl'edge
priv'y
  — coun'cil
  — coun'cil·or
  — purse
  — seal
  — sig'net
  — to'ken
  — ver'dict
prize
  — courts
pro
pro and con
prob'a·bil'i·ty
prob'a·ble
  — cause
  — con'se·quence
  — fu'ture pay'ments
  — ground
prob'a·bly
pro'bate'
  — bond
  — code
  — court
  — judge
  — ju'ris·dic'tion
pro·ba'ti·o'
  — mor'tu·a

  — vi'va
pro·ba'tion
  — of'fi·cer
pro·ba'tion·er
pro'ba·tive
  — facts
pro bo'no' et ma'-
  lo'
pro bono pub'li·co'
pro'ce·den'do'
pro·ce'dur·al law
pro·ce'dure
  — acts
pro·ceed'
pro·ceed'ing
  col·lat'er·al —
  ex·ec'u·to'ry —
  — in er'ror
  spe'cial —
  sum'ma·ry —
  sup'ple·men'ta·ry —
pro·ceed'ings
  — in bank'rupt·cy
  le'gal —
  or'di·nar'y —
pro'ceeds'
proc'ess'
  a·buse' of —
  com·pul'so·ry —
  ex·ec'u·to'ry —
  fi'nal —
  ir·reg'u·lar —
  ju·di'cial —
  le'gal —
  me·chan'i·cal —
  mesne —
  — of in'ter·plead'er
  — of law
  o·rig'i·nal —
  reg'u·lar —
  sum'ma·ry —
  trus·tee' —
  void —

pro·ces'sion
pro·ces'sion·ing
pro·chein'
 — a·mi' *or* a·my'
 — a·void'ance
pro·chron'ism
pro·claim'
proc'la·ma'tion
proc'la·ma'tor
pro con·fes'so'
pro'cre·a'tion
proc'tor
proc'u·ra·cy
proc'u·ra'tion
proc'u·ra'tor
proc'u·ra'trix'
pro·cure'
pro·cur'er
pro·cur'ing cause
prod'i·gal
pro·di'tion
pro·di'tor
pro'duce *n.*
pro·duce' *v.*
pro·duc'er
pro·duc'ing
 — cause
prod'uct
pro·duc'tion
pro e'o' quod
pro fac'to'
pro·fane'
pro·fane'ly
pro·fan'i·ty
pro·fess'
pro·fes'sion
pro·fes'sion·al
pro·fes'sor
pro·file'
prof'it
 — and loss
 — à pren'dre
 — à ren'dre

prof'i·teer'ing
prof'its
 mesne —
 net —
 pa'per —
 sur'plus —
pro for'ma
pro·gres'sion
pro hac vi·ce'
pro·hib'it
pro·hib'it·ed
 de·grees'
pro'hi·bi'tion
pro·hib'i·tive
 im·ped'i·ments
pro in'ter·es·se'
 su'o'
pro lae'si·o'ne'
 fi·de'i'
pro le·ga'to'
pro'les'
pro'le·tar'i·at *or*
 pro'le·tar'i·ate
pro'le·ta'ri·us
pro'li·cide'
pro·lix'i·ty
pro'lon·ga'tion
pro ma'jo·ri'
 cau'te·la
prom'ise
 fic·ti'tious —
 na'ked —
 new —
 — of mar'riage
 pa·rol' —
 — to pay the debt
  of an·oth'er
prom'i·see'
prom'i·sor'
prom'is·so'ry
 — es·top'pel
 — note
pro·mote'

pro·mot'er
prompt
 — de·liv'er·y
 — ship'ment
prompt'ly
prom'ul·gate'
prom'ul·ga'tion
pro non scrip'to'
pro·no'ta·ry
pro·nounce'
pro·nun'ci·a'tion
proof
 — be·yond' a
  rea'son·a·ble
  doubt
 — ev'i·dent or
  pre·sump'tion
  great
 — of will
pro o'pe·re' et
 la·bo're'
prop'a·gate'
pro par'ti·bus
 lib'er·an'dis
prop'er
 — par'ty
prop'er·ty
 com'mon —
 com·mu'ni·ty —
 mixed —
 per'son·al —
 real —
 spe'cial —
pro·pin'qui·ty
pro·po'nent
pro·pos'al
pro pos·ses'si·o'ne'
 prae·sum'i·tur' de
 ju're'
pro pos·ses·so're'
pro pos'se' su'o'
pro·pound'
pro·pri'e·tar'y

pro·pri′e·tas′
pro·pri′e·tor
pro·pri′e·ty
pro′pri·o′ vi·go′re′
prop′ter
— af·fec′tum
— de·fec′tum
— defectum
   san·gui′nis
— de·lic′tum
— hon·o′ris
   re·spec′tum
— im′po·ten′ti·am
— pri′vi·le′gi·um
pro que·ren′te′
pro ra′ta
pro·rate′
pro re na′ta
pro′ro·ga′tion
pro·rogue′
pro sa·lu′te′
   an′i·mae′
pro·scribed′
pro se
pros′e·cute′
pros′e·cu′tion
pros′e·cu′tor
— of the pleas
   pri′vate —
   pub′lic —
pros′e·cu′trix′
pro·se′qui′
pro·se′qui·tur′
pro so·li′do′
pro·spec′tive
— dam′ag·es
— law
pro·spec′tus
pros′ti·tu′tion
pros′ti·tute′
pro tan′to′
pro·tec′tion
pro·tec′tive tar′iff

pro·tec′tor·ate
pro tem·po′re′
pro′test′
   no′tice of —
   su′pra —
   waiv′er of —
pro′tes·tan′do′
Prot′es·tant
prot′es·ta′tion
pro·thon′o·tar′y
pro′to·col′
prov′a·ble
prove
pro·vide′
pro·vid′ed
— by law
prov′ince
pro·vi′sion
pro·vi′sion·al
pro·vi′sions
pro·vi′so′
   tri′al by —
pro·vi′sor
prov′o·ca′tion
pro·voke′
pro′vost′
pro′vost′ mar′shal
prox′i·mate
— cause
— con′se·quence′ or
   re·sult′
— dam′ag·es
prox′i·mate·ly
prox·im′i·ty
prox′y
pru′dence
pru′dent
prud′hommes′ or
   prodes hommes
pseu′do′
pseu′do·cy′e·sis
pseu′do·graph′
psy′cho·di′ag·-

no′sis
psy′cho·neu·ro′sis
psy′cho·path′
psy·cho′sis
psy′cho·ther′a·py
pto′maine′
pu′ber·ty
pub′lic n.
pub′lic adj.
— con·ven′ience
— in′ter·est
— lands
— place
— serv′ice
— use
— u·til′i·ty
— ways
— wel′fare′
pub′li·can
pub′li·ca′tion
pub′li·ci′ ju′ris
pub′li·cist
pub·lic′i·ty
pub′lic·ly
pub′lish
pub′lish·er
pu·dic′i·ty
puer·il′i·ty
puff′er
puff′ing
pu′gi·list
puis
— dar·rein′
   con·tin′u·ance
puis·ne′
pull′ing
pul·sa′tor
pum′my
punc′tu·a′tion
punc′tum tem·po′ris
pun′dit
pun′ish·a·ble
pun′ish·ment

pu'ni·tive
— dam'ag·es
— pow'er
— stat'ute
pu'pil
pur
pur au'tre vie
pur cause de
vi·ci·nage'
pur'chase
— mon'ey
— price
qua'si' —
words of —
pur'chase-mon'ey
— mort'gage
— se·cur'i·ty
in'ter·est
pur'chas·er
bo'na fide —
pur·ga'tion
purge
purg'ing con·tempt'
pur'lieu
pur·loin'
pur·part'
pur·part'y
pur·port' *n.*
pur·port' *v.*
pur'pose
pur·pose·ly
pur·pres'ture
pur·prise'
purse
purs'er
pur·su'ant
pur·sue'
pur·su'er
pur·suit'
pur tant que
pu'rus id'i·o'ta
pur·vey'or
pur'view

pu'ta·tive
puts and calls
py'ro·ma'ni·a
Pyx, trial of the

Q

qua
quack
quad'rant
quad'ri·par'tite'
quad'ri·par·ti'tus
quad·roon'
quad·ru'pli·ca'tion
quae est e·a'dem
quae ni'hil frus'tra
quae're'
quae'rens'
quaes'ti·o'
ca'dit —
— vex'a·ta
quaes'tus
Quak'er
qual'i·fi·ca'tion
qual'i·fied'
— ac·cep'tance
— en·dorse'ment
— priv'i·lege
qual'i·fy'
qual'i·ty
— of es·tate'
quam·di·u'
quan'do'
ac·cid'er·int
quan'ti' mi·no'ris
quan'tum
— mer'u·it
— va·le'bant
quar'an·tine'
qua're'

— clau'sum fre'git
quar'rel
quar'ry
quart
quar'ter
— ses'sions
quar'ter·ing
quar'ter·ly
— courts
quash
qua'si'
— con·trac'tus
— es·top'pel
— ju·di'cial
— post'hu·mous
child
quay
queen's bench
que es·tate'
que est le mesme
que·re'la
quer'u·lous
ques'ta
ques'tion
fed'er·al —
hy'po·thet'i·cal —
lead'ing —
qui'a ti'met
quib'ble
quick
— child
quick'en·ing
quid pro quo
qui'et
qui'e·ta're'
qui·e'tus
quit
qui tam
quit'claim'
— deed
quo an'i·mo'
quod re·cu'per·et
quod vi'de'

quo′rum
quo′ta
quo·ta′tion
quo′tient ver′dict
quo war·ran′to′

R

race
rack′et
rack′et·eer′
rack′et·eer′ing
rad′i·cals
ra′di·us
raf′fle
rail′road′
rail′way′
raise
— a pre·sump′tion
— an is′sue
rais′ing a use
range
rang′er
rank
ran′som
rape
rap′ine
ra′sure
rat′a·ble
rate
com·mod′i·ty —
— of ex·change′
— tar′iff
rat′i·fi·ca′tion
rat′i·fy′
ra′tio
— de′ci·den·di′
— le′gis
ra′tion·al doubt
ra′ti·o·nal′i·bus

de·vi′sis
ra′ti·o′ne′
— im′po·ten′ti·ae′
— ma·te′ri·ae′
— per·so′nae′
— priv′i·le′gi·i′
— so′li′
— ten′u·rae′
ra·vine′
rav′ish
rav′ished
rav′ish·er
rav′ish·ment
raze
re
read′ers
read′y and will′ing
re′af·for′est·ed
real
— chy·min′
— ev′i·dence
— law
re·al′i·ty
re′al·ize′
realm
re′al·ty
re′ap·prais′er
rear
re·ar′gu·ment
rea′son
rea′son·a·ble
— and prob′a·ble
cause
— crea′ture
— rule of cer′tain·ty
re·as·sur′ance
re·at·tach′ment
re′bate′
reb′el *n.*
re·bel′ *v.*
re·bel′lion
re·bel′lious
as·sem′bly

re·but′
— an eq′ui·ty
re·but′ta·ble
pre·sump′tion
re·but′tal
re·but′ter
re·but′ting
ev′i·dence
re·call′
— a judg′ment
re·cant′
re·cap′i·tal·i·za′tion
re·cap′tion
re·cap′ture
re·ceipt′
re·ceip′tor
re·ceive′
re·ceiv′er
— pen·den′te′ li′te′
re·ceiv′er·ship′
re′cess′
re·ces′sion
Recht
re·cid′i·vist
re·cip′ro·cal
— con′tract′
— wills
rec′i·proc′i·ty
re·cit′al
re·cite′
reck
reck′less
— dis′re·gard′ of
rights of oth′ers
— driv′ing
reck′less·ness
re·claim′
rec′la·ma′tion
re·clu′sion
rec′og·ni′tion
re·cog′ni·tors
re·cog′ni·zance
rec′og·nize′

rec'og·nized'
re·cog'ni·zee'
re·cog'ni·zor
rec'om·mend'
rec'om·men·da'tion
rec'om·men'-
    da·to'ry
rec'om·pense'
rec'on·cil'i·a'tion
re'con·duc'tion
re'con·struct'
re'con·struc'tion
re'con·tin'u·ance
re'con·ver'sion
re'con·vey'ance
re·cord' v.
rec'ord n.
    courts of —
    debts of —
    es·top'pel by —
    mat'ter of —
    — of ni'si' pri'us
    ti'tle of —
re·cord'er
re·cord'ing acts
re·coup' or
    re·coupe'
re·coup'ment
re'course'
re·cov'er
re·cov'er·ee'
re·cov'er·er
re·cov'er·y
rec're·ant
re·crim'i·na'tion
re·cruit'
re·cruit'ing
rec'ti·fi'er
rec'ti·fy'
rec'tor
rec'to·ry
rec'tum
    — es'se

rec'tus in cu'ri·a
re'cu·pe·ra'ti·o'
re·cus'ants
re'cuse'
red·den'dum
re·deem'
re·deem'a·ble
re'de·liv'er·y
re'de·mise'
re·demp'tion
    equity of —
    the right of —
red'-hand'ed
re'dis·sei'sin
re·dis'tri·bu'tion
re·di'tus
re'draft'
re·dress'
re·dub'bers
re·duce'
re·duc'ti·o' ad
    ab·sur'dum
re·duc'tion
    — to pos·ses'sion
re·dun'dan·cy
re'-en·act'
re-en'try
re'-es·tab'lish
reeve
re'-ex·am'i·na'tion
re'-ex·change'
re·fer'
ref'e·ree'
    court of —
    — in bank'rupt·cy
ref'er·ence
ref'er·en'dum
re'fi·nance'
re·fine'ment
re·form'
ref'or·ma'tion
re·for'ma·to·ry
re·fresh'ing

— the mem'o·ry
— the rec'ol·lec'tion
re·fund' v.
re'fund' n.
    — an·nu'i·ty
        con'tract'
re'fund'ing bond
re'funds'
re·fus'al
re·fuse' v.
ref'use n.
re·ga'lia
re·gard'
re'gen·cy
re'gent
re'gi·a vi'a
reg'i·cide'
re·gime'
re·gi'na
reg'is·ter
    — in bank'rupt·cy
    — of deeds
    — of land of'fice
    — of pat'ents
    — of ships
    — of the treas'ur·y
    — of wills
reg'is·tered
    — bond
    — trade'mark'
    — vot'ers
reg'is·trant
reg'is·trar'
reg'is·tra'tion
    — of stock
reg'is·try
    — of deeds
reg'nal years
reg'nant
re'grant'
re·gress'
reg'u·la
reg'u·lar

— army
— course of
  busi′ness
— on its face
— rate
reg′u·lar·ly
reg′u·lars
reg′u·late′
reg′u·la′tion
re′ha·bil′i·tate′
— a wit′ness
re′ha·bil′i·ta′tion
re·hear′ing
reif
re′im·burse′
re′in·state′
— a case
re′in·sur′ance
re·join′
re·join′der
re·join′ing grat′is
re·late′
re·lat′ed
re·la′tion
re·la′tions
rel′a·tive
re·la′tor
re·la′trix′
re·lax′a·re′
re·lax·a′ti·o′
re·lease′ *v.*
re·lease′ *n.*
— by way of en′try
  and feoff′ment
— by way of
  ex·tin′guish·ment
deed of —
— of dow′er
re′-lease′
re·leas′ee′
re·leas′er *or*
  re·lea′sor
rel′e·gate′

rel′e·ga′tion
rel′e·van·cy
rel′e·vant
— ev′i·dence
re·li′a·ble
rel′ict
re·lic′tion
re·lief′
re·lieve′
re·lig′ion
re·lig′ious free′dom
re·lin′quish
re·lin′quish·ment
re′lo·ca′tion
re·main′der
re·main′der·man
re·mand′
re·me′di·al
— ac′tion
— stat′ute
rem′e·dy
— o′ver
re·mise′
re·miss′
re·mis′sion
re·miss′ness
re·mit′
re·mit′ment
re·mit′tance
re′mit·tee′
re·mit′ter
re·mit′tit dam′na
re·mit′ti·tur′
— dam′na
— of rec′ord
re·mit′tor
rem′nant rule
re·mod′el
re·mon′strance
re·mote′
— cause
— dam′age
— pos′si·bil′i·ty

re·mote′ness
re·mov′al
— from of′fice
— of caus′es
order of —
— to a·void′ tax
— with·out′ prop′er
  cause
re·mov′er
re·mov′ing cloud
  from ti′tle
re·mu′ner·a′tion
ren·coun′ter
ren′der
— an ac·count′
— judg′ment
— ver′dict
ren′dez·vous′
ren′e·gade′
re·new′
re·new′al
— of note
re·nounce′
re′no·va′re′
rent
  fee farm —
  quit —
— roll
— seck
rent′age
rent′al
— val′ue
rents, is′sues, and
  prof′its
re·nun′ci·a′tion
ren′voi′
re′o ab·sen′te′
re·o′pen·ing a case
re·or′gan·i·za′tion
re·pair′
rep′a·ra′tion
re·pa′tri·a′tion
re·pay′

re·peal'
re·peat'ers
rep'e·ti'tion
re·place'
re·plead'
re·plead'er
re·ple·gi'a·re'
re·plev'in
  — bond
  per'son·al —
re·plev'y
rep'li·ca'tion
re·ply'
re·port'
re·port'er
rep're·sent'
rep're·sen·ta'tion
  false —
  ma·te'ri·al —
  prom'is·so'ry —
rep're·sen'ta·tive
re·prieve'
rep'ri·mand'
re·pri'sals
re·pris'es
re·pub'lic
re·pub'li·can
re'pub·li·ca'tion
re·pu'di·ate'
re·pu'di·a'tion
re·pug'nan·cy
re·pug'nant
rep'u·ta·ble
rep'u·ta'tion
re·put'ed
re·quest'
re·quire'
re·quire'ment
  con'tract'
req'ui·si'tion
res
  — der·e·lic'ta
  — ges'tae'
  — in'ter a'li·os'

  ac'ta
  — ip'sa lo'qui·tur'
  — ju'di·ca'ta
  — no'va
  — per'i·it do'mi·no'
  — pub'li·cae'
  — quo·tid'i·a'nae'
  — re·lig'i·o'sae'
re'sale'
re·scind'
re·scis'sion of
  con'tract'
re·script'
  — o·pin'ion
res'cue
  — doc'trine
re·scyt'
res'er·va'tion
re·serve'
re·served' land
re·set'
re·set'tle·ment
res'i·ance
res'i·ant
re·side'
res'i·dence
  le'gal —
res'i·dent
re·sid'u·al
re·sid'u·ar'y
  — be·quest'
  — clause
  — de·vise' and
    de·vi·see'
  — es·tate'
  — leg'a·cy
  — leg'a·tee'
res'i·due'
re·sid'u·um
res'ig·na'tion
re·sign·ee'
re·sil'ien·cy
re·sist'
re·sis'tance

re·sist'ing an
  of'fi·cer
res'o·lu'tion
  joint —
re·sort'
re'sourc'es
re·spec'tive
res'pite
re·spond'
re·spon'de·at'
  — ous'ter
  — su·pe'ri·or
re·spon'dent
re'spon·den'ti·a
re·spon'si·bil'i·ty
re·spon'si·ble
  — cause
re·spon'sive
res·seis·er'
rest
res'tau·rant
res'ti·tu'tion
re·strain'
re·straint'
  — of mar'riage
  — of trade
  — on al'ien·a'tion
re·strict'
re·strict'ed
re·stric'tion
re·stric'tive
  — en·dorse'ment
rests
re·sult'
re·sult'ing
  — trust
  — use
re·sum'mons
re·sump'tion
re·sur·ren'der
re'tail'
re'tail'er
re·tain'
re·tain'er

re·tak′ing
re·tal′i·a′tion
re·ten′tion
re·tire′
re·tor′sion
re·tract′
re′trac·ta′tion
re·trax′it
ret′ri·bu′tion
ret′ro′
ret′ro·ac′tive
  — law
  — stat′ute
ret′ro·spec′tive
rette
re·turn′
  — book
  fair —
  false —
re·turn′a·ble
re·turn′-day′
  gen′er·al —
re′us
reve
rev′el
re·ven′di·ca′tion
rev′e·nue′
re·ver′sal
re·verse′
re·vers′i·ble er′ror
re·ver′sion *or*
  es·tate′ in
  reversion
re·ver′sion·ar′y
  — in′ter·est
  — lease
re·ver′sion·er
re·vert′
re·vert′er
re·vest′
re·view′
re·vise′
re·vised′ stat′utes
re·vi′sion

re·viv′al
re·vive′
rev′o·ca·ble
rev′o·ca′tion
  — of will
re·voke′
re·volt′
rev′o·lu′tion
rev′o·lu′tion·ar′y
re·ward′
rex
Rho·di′an Laws
Rich′ard Roe
rid′er
  — roll
ridg′ling
ri·en′
  — culp
  — dit
right
  — and wrong test
  — of ac′tion
  — of en′try
  — of hab′i·ta′tion
  — of lo′cal self′-
    gov′ern·ment
  — of pos·ses′sion
  — of pri′va·cy
  — of prop′er·ty
  — of re·demp′tion
  — of rep′re·-
    sen·ta′tion and
    per·form′ance
  — of search
  — of way
  — pat′ent
  — to be·gin′
  — to re·deem′
rights
  — of per′sons
  — of things
  pe·ti′tion of —
  pri′vate —
rig′or mor′tis

ring
ri′ot
ri′ot·er
ri′ot·ous as·sem′bly
ri′ot·ous·ly
ri′pa
ri·par′i·a
ri·par′i·an
  — na′tions
  — own′er
  — pro·pri′e·tor
  — rights
  — wa′ter
ripe for judg′ment
ris′ing of court
risk
  as·sump′tion
    of —
  — in′ci·dent to
    em·ploy′ment
  ob′vi·ous —
  — of nav′i·ga′tion
  per·ceiv′a·ble —
ris·tourne′
rite
riv′er
rix′a·trix′
road
road′bed′
rob
rob′ba·tor
rob′ber
rob′ber·y
robes
rod
Roe, Rich′ard
ro·ga′re′
ro·ga′ti·o′
rog′a·to′ry let′ters
rogue
roll *n.*
  as·sess′ment —
  judg′ment —
  tax —

roll *v.*
roll′ing
— stock
— stock pro·tec′tion
act
rolls
mas′ter of the —
ob′late′ —
— of par′lia·ment
— of the
Ex′cheq′uer
— of the Tem′ple
— of′fice of the
Chan′cer·y
Ro′man Cath′o·lic
Roman Catholic
Church
Ro′man law
rood of land
room′er
root of de·scent′
ros′ter
ro′ta
round rob′in
rout
route
rou′tous·ly
roy
roy′al
— as·sent′
— pre·rog′a·tive
roy′al·ties
roy′al·ty
ru′bric
rude′ness
rule *v.*
rule *n.*
— ab′so·lute′
— a·gainst′
per′pe·tu′i·ties
— day
— dis·charged′
— in Shel′ley's
Case

— ni′si′
— of 1756
— of ap·por′-
tion·ment
— of four
— of Kent
— of law
— of len′i·ty
— of pre·sump′tion
— of prop′er·ty
— of the road
special —
— to plead
— to show cause
rules
cross —
— of course
— of court
— of prac′tice
— of pro·ce′dure
ru′mor
run
run′ning
— ac·count′
— days
— with the land
— with the
re·ver′sion
ruse de guerre
rus′ti·cum fo′rum
rus′tler

S

Sab′bath
sab′o·tage′
sac′cus
sac′ra·men′tum
sac′ri·lege
sa′dism
sae·vi′ti·a

safe
— con′duct
— de·pos′it
com′pa·ny
safe′guard′
sa′ga·man
sages de la ley
said
sail
sail′ing
— in·struc′tions
sail′ors
sake
sal′a·ble
sal′a·ry
sale
ab′so·lute′ —
— and re·turn′
bill of —
cash —
con·di′tion·al —
ex·clu′sive —
ex′e·cut′ed —
ex′e·cu′tion —
ex·ec′u·to′ry —
fair —
forced —
— in gross
ju·di′cial —
— on ap·prov′al
— on cred′it
pri′vate —
pub′lic —
sher′iff's —
tax —
— with all faults
sales′man
Sal′ic Law
sa′line′
— land
sa·loon′
sa·loon′keep′er
sal′us
sa·lute′

sal'vage
sal'vo'
sal'vor
sal'vus ple'gi·us
same
sam'ple
san'a·to'ri·um
sanc'tion
sanc'tu·ar'y
sand'bag'
sane
san'guine
san'i·tar'i·um
san'i·tar'y
san'i·ta'tion
san'i·ty
sans
 — ce·o' que
 — frais
 — jour
 — re·cours'
sap
sat'is·fac'tion
sat'is·fac'to·ry
sat'is·fy'
saun·ke·fin'
sau·va·gine'
save
sav'er de·fault'
sav'ing
 — clause
sav'ings
 — bank
 — bank trust
Sax'on lage
scale
 — tol'er·ance
scan'dal
scan'dal·ous mat'ter
sched'ule
scheme
schism
Schism Bill
school

 — board
 — dis'trict
dis'trict —
grade —
high —
 — lands
normal —
pri'vate —
 — pur'pos·es
school'mas'ter
schools
 com'mon —
 pub'lic —
sci·en'ter
scil'i·cet'
scin·til'la
 — ju'ris
 — of ev'i·dence
sci're' fa'ci·as
 — fe'ci'
site
scold
scope
scorn
scot
 — and lot
 — and lot vot'ers
scoun'drel
scri'ba
scrip
 — div'i·dend
script
scrip'tum
scriv'en·er
scroll
scur'ri·lous
sea
 — bed
 — brief
 — laws
 — let'ter
seal
 com'mon —
 cor'por·ate —

 — days
great —
 — of'fice
 — pa'per
pri'vate —
priv'y —
pub'lic —
quar'ter —
sealed
 — and de·liv'ered
 — in'stru·ment
 — ver'dict
seal'ing
 — up
seals
sea'men
sé'ance'
search
 — and seizure
 un·law'ful —
 un·rea'son·a·ble —
 — war'rant
search'er
seas
 high —
sea'shore'
sea'son·al
 em·ploy'ment
sea'ward *or* se'ward
sea'wor'thi·ness
sea'wor'thy
se·bas'to·ma'ni·a
sec'ond
 — lien
sec'on·dar'y *n.*
sec'on·dar'y *adj.*
 — boy'cott'
sec'ond-hand'
 ev'i·dence
sec'onds
se'cret
 — lien
 — serv'ice
sec're·tar'y

— of state
se·crete′
se′crets of state
sect
sec′ta
sec·tar′i·an
sec′tion
  — of land
sec′u·lar
se·cun′dum
  — ar′tem
  — le′gem
    com·mu′nem
  — nor′mam le′gis
  — reg′u·lam
se·cure′
se·cured′ cred′i·tor
se·cu′ri·ties
  mar′shal·ing —
  pub′lic —
  treas′ur·y —
se·cu′ri·ty
  col·lat′er·al —
  — coun′cil
  coun′ter —
  — de·pos′it
  — for costs
  — for good
    be·hav′ior
  per′son·al —
  real —
se′cus
se·da′to′ an′i·mo′
se·di′tion
se·di′tious li′bel
sed per cu′ri·am
sed quae′re′
se·duce′
se·duc′tion
sed vi′de′
see
seen
seign′ior

seign′ior·age
seign′ior·ess
seign′ior·y
seised *or* seized
seised in de·mesne′
  as of fee
sei′si′
sei′sin·a
seize
sei′zin *or* sei′sin
  actual —
  constructive —
  covenant of —
  — in deed
  — in fact
  — in law
  liv′er·y of —
  prim′er —
  qua′si′ —
seiz′ing of her′i·ots
sei′zure
  — quo·us′que
sel′da
se·lect′
  — coun′cil
se·lect′men
self′-deal′ing
self′-de·fense′
self′-de·struc′tion
self′-ex′e·cut′ing
sell
sell′er
sem·ble′
sem′i·nar′y
sem′per pa·ra′tus
sen′ate
sen′a·tor
se·nile′ de·men′ti·a
se·nil′i·ty
sen′ior
  — coun′sel
  — judge
sen·ior′i·ty

sen′sus
sen′tence
  in′de·ter′mi·nate —
  sus·pen′sion of —
sen′ten·ces
  cu′mu·la′tive —
  — to run
    con·cur′rent·ly
sep′a·ra·ble
sep′a·rate′ *v.*
sep′a·rate *adj.*
  — main′te·nance
sep′a·ra′tion
  — a men′sa et
    tho′ro′
  — of pat′ri·mo′ny
sep′a·ra·tists
sep′tum
sep′ul·cher
se·que′la
se·que′lae′
se′quels
se·ques′ter
se′ques·tra′tion
se′ques·tra′tor
serf
ser′geant *or*
  ser′jeant
  — at arms
  — at law
se·ri·ate′ly
se·ri·a′tim
se′ri·ous
  — and will′ful
    mis·con′duct
ser′jeant
ser′rat′ed
ser′vant
serve
serv′ice
  — by pub′li·ca′tion
  civ′il —
  con·struc′tive —

— of proc′ess
per′son·al —
sal′vage —
sub′sti·tut′ed —
ser′vi·ent
— ten′e·ment
ser·vi′ti·um
ser′vi·tude′
in·vol′un·tar′y —
pe′nal —
ser′vi·tus
ser′vus
sess
ses′si·o′
ses′sion
joint —
— laws
reg′u·lar —
ses′sions
quar′ter —
spe′cial —
set *n.*
— of ex·change′
set *v.*
— a·side′
— out
— up
set′off′
set′tle
set′tle·ment
fi′nal —
set′tler
set′tlor
sev′er
sev′er·a·ble
sev′er·al
sev′er·al·ly
sev′er·al·ty
es·tate′ in —
sev′er·ance
— dam′age
se·vere′
sew′age

se′ward
sew′er
sex
sex′u·al
— in′ter·course′
shaft
shall
sham
share *v.*
share *n.*
— cer·tif′i·cate
— of cor′po·rate
stock
share′hold′er
sharp
shave
sheep
sheep′-heaves′
sheep′skin′
Shel′ley's Case
shel′ter
sher′iff
dep′u·ty —
high —
pock′et —
sher′iff's
— court
— court in Lon′don
— ju′ry
sher′iff·wick′
shift′ing
— clause
— risk
— sev′er·al·ty
— stock of
mer′chan·dise′
— the bur′den of
proof
— use
shil′ling
ship *v.*
ship *n.*
— bro′ker

— chan′dler·y
— chan′nel
— mas′ter
— mon′ey
ship′ment
ship′per
ship′ping
ship's
— bill
— com′pa·ny
— hus′band
— pa′pers
ship′wreck′
shire
shock
shop
— right
shop′book′ rule
shop′books′
shop′keep′er
shore
— lands
short
— no′tice
— sale
shot
should
show *n.*
show *v.*
— cause
show′er
shrub
shy′ster
si i′ta est
si pri′us
sic
sick
sick′ness
side
side′-bar′ rules
side′walk′
sight
sign

sig′nal
sig′na·to′ry
sig′na·ture
sig′net
sig′ni·fi·ca′tion
sig′ni·fy′
si′lence
  es·top′pel by —
silk
sil′ver
sim′i·lar
si·mil′i·ter
sim′ple
sim·plic′i·ter
si′mul cum
sim′u·late′
sim′u·lat′ed
  con′tract′
sim′u·la′tion
si′mul·ta′ne·ous
since
si′ne′
si′ne·cure′
si′ne′ di′e′
si′ne′ hoc quod
si′ne′ prole
si′ne′ qua non
sin′gle
sin′gu·lar
sis′ter
sis′ter-in-law′
sit
site
sit′ting
sit′tings
  — in bank *or* en
    banc
  — in cam′er·a
sit′u·ate′
sit′u·a′tion
si′tus
six′-day′ li′cense
skel′e·ton bill

skid
skill
skilled wit′ness·es
slack′er
slan′der
  — of ti′tle
slan′der·er
slan′der·ous per se
slave
slave trade
slav′er·y
slay
sledge
slice
slick
slight
slip
slope
slough
sluice′way′
slum
slush fund
small claims courts
smart mon′ey
smelt′ing
smug′gling
smut
So help you God
soak′age
so′ber
soc′ag·er
so′cial clubs
so′cial′ism
so·ci·é·té′
  — an·o·nyme′
so·ci′e·ty
so′ci·o·path′ic
  per′son·al′i·ty
sod′o·mite′
sod′o·my
soil
soit
so′journ′ing

so′lar
  — day
  — month
so·la′ti·um
sold
  — note
sol′dier
sole
  — ac′tor doc′trine
  — and un′con·di′-
    tion·al own′er
sol′emn
so·lem′ni·ty
sol′em·nize′
so·lic′it
so·lic′i·ta′tion
so·lic′i·tor
  — gen′er·al
sol′i·dar′i·ty
so·li′dum
sol′i·tar′y
  con·fine′ment
sol′ven·cy
sol′vent
sol′vit
Som′er·sett's Case
som·nam′bu·lism
son
son as·sault′
  de·mesne′
son′-in-law′
sors
sough
sound *v.*
sound *adj.*
  — and dis·pos′ing
    mind and
    mem′o·ry
  — health
  — ju·di′cial
    dis·cre′tion
  — mind
sound′ing

— in dam'ag·es
sound'ness
source
— of in'come
sous
— seing pri·vé'
sov'er·eign
— im·mu'ni·ty
— peo'ple
— pow'er
— pre·rog'a·tive
— right
— states
sov'er·eign·ty
speak
speak'er
speak'ing
— de·mur'rer
— mo'tion
— or'der
— with pros'e·cu·tor
spe'cial
— act
— er'rors
— ex·am'in·er
— ex·cep'tion
— ex'e·cu'tion
— ex·ec'u·tor
— facts rule
— ju'ris·dic'tion
— law
— lien
— mat'ter
— pa'per
— place
— reg'is·tra'tion
— ver'dict
spe'cial·ist
spe'cial·ty
— debt
spe'cie
spe'cies
spe·cif'ic

spe·cif'i·cal·ly
spec'i·fi·ca'tion
spec'i·fy'
spec'i·men
spec'u·la'tion
spec'u·la'tive
dam'ages
spec'u·lum
speed'y
— ex'e·cu'tion
— rem'e·dy
— trial
spell'ing
spend
spend'thrift'
— trust
spe·ra'te'
spin'ster
spir'i·tu·al
spir'i·tu·ous liquors
spite fence
split sen'tence
split'ting a cause of
ac'tion
spo'li·a'tion
spo'li·a'tor
spon'sions
spon'sor
spon·ta'ne·ous
— com·bus'tion
— ex'cla·ma'tion
sport'ing house
spous'als
spouse
spring'-branch'
spring'ing use
spu'ri·ous
spur track
spy
square
squat'ter
squire
sta'bi·lize'

sta'ble
stag'num
stake
stake'hold'er
stale
— claim
— de·mand'
stall'age
stamp
— acts
— du'ties
stance
stand
stan'dard
— of weights and
meas'ures
stand'ing
— a·side' ju'rors
— by
— in lo'co'
pa·ren'tis
— mute
— or'ders
— seized to us'es
— to sue doc'trine
sta'ple
Staple Inn
star'board'
star'-cham'ber
sta're' de·ci'sis
state v.
state n.
— of facts
— of the case
stat'ed
state'ment
— of af·fairs'
— of claim
— of con·fes'sion
— of de·fense'
— of par·tic'u·lars
state's ev'i·dence
sta'tion

Sta'tion·er's
  Com'pa·ny
Sta'tion·er'y
sta'tist
sta·tis'tics
stat'us
  — of ir're·mov'-
    a·bil'i·ty
  — quo
stat'ute
  — of frauds
  — of lim'i·ta'tions
  — of us'es
  pe'nal —
  pu'ni·tive —
  re·me'di·al —
  re·vised' —
Stat'ute
  — of E·liz'a·beth
  — of Wills
stat'utes at large
stat'u·to'ry
  — bond
  — fore·clo'sure
  — re·lease'
  — sta'ple
sta·tu'tum
stay *v.*
stay *n.*
  — laws
  — of ex'e·cu'tion
  — of pro·ceed'ings
stead'y
steal
stealth
steam'ship'
steer'er
ste·nog'ra·pher
ste·nog'ra·phy
step
step'child'
step'fa'ther
step'moth'er

step'son'
ste·ril'i·ty
stet pro·ces'sus
ste've·dore'
stew'ard
stick'er
stick'ler
sti'fling a
  pros'e·cu'tion
still
still'born'
stint
sti'pend'
sti·pen'di·ar'y
sti'pes'
stip'u·late'
stip'u·lat'ed
stip'u·la'tion
stir'pes'
stock
  — as·so'ci·a'tion
  — bro'ker
  — cer·tif'i·cate
  com'mon —
  — cor'po·ra'tion
  — div'i·dend
  — ex·change'
  — in trade
  — job'ber
  — law dis'trict
  — life in·sur'ance
    com'pa·ny
  pre·ferred' —
  wa'tered —
stock'hold'er
stock'hold'er's
  — de·riv'a·tive suit
  — li'a·bil'i·ty
  — suit
stock'hold'ers'
  rep're·sen'ta·tive
  ac'tion
stocks

stop *v.*
stop *n.*
  — or'der
  — sign
stop'page
  — in tran·si'tu'
  — of work
stor'age
store
store'house'
store'room'
storm
stow'age
stow'a·way'
stowe
strad'dle
strag'gler
straight line
straight'-line'
  de·pre'ci·a'tion
stra·min'e·us ho'mo'
strand
strand'ing
stran'ger
  — in blood
strat'a·gem
stray
stream
street
  — rail'way'
strict
  — in·ter'pre·ta'tion
  — li'a·bil'i·ty
stric'ti' ju'ris
stric·tis'si·mi' ju'ris
strict'ly
  — con·strued'
  — min'is·te'ri·al
    du'ty
stric'to' ju're'
stric'tum jus
strike
  — suits

strike'break·er
strik'ing
— a ju'ry
— off the roll
strip
— mine
— min'ing
strong
— hand
struck
— ju'ry
struc'tur·al
al'ter·a'tion or
change
struc'ture
strum'pet
stul'ti·fy'
stump
stump'age
stur'geon
style
su'a·ble
su'a spon'te'
sub
sub·a'gent
sub·al'tern
sub co·lo're' ju'ris
sub con·di'ti·o'ne'
sub·con'tract'
sub·con'trac'tor
sub cu'ri·a
sub'di·vide'
sub'di·vi'sion
sub·duct'
sub·flow'
sub·ir'ri·gate'
sub·ja'cent sup'port
sub'ject
— mat'ter
— to
sub·jec'tion
sub'ject-mat'ter
ju'ris·dic'tion

sub ju'di·ce'
sub'lease'
sub'let'ting
sub·mer'gence
sub·mis'sion
sub·mit'
sub mo'do'
sub·mort'gage
sub nom
sub nom'i·ne'
sub·or'di·nate'
sub·orn'
sub'or·na'tion of
per'ju·ry
sub·orn'er
sub·poe'na
— ad tes'ti·fi·can'-
dum
— du'ces' te'cum
sub po'tes·ta'te'
sub'ro·ga'tion
sub·ro'gee'
sub·scribe'
sub·scrib'er
sub·scrib'ing
wit'ness
sub·scrip'tion
sub'se·quent
— con·di'tion
— cred'i·tor
sub'si·dy
sub si·len'ti·o'
sub·sis'tence
sub'soil'
sub'stance
sub·stan'tial
— com·pli'ance rule
— dam'ag·es
— jus'tice
— per·form'ance
sub·stan'tial·ly
sub·stan'ti·ate'
sub'stan·tive

— ev'i·dence
— fel'o·ny
— law
sub'sti·tute' v.
sub'sti·tute' n.
— de·fen'dant
sub'sti·tut'ed
— ex·ec'u·tor
— serv'ice
sub'sti·tu'tion
sub'sti·tu'tion·al
sub'sti·tu'tion·ar'y
— ev'i·dence
— ex·ec'u·tor
sub·ten'ant
sub'ter·fuge'
sub'ter·ra'ne·an
wa'ters
sub·trac'tion
suc·ces'sion
ar'ti·fi'cial —
he·red'i·tar'y —
in·tes'tate' —
ir·reg'u·lar —
le'gal —
nat'u·ral —
— tax
tes'ta·men'ta·ry —
va'cant —
suc·ces'sive
suc·ces'sor
suc·cinct'
such
sud'den
— af·fray'
— heat of pas'sion
— or vi'o·lent
in'ju·ry
— per'il rule
sue
suf'fer
suf'fer·ance
suf·fi'cient

— cause
— ev'i·dence
suf'fo·cate'
suf'frage
sug·gest'
sug·ges'tion
— of er'ror
sug·ges'tive
su'i·cide'
su'i gen'e·ris
su'i ju'ris
su'ing and la'bor·ing
  clause
suit
suit'a·ble
suite
suit'or
sum
— in gross
— pay'a·ble
— re·ceiv'a·ble
sum·ma'ri·ly
sum'ma·ry *n.*
sum'ma·ry *adj.*
— ju'ris·dic'tion
— pro·ceed'ing
— proc'ess'
sum'ming up
sum'mon
sum'mons
sum'mum jus
sump'tu·ar'y laws
sun'dries
sun'dry
sun'stroke'
su'o nom'i·ne'
su'o pe·ric'u·lo'
su·per'flu·ous
su'per·in·tend'
su'per·in·ten'dent
su·pe'ri·or *n.*
su·pe'ri·or *adj.*
— courts

— fel'low ser'vant
— force
su·pe'ri·or'i·ty
su'per·sede'
su'per·se'de·as
su'per·sed'ing cause
su'per·ven'ing
— cause
— neg'li·gence
su'per·vise'
su'per·vi'sion
su'per·vi'sor
su'per·vi'so·ry
su'per vi'sum
  cor'po·ris
sup'ple·ment
sup'ple·men'tal
sup'ple·men'ta·ry
sup'pli·ant
sup·plies'
sup·ply'
sup·port'
sup'po·si'tion
sup·press'
su'pra
sup'ra·ri·par'i·an
su·prem'a·cy
su·preme'
Su·preme' Court
— of Ju'di·ca·ture
sur'charge'
sure'ty
sure'ty·ship'
— de·fens'es
sur'face
— wa'ters
sur'geon
sur'ger·y
sur·mise'
sur'name'
sur'plus
sur'plus·age
sur·prise'

sur're·but'ter
sur're·join'der
sur·ren'der
sur·ren'der·ee'
sur·ren'der·or
sur·rep·ti'tious
sur'ro·gate'
sur'ro·gate's court
sur·round'
sur·sise'
sur·veil'lance
sur·vey' *v.*
sur'vey' *n.*
sur·vey'or
sur·viv'al stat'utes
sur·vive'
sur·viv'ing
sur·vi'vor
sur·vi'vor·ship'
sus·cep'ti·ble
sus·pect' *v.*
sus'pect' *n.*
sus·pend'
sus·pense'
sus·pen'sion
sus·pi'cion
sus·pi'cious
  char'ac·ter
sus·tain'
swamp
swear
sweat'ing
sweat'shop'
sweep'ing
sweep'stakes'
swell
swin'dler
swin'dling
switch
switch'yard'
  doc'trine
sworn
syl'la·bus

syl'lo·gism
sym·bol'ic
   de·liv'er·y
sym'me·try
Sy'mond's Inn
sym'pa·thet'ic strike
syn'al·lag·mat'ic
   con'tract'
syn'chro·nism
syn'chro·ni·za'tion
syn'dic
syn'di·cal·ism
syn'di·cate n.
syn'di·cate' v.
syn'di·cat'ing
syn'od
syn·on'y·mous
syn·op'sis
syph'i·lis
sys'tem

T

ta·bet'ic de·men'ti·a
ta'ble
   — of cas'es
tab'u·la
   — ra'sa
tac'it
   — ac·cept'ance
   — ded'i·ca'tion
   — law
   — mort'gage
   — re'lo·ca'tion
tac'i·te'
tack
tack'ing
tail
   — after pos'si·bil'-
      i·ty of is'sue
      ex·tinct'

es·tate' in —
   — fe'male'
   — gen'er·al
   — male
sev'er·al —
   — spe'cial
taint
take
   — a·way'
   — back
   — by stealth
   — care of
   — ef·fect'
   — o'ver
   — up
tak'er
tak'ing
ta'les'
tales'man
tal'lage or tai'lage
tal·la'gi·um
tal'ley or tal'ly
Tal'mud'
tal'weg'
tame
tam'per
tam quam
tan'gi·ble
   — prop'er·ty
tank
tank'age
tar'iff
tau·tol'o·gy
tav'ern
   — keep'er
tav'ern·er
tax v.
tax n.
   ad va·lo'rem —
   cap'i·ta'tion —
   — cer·tif'i·cate
   col·lat'er·al
      in·her'i·tance —

— deed
di·rect' —
es·tate' —
   — fer'rets
floor —
fran'chise' —
in'come' —
in·her'i·tance —
land —
   — lease
   — lev'y
li'cense —
   — lien
oc'cu·pa'tion —
per'son·al —
poll —
pub'lic —
   — pur'chas·er
   — roll
   — sale
sink'ing fund —
spe·cif'ic —
suc·ces'sion —
   — ti'tle
ton'nage —
tax'a·ble
   — year
tax·a'tion
dou'ble —
   — of costs
tax'es
   in'di·rect' —
   lo'cal —
   par'lia·men'ta·ry —
   pro·por'tion·al —
tax'i·cab'
tax'ing
   — pow'er
tax'pay'er
team
team'ster
tear'ing of will
tech'ni·cal

tel'e·gram'
tel'e·graph'
tel'e·phone'
Tel'e·type'
tel'e·vi'sion
tell'er
tell'tales'
tem'per·ance
tem'pest
tem'po·ra'lis
tem'po·ral'i·ties
tem'po·ral'i·ty
tem'po·ral lords
tem'po·rar'i·ly
tem'po·rar'y
tem'po·re'
tem'pus
  — u'ti·le'
ten'an·cy
  — by the en·tire'ty
  — in com'mon
  joint —
ten'ant
  — at suf'fer·ance
  — by the cur'te·sy
  — by the man'ner
  — for life
  — for years
  — from year to year
  — in cap'i·te'
  — in com'mon
  — in dow'er
  — in fee
  — in fee sim'ple
  — in sev'er·al·ty
  — in tail
  — in tail ex
    pro'vi·si·o'ne'
    vi'ri'
  — of the de·mesne'
  — par'a·vaile'
ten'ants
  — by the verge

joint —
ten·con'
tend
ten'der
ten'e·ment
te·ne're'
ten'et
ten'or
ten'u·it
ten'u·ra
ten'ure
  — in of'fice
term
  — for years
  gen'er·al —
  — in gross
  — in·sur'ance
  — of lease
  — of of'fice
  reg'u·lar —
termes de la ley
ter'mi·na·ble
ter'mi·nate'
ter'mi·na'tion
  — of em·ploy'ment
ter'min·er
ter'mi·ni'
ter'mi·nus
terms
  spe'cial —
  un'der —
ter'ra
ter'ri·er
ter'ri·to'ri·al
  — courts
  — ju'ris·dic'tion
ter'ri·to·ri·al'i·ty
ter'ri·to'ry
ter'ror
test
  — case
tes'ta·ble
tes'ta·cy

tes'ta de nev'il
tes'ta·ment
tes'ta·men'ta·ry
  — ca·pac'i·ty
  — caus'es
  — class
  — dis'po·si'tion
  — guard'i·an
  — paper or
    in'stru·ment
  — pow'er
  — suc·ces'sion
  — trus·tee'
tes'tate'
tes·ta'tion
tes·ta'tor
tes'ta·trix'
tes'te' of a writ
test'ed
tes'tes'
  tri'al per —
tes'ti·fy'
tes'ti·mo'ni·al
tes'ti·mo'ny
  ex'pert' —
tes'tis
text'book'
thane
thane'lands'
thane'ship'
Tha'vies Inn
the'a·ter *or* the'a·tre
theft
  — bote
  — by false pre'text'
theme
thence
the'o·ry of case
there'a·bout'
there·af'ter
there·by'
there·for'
there'fore'

there·in'
there'up·on'
thief
things
  — in ac'tion
third par'ty
  — ben'e·fi'ci·ar·y
  — claim pro·ceed'ing
thor'ough·fare'
thread
threat
threat'en·ing
through
thrust'ing
tick'et
  — of leave
tick'et-of-leave' man
tid'al
tide
  neap —
tide'land
tides'men'
tide'wa'ter
tide'way'
tie
ti·el'
ti·erce'
till'age
tim'ber
time
  — bar'gain
  — check
  cool'ing —
  — im'me·mo'ri·al
  — is of the es'sence
  — pol'i·cy
  rea'son·a·ble —
tip'pling house
tip'staff'
ti'ther
tithes
  great —
  mi·nute' —

mixed —
per'son·al —
pred'i·al —
  — rent charge
tith'ing
  — man
ti'tle
ab'so·lute' —
ab'stract' of —
ad·verse' —
  — by ad·verse'
    pos·ses'sion
  — by de·scent'
  — by pre·scrip'tion
chain of —
clear —
clear rec'ord —
col'or of —
cov'e·nants for —
  — deeds
  — de·fec'tive in
    form
doubt'ful —
eq'ui·ta·ble —
ex·am'i·na'tion of —
im·per'fect —
  — in·sur'ance
le'gal —
lu'cra·tive —
mar'ket·a·ble —
mer'chant·a·ble —
  — of a cause
  — of an act
  — of cler'gy·men
  — of dec'la·ra'tion
  — of en'try
on'er·ous —
pa'per —
pas'sive —
per'fect —
pre·sump'tive —
rec'ord —
re·ten'tion —

sin'gu·lar —
tax —
  — to or'ders
un·mar'ket·a·ble —
to have and to hold
to wit
to·bac'co·nist
to'ken
  — mon'ey
tol'er·ate'
tol'er·a'tion
toll *v.*
toll *n.*
  — and team
  — bridge
  — gath'er·er
  — road
  — thor'ough
  — trav'erse
  — turn
toll'age
toll'er
tolls
tomb
tomb'stone'
ton
ton'nage
  — du'ty
  — rent
ton'sure
took and car'ried
  a·way'
tool
tor·pe'do doc'trine
tort
  mar'i·time' —
  per'son·al —
  prop'er·ty —
  qua'si' —
  will'ful —
tort'-fea'sor
tor'tious
tor'ture

To′ry
to′tal
— de·pend′en·cy
— dis′a·bil′i·ty
— e·vic′tion
— loss
Tot′ten Trust
touch and stay
tourn
tout
— temps prist
— un sound
tow′age
— serv′ice
to·ward′
to·wards′
town
— clerk
— cri′er
— hall
— meet′ing
town′ship′
town′site′
tox′ic
tox·e′mi·a or
tox′i·ce′mi·a
tox′i·cal
tox′i·cant
tox′i·cate′
tox′i·col′o·gy
tox′i·co·ma′ni·a
tox′i·co′sis
tox′in
trac′ing
tracks
tract
trac′tor
trade v.
trade n.
— ac·cept′ance
— and com′merce
— a·gree′ment
— name

— se′cret
— un′ion
— us′age
trade′mark′
trad′er
trades′man
trad′ing
— cor′po·ra′tion
— part′ner·ship′
— stamps
— voy′age
tra·di′ti·o′
tra·di′tion
traf′fic
— reg′u·la′tions
trail′er
train
— wreck
trai′tor
trai′tor·ous·ly
tra′jec·ti′ti·a
pe·cu′ni·a
tram′mer
tramp
trans·act′
trans·act′ing
busi′ness
trans·ac′tion
tran′script′
— of rec′ord
trans·fer′ v.
trans′fer n.
— in con′tem·pla′tion
of death
— of a cause
— tax
— tick′et
trans·fer′a·ble
trans·fer·ee′
trans·fer′ence
trans·fer′or
trans·ship′ment
tran′sient n.

tran′sient adj.
— per′son
tran′sire′
tran′sit
— in rem
ju′di·ca′tam′
tran′si·tive
tran′si·to′ry
trans·la′tion
trans·mis′sion
trans′port′ n.
trans·port′ v.
trans′por·ta′tion
trap
trau′ma
trau·mat′ic
trau′ma·tism
tra·vail′
trav′el
trav′eled or
trav′elled
— place
— way
trav′el·er or
trav′el·ler
trav′el·er's check
trav′el·ing sales′man
trav′erse
— ju′ry
trav′ers·er
trav′ers·ing note
tread′mill′
trea′son
— fel′o·ny
high —
mis·pri′sion of —
pet′it —
trea′son·a·ble
treas′ure
treas′ur·er
treas′ure-trove′
treas′ur·y
— note

— se·cu′ri·ties
— stock
treat′ment
trea′ty
— of peace
tre′ble
— costs
— dam′ag·es
tres′pass
— de bo′nis
as′por·ta′tis
— for mesne
prof′its
— on the case
— qua′re′ clau′sum
fre′git
— to try ti′tle
— vi et ar′mis
tres′pass·er
— ab i·ni′ti·o′
tri′al
— a·mend′ment
— at bar
— at ni′si′ pri′us
— by grand as·size′
— by ju′ry
— by wa′ger of
bat′tel
— by wa′ger of law
— de no′vo′
fair and im·par′-
tial —
— list
new —
— per pais
speed′y —
— with as·ses′sors
trib′al
— lands
tribe
tri·bu′nal
trib′u·tar′y
trib′ute′

Trin′i·ty Term
trin′kets
tri′ors
tri·par′tite′
triv′i·al
tron′age
troops
tro′phy
tro′ver
troy weight
truce
truck
true
— ad·mis′sion
— bill
— cop′y
— val′ue rule
— ver′dict
trunk rail′way′
trust
— al·lot′ments
busi′ness —
ces·tui′ que —
char′i·ta·ble —
— com′pa·ny
com·plete′
vol′un·tar′y —
con·struc′tive —
con·tin′gent —
— deed
— de·pos′it
di·rect′ —
di·rec′to·ry —
dry —
ed′u·ca′tion·al —
— es·tate′
— ex de·lic′to′
ex′e·cut′ed —
ex·ec′u·to′ry —
— ex mal′e·fi′ci·o′
ex·press′—
ex·press′ ac′tive —
express pri′vate

pas′sive —
— fund
— fund doc′trine
im·per′fect —
im·plied′ —
— in in·vi′tum
in′stru·men′tal —
in·vol′un·tar′y —
— leg′a·cy
Mas′sa·chu′setts —
min′is·te′ri·al —
na′ked —
pas′sive —
prec′a·to′ry —
pri′vate —
— re·ceipt′
re·sult′ing —
sav′ings bank —
se′cret —
shift′ing —
sim′ple —
spe′cial —
spend′thrift′ —
trans·gres′sive —
vol′un·tar′y —
vot′ing —
trus·tee′
— ex mal′e·fi′ci·o′
— in bank′rupt·cy
— proc′ess′
qua·si′ —
tes′ta·men′ta·ry —
truth
try
tsar *or* czar
tu·i′tion
tu·mul′tu·ous
tun
tun′ing
tun′nage
tur′ba·ry
turf and twig
turn *or* tourn

turn′key′
turn′out′
turn′pike′
tur′pis
   — cau′sa
   — con·trac′tus
tur′pi·tude′
tur′pi·tu′do′
tu′te·lage
tu′tor
   — al·i·en′us
   — pro′pri·us
tu′tor·ship′
tu′trix′
twelve′-month′ bond
twen′ty-per·cent′ rule
twice in jeop′ard·y
two′-is′sue rule
ty′ing
type′writ′ing
ty′phoid′ fe′ver
tyr′an·ny
ty′rant
tythe
tyth′ing

U

u′bi jus, i′bi re·me′di·um
u·biq′ui·ty
ul′lage
ul·te′ri·or
ul′ti·ma ra′ti·o′
ul′ti·mate
   — facts
ul′ti·ma′tum
ul′tra
   dam′ag·es —

   — ma′re′
   — re·pris′es
   — vi′res′
um′pir·age
um′pire′
u′na vo′ce′
un·a′ble
un′ac·crued′
un′ad·just′ed
un·al′ien·a·ble
un′am·big′u·ous
u′na·nim′i·ty
u·nan′i·mous
un·as′cer·tained′
un′a·void′a·ble
un·bro′ken
un·cer′tain·ty
un·chas′ti·ty
un′cle
un·clean′ hands
un′con·di′tion·al
un·con′scion·a·ble
un·con′scious
un′con·sti·tu′tion·al
un′con·trol′la·ble
   — im′pulse′
un·cuth′
un′de·fend′ed
un′der
under and sub′ject
under con·trol′
un′der·cur′rent of sur′face stream
un′der·flow′ of surface stream
un′der·ground′ wa′ters
un′der·growth′
un′der-lease′
un′der-sher′iff
un′der·signed′
un′der·stand′
un′der·stand′ing

un′der·stood′
un′der·take′
un′der·tak′er
un′der·tak′ing
un′der·ten′ant
un′der·took′
un′der-tu′tor
un′der·write′
un′der·writ′er
un′dis·closed′ prin′ci·pal
un′dis·put′ed
un′di·vid′ed
un·due′
   — in′flu·ence
un·earned′ in′cre·ment
un·ed′u·cat′ed
un′em·ploy′ment
un′en·closed′ place
un·e′qual
un′e·quiv′o·cal
un·err′ing
un·eth′i·cal
un′ex·cep′tion·a·ble
un′ex·pect′ed
un′ex·pired′ term
un·fair′
   — com′pe·ti′tion
   — hear′ing
   — la′bor prac′tice
   — meth′ods of com′pe·ti′tion
un·faith′ful
un·fin′ished
un·fit′
un′fore·seen′
un·harmed′
U′ni·at′ Church *or* U′ni·ate′ Church
u′ni·fac′tor·al ob′li·ga′tion
u′ni·fied′

u'ni·form'
u'ni·for'mi·ty
u'ni·fy'
u'ni·lat'er·al
— con'tract'
— mis·take'
un'im·peach'a·ble
wit'ness
un'im·proved' land
un'in·fect'ed
un'in·tel'li·gi·ble
un'ion
— mort'gage clause
— shop
Un'ion Jack
u'nit
— of pro·duc'tion
u·nite'
u·nit'ed in in'ter·est
U·nit'ed Na'tions
U·nit'ed States
— bonds
— com·mis'sion·er
— courts
— cur'ren·cy
— notes
— of'fi·cer
u'ni·ty
— of in'ter·est
— of pos·ses'sion
— of sei'sin
— of time
— of ti'tle
u'ni·ver'sal
u'ni·ver'si·ty
un·just'
— en·rich'ment
un·law'ful
— as·sem'bly
— de·tain'er
— en'try
— pick'et·ing
un·law'ful·ly

un·less'
— lease
un·lim'i·ted
un·liq'ui·dat'ed
un·liv'er·y
un·load'ing
un·mar'ket·a·ble
ti'tle
un·mar'ried
un·nat'u·ral of·fense'
un·nec'es·sar'y
— hard'ship'
un·oc'cu·pied'
un·prec'e·dent'ed
un'pro·fes'sion·al
— con'duct
un'ques'
un·rea'son·a·ble
— re·straint' of
trade
— restraint on
al'ien·a'tion
— search
un·ru'ly and
dan'ger·ous
un·safe'
un·seat'ed land
un·sea'wor'thy
un·sol'emn war
un·sound'
— mind
un·thrift'
un·til'
un'to·ward'
un·true'
un·u'su·al
— cir'cum·stance'
un·val'ued
un·whole'some
— food
un·wor'thy
un·writ'ten
— law

up'keep'
up'lands'
up'per bench
up'set' price
ur'ban
— home'stead'
— ser'vi·tude'
ure
us'age
— of trade
use v.
use n.
— and hab'i·ta'tion
— and oc'cu·pa'tion
ces·tui' que —
char'i·ta·ble —
con·tin'gent —
ex·clu'sive —
ex'e·cut'ed —
ex·ec'u·to'ry —
ex·ist'ing —
feoff·ee' to —
of·fi'cial —
pas'sive —
per·mis'sive —
— plain'tiff
re·sult'ing —
sec'on·dar'y —
shift'ing —
spring'ing —
su'per·sti'tious —
us·ee'
use'ful
use'ful·ness
us'er
ad·verse' —
ush'er
us'ing mail to
de·fraud'
us'que'
u'su·al
— course
— cov'e·nants

— place of a·bode'
u·su·fruct'
  im·per'fect —
  le'gal —
  per'fect —
u·su·fruc'tu·ar'y
u·su'ri·ous
  — con'tract'
u·surp'
u'sur·pa'tion
  — of ad·vow'son
  — of fran'chise'
  — of of'fice
u·surp'er
u'su·ry
u·ten'sil
u'ter·ine
u·til'i·ty
ut·lage'
ut'most'
  — care
  — re·sis'tance
ut'ter *v.*
ut'ter *adj.*
  — bar
  — bar'ris·ter
ux'or'
ux·or'i·cide'

va'can·cy
va'cant
va'cate'
va·ca'tion
va·ca'tur'
vac'ci·na'tion
va'cu·a pos·ses'si·o'
va·cu'i·ty
vac'u·um

va'di·a're' du·el'lum
va·di'um
  — mor'tu·um
  — po'ne·re'
  — vi'vum
vag'a·bond'
va'gran·cy
va'grant
  — act
vague
va·len'ti·a
val'et
val'id
  — rea'son
val'i·date'
val'i·dat'ing stat'ute
va·lid'i·ty
  — of a stat'ute
  — of a trea'ty
  — of a will
val'ley
val'or
  — ben'e·fi·ci·o'rum
  — ma'ri·ta'gi·i'
val'u·a·ble
  — con·sid'er·a·ble
  — im·prove'ments
  — pa'pers
  — thing
val'u·a'tion
  — list
val'ue
  clear —
  face —
  fair —
  fair and eq'ui·ta·-
    ble —
  fair and rea'son·-
    a·ble —
  fair and reasonable
    mar'ket —
  fair cash —
  fair cash mar'ket —

  market —
  net —
  — of mat'ter in
    con'tro·ver'sy
  — re·ceived'
  true —
val'ued pol'i·cy
val'ue·less
val'u·er
van'dal·ism
van·ta'ri·us
var'i·ance
var'i·a'tion
var'i·ous
va·sec'to·my
vas'sal
vas'sal·age
vas'tum
vaude'ville
va'va·sor' *or*
  va'va·sour'
veg'e·ta·ble
ve'hi·cle
vei'es'
veil'ings
vein
ve'jours
vel non
ve'nal
ve·na'ri·a
ve·na'ti·o'
vend
vend·ee'
ven·det'ta
vend'i·ble
ven·di'tion
ven'di·ti·o'ni'
  ex·po'nas'
ven'di·tor'
ven'di·trix'
ven'dor
  — and pur'chas·er
    act

ven'dor's lien
ven'due
— mas'ter
ve·ne're·al
— dis·ease'
ve'ni·a
ve·ni're'
— de no'vo'
— fa'ci·as'
— facias ad
    res'pon·den'dum
— facias de no'vo'
— facias
    ju'ra·to'res'
ve·ni're·man
ve'nit et de·fen'dit
ve'nit et di'cit
ven'ter'
ven'ture
ven'ue
ve·ran'dah *or*
    ve·ran'da
ve·ray'
ver'ba
— pre·car'i·a
ver'bal
— act
— proc'ess'
ver'der·er *or*
    ver'de·ror
ver'dict
ad·verse' —
— by lot
chance —
com'pro·mise' —
— con'tra'ry to law
es·top'pel by —
ex·ces'sive —
false —
gen'er·al —
— of no cause of
    ac'tion
— of not guilt'y

— of not guilty by
    rea'son of
    in·san'i·ty
o'pen —
par'tial —
priv'y —
pub'lic —
quo'tient —
sealed —
spe'cial —
— sub'ject to
    o·pin'ion of court
vere'bot'
ve're·dic'tum
verge *or* virge
ver'i·fi·ca'tion
ver'i·fied'
— cop'y
— names
ver'i·fy'
ver'i·ly
ver'sus
ver'ti·cal price'-
    fix'ing con'tract'
ver'ti·go'
ve'rus
ver'y
ves'sel
vest
vest'ed
— de·vise'
— es·tate'
— gift
— in in'ter·est
— in pos·ses'sion
— in'ter·est
— leg'a·cy
— re·main'der
— rights
ves·tig'i·al words
ves·tig'i·um
vest'ing or'der
ves'try

ves'try·men
ves·tu'ra
— ter'rae'
ves'ture
— of land
vet'er·an
ve'te·ra sta·tu'ta
vet'er·i·nar'i·an
ve'to
pock'et —
— pow'er
vex
vex·a'ri'
vex·a'ta quaes'ti·o'
vex·a'tion
vex·a'tious
— ac'tions act
— de·lay'
— pro·ceed'ing
— re·fus'al to pay
vexed ques'tion
vi'a
— ex·ec'u·ti'va
— or'di·na'ri·a
— pub'li·ca
— re'gi·a
vi'a an·ti'qua vi'a
    est tu'ta
vi'a·bil'i·ty
vi'a·ble
vic'ar
vic'ar·age
vi·car'i·al
— tithes
vice *n.*
vice *adj.*
— ad'mi·ral
— chan'cel·lor
— con'sul
— mar'shal
— pres'i·dent
— prin'ci·pal
vice'roy'

vi′ce ver′sa
vic′i·nage
vi·cin′i·ty
vi′cious
 — pro·pen′si·ty
vi·con′ti·el *or*
 vi·coun′ti·el
 — ju′ris·dic′tion
vict′ual·ler
vict′uals
vic′tus
vi′de′
 — an′te′
 — in′fra
 — post
 — su′pra
vi·de′li·cet
vi·du′i·ty
vie
vi et ar′mis
view
 — and de·liv′er·y
 de·mand′ of —
 — of an in′quest′
view′ers
vig′il
vig′i·lance
vig′or
vil′lage
vil′lain
vil′lein
 — in gross
 — re·gar′dant
 — serv′ic·es
 — soc′age
vil′len·age
vil′len·ous
 judg′ment
vin·a′gi·um
vin′di·ca′re′
vi′nous
 — liq′uor
vint′ner

vi′o·la′tion
vi′o·lence
vi′o·lent
 — death
 — pre·sump′tion
vi′o·lent·ly
vir
vi′res′
vir·ga′ta
vir′gate′
virge
 ten′ant by —
vir′tu·al
 — rep′re·sen·ta′tion
vir′tu·ous
vir·tu·te′
 — cuj′us
 — of·fi′ci·i′
vis
 — ar·ma′ta
 — clan·des·ti′na
 — com·pul′si·va
 — ex·pul′si·va
 — im·pres′sa
 — in·er′mis
 — in·ju′ri·o′sa
 — la′i·ca
 — li·ci′ta
 — ma′jor
 — per·tu·ba·ti′va
 — prox′i·ma
 — sim′plex′
vi′sa
vis′count′
vi′sé′
vis′i·ble
vis′it
vis′i·ta′tion
 — books
vis′i·tor
visne
vi′sus
vi′tal

 — sta·tis′tics
vi′ta·min
vi′ti·ate′
vit·il′i·gate′
vit′re·ous
vi·var′i·um
vi′va·ry
vi′va vo′ce′
vi′vum va′di·um
viz
vo·cab′u·la ar′tis
vo·ca′tion
vo·cif′er·ous
vo′co′
void
 — con′tract′
 — in part
 — in to′to′
 — judg′ment
 — mar′riage
 — proc′ess′
void′a·ble
 — con′tract′
 — judg′ment
 — mar′riage
 — pref′er·ence
void′ance
voir dire
vo′lens′
vo·len′ti′ non fit
 in·ju′ri·a
vo·li′tion·al
vol′un·tar′i·ly
vol′un·tar′y
vol′un·teer′
vote
 cast′ing —
vot′er
votes and
 pro·ceed′ings
vot′ing
 — by bal′lot
 cu′mu·la′tive —

— trust
vouch
vouch·ee′
vouch′er
voy′age
vul′gar

wab′ble
wa·cre·our′
wa′di·a
wage
— earn′er
wa′ger
— of bat′tel
— of law
— pol′i·cy
wa′ger·ing
— con′tract
— gain
wag′es
wag′on
wag′on·age
wag′on·way′
waif
waive
waiv′er
— by e·lec′tion of
rem′e·dies
ex·press′ —
im·plied′ —
— of ex·emp′tion
— of im·mu′ni·ty
— of pro′test′
— of tort
walk′ers
wall
wam′pum
wan′der

want
— of con·sid′er·a′tion
— of ju′ris·dic′tion
— of re·pair′
want′age
wan′ton
— act
— acts and
o·mis′sions
— and fu′ri·ous
driv′ing
— and reck′less
mis·con′duct
— in′ju·ry
— mis·con′duct
— neg′li·gence
wan′ton·ness
wap′en·take′
war
ar′ti·cles of —
civ′il —
laws of —
— pow′er
ward
— in chan′cer·y
— mote
— pa′tient
— of ad′mi·ral·ty
— of court
war′da
ward′age
war′den
— of the Cinque
Ports
wards and liv′er·ies
ward′ship′
ware′house′
— re·ceipt′
ware′house′man
warn′ing
warp
war′rant *v.*
war′rant *n.*

bench —
death —
dis·tress′ —
— of ar·rest′
— of at·tor′ney
— of com·mit′ment
— of′fi·cer
— of mer′chant·a·bil′i·ty
search —
war′rant·ee′
war′ran·tor
war′ran·ty
af·firm′a·tive —
col·lat′er·al —
con·tin′u·ing —
cov′e·nant of —
— deed
ex·ec′u·to′ry —
ex·press′ —
gen′er·al —
im·plied′ —
lin′e·al —
— of fit′ness
— of fitness for a
par·tic′u·lar
pur′pose
— of mer′chant·a·bil′i·ty
per′son·al —
prom′is·so′ry —
spe′cial —
war′ren
wash
— bank
washed sale
waste
com·mis′sive —
dou′ble —
eq′ui·ta·ble —
im·peach′ment of —
nul —
per·mis′sive —
vol′un·tar′y —
wast′ing trust

watch *n*.
watch *v*.
  — and ward
watch′man
wa′ter
  de·vel′oped —
  — pow′er
  — right
  — right claim
  sur′plus —
wa′ter·course′
wa′tered stock
wa′ter·front′
wa′ter·mark′
wa′ters
  flood —
  for′eign —·
  nav′i·ga·ble —
  per′co·lat′ing —
  pri′vate —·
  pub′lic —
  sub′ter·ra′ne·an —
  sur′face —
  tide —
wa′ter·way′
way
  — of ne·ces′si·ty
  pri′vate —
  right of —
way′bill′
way′-go′ing crop
way′leave′
ways and means
way′war′den
wealth
weap′on
wear and tear
wear′ing ap·par′el
weath′er·ing
wed
wed′ding
wed′lock′
week

weigh′age
weight
  gross —
  min′er′s —
  — of ev′i·dence
weir
wel′fare′
  — of child
well know′ing
welsh′er
welsh′ing
wet
  — gas
  — oil
weth′er
whale
whal′er
wharf
wharf′age
wharf′in·ger
wharf′ing out
wheel′age
wheel′ers
whelps
when
  — and where
when·ev′er
where
where·as′
where·by′
where′up·on′
wher·ev′er
which
Whig
while
whip′lash′
  — in′ju·ry
whip′ping
whis′key *or* whis′ky
white a′cre
who·ev′er
whole
  — blood

  — gale
whole′sale′
  — deal′er
  — price
whole′sal′er
whole′some
whol′ly
  — and per′ma-·
    nent·ly dis·a′bled
  — de·pend′ent
  — dis·a′bled
whore
whore′mas′ter
wid′ow
wid′ow·er
wid′ow·hood′
wife
Wild's Case
will *v*.
will *n*.
  am′bu·la·to′ry —
  con·di′tion·al —
  con·joint′ —
  — con′test′
  coun′ter —
  dou′ble —
  es·tate′ at —
  hol′o·graph′ic —
  joint —
  joint and mu′tu-·
    al —
  mu′tu·al —
  non′in·ter·ven′-
    tion —
  nun′cu·pa′tive —
  re·cip′ro·cal —
  self′-proved′ —
  un′of·fi′cious —
will′ful
  — and ma·li′cious
    in′ju·ry
  — and wan′ton
    in′ju·ry

— in·dif′fer·ence to
the safe′ty of
oth′ers
— mis·con′duct
— mis·con′duct of
em·ploy′ee
— mur′der
— neg′li·gence
— tort
will′ing·ly
wind′storm′
wind up
wine
win′ter
wit
wit′am
with
with all faults
with·draw′
with·draw′al
— of charges
with·draw′ing a
ju′ror
with·hold′
with·in′
with·out′
with·out′ day
with·out′ de·lay′
with·out′ prej′u·dice
with·out′ re′course′
with prej′u·dice
wit′ness *v.*
wit′ness *n.*
ad·verse′ —
— a·gainst′ him·self′
at·test′ing —
com′pe·tent —
cred′i·ble —
ex′pert′ —
hos′tile —
pros′e·cut′ing —
sub·scrib′ing —
swift —

— to will
wit′ting·ly
wom′en
wood
woods
wood′work′
wood′work′er
words
— ac′tion·a·ble in
them·selves′
— of art
— of lim′i·ta′tion
— of pro′cre·a′tion
— of pur′chase
work
— of art
— prod′uct
— re·lief′
— week
work′a·way′
work′ing
— cap′i·tal
— days
work′man
work′men's
— com′pen·sa′tion
— compensation
acts
— compensation
loss
works
work′shop′
world
world′ly
— busi′ness
— em·ploy′ment
wor′ship
wor′sted
worth
wor′thi·er ti′tle
worth′less
wor′thy
would

wound
wound′ed feel′ings
wound′ing
wrath
wreck
wreck′er
wreck′free′
wrench
wres′tling
wrin′kle
wrist′drop′
writ
a′li·as —
close —
con·cur′rent —
ju·di′cial —
jun′ior —
— of as·sis′tance
— of at·tach′ment
— of det′i·nue′
— of e·ject′ment
— of en′try
— of er′ror
— of error co′ram
no′bis
— of for′me·don
— of main′prize′ *or*
main′prise′
— of man′da·mus
— of mesne
— of pos·ses′sion
— of pro′hi·bi′tion
— of re·cap′tion
— of re·plev′in
— of res′ti·tu′tion
— of su′per·se′de·as
o·rig′i·nal —
pat′ent —
per·emp′to·ry —
pre·rog′a·tive —
— pro re·tor′no′
ha·ben′do′
writ′ing

— o·blig′a·to′ry
writ′ten
  — con′tract′
  — in′stru·ment
  — law
wrong
  pri′vate —
  pub′lic —
wrong′do′er
wrong′ful
  — act
  — con′duct
  — death stat′utes
  — lev′y
wrong′ful·ly
  — in·tend′ing

X Y Z

xe′no·do′chi·um
xy′lon′
xe·rog′ra·phy
x′-¦ray′
x-ray
  — pho′to·graph′

yacht
yard
yard′man′
yea and nay
year
  — and a day
  — books
  — of mourn′ing
  — of Our Lord
year′ling
year to year
  ten′an·cy from —
yeas and nays
yeast

yel′low-dog′
  con′tract′
yeo′man
yeo′man·ry
yeo′men of the
  guard
Yid′dish
yield
  — up·on′
    in·vest′ment
York, stat′ute of
young′er chil′dren
youth

zeal′ot
zeal′ous
  — wit′ness
zone
  — of em·ploy′ment
zon′ing

LEGAL CITATIONS

This section is adapted from parts of the 12th edition of *A Uniform System of Citation,* which is the authoritative guide to legal citation. Readers interested in obtaining copies of this comprehensive guide should contact The Harvard Law Review Association, Gannett House, Cambridge, MA 02138.

I. Introduction

Most legal writing involves the use of "citation." A "citation" is an author's reference to the specific source of legal authority that substantiates a statement made in the text; essentially, it serves the same purpose as a footnote. The most common sources of legal authority are cases and statutes, and legal writers will "cite" to these sources, and others, to enable their readers to refer to the original source material.

It is useful to understand the difference between a statute and a case. A statute is a law duly passed by a legislative body (like the Congress or a state legislature) and approved by the chief executive (like the President or a governor). The Civil Rights Act of 1964 is an example of a federal statute. A case, on the other hand, is a judicial decision in a specific case before a court. The judge's decision in a case is sometimes set forth in a written opinion, and lawyers will often refer to these opinions — or cases — in legal writing. *Griggs v. Duke Power Co.* is an example of a case.

For example, a legal writer might wish to state in a brief or legal memorandum that federal law prohibits discrimination in employment because of a person's race, color, religion, sex, or national origin. The primary federal statute that makes such discrimination illegal is known as the Civil Rights Act of 1964. Federal statutes are compiled in a set of reference books called "The United States Code" (U.S.C.). The Civil Rights Act of 1964, for example, can be found in Volume 42 of the United States Code in section 2000e-2. The legal writer's statement, with the correct citation, is as follows:

> The Civil Rights Act of 1964 prohibits employment discrimination because of race, color, religion, sex, or national origin. Civil Rights Act of 1964, § 703, 42 U.S.C. § 2000e-2 (1970).

From the above statement and citation, a reader knows that the provision of federal law that prohibits employment discrimination because of race, color, religion, sex, or national origin was enacted as section 703 of the Civil Rights Act of 1964, and can be found at "42 U.S.C. § 2000e-2 (1970)." This citation means that the federal law prohibiting such discrimination is in Volume 42 of the United States Code (42 U.S.C.) at section 2000e-2 (§ 2000e-2). The date in parentheses indicates the edition of the codification.

Citation to cases is accomplished in much the same way. For example, a legal writer might wish to say that in a certain case, the United States Supreme Court interpreted Title VII of the Civil Rights Act of 1964 to mean that even unintentional discrimination by an employer is a violation of the law. The Supreme Court did, in fact, say this in the case of *Griggs v. Duke Power Co.* in 1971. The statement, and its proper citation, might be written as follows:

> In one case, the Supreme Court has stated that even unintentional discrimination by an employer is illegal. *Griggs v. Duke Power Co.*, 401 U.S. 424, 428 (1971).

This citation shows the reader that the opinion of the Supreme Court in the case of *Griggs v. Duke Power Co.* can be found in Volume 401 of a set of books called the "United States Reports" (401 U.S.), beginning at page 424. The precise issue in question is discussed at page 428, and the year the opinion was given was 1971.

A citation can be a separate citation "sentence" (beginning with a capital letter and ending with a period) after a regular sentence or an appositive clause within a regular sentence.

A typical citation sentence may read as follows:

> Title VII of the Civil Rights Act of 1964 prohibits employment discrimination because of race, color, religion, sex, or national origin. Civil Rights Act of 1964, § 703, 42 U.S.C. § 2000e-2 (1970).

A typical citation clause may read as follows:

> The Civil Rights Act of 1964 prohibits discrimination because of race, color, religion, sex, or national origin, 42 U.S.C. § 2000e-2 (1970), and has been interpreted to mean that . . .

In addition to citations to statutes and cases, legal writers also cite to books, periodicals, congressional reports, treaties, constitutions, newspapers, and other sources. In order to make citations uniform and understandable by all legal readers, a "uniform system of citation" has been developed by various law reviews. It is published as a handbook titled *A Uniform System of Citation*, commonly referred to as the "Bluebook." All citations should conform to the uniform system of citation, and examples of the most commonly used citations are given below.

II. Proper Citation Form

A. Statutes

Statutes are cited in several ways, depending on where the statute is found. Statutes currently in force are usually found in a codification or code (e.g., "United States Code" is a large set of books containing current federal statutes).

Codes are generally organized according to the subject matter of the statutes. If the statute was recently enacted, however, it is probably not yet found in the code. In this event, the statute is cited to the "session law." Session laws report statutes chronologically as they are enacted. Eventually, most session laws can be found in the code, but it takes about a year for the code to be updated with the laws enacted during each session of Congress.

Statutes may also be found in "secondary sources." A secondary source is any source other than a code or session law that contains the text of a statute.

A citation to the current code must include the name of the code, the code section number, and a parenthetical that contains the year of the codification. In a citation to the current code, the name of the statute and the original section number (found in the appropriate session laws) are given only if the statute is usually cited by its name and original sections or if they would otherwise aid in identification. An official name, a popular name, or both may be used. For example, Labor Management Relations (Taft-Hartley) Act § 301(a), 29 U.S.C. § 185(a) (1970).

A citation to any other source must include the name of the act, the public law or chapter number, the original section number, the published source in which the statute is found, if any, and a parenthetical containing the year of enactment. When a statute has been amended or repealed or is otherwise no longer in force as cited, the statute's relevant history must be explained parenthetically. If a statute has no official or popular name, ''Act of'' with the full date of enactment should be used, for example, Act of Apr. 25, 1957, Pub. L. No. 85-24, § 3, 71 Stat. 25. The section number follows the public law or chapter number, not the name of the act, for example, Clayton Act, ch. 323, § 7, 38 Stat. 730 (1914).

Thus, the proper citation of statutes is as follows:

cited to current code	National Environmental Policy Act of 1969, § 102, 42 U.S.C. § 4332 (1970)

or

42 U.S.C. § 4332 (1970)

cited to session laws	National Environmental Policy Act of 1969, Pub. L. No. 91-190, § 102, 83 Stat. 852 (1970) (prior to 1975 amendment)
cited to secondary source	Act of Aug. 9, 1975, Pub. L. No. 94-83, § 1, 5 Envir. L. Rep. 41,014 (1975) (to be codified in 42 U.S.C. § 4332)

B. Cases

All case citations *must* give the following information so that the reader can find the source easily:

1. Name of the case
2. Location of the printed decision (name of reporter, volume number, and page number)
3. Date of decision
4. Jurisdiction and court of decision. United States courts of appeals for numbered circuits, regardless of year, are indicated: 2d Cir., *not* C.C.A. 2d, and *not* C.A.2. The Court of Appeals for the District of Columbia and all its predecessors are cited: D.C. Cir. For district court cases, give the district but not the division. Thus:
S.D. Cal., *not* S.D. Cal. C.D. Cite the old circuit courts (abolished 1912): C.C.S.D.N.Y. And cite the Judicial Panel on Multi-District Litigation: J.P.M.D.L.

A typical case citation might look like this:

Dodd v. Smith, 526 F.2d 35 (1st Cir. 1976)

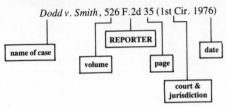

In addition, a case citation may give other important information that would be helpful to the reader. This information might include reference to specific pages within the reported decision, prior or subsequent history of the case, or specific details concerning the case.

A case citation, with helpful additional information, might look like this:

Dodd v. Smith, 526 F.2d 35 (37) (1st Cir. 1976) *aff'g* 389 F. Supp. 154 (D. Mass. 1975) (applying Pennsylvania law).

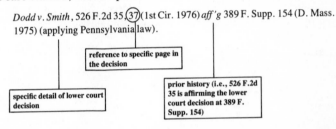

Following are typical case citation forms for the various stages of litigation, beginning when the case is first filed, all the way through to an appeal to, and decision by, the United States Supreme Court. Note that these examples are of cases in federal courts. The same format, however, can be used for state court decisions. The examples marked by an asterisk are the most commonly used.

filed but not decided	*Dodd v. Smith*, No. 74-329 (D. Mass., filed Sept. 9, 1974)
unpublished interim order	*Dodd v. Smith*, No. 74-329 (D. Mass., Oct. 10, 1974) (order granting preliminary injunction)
published interim order	*Dodd v. Smith*, 377 F. Supp. 321 (D. Mass. 1974) (order granting preliminary injunction)
unpublished decision	*Dodd v. Smith*, No. 74-329 (D.Mass., Jan. 21, 1975)
decision published in service only	*Dodd v. Smith*, [1975] Fed. Sec. L. Rep. (CCH) ¶95,098 (D. Mass., Jan. 21, 1975)
*published decision	*Dodd v. Smith*, 389 F. Supp. 154 (D. Mass. 1975)
appeal docketed	*Dodd v. Smith*, 389 F. Supp. 154 (D. Mass. 1975), appeal docketed, No. 75-699 (1st Cir. Feb. 10, 1975)

disposition on appeal	*Dodd v. Smith,* 389 F. Supp. 154 (D. Mass. 1975), *aff'd,* 526 F.2d 35 (1st Cir. 1976)
*appellate opinion	*Dodd v. Smith,* 526 F.2d 35 (1st Cir. 1976)
brief, record, or appendix	Brief for Appellee, *Dodd v. Smith,* 526 F.2d 35 (1st Cir. 1976)
*Supreme Court opinion	*Dodd v. Smith,* 428 U.S. 1011 (1977)

or

Dodd v. Smith, 428 U.S. 1011, 93 S. Ct. 1480 (1977)

Aside from statutes and cases, legal writers often cite the Constitution, newspapers, periodicals, and other specialized sources. Such citations must also conform to proper citation form as the following examples show:

C. Constitutions

U.S. Const. art. I, § 9, cl. 2
U.S. Const. amend. XIV, § 2

D. Books

6 C. Wright & A. Miller, *Federal Practice and Procedure* § 1417 (1971)

E. Periodicals

Hertz, *Limits to the Naturalization Power,* 64 Geo. L.J. 1007 (1976)

F. Newspapers

Washington Post, Oct. 14, 1977, at 4, col. 2

G. Legislative Materials

1. Bills
S. 383, 83d Cong., 2d Sess. (1954)
H.R. 136, 79th Cong., 1st Sess. (1945)

2. Reports
H.R. Rep. No. 353, 82d Cong., 1st Sess. 2 (1951)
S. Rep. No. 148, 91st Cong., 2d Sess. 181 (1973)

3. U.S. Code Congressional & Administrative News
H.R. Rep. No. 98, 92d Cong., 1st Sess. 4 *reprinted in* [1971] U.S. Code Cong. & Ad. News 1017

4. Congressional Record
103 Cong. Rec. 1728 (1975)
123 Cong. Rec. H12,575 (daily ed. Nov. 27, 1977)

H. Regulations

1. Code of Federal Regulations
10 C.F.R. § 481.11 (1976)

2. Federal Register
49 Fed. Reg. 11,234 (1977)

I. Taxation Materials

I.R.C. § 161
Treas. Reg. § 1.732 (1976)
Rev. Rul. 77-108

J. Other Sources

1. Uniform Commercial Code
U.C.C. § 2-207

2. Federal Rules of Evidence
Fed. R. Evid. 911

3. Federal Rules of Civil Procedure
Fed. R. Civ. P. 61(a)

4. Local Court Rules
1st Cir. R. 10(b)

5. Bible
2 *Kings* 12:19

6. Miscellaneous
9 ABA Antitrust Section 111 (1936)

ABA Canons of Professional Ethics No. 11

ABA Comm. on Professional Ethics, Opinions No. 105 (1934)

ABA-ALI Model Bus. Corp. Act. § 15 (1953)

12 Am. Jr. *Contracts* § 74 (1938)

ALI Fed. Income Tax Stat. § X105(a) (Feb. 1954 Drafts)

10 ALI Proceedings 256 (1931-1932)

5 American Law of Property § 22.30 (A.J. Casner ed. 1952)

Black's Law Dictionary 712 (4th ed. 1951)

88 C.J.S. *Trial* &192 (1955)

Model Penal Code § 305.17, Comment (Tent. Draft No. 5, 1956)

6 Moore's Federal Practice ¶ 56.07, at 2044 (2d ed. 1973)

Restatement (Second) of Agency § 20 (1957)

Restatement (Second) of Conflict of Laws § 305, Comment b, Illustration 1 (1971)

Restatement of Torts, Explanatory Notes § 3-40, Comment a at 118 (Tent. Draft No. 17, 1938)

The Federalist No. 23 (A. Hamilton)

III. General Rules For Citations

A. Generally. Citation sentences begin with a capital letter and end with a period.

B. Underlining. Proper legal writing style requires that certain words in citations and text be italicized. As a general rule, in typewritten manuscript to indicate this, *always underline the following:*

1. Case Names

Griggs v. Duke Power Co., 401 U.S. 424 (1971)

2. Book Titles

6 C. Wright & A. Miller, *Federal Practice and Procedure* § 1417 (1971)

3. Titles of Articles in Periodicals

Hertz, *Limits to the Naturalization Power,* 64 Geo. L.J. 1007 (1976)

4. Names of Newspapers

Washington Post, Dec. 3, 1977, at 2, col. 1

5. Signals and Explanatory Phrases

Sometimes a legal writer will insert additional words in a citation sentence to explain to the reader the significance of the citation (See pages 131-134). Always underline the following words when used in a citation:

E.g., or *e.g.,*
Accord,
See (or *see, e.g.,*)
See also
Cf.
Compare . . . [and] . . . with . . . . [and]
Contra
But see
But cf.
See generally
Ibid. or *id.*
Reprinted in
Passim
Semble
Sub nom.

6. Latin Words and Phrases

Always underline the following words in typewritten manuscript when used in a citation or text:

infra
inter alia
inter se
qua
sic
supra

C. **Spacing Between Certain Abbreviations.** In some instances, *there should be no space between two abbreviated words*. The rule is that whenever two adjacent abbreviated words have been abbreviated to single capital letters, there is no space between the letters. For this purpose, numerical designation such as "2nd" and "3d" are considered single capital letters.

> *Examples:*
> A.L.R.2d
> D.C.
> D.R.I.
> F.R.D.
> F.2d
> I.C.C.
> N.Y.
> S.D.N.Y.
> ˙U.S.
> *But:*
> Cal. 3d
> F. Supp.
> So. 2d

D. **More than One Citation — "String" Citations.** When there is more than one citation within a citation sentence or clause, they are separated by a semicolon.

> *Example:*
> A familiar rule of law is that a final order of a court of competent jurisdiction having jurisdiction over the subject matter and the parties cannot be attacked in a collateral proceeding. *See, e.g., United States v. Throckmorton*, 98 U.S. 61, 67 (1878); *Goodwin v. Home Buying Investment Co.*, 352 F. Supp. 413, 414 (D.D.C. 1973).

E. **Punctuation Marks in Quoted Material.** Commas and periods are always placed inside the quotation marks; other punctuation marks are placed inside the quotation marks only if they are part of the quoted matter.

IV. INTRODUCTORY SIGNALS

A. Explanation

"Introductory signals" are the words or phrases used by legal writers in a citation to emphasize the importance the writer ascribes to the cited authority or for purposes of comparison or general background information. They precede or "introduce," the authorities that they explain and "signal" the reader how to interpret the material that follows and apply it to the authorities in the citation.

1. Signals That Indicate Specific Support:

When *no signal* appears, this means that the cited authority (a) directly supports the statement in the text, (b) identifies the source of a quotation, or (c) identifies an authority referred to in the text.

E.g.,: This signal means that there are other examples directly supporting the statement in the text, but citation to them would not be helpful. ("*E.g.,*" may also be used in combination with other signals, preceded by a comma: "*See, e.g.,*" "*But see, e.g.,*").

Accord,: This signal means that the cited authority directly supports the statement, but in a slightly different way than the authority(ies) first cited. "*Accord,*" is commonly used when two or more cases are on the point but the text refers to only one; the others are then introduced by "*accord,.*" Similarly, the law of one jurisdiction may be cited as in accord with that of another.

See: This signal means that the cited authority constitutes the basic source material supporting the proposition. "*See*" is used when the proposition is not stated by the cited authority but follows from it.

Cf.: This signal means that the cited authority supports a proposition different from that in the text but is sufficiently analogous to lend support. "*Cf.*" means "compare." "*Cf.*" should always be used with an explanatory parenthetical.

2. **Signals That Suggest a Profitable Comparison:** *Compare. . . [and] . . . with . . . [and] . . .:* This signal means that comparison of authorities cited will offer support for, or illustrate, a statement in the text.

3. **Signals That Indicate Specific Contradiction:**
   Contra: This signal means that the cited authority directly supports a contrary statement.

   But see: This signal means that the cited authority suggests a contrary statement.

   But cf.: This signal means that the cited authority supports a proposition analogous to the contrary of the position stated in the text. "*But cf.*" should always be used with an explanatory parenthetical.

4. **Signals That Indicate Background Material:**
   See generally: This signal means that the cited authority provides background to the question examined in the text, without providing support for the specific conclusion reached.

   See also: This signal means that the cited authority provides background to a question analogous to that examined in the text and can be profitably compared.

B. Order of Signals

When more than one signal is used in a citation, the signals (together with the authorities they introduce) should appear in the order listed above.

C. Order Within a Given Signal

Within a signal, authorities should be cited in the following order, subject to alteration for any good reason.

Cases are arranged within a signal according to the courts issuing the cited opinions; subsequent and prior history is irrelevant to the order of citation. Cases decided by the same court are arranged in reverse chronological order; for this purpose the several United States courts of appeals are treated as one court and all federal district courts are treated as one court. The ordering system is as follows:

Federal:

1. Supreme Court,
2. courts of appeals, Emergency Court of Appeals,
3. district courts,
4. Court of Claims,
5. Court of Customs and Patent Appeals, Court of Military Appeals, Customs Court, Tax Court (including Board of Tax Appeals),
6. administrative agencies (alphabetically by agency).

State (alphabetically by state):

7. courts (by rank within each state),
8. agencies (alphabetically by agency within each state).

Non-United States:

9. common-law jurisdictions (as for states),
10. civil-law jurisdictions (as for states).

Cite **statutes** according to jurisdiction in the following order:

Federal:

1. statutes in U.S.C. or U.S.C.A. (by progressive order of U.S.C. title),
2. statutes currently in force but not in U.S.C. or U.S.C.A. (by reverse chronological order of enactment),
3. repealed statutes (by reverse chronological order of enactment).

State: (alphabetically by state)

4. statutes in current codification (by order in the codification),
5. statutes currently in force but not in current codification (by reverse chronological order of enactment,
6. repealed statutes (by reverse chronological order of enactment).

Non-United States: (alphabetically by jurisdiction)

7. statutes currently in force,
8. repealed statutes.

International agreements, bills, and resolutions are cited in that order, in reverse chronological order within each classification.

Rules and administrative materials are cited in the following order:

Rules:

1. federal,
2. state (alphabetically by state),
3. non-United States (alphabetically by jurisdiction). These are followed by

Federal administrative regulations and rulings:

4. Exec. Orders,
5. current Treas. Regs., Proposed Treas. Regs.,

6. all others currently in force (by progressive order of C.F.R. title),
7. all repealed regulations and rulings (by reverse chronological order of promulgation). These are followed by

Other administrative regulations and rulings:

8. state (alphabetically by state), currently in force, then repealed;
9. non-United States (alphabetically by jurisdiction), currently in force, then repealed.

Records, briefs, and petitions are cited in that order and within each classification by order of court in which filed.

Secondary sources are cited in the following order:

1. books and essays in a collection of a single author's essays (alphabetically by author — if none, by first word of title),
2. articles and essays in a collection of various authors' essays (alphabetically by author),
3. student-written law review material — special student projects, then long works such as notes, then short commentaries on recent developments (alphabetically by periodical as abbreviated in citation),
4. signed book reviews (alphabetically by reviewer),
5. student-written book reviews (alphabetically by periodical as abbreviated in citation),
6. unpublished material and other material of limited circulation (alphabetically by author — if none, by first word of title).

V. ABBREVIATIONS

Following are proper abbreviations for the most commonly used sources for both cases and statutes (see page 124 for a discussion of the difference between cases and statutes).

A. Case Reporters and Statutory Compilations:

1. Federal Courts

United States Supreme Court

United States Reports	__ U.S. __
Supreme Court Reporter	__ S. Ct. __
United States Supreme Court Reports (Lawyers' Edition)	__ L. Ed. __
(second series)	__ L. Ed. 2d __
United States Law Week	__ U.S.L.W. __

United States Courts of Appeals

a. Federal Reporter (1880-date) (second series)	__ F. __
b. Federal Cases (1789-1800)	__ F. Cas. __

United States District Courts

Federal Supplement	___ F. Supp. ___
Federal Rules Decisions	___ F.R.D. ___

Court of Claims and Customs Court

Court of Claims Reports	___ Ct. Cl. ___
Customs Court Reports	___ Cust. Ct. ___

Court of Customs and Patent Appeals

Court of Customs and Patent Appeals Reports	___ C.C.P.A. ___

Tax Court and Board of Tax Appeals

Tax Court of the United States Reports	___ T.C. ___
Board of Tax Appeals Reports	___ B.T.A. ___
Tax Court Memorandum Decisions	___ T.C.M. ___ (CCH) [or (P-H)]
Board of Tax Appeals Memorandum Decisions	___ B.T.A.M. (P-H)

Court of Military Appeals

a. Court of Military Appeals Reports	___ C.M.A. ___
b. Military Justice Reports	___ M.J. ___
c. Court-Martial Reports	___ C.M.R.___

2. Federal Statutes

United States Code	___ U.S.C. § ___
Internal Revenue Code of 1954	I.R.C. §
United States Code Annotated	___ U.S.C.A. § ___
United States Statutes at Large	___ Stat. ___

3. Regional Reporters (state court decisions)

Regional reporters, published by the West Publishing Company, contain virtually all opinions of the highest courts of all fifty states and the District of Columbia.

Atlantic Reporter	___ A. ___
(second series)	___ A.2d ___
North Eastern Reporter	___ N.E. ___
(second series)	___ N.E. 2d ___
North Western Reporter	___ N.W. ___
(second series)	___ N.W.2d ___
Pacific Reporter	___ P. ___
(second series)	___ P.2d ___
Southern Reporter	___ So. ___
(second series)	___ So. 2d ___
South Eastern Reporter	___ S.E. ___
(second series)	___ S.E.2d. ___
South Western Reporter	___ S.W. ___
(second series)	___ S.W.2d ___

4. Table of State Supreme Courts and Statutory Compilations

Almost every state publishes the decisions of its highest court in a separate set of books such as "Alabama Reports" (Ala. or "Arizona Reports" (Ariz.). In those states where there is no official state reporter it is necessary to cite to the regional reporter (e.g., Alaska Supreme Court decisions are cited to P.2d).

In addition, each state compiles its statutes in a set of books such as "Ala. Code" (Alabama Code) and "Ariz. Rev. Stat. Ann." (Arizona Revised Statutes Annotated).

Following is a table of the proper abbreviations for the source of opinions of each state's highest (a supreme) court as well as the abbreviations for each state's statutory compilation.

	Supreme Court	Statutory Compilation
Alabama	___ Ala. ___	Ala. Code tit. ___, § ___
Alaska	(Cite to P.2d)	Alaska Stat. § ___
Arizona	___ Ariz. ___	Ariz. Rev. Stat. Ann. § ___
Arkansas	___ Ark. ___	Ark. Stat. Ann. § ___
California	___ Cal. [2d] [3d] ___	Cal.[subject] Code § ___
Colorado	___ Colo. ___	Colo. Re. Stat. § ___
Connecticut	___ Conn. ___*	Conn. Gen. Stat. § ___ Conn. Gen. Stat. Ann. § ___ (West)
Delaware	___ Del. ___	Del. Code Ann. tit. ___, § ___
District of Columbia	(Cite to A.2d)**	D.C. Code Ann. § ___
Florida	___ Fla. ___	Fla. Stat. § ___
Georgia	___ Ga. ___	Ga. Code § ___
Hawaii	___ Haw. ___	Haw. Rev. Stat.§ ___
Idaho	___ Idaho ___	Idaho Code § ___
Illinois	___ Ill. [2d] ___	Ill. Ann. Stat. ch. ___, § ___ (Smith-Hurd)
Indiana	___ Ind. ___	Ind. Code § ___ Ind. Code Ann. § ___ (Burns)
Iowa	___ Iowa ___	Iowa Code § ___ Iowa Code Ann. § ___ (West)
Kansas	___ Kan. ___	Kan. Stat. § ___ Kan. U.C.C. Ann. § ___ (Vernon) Kan. Civ. Pro. Stat. Ann. § ___ (Vernon) Kan. Crim. Code & Code of Crim. Proc. § ___ (Vernon)

*Supreme Court of Errors
**Court of Appeals
***Supreme Judicial Court

	Supreme Court	**Statutory Compilation**
Kentucky	__ Ky. __ (1879-1951) (Cite to Ky. and S.W. or S.W.2d)	Ky. Rev. Stat. § __ Ky. Rev. Stat. Ann. § __ (Baldwin)

Louisiana	__ La. __	La. Rev. Stat. Ann. § __
		    (West)
		La. Civ. Code Ann.
		    art. __ (West)
		La. Code Crim. Pro. Ann.
		    art. __ (West)

Maine	__ Me. __ (1820-1965)*** (Cite to Me. and A. or A.2d)	Me. Rev. Stat. tit. __, § __
Maryland	__ Md. __**	Md. [subject] Code Ann. § __ Md. Ann. Code art. __, § __

Massachusetts	__ Mass. __***	Mass. Gen. Laws Ann.
		    ch. __, § __ (West)
		Mass. Ann. Laws Ch. __,
		    §__ (Michie Law. Co-op)

Michigan	__ Mich. __	Mich. Comp. Laws § __ Mich. Comp. Laws Ann. § __ Mich. Stat. Ann. § __
Minnesota	__ Minn. __	Minn. Stat. § __ Minn. Stat. Ann. § __ (West)
Mississippi	__ Miss. __ (1850-1966) (Cite to Miss. and So. or So.2d)	Miss. Code Ann. § __
Missouri	__ Mo. __ (1821-1956) (Cite to Mo. and S.W. or S.W.2d)	Mo. Rev. Stat. § __ Mo. Ann. Stat. § __ (Vernon)
Montana	__ Mont. __	Mont. Rev. Codes Ann. § __
Nebraska	__ Neb. __	Neb. Rev. Stat. § __
Nevada	__ Nev. __	Nev. Rev. Stat. § __
New Hampshire	__ N.H. __	N.H. Rev. State. Ann. § __
New Jersey	__ N.J. __	N.J. Rev. Stat. § __ N.J. Stat. Ann. § __ (West)
New Mexico	__ N.M. __	N.M. Stat. Ann. § __

New York	__ N.Y. [2d] __**	N.Y. [subject] Law
		    (McKinney)
		N.Y. [subject] Law
		    (Consol.)

	Supreme Court	Statutory Compilation
North Carolina	___ N.C. ___	N.C. Gen. Stat. § ___
North Dakota	___ N.D. ___ (1890-1953) (Cite to N.D. and N.W. or N.W.2d)	N.D. Cent. Code § ___
Ohio	___ Ohio St. [2d] ___	Ohio Rev. Code Ann. § ___ (Page) Ohio Rev. Code Ann. § ___ (Baldwin) Ohio Rev. Code Ann. § ___ (Anderson)
Oklahoma	___ Okla. ___ (1890-1953) (Cite to Okla. and P. or P.2d)	Okla. Stat. tit. ___, § ___ Okla Stat. Ann. tit. ___, § ___ (West)
Oregon	___ Or. ___	Or. Rev. Stat. § ___
Pennsylvania	___ Pa. ___	___ Pa. Cons. Stat. § ___ ___ Pa. Cons. Stat. Ann. § ___ (Purdon) Pa. Stat. Ann. tit. ___, § ___ (Purdon)
Puerto Rico	___ P.R.R. ___	P.R. Laws Ann. tit. ___, § ___
Rhode Island	___ R.I. ___	R.I. Gen. Laws § ___
South Carolina	___ S.C. ___	S.C. Code § ___
South Dakota	___ S.D. ___	S.D. Compiled Laws Ann. § ___ S.D. Uniform Prob. Code § ___
Tennessee	___ Tenn. ___	Tenn. Code Ann. § ___
Texas	___ Tex. ___ (1846-1962) (Cite to Tex. and or S.W.2d)	Tex. [subject] Code Ann. tit. ___, § ___ (Vernon) Tex. Stat. Ann. § ___
Utah	___ Utah [2d] ___	Utah Code Ann. § ___
Vermont	___ Vt. ___	Vt. Stat. Ann. tit. ___, § ___
Virginia	___ Va. ___	Va. Code § ___
Washington	___ Wash. [2d] ___	Wash. Rev. Code § ___ Wash. Rev. Code Ann. § ___
West Virginia	___ W. Va. ___	W. Va. Code § ___
Wisconsin	___ Wis. ___	Wis. Stat. § ___ Wis. Stat. Ann. § ___ (West)
Wyoming	___ Wyo. ___ (1870-1959) (Cite to Wyo. and P. or P.2d)	Wyo. Stat. § ___

B. Case Names:

In case names that appear in footnotes, the following words are abbreviated as indicated below. Never abbreviate "United States" or the first word of a party name. For example, a case titled *"American Brotherhood of Chemical Engineers v. General Hospital Corporation"* would be written *"American Bhd. of Chem. Eng'rs v. General Hosp. Corp."* However, always abbreviate Co., Corp., Inc., Ltd., No., and & as well as commonly used abbreviations of organizations (e.g., NAACP or UMW).

Administrator	Adm'r	Exchange	Exch.	Savings	Sav.
Administratrix	Adm'x	Executor	Ex'r	Securities	Sec.
American	Am.	Executrix	Ex'x	Service	Serv.
Associate	Assoc.	Federal	Fed.	Society	Soc'y
Association	Ass'n	Federation	Fed'n	South	S.
Atlantic	Atl.	Finance	Fin.	Southern	S.
Authority	Auth.	General	Gen.	Steamship	S.S.
Automobile	Auto.	Government	Gov't	Street	St.
Avenue	Ave.	Guaranty	Guar.	Surety	Sur.
Board	Bd.	Hospital	Hosp.	System	Sys.
Brotherhood	Bhd.	Housing	Hous.	Telegraph	Tel.
Brothers	Bros.	Incorporated	Inc.	Telephone	Tel.
Building	Bldg.	Indemnity	Indem.	Transport	Transp.
Casualty	Cas.	Industrial	Indus.	Transportation	Transp.
Central	Cent.	Industries	Indus.	University	Univ.
Chemical	Chem.	Industry	Indus.	Utility	Util.
Commission	Comm'n	Insurance	Ins.	West	W.
Commissioner	Comm'r	Institute	Inst.	Western	W.
Committee	Comm.	Institution	Inst.		
Company	Co.	International	Int'l		
Consolidated	Consol.	Investment	Inv.		
Construction	Constr.	Liability	Liab.		
Cooperative	Coop.	Limited	Ltd.		
Corporation	Corp.	Machine	Mach.		
Department	Dep't	Machinery	Mach.		
Development	Dev.	Manufacturer	Mfr.		
Distribute	Distrib.	Manufacturing	Mfg.		
Distributing	Distrib.	Market	Mkt.		
Distributor	Distrib.	Municipal	Mun.		
District	Dist.	Mutual	Mut.		
Division	Div.	National	Nat'l		
East	E.	North	N.		
Eastern	E.	Northern	N.		
Education	Educ.	Pacific	Pac.		
Educational	Educ.	Product	Prod.		
Electric	Elec.	Production	Prod.		
Electricity	Elec.	Public	Pub.		
Electronic	Elec.	Railroad	R.R.		
Engineer	Eng'r	Railway	Ry.		
Engineering	Eng'r	Refining	Ref.		
Equipment	Equip.	Road	Rd.		

C. Names of Courts:

When citing to cases, it is essential to tell the reader the name of the court deciding the case. This is accomplished by placing the name of the court, properly abbreviated, in parentheses after the name of the case. For example, the case of *Fitzgerald v. Reeves*, decided by the District of Columbia Municipal Court of Appeals in 1962, might be cited as follows:

Fitzgerald v. *Reeves*, 281 A.2d 422 (D.C. Mun. Ct. App. 1962).
Following are abbreviations for court names and designations:

Admiralty Court or Division	Adm.
Appellate Department	App. Dep't.
Appellate Division	App. Div.
Board of Tax Appeals	B.T.A.
Chancery Court or Division	Ch.
Children's Court	Child. Ct.
Circuit Court (old federal)	C.C.
Circuit Court (state)	Cir. Ct.
Circuit Court of Appeal (state)	Cir. Ct. App.
Circuit Court of Appeals (federal)	Cir.
City Court	[name city] City Ct.
Civil Appeals	Civ. App.
Civil Court of Record	Civ. Ct. Rec.
Common Pleas	C.P. [when appropriate, name county or similar subdivision]
Commonwealth Court	Commw. Ct.
County Court	[name county] County Ct.
County Judge's Court	County J. Ct.
Court of Appeals (federal)	Cir.
Court of Appeal[s] (state)	Ct. App.
Court of Claims	Ct. Cl.
Court of Criminal Appeals	Crim. App.
Court of Customs and Patent Appeals	C.C.P.A.
Court of Customs Appeals	Ct. Cust. App.
Court of Errors and Appeals	Ct. Err. & App.
Court of Military Appeals	C.M.A.
Court of Military Review	C.M.R.
Court of [General, Special] Sessions	Ct. [Gen., Spec.] Sess.
Criminal Appeals	Crim. App.
Customs Court	Cust. Ct.
District Court (federal)	D.
District Court (state)	Dist. Ct.
District Court of Appeal	Dist. Ct. App.
Domestic Relations Court	Dom. Rel. Ct.
Emergency Court of Appeals	Emer. Ct. App.
Equity Court or Division	Eq.
Justice of the Peace's Court	J.P. Ct.
Juvenile Court	Juv. Ct.
Law Court or Division	L. Ct., Div.
Magistrate's Court	Magis. Ct.

Municipal Court	[name city] Mun. Ct.
Orphan's Court	Orphan's Ct.
Probate Court	P. Ct.
Police Justice's Court	Police J. Ct.
Public Utilities Commission	P.U.C.
Real Estate Commission	Real Est. Comm'n
Superior Court	Super. Ct.
Supreme Court	Sup. Ct.
Supreme Court, Appellate Division	App. Div.
Supreme Court, Appellate Term	App. T.
Supreme Judicial Court	Sup. Jud. Ct.
Surrogate's Court	Sur. Ct.
Tax Court	T.C.
Workmen's Compensation Division	Workmen's Comp. Div.
Youth Court	Youth Ct.

LEGAL FORMS

The following are suggested formats for typing some legal documents. As local rules regarding the style of forms may vary between courts, districts, and divisions, it is important to check local rules before filing any document.

All papers filed in connection with a case in court must contain a "caption." The caption is the heading on a document that shows the following: 1) name of the court, including the district or division, if any; 2) names of the parties (i.e., plaintiff and defendant); and 3) the case's number on the court docket or calendar.

IN THE UNITED STATES DISTRICT COURT
FOR
THE _____ **DISTRICT OF** _____
_____ **DIVISION**   **(if applicable)**

A.B., Plaintiff

       v.   Civil Action No. _____

C.D., Defendant

(Designation of paper to be filed, i.e., Complaint, Summons, Answer, Interrogatories, Motion for Summary Judgment, etc.)

Virtually all papers filed in connection with a case in court must be sent to, or "served on," all other parties connected with the case. Accordingly, it is necessary to certify to the court that the paper was served on the other parties and a certificate of service is used for this purpose. The certificate of service is usually the last paragraph of the document filed with the court.

CERTIFICATE OF SERVICE

I hereby certify that the foregoing _____
(designation of paper to be filed, i.e.,

_____ was mailed, postage prepaid, this _____day of
Answer, Interrogatories, etc.)

_____, 19___, to _____, attorney
(name and address)

for _____.
(Plaintiff, Defendant, etc.)

_____

Every complaint filed in a court must contain an allegation of jurisdiction. The allegation of jurisdiction informs the court by what statutory authority the court has to hear the case.

ALLEGATION OF JURISDICTION

(a) Jurisdiction founded on diversity of citizenship and amount.

Plaintiff is a [citizen of the State of Connecticut] [1] [corporation incorporated under the laws of the State of Connecticut having its principal place of business in the State of Connecticut] and defendant is a corporation incorporated under the laws of the State of New York having its principal place of business in a State other than the State of Connecticut. The matter in controversy exceeds, exclusive of interest and costs, the sum of ten thousand dollars.

(b) Jurisdiction founded on the existence of a Federal question and amount in controversy.

The action arises under [the Constitution of the United States, Article ____, Section ____]; [the ____ Amendment to the Constitution of the United States, Section ____]; [the Act of ____, ____ Stat. ____; U.S.C., Title ____, § ____]; [the Treaty of the United States (here describe the treaty)], [2] as hereinafter more fully appears. The matter in controversy exceeds, exclusive of interest and costs, the sum of ten thousand dollars.

(c) Jurisdiction founded on the existence of a question arising under particular statutes.

The action arises under the Act of ____, ____ Stat. ____; U.S.C., Title ____, § ____, as hereinafter more fully appears.

(d) Jurisdiction founded on the admiralty or maritime character of the claim.

This is a case of admiralty and maritime jurisdiction, as hereinafter more fully appears. [If the pleader wishes to invoke the distinctively maritime procedures referred to in Rule 9(h), add the following or its substantial equivalent: This is an admiralty or maritime claim within the meaning of Rule 9(h).]

---

[1] Form for natural person.

[2] Use the appropriate phrase or phrases. The general allegation of the existence of a Federal question is ineffective unless the matters constituting the claim for relief as set forth in the complaint raise a Federal question.

[CAPTION]

COMPLAINT ON A PROMISSORY NOTE

1. [Allegation of jurisdiction]
2. Defendant on or about June 1, 1935, executed and delivered to plaintiff a promissory note [in the following words and figures: (here set out the note verbatim)]; [a copy of which is hereto annexed as Exhibit A]; [whereby defendant promised to pay to plaintiff or order on June 1, 1936 the sum of _____ dollars with interest thereon at the rate of six percent per annum].
3. Defendant owes to plaintiff the amount of said note and interest.

Wherefore plaintiff demands judgment against defendant for the sum of _____ dollars, interest, and costs.

Signed: _____
                              Attorney for Plaintiff
Address: _____

[CAPTION]

COMPLAINT ON AN ACCOUNT

1. [Allegation of jurisdiction]
2. Defendant owes plaintiff _____ dollars according to the account hereto annexed as Exhibit A.

Wherefore plaintiff demands judgment against defendant for the sum of _____ dollars, interest, and costs.

Signed: _____
                              Attorney for Plaintiff
Address: _____

147

[CAPTION]

COMPLAINT FOR GOODS SOLD AND DELIVERED

1. [Allegation of jurisdiction]
2. Defendant owes plaintiff _____ dollars for goods sold and delivered by plaintiff to defendant between June 1, 1936 and December 1, 1936.

Wherefore plaintiff demands judgment against defendant for the sum of _____ dollars, interest, and costs.

Signed: _____
Attorney for Plaintiff

Address: _____

[CAPTION]

COMPLAINT FOR MONEY LENT

1. [Allegation of jurisdiction]
2. Defendant owes plaintiff _____ dollars for money lent by plaintiff to defendant on June 1, 1936.

Wherefore plaintiff demands judgment against defendant for the sum of _____ dollars, interest, and costs.

Signed: _____
Attorney for Plaintiff

Address: _____

[CAPTION]

COMPLAINT FOR MONEY PAID BY MISTAKE

1. [Allegation of jurisdiction]
2. Defendant owes plaintiff _____ dollars for money paid by plaintiff to defendant by mistake on June 1, 1936, under the following circumstances: [here state the circumstances with particularity—see Rule 9(b)].

Wherefore plaintiff demands judgment against defendant for the sum of _____ dollars, interest, and costs.

Signed: _____
Attorney for Plaintiff

Address: _____

[CAPTION]

COMPLAINT FOR MONEY HAD AND RECEIVED

1. [Allegation of jurisdiction]
2. Defendant owes plaintiff _____ dollars for money had and received from one G. H. on June 1, 1936, to be paid by defendant to plaintiff.

Wherefore plaintiff demands judgment against defendant for the sum of _____ dollars, interest, and costs.

Signed: _____

Attorney for Plaintiff

Address: _____

[CAPTION]

ANSWER TO COMPLAINT FOR MONEY HAD AND RECEIVED WITH COUNTERCLAIM FOR INTERPLEADER

Defense

Defendant admits the allegations stated in paragraph 1 of the complaint; and denies the allegations stated in paragraph 2 to the extent set forth in the counterclaim herein.

Counterclaim for Interpleader

1. Defendant received the sum of _____ dollars as a deposit from E. F.

2. Plaintiff has demanded the payment of such deposit to him by virtue of an assignment of it which he claims to have received from E. F.

3. E. F. has notified the defendant that he claims such deposit, that the purported assignment is not valid, and that he holds the defendant responsible for the deposit.

Wherefore defendant demands:

(1) That the court order E. F. to be made a party defendant to respond to the complaint and to this counterclaim.[1]

(2) That the court order the plaintiff and E. F. to interplead their respective claims.

(3) That the court adjudge whether the plaintiff or E. F. is entitled to the sum of money.

(4) That the court discharge defendant from all liability in the premises except to the person it shall adjudge entitled to the sum of money.

(5) That the court award to the defendant its costs and attorney's fees.

---

[1] Rule 13(h) provides for the court ordering parties to a counterclaim, but who are not parties to the orginal action, to be brought in as defendants.

[CAPTION]

COMPLAINT FOR NEGLIGENCE

1.   [Allegation of jurisdiction]
2.   On June 1, 1936, in a public highway called Bolyston Street in Boston, Massachusetts, defendant negligently drove a motor vehicle against plaintiff who was then crossing said highway.
3.   As a result plaintiff was thrown down and had his leg broken and was otherwise injured, was prevented from transacting his business, suffered great pain of body and mind, and incurred expenses for medical attention and hospitalization in the sum of one thousand dollars.

Wherefore plaintiff demands judgment against defendant in the sum of _____ dollars and costs.

[CAPTION]

COMPLAINT FOR CONVERSION

1.   [Allegation of jurisdiction]
2.   On or about December 1, 1936, defendant converted to his own use ten bonds of the _____ Company (here insert brief identification as by number and issue) of the value of _____ dollars, the property of plaintiff.

Wherefore plaintiff demands judgment against defendant in the sum of _____ dollars, interest, and costs.

[CAPTION]

COMPLAINT FOR SPECIFIC PERFORMANCE OF CONTRACT TO CONVEY LAND

1. [Allegation of jurisdiction]

2. On or about December 1, 1936, plaintiff and defendant entered into an agreement in writing a copy of which is hereto annexed as Exhibit A.

3. In accord with the provisions of said agreement plaintiff tendered to defendant the purchase price and requested a conveyance of the land, but defendant refused to accept the tender and refused to make the conveyance.

4. Plaintiff now offers to pay the purchase price.

Wherefore plaintiff demands (1) that defendant be required specifically to perform said agreement, (2) damages in the sum of one thousand dollars, and (3) that if specific performance is not granted plaintiff have judgment against defendant in the sum of _____ dollars.

[CAPTION]

COMPLAINT ON CLAIM FOR DEBT AND TO SET ASIDE FRAUDULENT CONVEYANCE UNDER RULE 18(b)

1. [Allegation of jurisdiction]

2. Defendant C. D. on or about _____ executed and delivered to plaintiff a promissory note [in the following words and figures: (here set out the note verbatim)] ; [a copy of which is hereto annexed as Exhibit A] ; [whereby defendant C. D. promised to pay to plaintiff or order on _____ the sum of five thousand dollars with interest thereon at the rate of _____ percent per annum].

3. Defendant C. D. owes to plaintiff the amount of said note and interest.

4. Defendant C. D. on or about _____ conveyed all his property, real and personal [or specify and describe] to defendant E. F. for the purpose of defrauding plaintiff and hindering and delaying the collection of the indebtedness evidenced by the note above referred to.

Wherefore plaintiff demands:

(1) That plaintiff have judgment against defendant C. D. for _____ dollars and interest; (2) that the aforesaid conveyance to defendant E. F. be declared void and the judgment herein be declared a lien on said property; (3) that plaintiff have judgment against the defendants for costs.

[CAPTION]

MOTION TO DISMISS, PRESENTING DEFENSES OR FAILURE TO STATE A CLAIM, OF LACK OF SERVICE OF PROCESS, OF IMPROPER VENUE, AND OF LACK OF JURISDICTION UNDER RULE 12(b)

The defendant moves the court as follows:

1. To dismiss the action because the complaint fails to state a claim against defendant upon which relief can be granted.

2. To dismiss the action or in lieu thereof to quash the return of service of summons on the grounds (a) that the defendant is a corporation organized under the laws of Delaware and was not and is not subject to service of process within the Southern District of New York, and (b) that the defendant has not been properly served with process in this action, all of which more clearly appears in the affidavits of M. N. and X. Y. hereto annexed as Exhibit A and Exhibit B respectively.

3. To dismiss the action on the ground that it is in the wrong district because (a) the jurisdiction of this court is invoked solely on the ground that the action arises under the Constitution and laws of the United States and (b) the defendant is a corporation incorporated under the laws of the State of Delaware and is not licensed to do or doing business in the Southern District of New York, all of which more clearly appears in the affidavits of K. L. and V. W. hereto annexed as Exhibit C and D respectively.

4. To dismiss the action on the ground that the court lacks jurisdiction because the amount actually in controversy is less than ten thousand dollars exclusive of interest and costs.

Signed: _____

Attorney for Defendant

Address: _____

Notice of Motion

To: _____

Attorney for Plaintiff

_____

Please take notice, that the undersigned will bring the above motion on for hearing before this Court at Room _____, United States Court House, Foley Square, City of New York, on the _____ day of _____, 19__, at 10 o'clock in the forenoon of that day or as soon thereafter as counsel can be heard.

Signed: _____

Attorney for Defendant

Address: _____

[CAPTION]

ANSWER PRESENTING DEFENSES UNDER RULE 12(b)

First Defense

The complaint fails to state a claim against defendant upon which relief can be granted.

Second Defense

If defendant is indebted to plaintiffs for the goods mentioned in the complaint, he is indebted to them jointly with G. H. G. H. is alive; is a citizen of the State of New York and a resident of this district, is subject to the jurisdiction of this court, as to both service of process and venue; can be made a party without depriving this court of jurisdiction of the present parties, and has not been made a party.

Third Defense

Defendant admits the allegation contained in paragraphs 1 and 4 of the complaint; alleges that he is without knowledge or information sufficient to form a belief as to the truth of the allegations contained in paragraph 2 of the complaint; and denies each and every other allegation contained in the complaint.

Fourth Defense

The right of action set forth in the complaint did not accrue within six years next before the commencement of this action.

Counterclaim

(Here set forth any claim as a counterclaim in the manner in which a claim is pleaded in a complaint. No statement of the grounds on which the court's jurisdiction depends need be made unless the counterclaim requires independent grounds of jurisdiction.)

Cross-Claim Against Defendant M. N.

(Here set forth the claim constituting a cross-claim against defendant M. N. in the manner in which a claim is pleaded in a complaint. The statement of grounds upon which the court's jurisdiction depends need not be made unless the cross-claim requires independent grounds of jurisdiction.)

[CAPTION]

NOTICE TO TAKE ORAL DEPOSITION

TO: Defendant (or Plaintiff) _____
(name and address)

   and his attorney, _____
(name and address)

   PLEASE TAKE NOTICE that the Plaintiff, _____ ,
(name)

in the above-captioned matter, will take the depositions of the following person
at _____
(address)

_____

at the time and date set forth below, said deposition to continue from day to
day until completed. Such deposition will be taken upon oral examination for
the purpose of discovery, or as evidence, or both, pursuant to the Federal
Rules of Civil Procedure, before an officer authorized by law to administer
oaths.

   The said witness will please bring with him to the deposition, all correspondence, files, drawings, notes, reports, memoranda, documents, logs, contracts,
agreements or other writings of any kind or character relating to _____

_____ .
(the subject of the oral deposition)

   You are invited to attend and participate if you desire to do so.

Person to be Deposed   Deposition Date   Time
_____   _____   _____

By: _____

[CAPTION]

SUMMONS

To the above-named Defendant:

You are hereby summoned and required to serve upon _____, plaintiff's attorney, whose address is _____, an answer to the complaint which is herewith served upon you, within 20[1] days after service of this summons upon you, exclusive of the day of service. If you fail to do so, judgment by default will be taken against you for the relief demanded in the complaint.

_____,

Clerk of Court

[Seal of the U. S. District Court]

Dated _____

---

[1] If the United States or an officer or agency thereof is a defendant, the time to be inserted as to it is 60 days.

[CAPTION]

SUMMONS AGAINST THIRD-PARTY DEFENDANT

A. B., Plaintiff

      v.

C. D., Defendant and

Third-Party Plaintiff   *Summons*

      v.

E. F., Third-Party

   Defendant

To the above-named Third-Party Defendant:

You are hereby summoned and required to serve upon _____, plaintiff's attorney whose address is _____, and upon _____, who is attorney for C. D., defendant and third-party plaintiff, and whose address is _____, an answer to the third-party complaint which is herewith served upon you within 20 days after the service of this summons upon you exclusive of the day of service. If you fail to do so, judgment by default will be taken against you for the relief demanded in the third-party complaint. There is also served upon you herewith a copy of the complaint of the plaintiff which you may but are not required to answer.

_____,

Clerk of Court

[Seal of District Court]

Dated _____

[CAPTION]

COMPLAINT AGAINST THIRD-PARTY DEFENDANT

A. B., Plaintiff

v.

C. D., Defendant and
Third-Party Plaintiff   *Third-Party Complaint.*

v.

E. F., Third-Party
  Defendant

1.   Plaintiff A. B. has filed against defendant C. D. a complaint, a copy of which is hereto attached as "Exhibit A."

2.   (Here state the grounds upon which C. D. is entitled to recover from E. F., all or part of what A. B. may recover from C. D. The statement should be framed as in an original complaint.)

Wherefore C. D. demands judgment against third-party defendant E. F. for all sums[1] that may be adjudged against defendant C. D. in favor of plaintiff A. B.

Signed: _____

Attorney for C. D.,
Third-Party Plaintiff

Address: _____

---

[1] Make appropriate change where C. D. is entitled to only partial recovery-over against E. F.

[CAPTION]

MOTION TO BRING IN THIRD-PARTY DEFENDANT

Defendant moves for leave, as third-party plaintiff, to cause to be served upon E. F. a summons and third-party complaint, copies of which are hereto attached as Exhibit X.

Signed: _____
                                        Attorney for Defendant C. D.

Address: _____

Notice of Motion

To: _____
            Attorney for Plaintiff

_____

Please take notice, that the undersigned will bring the above motion on for hearing before this Court at Room _____, United States Court House, Foley Square, City of New York, on the _____ day of _____, 19___, at 10 o'clock in the forenoon of that day or as soon thereafter as counsel can be heard.

Signed: _____
                                    Attorney for Defendant

Address: _____

[CAPTION]

REQUEST FOR PRODUCTION OF DOCUMENTS, ETC., UNDER RULE 34

Plaintiff A. B. requests defendant C. D. to respond within _____ days to the following requests:

(1) That defendant produce and permit plaintiff to inspect and to copy each of the following documents:

(Here list the documents either individually or by category and describe each of them.)

(Here state the time, place, and manner of making the inspection and performance of any related acts.)

(2) That defendant produce and permit plaintiff to inspect and to copy, test, or sample each of the following objects:

(Here list the objects either individually or by category and describe each of them.)

(Here state the time, place, and manner of making the inspection and performance of any related acts.)

(3) That defendant permit plaintiff to enter (here describe property to be entered) and to inspect and to photograph, test, or sample (here describe the portion of the real property and the objects to be inspected).

(Here state the time, place, and manner of making the inspection and performance of any related acts.)

Signed: _____
                    Attorney for Plaintiff

Address: _____

[CAPTION]

REQUEST FOR ADMISSION UNDER RULE 36

Plaintiff A. B. requests defendant C. D. within _____ days after service of this request to make the following admissions for the purpose of this action only and subject to all pertinent objections to admissibility which may be interposed at the trial:

1. That each of the following documents, exhibited with this request, is genuine.

(Here list the documents and describe each document.)

2. That each of the following statements is true.

(Here list the statements.)

Signed: _____
                      Attorney for Plaintiff

Address: _____

[CAPTION]

JUDGMENT ON JURY VERDICT

This action came on for trial before the Court and a jury, Honorable John Marshall, District Judge, presiding, and the issues having been duly tried and the jury having duly rendered its verdict,

It is Ordered and Adjudged

[that the plaintiff A. B. recover of the defendant C. D. the sum of _____, with interest thereon at the rate of _____ per cent as provided by law, and his costs of action.]

[that the plaintiff take nothing, that the action be dismissed on the merits, and that the defendant C. D. recover of the plaintiff A. B. his costs of action.]

Dated at New York, New York, this _____ day of _____, 19___.

_____,
                           Clerk of Court

[CAPTION]

JUDGMENT ON DECISION BY THE COURT

This action came on for [trial] [hearing] before the Court, Honorable John Marshall, District Judge, presiding, and the issues having been duly [tried] [heard] and a decision having been duly rendered,

It is Ordered and Adjudged

[that the plaintiff A. B. recover of the defendant C. D. the sum of _____, with interest thereon at the rate of _____ per cent as provided by law, and his costs of action.]

[that the plaintiff take nothing, that the action be dismissed on the merits, and that the defendant C. D. recover of the plaintiff A. B. his costs of action.]

Dated at New York, New York, this _____ day of _____, 19___.

_____,
Clerk of Court

AFFIDAVITS

General forms of affidavits

State of _____,
County of _____, Sct.

E. F., after being first duly sworn, makes this his affidavit and states: [allegations].

This [date]

[Signature of affiant]

The foregoing was subscribed and sworn to before me by E. F. this [date].

(SEAL)

G. H., Notary Public
My commission expires [date].

Alternate form

State of _____,
County of _____, ss.

E. F., being first duly sworn, says that _____ [allegations].

Sworn to before me and subscribed in my presence by E. F. this _____ day of _____, 19___.

(SEAL)

G. H., Notary Public
My commission expires [date].

Specimen form of affidavit in legal proceeding

[CAPTION]

Affidavit of E. F.

State of _____,
County of _____, Sct.

E. F., being first duly sworn, makes this his affidavit and states: [allegations].

[Signature of affiant]

The foregoing was subscribed and sworn to before me by E. F. this _____ day of _____, 19___.

(SEAL)

G. H., Notary Public
My commission expires [date].

ABBREVIATIONS

A

a., an., or **anon.** anonymous

A. [2d] Atlantic Reporter [second series]

A.B.A. or **ABA** American Bar Association

ABA-ALI American Bar Association-American Law Institute

Abb. N. Cas. Abbott's New Cases (New York)

Abb. Pr. [n.s.] Abbott's Practice Reports [new series] (New York)

abr. abridged; abridgement

A.B.R. Army Board of Review

acc'g accounting

acct. account

A.C.M.R. Army Court of Military Review

A.D. [2d] Appellate Division Reports [second series] (New York)

Ad. L. [2d] Administration Law Reporter [second]

Adm. Admiralty Court; Admiralty Division

adm'r administrator

adm'x administratrix

AEC Atomic Energy Commission

A.E.C. Atomic Energy Commission; Atomic Energy Commission Reports

A.F.B.R. Air Force Board of Review

A.F.C.M.R. Air Force Court of Military Review

aff'd affirmed

aff'g affirming

A.F. JAG L. REV. Air Force JAG Law Review

Agric. Dec. Agricultural Decisions

Aik. Aikens' Reports (Vermont Supreme Court)

Ala. Alabama; Alabama Reports (Supreme Court)

Ala. Acts Acts of Alabama

Ala. App. Alabama Appellate Court Reports

Ala. Code Code of Alabama

Alaska Sess. Laws Alaska Session Laws

Alaska Stat. Alaska Statutes

A.L.I. or **ALI** American Law Institute

All State Sales Tax Rep. All State Sales Tax Reporter

Am. America; American

amend. amendment

amends. amendments

Am. Jur. [2d] American Jurisprudence [second edition]

Am. Stock Ex. Guide American Stock Exchange Guide

an. anonymous

ann. annotated

ANNALS Annals of the American Academy of Political and Social Science

anon. anonymous

Antitrust & Trade Reg. Rep. Antitrust & Trade Regulation Report

app. appendix

App. D.C. Appeal Cases, District of Columbia

App. Dep't Appellate Department

App. Div. Appellate Division; Supreme Court, Appellate Division

apps. appendixes

App. T. Supreme Court, Appellate Term

App. Term Appellate Term

arb. arbitrator

Ariz. Arizona; Arizona Reports (Supreme Court)

Ariz. App. Arizona Appeals Reports

Ariz. Legis. Serv. Arizona Legislative Service

Ariz. Rev. Stat. Ann. Arizona Revised Statutes Annotated

Ariz. Sess. Laws Session Laws, Arizona

Ark. Arkansas; Arkansas Reports

Ark. Acts General Acts of Arkansas

Ark. Stat. Ann. Arkansas Statutes Annotated

art. article

arts. articles

AS, A/S, or **A/s** account sales; after sight; at sight

ASCAP American Society of Composers, Authors and Publishers

ASCAP Copyright L. Symp. Copyright Law Symposium (American Society of Composers, Authors and Publishers)

A.S. Code American Samoa Code

Ass'n Association

Assoc. Associate

Atl. Atlantic

Atom. En. L. Rep. Atomic Energy Law Reporter

Auth. Authority

Auto. Automobile

Auto. Cas. [2d] Automobile Cases [second]

Auto. Ins. Cas. Automobile Insurance Cases

Auto. L. Rep. Automobile Law Reporter

Av. Cases Aviation Cases

Ave. Avenue

Av. L. Rep. Aviation Law Reporter

B

B. Baron; British

Bankr. L. Rep. Bankruptcy Law Reporter

Barb. Barbour's Supreme Court Reports (New York)

Barb. Ch. Barbour's Chancery Reports (New York)

B.C. Bail Court; Bankruptcy Cases; before Christ; British Columbia

BCA or **B.C.A.** Board of Contract Appeals; Board of Contract Appeals Decisions

Bd. Board

Bhd. Brotherhood

Binn. Binney's Reports (Pennsylvania Supreme Court)

bk. bank; block; book

bks. banks; blocks; books

Blackf. Blackford's Reports (Indiana Supreme Court)

bldg. building

Blue Sky L. Rep. Blue Sky Law Reporter

B.R. or **BR** Board of Review

Bradf. Bradford's Reports (Iowa Supreme Court)

Brayt. Brayton's Reports (Vermont Supreme Court)

Bros. Brothers

B.T.A. United States Board of Tax Appeals

B.T.A.M. Board of Tax Appeals Memorandum Decisions

Bur. Burnett's Reports (Wisconsin Supreme Court)

C

c. or **ct.** cent

C. Chancellor

C.A.A. Civil Aeronautics Authority

CAB or **C.A.B.** Civil Aeronautics Board; Civil Aeronautics Board Reports

C.A.F. cost and freight

Cai. Cas. Caines' Cases in Error (New York)

Cai. R. Caines' Reports (New York)

Cal. [2d; 3d] California Reports [second, third series]

Cal. Adv. Legis. Serv. California Advance Legislative Service (Deering)

Cal. App. Supp. [2d; 3d] California Appellate Reports Supplement [second, third supplement]

Cal. [subject] * **Code Ann. (Deering)** Deering's Annotated California Code

Cal. [subject] * **Code Ann. (West)** West's Annotated California Code

* [Subject Abbreviations]

Bus. & Prof. Business and Professions

Civ. Civil

Civ. Proc. Civil Procedure

Com. Commercial

Corp. Corporations

Educ. Education

Elec. Elections

Evid. Evidence

Fin. Financial

Fish & Game Fish & Game

Food & Agric. Food & Agricultural

Gov't Government

Harb. & Nav. Harbors & Navigation

Health & Safety Health & Safety

Ins. Insurance

Lab. Labor

Mil. & Vet. Military & Veterans

Penal Penal

Prob. Probate

Pub. Res. Public Resources

Pub. Util. Public Utilities

Rev. & Tax. Revenue & Taxation

Sts. & Hy. Streets & Highways

U. Com. Uniform Commercial

Unemp. Ins. Unemployment Insurance

Veh. Vehicle

Water Water

Welf. & Inst. Welfare & Institutions

Cal. Gen. Laws Ann. Deering's California General Laws Annotated

Calif. L. Rev. California Law Review

Cal. Legis. Serv. California Legislative Service (West)

Cal. Rptr. West's California Reporter

Cal. Stats. Statutes of California

Cal. Unrep. California Unreported Cases

cas. casualty

ca. sa. capias ad satisfaciendum (*a writ of execution*)

c.a.v. curia advisari vult (*the court will be advised*)

c.b. common bench; chief baron

C.B. Cumulative Bulletin

C.C. Circuit Court (old Federal); United States Circuit Courts

C.C.P.A. (United States) Court of Customs and Patent Appeals

cent. central

cf. confer (*compare*)

c. & f. cost and freight

c.f.i. or **C.F.I.** cost, freight, and insurance

ch. chaplain; chapter; check; chief; child; children; church

Ch. Chancery; Chancery Court; Chancery Division

Chand. Chandler's Reports (Wisconsin Supreme Court)

chem. chemical

Child. Ct. Children's Court

chs. chapters

c.i.f. or **C.I.F.** price covers the cost of goods, insurance, and freight

Cir. Circuit Court of Appeals (federal); Court of Appeals (federal)

Cir. Ct. Circuit Court (state)

Cir. Ct. App. Circuit Court of Appeal (state)

City Civ. Ct. Act New York City Civil Court Act (29A)

City Crim. Ct. Act New York City Criminal Court Act (29A)

Civ. App. Civil Appeals

Civ. Ct. Rec. Civil Court of Record

C.J. Chief Judge; Chief Justice

C.J.S. Corpus Juris Secundum

cl. clause

C.L. Civil Law

Cl. Ch. Clarke's Chancery Reports (New York)

cls. clauses

C.M.A. Court of Military Appeals

C.M.R. Court-Martial Reports; Court of Military Review

c/o care of

Co. Company

COD or **C.O.D.** cash on delivery; collect on delivery

Code Crim. Proc. Code of Criminal Procedure (66) (New York)

Cole. & Cai. Cas. Coleman & Caines' Cases (New York)

Cole. Cas. Coleman's Cases (New York)

Colo. Colorado; Colorado Reports (Supreme Court)

Colo. App. Colorado Court of Appeal Reports

Colo. Rev. Stat. Colorado Revised Statutes

Colo. Sess. Laws Colorado Session Laws

comm. committee

Comm. Ct. United States Commerce Court

Comm. Fut. L. Rep. Commodity Futures Law Reporter

Comm'n Commission

Comm'r Commissioner

Commw. Ct. Commonwealth Court

comp. compilation; compiled

Comp. Gen. Decision of the Comptroller General

Condit. Sale–Chat. Mort. Rep. Conditional Sale–Chattel Mortgage Reporter

Conn. Connecticut; Connecticut Reports (Supreme Court of Errors)

Conn. Cir. Ct. Connecticut Circuit Court Reports

Conn. Gen. Stat. General Statutes of Connecticut

Conn. Gen. Stat. Ann. Connecticut General Statutes Annotated

Conn. Legis. Serv. Connecticut Legislative Service

Conn. Pub. Acts Connecticut Public Acts

Conn. Supp. Connecticut Supplement

Cons. Cred. Guide Consumer Credit Guide

consol. consolidated

consols. consolidated annuities

constr. construction

Cont. Cas. Fed. Contract Cases Federal

Conv. [n.s.] Conveyancer & Property Lawyer [new series]

coop. cooperative

Copy. Dec. Copyright Decisions

Corp. Corporation

Corp. Guide Corporation Guide

Corp. L. Guide Corporation Law Guide

Cost Acc'g Stand. Guide Cost Accounting Standards Guide

County Ct. County Court

County J. Ct. County Judge's Court

Cow. Cowen's Reports (New York)

C.P. common pleas; Court of Common Pleas

C.P.A. Certified Public Accountant

c.r. chancery reports; curia regis (*the king's court*)

Crim. App. Court of Criminal Appeals; Criminal Appeals

crim. con. criminal conversation

Crim. L. Rep. Criminal Law Reporter

C.S.C. Civil Service Commission

ct. cent

c.t.a. cum testamento annexo (*with the will annexed*)

Ct. App. Court of Appeals (state)

Ct. Cl. United States Court of Claims

Ct. Cl. Act Court of Claims Act (29A) (New York)

Ct. Cust. App. Court of Customs Appeals

Ct. Err. & App. Court of Errors and Appeals

Ct. Gen. Sess. Court of General Sessions

Ct. Spec. Sess. Court of Special Sessions

Current Med. Current Medicine for Attorneys

Cust. B. & Dec. Customs Bulletin and Decisions

Cust. Ct. Customs Court

cwt. hundredweight

C.Z. Code Canal Zone Code

D

D. District (state); District Court (federal)

Dall. Dallas' Reports (Pennsylvania Supreme Court)

Day Day's Reports (Connecticut Supreme Court of Errors)

d.b.a. or **d/b/a** doing business as

D.C. District Court; District of Columbia

D.C. Cir. United States Court of Appeals for the District of Columbia

D.C. Code Ann. District of Columbia Code Annotated

D.C. Code Encycl. District of Columbia Code Encyclopedia

D.C. Code Legis. & Ad. Serv. D.C. Code Legislative and Administrative Service (West)

D.C. (Cranch) District of Columbia Reports (Cranch)

D. Chip. D. Chipman's Reports (Vermont Supreme Court)

D.C. (MacArth.) District of Columbia Reports (MacArthur)

D.C. (MacArth. & M.) District of Columbia Reports (MacArthur and Mackey)

D.C. (Mackey) District of Columbia Reports (Mackey)

D.C. (Tuck. & Cl.) District of Columbia Reports (Tucker and Clephane)

dec. decision

Dec. Com. Pat. Patents Decisions of the Commissioner and of U.S. Courts

Dec. Fed. Mar. Comm'n Decisions of the Federal Maritime Commission

decs. decisions

Dec. U.S. Mar. Comm'n Decision of the United States Maritime Commission

Del. Delaware; Delaware Reports (Court of Errors and Appeals)

Del. (Boyce) Delaware Reports (Boyce)

Del. Cas. Delaware Cases

Del. Ch. Delaware Chancery Reports

Del. Code Ann. Delaware Code Annotated

Del. (Harr.) Delaware Reports (Harrington)

Del. (Hous.) Delaware Reports (Houston)

Dell. Dellam's Opinions (Texas Supreme Court)

Del. Laws Laws of Delaware

Del. (Marv.) Delaware Reports (Marvel)

Del. (Penne.) Delaware Reports (Pennewill)

dem. demise

Denio Denio's Reports (New York)

Dep't or **Dept.** Department

Dep't State Bull. United States Department of State Bulletin

dev. development

dies non dies non juridicus (*not a court day*)

Dig. Digest

Dist. District

Dist. Ct. District Court (state)

Dist. Ct. App. District Court of Appeal

distrib. distribute; distributing

Div. Division

D.J. District Judge

Dom. Proc. or **D.P.** Domus Procerum (*House of Lords*)

Doug. Douglas' Reports (Michigan Supreme Court)

D.P. Also **Dom. Proc.** Domus Procerum (*House of Lords*)

dr. debtor

Dr. Doctor

Duq. Duquesne

d.w.i. died without issue; driving while under the influence

E

E. East; Eastern

econ. economic; economics; economy

Econ. Cont. Economic Controls

ed. edition; editor

educ. education; educational

Edw. Ch. Edward's Chancery Reports (New York)

EEOC or **E.E.O.C.** Equal Employment Opportunity Commission

EEOC Compl. Man. Equal Employment Opportunity Commission Compliance Manual

e.g. exempli gratia (*for example*)

elec. electric; electricity; electronic; electronics

Emer. Ct. App. United States Emergency Court of Appeals

Empl. Comp. App. Bd. Decisions of the Employees' Compensation Appeals Board

Empl. Prac. Dec. Employment Practices Decisions

Empl. Prac. Guide Employment Practices Guide

Eng. England; English

Eng'r Engineer; Engineering

Envir. Rep. Environment Reporter

envt'l environmental

e.o.e. errors and omissions excepted

Eq. Equity Court; Equity Division

equip. equipment

est. established; estimate; estimated

Est. Estate; Estates

et al. et alii (*and others*)

etc. et cetera (*and so forth*)

et seq. et sequentia (*and the following*)

et ux. et uxor (*and wife*)

Exch. Exchange

Ex'r Executor

Ex'x Executrix

F

F. Forum

F. [2d] Federal Reporter [second series]

FAA or **F.A.A.** Federal Aviation Administration

Fair Empl. Prac. Cas. Fair Employment Practices Cases

fam. family

Fam. Ct. Family Court

Fam. Ct. Act Family Court Act (29A) (New York)
Fam. L. Rep. Family Law Reporter
f.a.s. free alongside ship
F. Cas. Federal Cases
FCC or **F.C.C.** Federal Communications Commission; Federal Communication Commission Reports
FDA or **F.D.A.** Food and Drug Administration
Fed. Federal
Fed. Banking L. Rep. Federal Banking Law Reporter
Fed. Carr. Cas. Federal Carriers Cases
Fed. Carr. Rep. Federal Carriers Reporter
Fed. Est. Gift Tax Rep. Federal Estate and Gift Tax Reporter
Fed. Ex. Tax. Rep. Federal Excise Tax Reporter
Fed'n Federation
Fed. Res. Bull. Federal Reserve Bulletin
Fed. Sec. L. Rep. Federal Securities Law Reporter
Fed. Taxes Federal Taxes
Fed. Taxes: Est. & Gift Federal Taxes: Estate and Gift Taxes
Fed. Taxes: Excise Federal Taxes: Excise Taxes
fi. fa. fieri facias (*a writ of execution*)
fin. finance
Fire & Casualty Cas. Fire & Casualty Cases
Fla. Florida; Florida Reports (Supreme Court)
Fla. Laws Laws of Florida
Fla. Sess. Law Serv. Florida Session Law Service
Fla. Stat. Florida Statutes (1975)
Fla. Stat. Ann. Florida Statutes

Annotated (West)
Fla. Supp. Florida Supplement
F.O.B. or **f.o.b.** free on board
fol. folio
fols. folios
Food Drug Cos. L. Rep. Food Drug Cosmetic Law Reporter
for. forensic
fort. fortnightly
FORUM The Forum
FPC or **F.P.C.** Federal Power Commission; Federal Power Commission Reports
F.R.D. Federal Rule Decisions
F. Supp. Federal Supplement
F.T.C. Federal Trade Commission; Federal Trade Commission Decision

G

Ga. Georgia; Georgia Reports (Supreme Court)
Ga. App. Georgia Appeals Reports
Ga. Code Code of Georgia (1975)
Ga. Code Ann. Code of Georgia Annotated
Ga. Laws Georgia (session) Laws
GAO or **G.A.O.** General Accounting Office
gdn. guardian
Gen. General
Geo. Georgetown
Geo. Wash. George Washington
Gill Gill's Reports (Maryland Court of Appeals)
G. & J. Gill's and Johnson's Reports (Maryland Court of Appeals)
G. L. General Laws
Gonz. Gonzaga
Gov't Government
Gov't Cont. Rep. Government Contracts Reporter
Gov't Empl. Rel. Rep. Government Employee Relations Report

Greene Greene's Reports (Iowa Supreme Court)

GSA or **G.S.A.** General Services Administration

Guam Civ. Code Guam Civil Code

Guam Code Civ. Pro. Guam Code of Civil Procedure

Guam Gov't Code Guam Government Code

Guam Prob. Code Guam Probate Code

guar. guaranty

H

h.a. hoc anno (*this year; in this year*)

Harv. Harvard

Haw. Hawaii; Hawaii Reports (Supreme Court)

Haw. Rev. Stat. Hawaii Revised Statutes

Haw. Sess. Laws Session Laws of Hawaii

H.B. House Bill

h.c. habeas corpus (*you have the body*)

H.C. House of Commons

H. & G. Harris' & Gill's Reports (Maryland Court of Appeals)

Hill Hill's Reports (New York)

Hill & Den. Hill and Denio Supplement (Lalor) (New York)

hist. historical; history

H. & J. Harris' and Johnson's Reports (Maryland Court of Appeals)

H.L. House of Lords

H. & McH. Harris' and McHenry's Reports (Maryland Court of Appeals)

Hoff. Ch. Hoffman's Chancery Reports (New York)

Hopk. Ch. Hopkins' Chancery Reports (New York)

hosp. hospital

hous. housing

Hous. Houston

Hous. & Dev. Rep. Housing & Development Reporter

How. Howard

How. Pr. [n.s.] Howard's Practice Reports [new series] (New York)

H.R. House of Representatives

h.v. hoc verbo or hac voce (*this word* or *under this word*)

I

ib., ibid., or **id.** ibidem (*in the same place*)

I.C.C. Indian Claims Commission; Interstate Commerce Commission; Interstate Commerce Commission Reports

I.C.C. Valuation Rep. Interstate Commerce Commission Valuation Reports

Idaho Idaho Reports (Supreme Court)

Idaho Sess. Laws Idaho Session Laws

i.e. id est (*that is*)

Ill. [2d] Illinois Reports [second series] , Supreme Court

Ill. Ann. Stat. Smith-Hurd Illinois Annotated Statutes

Ill. App. [2d; 3d] Illinois Appellate Court Reports [second, third series]

Ill. (Bresse) Illinois Reports (Bresse)

Ill. Ct. Cl. Illinois Court of Claims Reports

Ill. (Gilm) Illinois Reports (Gilman)

Ill. Laws Laws of Illinois (Session Laws)

Ill. Legis. Serv. Illinois Legislative Service (West)

Ill. Rev. Stat. Illinois Revised Statutes (1973; Supplement 1974)

Ill. (Scam.) Illinois Reports (Scammon)

inc. income; incorporated

Inc. Incorporated

Ind. Indiana; Indiana Reports (Supreme Court)

Ind. Acts Indiana Acts (Session Laws)

Ind. App. Indiana Court of Appeals Reports

Ind. Code Indiana Code (1971)

Ind. Code Ann. Burns' Indiana Statutes Annotated Code Edition

I. & N. Dec. Immigration and Naturalization Administrative Decisions

indem. indemnity

Ind. Rel. Industrial Relations

indus. industrial; industries; industry

Ins. Insurance

Inst. Institute; Institution

Insur. L. Rep. Insurance Law Reporter

Interior Dec. Decisions of the Department of the Interior

int'l international

intra. intramural

inv. investment

IOU I owe you

Iowa Iowa Reports (Supreme Court)

Iowa Acts Acts and Joint Resolutions of the State of Iowa

Iowa Code Code of Iowa (1971)

Iowa Code Ann. Iowa Code Annotated

Iowa Legis. Serv. Iowa Legislative Service (West)

Ir. Irish

I.R.C. Internal Revenue Code of 1954

IRS or **I.R.S.** Internal Revenue Service

J

J. Journal; Judge; Justice

J.A. Judge Advocate

JAG Judge Advocate General

JAG J. JAG Journal

J. Am. Soc'y C.L.U. Journal of American Society of Chartered Life Underwriters

J. Crim. L. C. & P.S. Journal of Criminal Law, Criminology, and Police Science

JJ. Judges; Justices

J. Mar. John Marshall

Johns. Johnson's Reports (New York)

Johns. Cas. Johnson's Cases (New York)

Johns. Ch. Johnson's Chancery Reports (New York)

J.P. Ct. Justice of the Peace's Court

jud. judicature

JUDICATURE Judicature

jur. juridical; jurist

Juris. Jurisprudence

Just. Justice

Just. Ct. Act Justice Court Act (29A) (New York)

Just. P. Justice of the Peace and Local Government Review

juv. juvenile

Juv. Ct. Juvenile Court

K

Kan. Kansas; Kansas Reports (Supreme Court)

Kan. Civ. Pro. Stat. Ann. Kansas Code of Civil Procedure

Kan. Crim. Code & Code of Crim. Proc. Kansas Criminal Code and Code of Criminal Procedure (Vernon)

Kan. Sess. Laws Session Laws of Kansas

Kan. Stat. Kansas Statutes (Supplement 1975)

Kan. U.C.C. Ann. Vernon's Kansas Statutes Annotated Uniform Commercial Code

K.B. King's Bench

K.C. King's Counsel

Ky. Kentucky; Kentucky Reports (Supreme Court, formerly Court of Appeals)

Ky. Acts Kentucky Acts (Session Laws)

Ky. (A.K. Marsh.) Kentucky Reports (A.K. Marshall)

Ky. (Bibb) Kentucky Reports (Bibb)

Ky. (B. Mon.) Kentucky Reports (Ben Monroe)

Ky. (Bush) Kentucky Reports (Bush)

Ky. (Dana) Kentucky Reports (Dana)

Ky. (Duv.) Kentucky Reports (Duvall)

Ky. (Hard.) Kentucky Reports (Hardin)

Ky. (Hughes) Kentucky Reports (Hughes)

Ky. (J.J. Marsh.) Kentucky Reports (J.J. Marshall)

Ky. (Litt.) Kentucky Reports (Littell)

Ky. (Met.) Kentucky Reports (Metcalf)

Ky. Rev. Stat. Kentucky Revised Statutes (1970)

Ky. Rev. Stat. Ann. Baldwin's Kentucky Revised Statutes Annotated

Ky. Rev. Stat. & Rules Serv. Kentucky Revised Statutes and Rules Service

Ky. (Sneed) Kentucky Reports (Sneed)

Ky. (T.B. Monroe) Kentucky Reports (T.B. Monroe)

L

L. Law; *Long Quinto* (one of the parts of the Year Books).

La. Louisiana; Louisiana Reports (Supreme Court)

L.A. Los Angeles

La. Acts State of Louisiana: Acts of the Legislature

La. Ann. Louisiana Annual Reports (Supreme Court)

La. App. Louisiana Courts of Appeal Reports

lab. labor

Lab. Arb. Awards Labor Arbitration Awards

Lab. Arb. & Disp. Settl. Labor Arbitration and Dispute Settlements

Lab. Arb. Serv. Labor Arbitration Service

Lab. Cas. Labor Cases

Lab. L. Rep. Labor Law Reporter

Lab. Rel. Rep. Labor Relations Reporter

La. Civ. Code Ann. West's Louisiana Civil Code Annotated

La. Code Civ. Pro. Ann. West's Louisiana Code of Civil Procedure Annotated

La. Code Crim. Pro. Ann. West's Louisiana Code of Criminal Procedure Annotated

Lans. Lansing's Reports (New York Supreme Court, Appellate Division)

La. Rev. Stat. Ann. West's Louisiana Revised Statutes Annotated

La. Sess. Law Serv. Louisiana Session Law Service

law. lawyer

Law. & Banker Lawyer and Banker and Central Law Journal

L.C. Leading Cases; Lord Chancellor; Lower Canada

L. Ct. Law Court

L. Div. Law Division

legis. legislation; legislative; legislature

L.F. Law French

liab. liability

lib. library

Life Cas. [2d.] Life (Health, Accident) Cases [second]

L.J. Law Journal; Law Judge; Lord Justice

ll. laws

L.L. Law Latin

LL.B. bachelor of law

LL.D. doctor of law

LL.M. master of law

Lock. Rev. Cas. Lockwood's Reversed Cases (New York)

Loy. Loyola

Loy. Chi. L. J. Loyola University of Chicago Law Journal

Loy L.A. L. Rev. Loyola University of Los Angeles Law Review

Loy L. Rev. Loyola Law Review (New Orleans)

L.R. Law Reports

L.R.R.M. Labor Relations Reference Manual

L.S. locus sigilli (*the place of the seal*)

Ltd. Limited

l.w. low water

M

mach. machine; machinery

Magis. Ct. Magistrate's Court

Man. Manhattan

mar. maritime

Marq. Marquette

marr. marriage

Mart. [n.s.] Martin's Louisiana Term Reports [new series] (Louisiana Supreme Court)

Mass. Massachusetts; Massachusetts Reports (Supreme Judicial Report)

Mass. Acts Acts and Resolves of Massachusetts

Mass. Adv. Legis. Serv. Massachusetts Advance Legislative Service (Lawyers Co-op)

Mass. Adv. Sh. Massachusetts Supreme Judicial Court Advance Sheets

Mass. (Allen) Massachusetts Reports (Allen)

Mass. Ann. Laws Annotated Laws of Massachusetts (Michie/Law. Co-op)

Mass. App. Ct. Massachusetts Appeals Court Reports

Mass. App. Ct. Adv. Sh. Massachusetts Appeals Court Advance Sheets

Mass. App. Dec. Appellate Decisions (Appellate Division of Massachusetts District Courts)

Mass. App. Div. Appellate Division Reports (Appellate Division of Massachusetts District Courts)

Mass. (Cush.) Massachusetts Reports (Cushing)

Mass. Gen. Laws Ann. Massachusetts General Laws Annotated (West)

Mass. (Gray) Massachusetts Reports (Gray)

Mass. (Met.) Massachusetts Reports (Metcalf)

Mass. (Pick.) Massachusetts Reports (Pickering)

M.C.C. Motor Carrier Cases

McCahon McCahon's Reports (Kansas Supreme Court)

McGl. McGloin's Louisiana Court of Appeals Reports

Md. Maryland; Maryland Reports (Court of Appeals)

M.D. Doctor of Medicine; Middle District

Md. Ann. Code Annotated Code of Maryland (1957)

Md. App. Maryland Appellate Reports

Md. [subject] * **Code Ann.** Annotated Code of Maryland
*[Subject Abbreviations]

Agric. Agriculture (1974)

Bus. Reg. Business Regulation

Com. Law Commercial Law (1975)

Corp. & Ass'ns Corporations and Associations (1975)

Crim. Law Criminal Law

Cts. & Jud. Proc. Courts and Judicial Proceedings (1974)

Educ. Education

Elec. Elections

Est. & Trusts Estates and Trusts (1974)

Fam. Law Family Law

Gen. Prov. General Provisions

Local Gov't Local Government

Nat. Res. Natural Resources (1974)

Occ. & Prof. Occupations and Professions

Pub. Health Public Health

Pub. Safety Public Safety

Real Prop. Real Property (1974)

Soc. Serv. Social Services

State Gov't State Government

Tax. & Rev. Taxation and Revenue

Transp. Transportation

Me. Maine; Maine Reports (Supreme Judicial Court)

Me. Acts Acts, Resolves, and Constitutional Resolutions of the State of Maine

med. mediator; medical; medicine

Melb. Melbourne

Me. Legis. Serv. Maine Legislative Service

Mem. Memphis

Me. Rev. Stat. Maine Revised Statutes

m.f.b.m. 1,000 feet board measure

Mfr. Manufacturer

Mich. Michigan; Michigan Reports (Supreme Court)

Mich. App. Michigan Appeals Reports

Mich. Comp. Laws Michigan Compiled Laws (1970)

Mich. Comp. Laws Ann. Michigan Compiled Laws Annotated

Mich. Legis. Serv. Michigan Legislative Service (West)

Mich. Pub. Acts Public and Local Acts of the State of Michigan

Mich. Stat. Ann. Michigan Statutes Annotated

mil. military

min. mineral

Minn. Minnesota; Minnesota Reports (Supreme Court)

Minn. Laws Laws of Minnesota (Session Laws)

Minn. Sess. Law Serv. Minnesota Session Law Service (West)

Minn. Stat. Minnesota Statutes

Minn. Stat. Ann. Minnesota Statutes Annotated (West)

Minor Minor's Reports (Alabama Supreme Court)

Misc. [2d] New York Miscellaneous Reports [second series]

Miss. Mississippi; Mississippi Reports (Supreme Court)

Miss. Code Ann. Mississippi Code Annotated (1972)

Miss. (Howard) Howard's Reports (Mississippi Supreme Court)

Miss. Laws General Laws of Mississippi (Session Laws)

Miss. (S. & M.) Smedes' and Marshall's Reports (Mississippi Supreme Court)

Miss. (Walker) Walker's Reports (Mississippi Supreme Court)

M.J. Military Justice Reports

mkt. market

mkts. markets

Mo. Missouri; Missouri Reports (Supreme Court)

Mo. Ann. Stat. Vernon's Annotated Missouri Statutes

Mo. App. Missouri Appeals Reports

mod. modern

Mo. Laws Laws of Missouri (Session Laws)

Mo. Legis. Serv. Missouri Legislative Service (Vernon)

Mont. Montana; Montana Reports (Supreme Court)

Mont. Laws Laws of Montana (Session Laws)

Mont. Rev. Codes Ann. Revised Codes of Montana Annotated

Mo. Rev. Stat. Missouri Revised Statutes

Morris Morris' Reports (Iowa Supreme Court)

M.R. Master of the Rolls

ms. manuscript

M.T. Michaelmas Term

Mun. Municipal

Mun. Ct. Municipal Court

Mut. Mutual

Mut. Funds Guide Mutual Funds Guide

N

n. natus (*born*); note

N. North; Northern

n.a. non allocatur (*it is not allowed*)

NASA or **N.A.S.A.** National Aeronautics and Space Administration

nat. natural

Nat'l National

n.b. nota bene (*note well*); nulla bona (*no goods*)

N.B.R. Navy Board of Review

N.C. North Carolina; North Carolina Reports (Supreme Court)

N.C. Adv. Legis. Serv. North Carolina Advance Legislative Service (Michie)

N.C. App. North Carolina Court of Appeals Reports

N.C. (Busb.) North Carolina Reports (Busbee's Law)

N.C. (Busb. Eq.) North Carolina Reports (Busbee's Equity)

N.C. (Cam. & Nor.) North Carolina Reports (Conference by Cameron & Norwood)

N.C. (Car. L. Rep.) North Carolina Reports (Carolina Law Repository)

N.C. (Dev.) North Carolina Reports (Devereux's Law)

N.C. (Dev. & Bat.) North Carolina Reports (Devereux & Battle's Law)

N.C. (Dev. & Bat. Eq.) North Carolina Reports (Devereux & Battle's Equity)

N.C. (Dev. Eq.) North Carolina Reports (Devereux's Equity)

N.C. Gen. Stat. General Statutes of North Carolina

N.C. (Hawks) North Carolina Reports (Hawks)

N.C. (Hayw.) North Carolina Reports (Haywood)

N. Chip. N. Chipman's Reports (Vermont Supreme Court)

N.C. (Ired.) North Carolina Reports (Iredell's Law)

N.C. (Ired. Eq.) North Carolina Reports (Iredell's Equity)

N.C. (Jones) North Carolina Reports (Jones' Law)

N.C. (Jones Eq.) North Carolina Reports (Jones' Equity)

N.C. (Mart.) North Carolina Reports (Martin)

N.C.M.R. Navy Court of Military Review

N.C. (Mur.) North Carolina Reports (Murphey)

N.C. (Phil. Eq.) North Carolina Reports (Phillips' Equity)

N.C. (Phil. Law) North Carolina Reports (Phillips' Law)

N.C. Sess. Laws Session Laws of North Carolina

N.C. (Tay.) North Carolina Reports (Taylor)

N.C. (Term) North Carolina Reports (Term Reports)

N.C. (Win.) North Carolina Reports (Winston)

N.D. North Dakota; North Dakota Reports (Supreme Court)

N.D. Cent. Code North Dakota Century Code

N.D. Sess. Laws Laws of North Dakota (Session Laws)

N.E. or NE Northeast; Northeastern

N.E. [2d] Northeastern Reporter [second series]

Neb. Nebraska; Nebraska Reports (Supreme Court)

Neb. Laws Nebraska Laws (Session Laws)

Neb. Rev. Stat. Revised Statutes of Nebraska

Negl. Cas. [2d] Negligence Cases [second]

Nev. Neveda; Nevada Reports (Supreme Court)

Nev. Rev. Stat. Nevada Revised Statutes

Nev. Stats. Statutes of Nevada (Session Laws)

N.H. New Hampshire; New Hampshire Reports (Supreme Court)

N.H. Laws Laws of the State of New Hampshire (Session Laws)

N.H. Rev. Stat. Ann. New Hampshire Revised Statutes Annotated

NIH or N.I.H. National Institute of Health

N. IR. L. Q. Northern Ireland Legal Quarterly

N.J. New Jersey; New Jersey Reports (Supreme Court, previously Court of Errors and Appeals)

N.J. Eq. New Jersey Equity Reports

N.J. L. New Jersey Law Reports

N.J. Laws Laws of New Jersey (Session Laws)

N.J. Misc. New Jersey Miscellaneous Reports

N.J. Rev. Stat. New Jersey Revised Statutes (1937)

N.J. Sess. Law Serv. New Jersey Session Law Service

N.J. Stat. Ann. New Jersey Statutes Annotated (West)

N.J. Super. New Jersey Superior Court Reports

NLRB or N.L.R.B. National Labor Relations Board

NLRB Dec. National Labor Relations Board Decisions

N.M. New Mexico; New Mexico Reports (Supreme Court)

N.M. (Gild., E.W.S. ed.) New Mexico Supreme Court Reports (edited by E.W.S. Gildersleeve)

N.M. Laws Laws of New Mexico (Session Laws)

N.M. Stat. Ann. New Mexico Statutes Annotated

nn. notes

no. number

NOLPE School L. J. NOLPE School Law Journal

nos. numbers

n.o.v. non obstante veredicto (*not withstanding the verdict*)

N.P. Notary Public

NRAB or **N.R.A.B.** National Railroad Adjustment Board; National Railroad Adjustment Board Decisions

n.s. new series

N. Trans. S. Dec. National Transportation Safety Board Decisions

N.W. Northwest; Northwestern

N.W. [2d] Northwestern Reports [second series]

N.Y. [2d] New York Reports [second series] (Court of Appeals)

N.Y. [subject] * **Law (Consol.)** Consolidated Laws Service (New York)

N.Y. [subject] * **Law (McKinney)** McKinney's Consolidated Laws (New York)

   *[Subject Abbreviations]

   Aband. Prop. Abandoned Property

   Agric. Conserv. & Adj. Agricultural Conservation and Adjustment

   Agric. & Mkts. Agriculture & Markets

   Alco. Bev. Cont. Alcoholic Beverage Control

   Alt. County Gov't Alternative County Government

   Banking Banking

   Ben. Ord. Benevolent Orders

   Bus. Corp. Business Corporation

   Canal Canal

   Civ. Prac. Civil Practice Law & Rules

Civ. Rights Civil Rights

Civ. Serv. Civil Service

Com. Commerce

Condem. Condemnation

Coop. Corp. Cooperative Corporations

Correc. Correction

County County

Crim. Proc. Criminal Procedure

Debt. & Cred. Debtor & Creditor

Dom. Rel. Domestic Relations

Educ. Education

Elec. Election

Empl'rs Liab. Employers' Liability

Envir. Conserv. Environmental Conservation

Est., Powers & Trusts Estates, Powers & Trusts

Exec. Executive

Gen. Ass'ns General Associations

Gen. Bus. General Business

Gen. City General City

Gen. Constr. General Construction

Gen. Mun. General Municipal

Gen. Oblig. General Obligations

High. Highway

Indian Indian

Ins. Insurance

Jud. Judiciary

Lab. Labor

Legis. Legislative

Lien Lien

Local Fin. Local Finance

Mental Hyg. Mental Hygiene

Mil. Military

Mult. Dwell. Multiple Dwelling

Mult. Resid. Multiple Residence

Mun. Home Rule Municipal Home Rule

Nav. Navigation

Not-For-Profit Corp. Not-for-Profit Corporation

Opt. County Gov't Optional County Government

Parks & Rec. Parks & Recreation

Partnership Partnership

Penal Penal

Pers. Prop. Personal Property

Priv. Hous. Fin. Private Housing Finance

Pub. Auth. Public Authorities

Pub. Bldgs. Public Buildings

Pub. Health Public Health

Pub. Hous. Public Housing

Pub. Lands Public Lands

Pub. Off. Public Officers

Pub. Serv. Public Service

Rapid Trans. Rapid Transit

Real Prop. Real Property

Real Prop. Acts. Real Property Actions & Proceedings

Real Prop. Tax Real Property Tax

Relig. Corp. Religious Corporations

Retire. & Soc. Sec. Retirement & Social Security

R.R. Railroad

Rural Elec. Coop. Rural Electric Cooperative

Salt Springs Salt Springs

Second Class Cities Second Class Cities

Soc. Serv. Social Services

Soil & Water Conserv. Dist. Soil and Water Conservation Districts

State State

State Fin. State Finance

State Print. State Printing

Stat. Local Gov'ts Statute of Local Governments

Tax Tax

Town Town

Transp. Transportation

Transp. Corp. Transportation Corporations

Veh. & Traf. Vehicle & Traffic

Village Village

Vol. Fire. Ben. Volunteer Firemen's Benefit

Work. Comp. Workmen's Compensation

N.Y. Laws Laws of New York (Session Laws)

N.Y.S. [2d] West's New York Supplement [second series]

NYSE New York Stock Exchange

NYSE Guide New York Stock Exchange Guide

N.Y. Sup. Ct. Supreme Court Reports (New York)

O

OEO or **O.E.O.** Office of Economic Opportunity

Off. Office

Off. Gaz. Pat. Off. Official Gazette of the Patent Office

Ohio Ohio Reports (Supreme Court)

Ohio App. [2d] Ohio Appellate Reports [second series]

Ohio C.C. Ohio Circuit Court Reports (Jahn)

Ohio C.C. Dec. Ohio Circuit Court Decisions

Ohio C.C. (n.s.) Ohio Circuit Court Reports (new series)

Ohio Cir. Dec. Ohio Circuit Decisions

Ohio Dec. Ohio Decisions

Ohio Dec. Reprint Ohio Decisions (reprint)

Ohio Dep't Ohio Department Reports

Ohio Gov't Ohio Government Reports

Ohio Laws State of Ohio: Legislative Acts Passed and Joint Resolutions Adopted

Ohio Legis. Bull. Ohio Legislative Bulletin (Anderson)

Ohio Misc. Ohio Miscellaneous (case reports)

Ohio N.P. [n.s.] Ohio Nisi Prius Reports [new series]

Ohio Op. [2d] Ohio Opinions [second series]

Ohio Rev. Code Ann. (Anderson) Ohio Revised Code Annotated (Anderson)

Ohio Rev. Code Ann. (Baldwin) Ohio Revised Code Annotated (Baldwin)

Ohio Rev. Code Ann. (Page) Ohio Revised Code Annotated (Page)

Ohio St. [2d] Ohio State Reports [second series] (Supreme Court)

Okla. Oklahoma; Oklahoma Reports (Supreme Court)

Okla. Crim. Oklahoma Criminal Reports

Okla. Sess. Laws Oklahoma Session Laws

Okla. Sess. Law Serv. Oklahoma Session Law Service (West)

Okla. Stat. Oklahoma Statutes (1971 & Supplement 1975)

Okla. Stat. Ann. Oklahoma Statutes Annotated (West)

Op. Att'y Gen. Opinions of the Attorney General

Op. Solic. P.O. Dep't Official Opinion of the Solicitor for the Post Office Department

Or. Oregon; Oregon Reports (Supreme Court)

Or. App. Oregon Reports, Court of Appeal

Ord. Order

Or. Laws Oregon Laws and Resolutions (Session Laws)

Or. Laws Adv. Sh. No. Oregon Laws and Resolutions Advance Sheet Number

Or. Laws Spec. Sess. Oregon Laws and Resolutions, Special Session

Orphans' Ct. Orphans' Court

Or. Rev. Stat. Oregon Revised Statutes

Or. T.R. Oregon Tax Reporter

o.s. old style; old series

P

p. page

P. [2d] Pacific Reporter [second series]

Pa. Pennsylvania State Reports (Supreme Court)

Pac. Pacific

Pa. Commw. Ct. Pennsylvania Commonwealth Court Reports

Pa. Cons. Stat. Pennsylvania Consolidated Statutes

Pa. Cons. Stat. Ann. Pennsylvania Consolidated Statutes Annotated (Purdon)

Pa. D. & C. [2d] Pennsylvania District and County Reports [second series]

Pa. Fiduc. Pennsylvania Fiduciary Reporter

Paige Ch. Paige's Chancery Reports (New York)

Pa. Laws Laws of the General Assembly of the Commonwealth of Pennsylvania (Session Laws)

Pa. Legis. Serv. Pennsylvania Legislative Service (Purdon)

par. paragraph

pars. paragraphs

Pa. Stat. Ann. (Purdon) Purdon's Pennsylvania Statutes Annotated

Pa. Super. Ct. Pennsylvania Superior Court Reports

Pat. Patent

P.C. Parliamentary Cases; Patent

Cases; Penal Code; Pleas of the Crown; Political Code; Practice Cases; Privy Council
P. Ct. Probate Court
Pelt. Peltier's Orleans Reports (Louisiana)
Pens. Plan Guide Pension Plan Guide
Pen. & W. Penrose and Watts' Reports (Pennsylvania Supreme Court)
perm. permanent
PHA or **P.H.A.** Public Housing Administration
Phil. Philadelphia
Pin. Pinney's Reports (Wisconsin Supreme Court)
Pitt. Pittsburgh
Plan. Planning
p.o. post office; public officer
Pol. Politics
Police J. Ct. Police Justice's Court
pol'y policy
Port. Porter's Reports (Alabama Supreme Court)
Pov. L. Rep. Poverty Law Reporter
p.p. pages; propria persona (*in his proper person*)
p.p.i. policy proof of interest
prac. practical; practice; practitioners'
Priv. Found. Rep. Private Foundations Reporter
P.R. Laws Ann. Puerto Rico Laws Annotated
Prob. Probate; Problems
Proc. Procedures; Proceedings
prod. product; production
Prod. Liab. Rep. Products Liability Reporter
Prop. Property
P.R.R. Puerto Rico Reports (all courts)
p.s. postscript

P.S. Public Statutes
Psych. Psychiatry; Psychology
pt. part
pts. parts
Pub. Public
Pub. Lands Dec. Decisions of the Department of the Interior relating to Public Lands
Pub. U. Rep. Public Utilities Reports
PUC or **P.U.C.** Public Utilities Commission

Q

Q. Quarterly
Q.B. Queen's Bench
Q.B.D. Queen's Bench Division
Q.C. Queen's Counsel
q.c.f. or **qu. cl. fr.** quare clausum fregit (*breaking a close*)
q.d. quasi dicat (*as if he should say*)
q.e.n. quare executionem non (*execution should not be issued*)
Q.S. Quarter Sessions
q.t. qui tam (*who as well*)
Queensl. Queensland
q.v. quod vide (*which see*)

R

Rad. Reg. Radio Regulation
Rawle Rawle's Reports (Pennsylvania Supreme Court)
Rd. Road
Real Est. Comm'n Real Estate Commission
Rec. Record
Ref. Referee; Referee's; Refining; Reform
Ref. J. Journal of National Conference of Referees in Bankruptcy
Reg. Register; Regulation
Rel. Relations
Reorg. Reorganization
Rep. Reporter; Reports
repl. replacement

Res. Reserve
rev. revised; revision
Rev. Review
Rev. C. Abo. P.R. Revista del Colegio de Abogados de Puerto Rico
Rev. Jur. U. P.R. Revista Juridica de la Universidad de Puerto Rico
Rev. P.R. Revista de Derecho Puertorrinqueño
R.I. Rhode Island; Rhode Island Reports (Supreme Court)
Rich. Richmond
R.I. Gen. Laws General Laws of Rhode Island
R.I. Pub. Laws Public Laws of Rhode Island (Session Laws)
R.L. Revised Laws; Roman Laws
Rob. Robinson's Reports (Louisiana Supreme Court)
Rocky Mtn. Rocky Mountain
Root Root's Reports (Connecticut Supreme Court of Errors)
R.R. Railroad
R.S. Revised Statutes
Rut.-Cam. Rutgers-Camden
Ry. Railway

S

S. South; Southern
Sand. Ch. Sandford's Chancery Reports (New York)
San Fern. V. San Fernando Valley
Sarat. Ch. Sent. Saratoga Chancery Sentinel (New York)
Sask. Saskatchewan
Sav. Savings
S.B. Senate Bill
SBA or **S.B.A.** Small Business Administration
s.c. same case; select cases; supreme court
S.C. South Carolina Reports (Supreme Court); Supreme Court

S.C. Acts Acts and Joint Resolutions, South Carolina (Session Laws)
S.C. Code Code of Laws of South Carolina
S.C. Eq. South Carolina Equity Reports
S.C. Eq. (Bail. Eq.) South Carolina Equity Reports (Bailey's Equity)
S.C. Eq. (Chev. Eq.) South Carolina Equity Reports (Cheves' Equity)
S.C. Eq. (Des.) South Carolina Equity Reports (Desaussure's Equity)
S.C. Eq. (Dud. Eq.) South Carolina Equity Reports (Dudley's Equity)
S.C. Eq. (Harp. Eq.) South Carolina Equity Reports (Harper's Equity)
S.C. Eq. (Hill Eq.) South Carolina Equity Reports (Hill's Chancery)
S.C. Eq. (McCord Eq.) South Carolina Equity Reports (McCord's Chancery)
S.C. Eq. (McMul. Eq.) South Carolina Equity Reports (McMullan's Equity)
S.C. Eq. (Rice Eq.) South Carolina Equity Reports (Rice's Equity)
S.C. Eq. (Rich. Cas.) South Carolina Equity Reports (Richardson's Cases)
S.C. Eq. (Rich. Eq.) South Carolina Equity Reports (Richardson's Equity)
S.C. Eq. (Ril.) South Carolina Equity Reports (Riley's Chancery)
S.C. Eq. (Speers Eq.) South Carolina Equity Reports (Speers' Equity)
S.C. Eq. (Strob. Eq.) South Carolina Equity Reports (Strobhart's Equity)
Sch. School
Sci. Science; Sciences

S.C.L. South Carolina Law Reports

S.C.L. (Bail.) South Carolina Law Reports (Bailey)

S.C.L. (Bay) South Carolina Law Reports (Bay)

S.C.L. (Brev.) South Carolina Law Reports (Brevard)

S.C.L. (Chev.) South Carolina Law Reports (Cheves)

S.C.L. (Harp.) South Carolina Law Reports (Harper)

S.C.L. (Hill) South Carolina Law Reports (Hill)

S.C.L. (McCord) South Carolina Law Reports (McCord)

S.C.L. (McMul.) South Carolina Law Reports (McMullan)

S.C.L. (Mill) South Carolina Law Reports (Mill's Constitutional Court Reports)

S.C.L. (Nott & McC.) South Carolina Law Reports (Nott and McCord)

S.C.L. (Rice) South Carolina Law Reports (Rice)

S.C.L. (Rich.) South Carolina Law Reports (Richardson)

S.C.L. (Ril.) South Carolina Law Reports (Riley)

S.C.L. (Speers) South Carolina Law Reports (Speers)

S.C.L. (Strob.) South Carolina Law Reports (Strobhart)

Scot. L. Rev. Scottish Law Review and Sheriff Court Reports

S. Ct. Supreme Court Reporter

S.D. South Dakota; South Dakota Reports (Supreme Court); Southern District

S/D B/L sight draft—bill of lading attached

S.D. Compiled Laws Ann. South Dakota Compiled Laws Annotated

S.D. Sess. Laws Laws of South Dakota (Session Laws)

S.D. Uniform Prob. Code South Dakota Uniform Probate Code

S.E. [2d] Southeastern Reporter [second series]

SEC or **S.E.C.** Securities and Exchange Commission

Sec. Securities

S.E.C. Securities and Exchange Commission; Securities and Exchange Commission Decisions and Reports

Sec. Reg. Guide Securities Regulation Guide

Sec. Reg. & L. Rep. Securities Regulation and Law Report

Sel. Serv. L. Rep. Selective Service Law Reporter

ser. serial; serials; series

Ser. Series

Serg. & Rawl. Sergeant and Rawle's Reports (Pennsylvania Supreme Court)

Serv. Service

S.F. San Francisco

s.f.s. sine fraude sua (*without fraud on his part*)

S.J.C. Supreme Judicial Court

S.L. Session Laws

So. [2d] Southern Reporter [second series]

Soc. Social; Sociological; Sociology

Soc'y Society

s.p. sine prole (*without issue*)

spec. special

ss. scilicet (*to wit*)

S.S. Steamship

SSA or **S.S.A.** Social Security Administration

SSS or **S.S.S.** Selective Service System

St. State; Street

Stan. Stanford

Stand. Ex. Prof. Tax Rep. Standard Excess Profits Tax Reporter

Stand. Fed. Tax Rep. Standard Federal Tax Reporter

Stat. United States Statutes at large

State Tax Cas. State Tax Cases

State Tax Cas. Rep. State Tax Cases Reporter

State & Loc. Taxes State and Local Taxes

State Mot. Carr. Guide State Motor Carrier Guide

Stew. Stewart's Reports (Alabama Supreme Court)

Stew. & P. Stewart and Porter's Reports (Alabama Supreme Court)

Stud. Studies

Sup. Ct. Supreme Court

Super. Ct. Superior Court

Sup. Jud. Ct. Supreme Judicial Court

Sur. Surety

Sur. Ct. Surrogate's Court

Sur. Ct. Proc. Act Surrogate's Court Procedure Act (58A) (New York)

s.v. sub voce (*under the voice*)

S.W. Southwest; Southwestern

S.W. [2d] Southwestern Reporter [second series]

Symp. Symposium

Sys. System

T

Tax. Taxation

Tax Ct. Mem. Dec. Tax Court Memorandum Decisions

Tax Ct. Rep. Tax Court Reporter

Tax Ct. Rep. Dec. Tax Court Reported Decisions

Tax-Exempt Orgs. Tax-Exempt Organizations

Tax Mngm't Tax Management

T.C. United States Tax Court

Tchr. Teacher

Tchrs. Teachers

T.C.M. Tax Court Memorandum Decisions

Tech. Technical; Technique; Technology

Teiss. Teisser's Court of Appeal, Parish of Orleans Reports (Louisiana)

Tel. Telegram; Telegraph; Telephone

temp. temporary

Temp. Temple

Temp. Emer. Ct. App. United States Temporary Emergency Court of Appeals

Tenn. Tennessee; Tennessee Reports (Supreme Court)

Tenn. Code Ann. Tennessee Code Annotated

Tenn. (Cold.) Tennessee Supreme Court Reports (Coldwell)

Tenn. (Cooke) Tennessee Supreme Court Reports (Cooke)

Tenn. (Hay.) Tennessee Supreme Court Reports (Haywood)

Tenn. (Head) Tennessee Supreme Court Reports (Head)

Tenn. (Heisk.) Tennessee Supreme Court Reports (Heiskell)

Tenn. (Hum.) Tennessee Supreme Court Reports (Humphreys)

Tenn. (Mart. & Yer.) Tennessee Supreme Court Reports (Martin and Yerger)

Tenn. (Meigs) Tennessee Supreme Court Reports (Meigs)

Tenn. (Overt.) Tennessee Supreme Court Reports (Overton)

Tenn. (Peck) Tennessee Supreme Court Reports (Peck)

Tenn. Pub. Acts Public Acts of the State of Tennessee (Session Laws)

185

Tenn. (Sneed) Tennessee Supreme Court Reports (Sneed)

Tenn. (Swan) Tennessee Supreme Court Reports (Swan)

Tenn. (Yer.) Tennessee Supreme Court Reports (Yerger)

Tex. Texas; Texas Reports (Supreme Court)

Tex. Bus. Corp. Act Ann. Texas Business Corporation Act Annotated

Tex. Civ. App. Texas Civil Appeals Reports

Tex. Civ. Cas. Texas Court of Appeals Decisions, Civil Cases (White & Willson)

Tex. [subject] * Code Ann. Texas Codes Annotated (Vernon)

[Subject Abbreviations] *

Agric. Agriculture

Alco. Bev. Alcoholic Beverage

Bus. & Com. Business and Commerce (1968)

Civ. Civil

Corp. & Ass'ns Corporations and Associations

Crim. Pro. Criminal Procedure,

Educ. Education (1972)

Elec. Election

Fam. Family (1975)

Fin. Financial

Gov't Government

Health & Safety Health & Safety

High. Highway

Ins. Insurance

Lab. Labor

Occ. Occupations

Parks & Wild. Parks & Wildlife (1976)

Penal Penal (1974)

Prob. Probate

Prop. Property

Res. Resources

Tax Tax

Util. Utilities

Veh. Vehicles

Water Water (1972)

Welf. Welfare

Tex. Code Crim. Proc. Ann. Texas Code of Criminal Procedure of 1965 Annotated (Vernon)

Tex. Crim. Texas Criminal Reports (Texas Court of Appeals Reports)

Tex. Elec. Code Ann. Texas Election Code of 1951 Annotated (Vernon)

Tex. Gen. Laws General and Special Laws of the State of Texas (Session Laws)

Tex. Ins. Code Ann. Texas Insurance Code of 1951 Annotated (Vernon)

Tex. Prob. Code Ann. Texas Probate Code of 1955 Annotated (Vernon)

Tex. Rev. Civ. Stat. Ann. Texas Revised Civil Statutes Annotated (Vernon)

Tex. Sess. Law Serv. Texas Session Law Service (Vernon)

Tex. Stat. Ann. Texas Statutes Annotated

Tex. Tax-Gen. Ann. Texas Tax-General Annotated (Vernon)

tit. title

tits. titles

Tol. Toledo

T.M. Trademark

Tr. Trust

Trademark Bull. (n.s.) Bulletin of United States Trademark Association (new series)

Trade Reg. Rep. Trade Regulation Reporter

trans. translation; translator

Transnat'l Transnational

transp. transportation

Treas. Dec. Treasury Decisions under Customs and Other Laws

Treas. Dec. Int. Rev. Treasury Decisions under the Internal Revenue Laws

Tul. Tulane

Tyl. Tyler's Reports (Vermont Supreme Court)

U

U. University; Universities

U.C.C. Uniform Commercial Code

Unauth. Unauthorized

Unconsol. Laws Unconsolidated Laws (New York)

Unempl. Ins. Rep. Unemployment Insurance Reporter

Uniform City Ct. Act Uniform City Court Act (New York)

Univ. University; Universities

urb. urban

Urb. Aff. Rep. Urban Affairs Reporter

U.S. United States; United States Supreme Court Reports

U.S. App. D.C. United States Court of Appeals for District of Columbia Circuit

U.S. (Black) United States Supreme Court Reports 1861–1862 (reported by Black)

U.S.C. [A.] United States Code [Annotated]

U.S. (Cranch) United States Supreme Court Reports 1801–1815 (reported by Cranch)

U.S. (Dall.) United States Supreme Court Reports 1790–1800 (reported by Dallas)

Users Rep. Energy Users Report

U.S. (How.) United States Supreme Court Reports 1843–1860 (reported by Howard)

U.S.L.W. United States Law Week

U.S. (Pet.) United States Supreme Court Reports 1828–1842 (reported by Peters)

U.S. P. Q. United States Patent Quarterly

U.S. Tax Cas. United States Tax Cases

U.S. (Wall.) United States Supreme Court Reports 1863–1874 (reported by Wallace)

U.S. (Wheat.) United States Supreme Court Reports 1816–1827 (reported by Wheaton)

Utah [2d] Utah Reports (Supreme Court) [second series]

Utah Code Ann. Utah Code Annotated

Utah Laws Laws of Utah (Session Laws)

Util. Utility; Utilities

Util. L. Rep. Utilities Law Reporter

V

v. verb; versus; vide (*see*); voce (*voice*); volume

V. Victoria

Va. Virginia; Virginia Reports (Supreme Court, previously Supreme Court of Appeals)

Va. Acts Acts of the General Assembly of the Commonwealth of Virginia (Session Laws)

Va. (Call) Virginia Supreme Court Reports (Call)

Va. Code Code of Virginia

Va. (Gilmer) Virginia Supreme Court Reports (Gilmer)

Va. (Gratt.) Virginia Supreme Court Reports (Grattan)

Va. (Hen. & M.) Virginia Supreme Court Reports (Hening & Munford)

Val. Valparaiso

Va. (Leigh) Virginia Supreme Court (Leigh)

Va. (Munf.) Virginia Supreme Court (Munford)

Vand. Vanderbilt

Va. (Rand.) Virginia Supreme Court Reports (Randolph)

Va. (Rob.) Virginia Supreme Court (Robinson)

Va. (Va. Cas.) Virginia Supreme Court Reports (Virginia Cases, Criminal)

Va. (Wash.) Virginia Supreme Court Reports (Washington)

V.C. Vice Chancellor

V.I. Virgin Islands; Virgin Island Reports (all courts)

V.I. Code Ann. Virgin Islands Code Annotated

Vict. Victoria

Vill. Villanova

vol. volume

vols. volumes

vs. versus

Vt. Vermont; Vermont Reports (Supreme Court)

Vt. Acts Laws of Vermont (Session Laws)

Vt. Stat. Ann. Vermont Statutes Annotated

W

W. West; Western; Westminster; William

Wage and Hour Cas. Wage & Hour Cases

Wash. [2d] Washington; Washington Reports (Supreme Court) [second series]

Wash. App. Washington Appellate Reports

Wash. Laws Laws of Washington (Session Laws)

Wash. Legis. Serv. Washington Legislative Service (West)

Wash. Rev. Code Revised Code of Washington (1974)

Wash. Rev. Code Ann. Revised Code of Washington Annotated

Wash. Terr. Washington Territory Reports

W.D. Western District

Wills, Est., Tr. Wills, Estates, Trusts

Wis. Wisconsin; Wisconsin Reports (Supreme Court)

Wis. Laws Laws of Wisconsin (Session Laws)

Wis. Legis. Serv. Wisconsin Legislative Service (West)

Wis. Stat. Wisconsin Statutes

Wis. Stat. Ann. (West) Wisconsin Statutes Annotated (West)

Wm. & Mary William and Mary

Workmen's Comp. Div. Workmen's Compensation Division

Workmen's Comp. L. Rep. Workmen's Compensation Law Reporter

W. Va. West Virginia; West Virginia Reports (Supreme Court of Appeals)

W. Va. Acts Acts of the Legislature of West Virginia (Session Laws)

W. Va. Code West Virginia Code

Wyo. Wyoming; Wyoming Reports (Supreme Court)

Wyo. Sess. Laws Session Laws of Wyoming

Wyo. Stat. Wyoming Statutes

Y

Y.B. Yearbook

Youth Ct. Youth Court

THE UNITED STATES COURT DIRECTORY

Supreme Court of the United States

United States Courts of Appeals

Special Courts

Judicial Panel on Multidistrict Litigation

United States Court of Military Appeals

United States District Courts

Federal Judicial Center

Administrative Office of the United States Courts

SUPREME COURT OF THE UNITED STATES
1 FIRST STREET, N.E.
WASHINGTON, D.C. 20543

Chief Justice
Warren E. Burger

Associate Justices
William J. Brennan, Jr.
Potter Stewart
Byron R. White
Thurgood Marshall
Harry A. Blackmun
Lewis F. Powell, Jr.
William H. Rehnquist
John Paul Stevens

Retired Justices
Stanley Reed
William O. Douglas

Clerk
Michael Rodak, Jr.

UNITED STATES COURTS OF APPEALS*

Circuit

District of Columbia Circuit

Clerk
U.S. Courthouse
3rd and Constitution Avenue, N.W.
Washington, D.C. 20001

First Circuit —
Maine, Massachusetts,
New Hampshire, Rhode Island,
Puerto Rico

Clerk
1606 John W. McCormack
    Post Office and Courthouse Building
Boston, Massachusetts 02109

Second Circuit —
Connecticut, New York, Vermont

Clerk
U.S. Courthouse
Foley Square
New York, New York 10007

Third Circuit —
Delaware, New Jersey, Pennsylvania,
Virgin Islands

Clerk
21400 U.S. Courthouse
601 Market Street
Philadelphia, Pennsylvania 19106

*The name of the court should be included in the address.
  For example: Clerk
                 U.S. Court of Appeals
                 U.S. Courthouse
                 Foley Square
                 New York, New York 10007

Fourth Circuit —
Maryland, North Carolina,
South Carolina, Virginia,
West Virginia

Clerk
U.S. Courthouse, Rm. 249
Tenth and Main Streets
Richmond, Virginia 23219

Fifth Circuit —
Alabama, Florida, Georgia,
Louisiana, Mississippi, Texas,
Canal Zone

Clerk
Rm. 100, 600 Camp Street,
New Orleans, Louisiana 70130

Sixth Circuit —
Kentucky, Michigan, Ohio,
Tennessee

Clerk
516 U.S. Post Office and Courthouse
   Building
Cincinnati, Ohio 45202

Seventh Circuit —
Illinois, Indiana, Wisconsin

Clerk
U.S. Courthouse and Federal Office
   Building
219 South Dearborn Street
Chicago, Illinois 60604

Eighth Circuit —
Arkansas, Iowa, Minnesota,
Missouri, Nebraska, North Dakota,
South Dakota

Clerk
511 U.S. Court and Customs House
St. Louis, Missouri 63101

Ninth Circuit —
Arizona, California, Idaho, Montana,
Nevada, Oregon, Washington,
Alaska, Hawaii, Guam

Clerk
P.O. Box 547
San Francisco, California 94101

Tenth Circuit —
Colorado, Kansas, New Mexico,
Oklahoma, Utah, Wyoming

Clerk
469 U.S. Courthouse
Denver, Colorado 80294

United States Court of Appeals
Temporary Emergency Court of Appeals
Rm. 2400, U.S. Courthouse
Washington, D.C. 20001

SPECIAL COURTS

Court

United States Court of Claims
717 Madison Place, N.W.
Washington, D.C. 20005

United States Court of Customs and Patent Appeals
717 Madison Place, N.W.
Washington, D.C. 20439

United States Customs Court
One Federal Plaza
New York, New York 10007

JUDICIAL PANEL ON MULTIDISTRICT LITIGATION

1030 15th Street, N.W.
320 Executive Building
Washington, D.C. 20005

UNITED STATES COURT OF MILITARY APPEALS

450 E Street, N.W.
Washington, D.C. 20442

UNITED STATES DISTRICT COURTS*

District

ALABAMA

Northern

Clerk
311 Federal Court House
Birmingham, Alabama 35203

Middle

Clerk
P.O. Box 711
Montgomery, Alabama 36101

Southern

Clerk
213 U.S. Court House
and Custom House Building
Mobile, Alabama 36602

*The name of the court should be included in the address.
For example: Clerk
U.S. District Court
311 Federal Court House
Birmingham, Alabama 35203

ALASKA

Clerk
Room 166
U.S. Courthouse
605 W. 4th Avenue
Anchorage, Alaska 99501

*Divisional Offices with Resident
Deputy in Charge:*
Box 1350
Fairbanks, Alaska 99707

Box 349
Juneau, Alaska 99801

Room 400
415 Main Street
Ketchikan, Alaska 99901

Box 130
Nome, Alaska 99762

ARIZONA

Clerk
Room 6218, Federal Building
Phoenix, Arizona 85025

*Divisional Office with Resident
Deputy in Charge:*
Room 238, U.S. Courthouse
Tucson, Arizona 85701

ARKANSAS

Eastern
Clerk
P.O. Box 869
Little Rock, Arkansas 72203

*Divisional Office with Resident
Deputy in Charge:*
P.O. Box 8307
Pine Bluff, Arkansas 71611

Western
Clerk
P.O. Box 1523
Fort Smith, Arkansas 72902

*Divisional Offices with Resident
Deputy in Charge:*
P.O. Box 2746
Texarkana, Arkansas 75501

P.O. Drawer I
Hot Springs, Arkansas 71901

P.O. Box 1566
El Dorado, Arkansas 71730

Room 523, Federal Building
and U.S. Courthouse
Fayetteville, Arkansas 72701

CALIFORNIA

Northern
Clerk
U.S. Courthouse
P.O. Box 36060
San Francisco, California 94102

*Divisional Office with Resident
Deputy in Charge:*
U.S. Courthouse
175 W. Taylor Street
San Jose, California 95110

Eastern
Clerk
2546 U.S. Courthouse
650 Capitol Mall
Sacramento, California 95814

*Divisional Office with Resident
Deputy in Charge:*
5408 U.S. Courthouse
1130 "O" Street
Fresno, California 93721

Central
Clerk
U.S. Courthouse
312 North Spring Street
Los Angeles, California 90012

Southern

Clerk
U.S. Courthouse, Room 1N20
940 Front Street
San Diego, California 92189

CANAL ZONE, DISTRICT COURT OF THE

Clerk
Box 2006
Balboa Heights, Canal Zone

Divisional Office with Resident Deputy in Charge:
Box 1175
Cristobal, Canal Zone

COLORADO

Clerk
Room 145, U.S. Courthouse
1929 Stout Street
Denver, Colorado 80294

CONNECTICUT

Clerk
141 Church Street
Federal Building
New Haven, Connecticut 06505

Divisional Offices with Resident Deputy in Charge:
450 Main Street
Hartford, Connecticut 06103

915 Lafayette Boulevard
Bridgeport, Connecticut 06604

DELAWARE

Clerk
Lockbox 18
Federal Building
844 King Street
Wilmington, Delaware 19801

DISTRICT OF COLUMBIA

Clerk
U.S. Courthouse
3rd and Constitution Avenue N.W.
Washington, D.C. 20001

FLORIDA

Northern

Clerk
P.O. Box 958
Tallahassee, Florida 32302

Divisional Office with Resident Deputy in Charge:
P.O. Box 990
Pensacola, Florida 32502

Middle

Clerk
P.O. Box 53558
Jacksonville, Florida 32201

Divisional Offices with Resident Deputy in Charge:
Room 611, Federal Office
and U.S. Courthouse

80 N. Hughey Avenue
Orlando, Florida 32801

P.O. Box 3270
Tampa, Florida 33601

Southern

Clerk
P.O. Box 010669
Flagler Station
Miami, Florida 33101

Divisional Offices with Resident Deputy in Charge:
301 N. Andrews Avenue
Ft. Lauderdale, Florida 33301

Federal Building
701 Clematis Street
West Palm Beach, Florida 33401

GEORGIA

Northern

Clerk
U.S. Courthouse
Room 100
56 Forsyth Street N.W.
Atlanta, Georgia 30303

*Divisional Offices with Resident
Deputy in Charge:*
Post Office Building
P.O. Box 1186
Rome, Georgia 30161

Federal Building
P.O. Box 939
Newnan, Georgia 30263

Room 201, Federal Building
Gainesville, Georgia 30501

Middle

Clerk
P.O. Box 128
Macon, Georgia 31202

*Divisional Offices with Resident
Deputy in Charge:*
P.O. Box 1906
Albany, Georgia 31702

P.O. Box 124
Columbus, Georgia 31902

P.O. Box 9
Thomasville, Georgia 31792

P.O. Box 68
Valdosta, Georgia 31601

Southern

Clerk
P.O. Box 8286
Savannah, Georgia 31402

*Divisional Offices with Resident
Deputy in Charge:*
P.O. Box 1130
Augusta, Georgia 30903

P.O. Box 1636
Brunswick, Georgia 31520

GUAM, DISTRICT COURT OF

Clerk
P.O. Box DC
Agana, Guam 96910

HAWAII

Clerk
P.O. Box 3193
Honolulu, Hawaii 96801

IDAHO

Clerk
U.S. Courthouse
P.O. Box 039
550 West Fort Street
Boise, Idaho 83724

ILLINOIS

Northern

Clerk
U.S. Courthouse
219 South Dearborn Street
Chicago, Illinois 60604

*Divisional Office with Resident
Deputy in Charge:*
206 Federal Building
Freeport, Illinois 61032

Eastern

Clerk
P.O. Box 786
Danville, Illinois 61832

*Divisional Offices with Resident
Deputy in Charge:*
P.O. Box 249
East St. Louis, Illinois 62201

U.S. Courthouse and
   Post Office Building
Benton, Illinois 62812

Southern

Clerk
P.O. Box 238
Peoria, Illinois 61601

Divisional Offices with Resident Deputy in Charge
Room 40, Post Office Building
Rock Island, Illinois 61201

P.O. Box 315
Springfield, Illinois 62705

Federal Building
501 Belle Street
Alton, Illinois 62002

INDIANA

Northern

Clerk
Federal Building
507 State Street
P.O. Box 645
Hammond, Indiana 46325

Divisional Offices with Resident Deputy in Charge:
Federal Building
1300 South Harrison
P.O. Box 59
Fort Wayne, Indiana 46801

Federal Building
204 South Main Street
South Bend, Indiana 46601

Federal Building
232 North 4th Street
P.O. Box 524
Lafayette, Indiana 47902

Southern

Clerk
U.S. Courthouse
Room 105
46 East Ohio Street
Indianapolis, Indiana 46204

Divisional Offices with Resident Deputy in Charge:
304 Federal Building
Evansville, Indiana 47708

210 Federal Building
New Albany, Indiana 47150

210 Federal Building
Terre Haute, Indiana 47808

Western

Clerk
230 U.S. Courthouse Building
Louisville, Kentucky 40202

Divisional Offices with Resident Deputy in Charge:
Federal Building
Paducah, Kentucky 42001

P.O. Box 538
Federal Building
Owensboro, Kentucky 42301

213 Federal Building
Bowling Green, Kentucky 42101

IOWA

Northern

Clerk
Federal Building
P.O. Box 4411
Cedar Rapids, Iowa 52407

Divisional Offices with Resident Deputy in Charge:
Federal Post Office Building
P.O. Box 1348
Sioux City, Iowa 51101

Federal Post Office Building
P.O. Box 1057
Fort Dodge, Iowa 50501

Southern

Clerk
Room 200, U.S. Courthouse
East 1st and Walnut Streets
Des Moines, Iowa 50309

Divisional Offices with Resident Deputy in Charge:
P.O. Box 307
Council Bluffs, Iowa 51501

P.O. Box 256
Davenport, Iowa 52805

KANSAS

Clerk
P.O. Box 2201
Wichita, Kansas 67201

Divisional Offices with Resident Deputy in Charge:
Room 142, Federal Building
Kansas City, Kansas 66101

444 S.E. Quincy
Topeka, Kansas 66683

KENTUCKY

Eastern

Clerk
P.O. Box 741
Lexington, Kentucky 40501

Divisional Offices with Resident Deputy in Charge:
P.O. Box 1073
Covington, Kentucky 41012

P.O. Box 689
London, Kentucky 40741

P.O. Box 355
Catlettsburg, Kentucky 41129

P.O. Box 131
Pikeville, Kentucky 41501

LOUISIANA

Eastern

Clerk
U.S. Courthouse
Chambers C-151
500 Camp Street
New Orleans, Louisiana 70130

Middle

Clerk
Room 308, 707 Florida Avenue
Federal Building and U.S. Courthouse
Baton Rouge, Louisiana 70801

Western

Clerk
P.O. Box 106
Shreveport, Louisiana 71161

Divisional Offices with Resident Deputy in Charge:
P.O. Box 2722
Lafayette, Louisiana 70501

P.O. Box 1116
Opelousas, Louisiana 70570

P.O. Box 393
Lake Charles, Louisiana 70601

P.O. Box 1269
Alexandria, Louisiana 71301

MAINE

Clerk
156 Federal Street
P.O. Box 4820
Portland, Maine 04112

Divisional Office with Resident Deputy in Charge:
212 Harlow Street
Bangor, Maine 04401

MARYLAND

Clerk
U.S. Courthouse
101 West Lombard Street
Baltimore, Maryland 21202

MASSACHUSETTS

Clerk
McCormack Post Office and
    Courthouse Building
Boston, Massachusetts 02109

MICHIGAN

Eastern

Clerk
Room 133
Federal Building
Detroit, Michigan 48226

*Divisional Offices with Resident
Deputy in Charge:*
214 Post Office Building
Bay City, Michigan 48706

600 Church Street
Flint, Michigan 48502

Western

Clerk
110 Michigan Street, N.W.
458 Federal Building
Grand Rapids, Michigan 49503

*Divisional Offices with Resident
Deputy in Charge:*
229 Post Office Building
Marquette, Michigan 49855

MINNESOTA

Clerk
708 Federal Building
316 North Robert Street
St. Paul, Minnesota 55101

*Divisional Offices with Resident
Deputy in Charge:*
514 U.S. Courthouse
110 South 4th Street
Minneapolis, Minnesota 55401

417 U.S. Courthouse
Duluth, Minnesota 55802

MISSISSIPPI

Northern

Clerk
P.O. Box 727
Oxford, Mississippi 38655

*Divisional Offices with Resident
Deputy in Charge:*
P.O. Box 190
Clarksdale, Mississippi 38614

P.O. Box 704
Aberdeen, Mississippi 39730

P.O. Box 190
Greenville, Mississippi 38701

Southern

Clerk
P.O. Box 769
Jackson, Mississippi 39205

*Divisional Offices with Resident
Deputy in Charge:*
Box 369
Biloxi, Mississippi 39533

Box 1186
Meridian, Mississippi 39301

Box 511
Hattiesburg, Mississippi 39401

MISSOURI

Eastern

Clerk
U.S. Court and Custom House
1114 Market Street
St. Louis, Missouri 63101

*Divisional Office with Resident
Deputy in Charge:*
Federal Building
339 Broadway
Cape Girardeau, Missouri 63701

Western

Clerk
U.S. Courthouse
811 Grand Avenue, Room 445
Kansas City, Missouri 64106

Divisional Offices with Resident
Deputy in Charge:
206 U.S. Courthouse
302 Joplin Street
Joplin, Missouri 64801

310 U.S. Courthouse
131 West High Street
Jefferson City, Missouri 65102

229 U.S. Courthouse
201 South Eight Street
St. Joseph, Missouri 64501

305 U.S. Courthouse
870 Boonville Street
Springfield, Missouri 65801

MONTANA

Clerk
P.O. Box 8537
Missoula, Montana 59807

Divisional Offices with Resident
Deputy in Charge:
Room 5405, Federal Building
316 North 26th Street
Billings, Montana 59101

Federal Building
Butte, Montana 59701

NEBRASKA

Clerk
9000 U.S. Courthouse and
    Post Office Building
P.O. Box 129
Downtown Station
Omaha, Nebraska 68101

Divisional Office with Resident
Deputy in Charge:
593 Federal Building
100 Centennial Mall North
Lincoln, Nebraska 68508

NEVADA

Clerk
Room 3-632
300 Las Vegas Boulevard, South
Las Vegas, Nevada 89101

Divisional Office with Resident
Deputy in Charge:
300 Booth Street
Room 5003
Reno, Nevada 89502

NEW HAMPSHIRE

Clerk
P.O. Box 1498
Concord, New Hampshire 03301

NEW JERSEY

Clerk
U.S. Post Office
    and Courthouse
Trenton, New Jersey 08605

Divisional Offices with Resident
Deputy in Charge:
U.S. Post Office
    and Courthouse
Newark, New Jersey 07102

U.S. Post Office
    and Courthouse
Camden, New Jersey 08102

NEW MEXICO

Clerk
P.O. Box 689
Albuquerque, New Mexico 87103

NEW YORK

Northern

Clerk
Box 950
Post Office and
    Courthouse Building
Albany, New York 12201

*Divisional Office with Resident
Deputy in Charge:*
Box 417
Post Office and
   Courthouse Building
Utica, New York 13503

Southern

Clerk
U.S. Courthouse
Foley Square
New York, New York 10007

Eastern

Clerk
U.S. Courthouse
225 Cadman Plaza East
Brooklyn, New York 11201

Western

Clerk
604 U.S. Courthouse
Buffalo, New York 14202

NORTH CAROLINA

Eastern

Clerk
P.O. Box 25670
Raleigh, North Carolina 27611

*Divisional Offices with Resident
Deputy in Charge:*
P.O. Box 43
Fayetteville, North Carolina 28302

P.O. Box 1336
New Bern, North Carolina 28560

P.O. Box 338
Wilmington, North Carolina 28401

Middle

Clerk
P.O. Box V-1
Greensboro, North Carolina 27402

Western

Clerk
Post Office Building
P.O. Box 92
Asheville, North Carolina 28802

*Divisional Offices with Resident
Deputy in Charge:*
Post Office and Courthouse
P.O. Box 1266
Charlotte, North Carolina 28231

Post Office and Courthouse
P.O. Box 466
Statesville, North Carolina 28677

NORTH DAKOTA

Clerk
P.O. Box 1193
Bismark, North Dakota 58501

*Divisional Office with Resident
Deputy in Charge:*
P.O. Box 870
Fargo, North Dakota 58102

OHIO

Northern

Clerk
328 U.S. Courthouse
Cleveland, Ohio 44114

*Divisional Offices with Resident
Deputy in Charge:*
201 U.S. Courthouse
Toledo, Ohio 43624

332 U.S. Post Office Building
Youngstown, Ohio 44501

568 U.S. Courthouse
Akron, Ohio 44308

Southern

Clerk
328 U.S. Courthouse
85 Marconi Boulevard
Columbus, Ohio 43215

*Divisional Offices with Resident
Deputy in Charge:*
832 U.S. Courthouse
  and Post Office Building
5th and Walnut Streets
Cincinnati, Ohio 45202

P.O. Box 970
Mid-City Station
Dayton, Ohio 45402

OKLAHOMA

Northern

Clerk
Room 411, U.S. Courthouse
Tulsa, Oklahoma 74103

Eastern

Clerk
P.O. Box 607
U.S. Courthouse
Muskogee, Oklahoma 74401

Western

Clerk
Room 3210, U.S. Courthouse
Oklahoma City, Oklahoma 73102

OREGON

Clerk
P.O. Box 1150
Portland, Oregon 97207

PENNSYLVANIA

Eastern

Clerk
2609 U.S. Courthouse
601 Market Street
Philadelphia, Pennsylvania 19106

*Divisional Office with Resident
Deputy in Charge:*
Room 444
American Bank Building
35 North 6th Street
Reading, Pennsylvania 19601

Middle

Clerk
P.O. Box 1148
Scranton, Pennsylvania 18501

*Divisional Office with Resident
Deputy in Charge:*
P.O. Box 983
Harrisburg, Pennsylvania 17108

Box 540
Williamsport, Pennsylvania 17701

Room 203, Federal Building
197 South Main Street
Wilkes-Barre, Pennsylvania 18701

Western

Clerk
P.O. Box 1805
Pittsburgh, Pennsylvania 15230

*Divisional Office with Resident
Deputy in Charge:*
227 U.S. Courthouse
Erie, Pennsylvania 16501

PUERTO RICO

Clerk
P.O. Box 3671
San Juan, Puerto Rico 00904

RHODE ISLAND

Clerk
Providence, Rhode Island 02901

SOUTH CAROLINA

Clerk
P.O. Box 867
Columbia, South Carolina 29202

*Divisional Offices with Resident
Deputy in Charge:*
P.O. Box 835
Charleston, South Carolina 29402

P.O. Box 10250
Greenville, South Carolina 29601

SOUTH DAKOTA

Clerk
Room 220, Federal Building
   and U.S. Courthouse
400 South Phillips Avenue
Sioux Falls, South Dakota 57102

*Divisional Offices with Resident
Deputy in Charge:*
Room 302, Federal Building
   and U.S. Courthouse
515 9th Street
Rapid City, South Dakota 57701

Room 405, Post Office and
   U.S. Courthouse
Pierre, South Dakota 57501

TENNESSEE

Eastern

Clerk
P.O. Box 2348
Knoxville, Tennessee 37901

*Divisional Offices with Resident
Deputy in Charge:*
P.O. Box 591
Chattanooga, Tennessee 37401

P.O. Box 149
Greenville, Tennessee 37743

Middle

Clerk
800 U.S. Courthouse
Nashville, Tennessee 37203

Western

Clerk
850 Federal Building
167 North Main Street
Memphis, Tennessee 38103

*Divisional Office with Resident
Deputy in Charge:*
P.O. Box 756
Jackson, Tennessee 38301

TEXAS

Northern

Clerk
U.S. Courthouse
Room 15C22
1100 Commerce Street
Dallas, Texas 75242

*Divisional Offices with Resident
Deputy in Charge:*
P.O. Box 1218
Abilene, Texas 79604

P.O. Box 886
Amarillo, Texas 79105

202 U.S. Courthouse
Fort Worth, Texas 76102

C-221 U.S. Courthouse
1205 Texas Avenue
Lubbock, Texas 79401

Twohig and Oaks Streets
Room 202
San Angelo, Texas 76901

P.O. Box 1234
Wichita Falls, Texas 76307

Southern

Clerk
P.O. Box 61010
Houston, Texas 77208

*Divisional Offices with Resident
Deputy in Charge:*
P.O. Box 2299
Brownsville, Texas 78520

P.O. Box 2567
Corpus Christi, Texas 78403

611 P.O. Building
Galveston, Texas 77550

P.O. Box 597
Laredo, Texas 78040

P.O. Box 1541
Victoria, Texas 77901

Eastern

Clerk
P.O. Box 231
Beaumont, Texas 77704

*Divisional Offices with Resident
Deputy in Charge:*
Federal Building
Sherman, Texas 75990

P.O. Box 2667
Texarkana, Texas 75501

P.O. Box 539
Tyler, Texas 75701

Western

Clerk
Hemisfair Plaza
655 East Durango Boulevard
San Antonio, Texas 78206

*Divisional Offices with Resident
Deputy in Charge:*
U.S. Courthouse
200 West 8th Street
Austin, Texas 78701

P.O. Box 1349
Del Rio, Texas 78840

Room 108, U.S. Courthouse
El Paso, Texas 79901

P.O. Box 608
Waco, Texas 76703

P.O. Box 191
Pecos, Texas 79772

UTAH

Clerk
U.S. Post Office and Courthouse
Salt Lake City, Utah 84101

VERMONT

Clerk
P.O. Box 945
Federal Building
Burlington, Vermont 05401

*Divisional Office with Resident
Deputy in Charge:*
P.O. Box 607
Federal Building
Rutland, Vermont 05701

VIRGIN ISLANDS, DISTRICT COURT OF THE

Clerk
Charlotte Amalie
St. Thomas, Virgin Islands 00801

*Divisional Office with Resident
Deputy in Charge:*
Christiansted
St. Croix, Virgin Islands 00820

VIRGINIA

Eastern

Clerk
P.O. Box 1318
Norfolk, Virginia 23501

*Divisional Offices with Resident
Deputy in Charge:*
P.O. Box 2-Ad
Richmond, Virginia 23205

P.O. Box 709
Alexandria, Virginia 22313

P.O. Box 494
Newport News, Virginia 23607

Western

Clerk
P.O. Box 1234
Roanoke, Virginia 24006

*Divisional Offices with Resident
Deputy in Charge:*
P.O. Box 398
Abingdon, Virginia 24210

P.O. Box 135
Charlottesville, Virginia 22902

P.O. Box 52
Danville, Virginia 24540

P.O. Box 1207
Harrisonburg, Virginia 22801

P.O. Box 744
Lynchburg, Virginia 24505

WASHINGTON

Eastern

Clerk
P.O. Box 1493
Spokane, Washington 99210

Western

Clerk
308 U.S. Courthouse
Seattle, Washington 98104

Divisional Offices with Resident Deputy in Charge:
P.O. Box 1935
Tacoma, Washington 98401

WEST VIRGINIA

Northern

Clerk
P.O. Box 1518
Elkins, West Virginia 26241

Divisional Offices with Resident Deputy in Charge:
P.O. Box 471
Wheeling, West Virginia 26003

P.O. Box 1526
Parkersburg, West Virginia 26101

Southern

Clerk
P.O. Box 2546
Charleston, West Virginia 25329

Divisional Offices with Resident Deputy in Charge:
Federal Station Box 4128
Bluefield, West Virginia 24702

P.O. Box 1570
Huntington, West Virginia 25716

WISCONSIN

Eastern

Clerk
Room 362 U.S. Courthouse
517 East Wisconsin Avenue
Milwaukee, Wisconsin 53202

Western

Clerk
P.O. Box 432
Madison, Wisconsin 53701

WYOMING

Clerk
P.O. Box 727
Cheyenne, Wyoming 82001

FEDERAL JUDICIAL CENTER

Dolley Madison House
1520 H Street, N.W.
Washington, D.C. 20005

ADMINISTRATIVE OFFICE OF THE UNITED STATES COURTS

Washington, D.C. 20544

DIRECTORY OF U.S. COUNTIES
AND COUNTY SEATS

ALABAMA

County	County Seat	Zip Code
Autauga	Prattville	36067
Baldwin	Bay Minette	36507
Barbour	Clayton	36016
Bibb	Centreville	35042
Blount	Oneonta	35121
Bullock	Union Springs	36089
Butler	Greenville	36037
Calhoun	Anniston	36201
Chambers	Lafayette	36862
Cherokee	Centre	35960
Chilton	Clanton	35045
Choctaw	Butler	36904
Clarke	Grove Hill	36451
Clay	Ashland	36251
Cleburne	Heflin	36264
Coffee	Elba	36323
Colbert	Tuscumbia	35674
Conecuh	Evergreen	36401
Coosa	Rockford	35136
Covington	Andalusia	36420
Crenshaw	Luverne	36049
Cullman	Cullman	35055
Dale	Ozark	36360
Dallas	Selma	36701
De Kalb	Fort Payne	35967
Elmore	Wetumpka	36092
Escambia	Brewton	36426
Etowah	Gadsden	35901-05
Fayette	Fayette	35555
Franklin	Russellville	35653
Geneva	Geneva	36340
Greene	Eutaw	35462
Hale	Greensboro	36744
Henry	Abbeville	36310
Houston	Dothan	36301
Jackson	Scottsboro	35768
Jefferson	Birmingham	35201-43
Lamar	Vernon	35592

County	County Seat	Zip Code
Lauderdale	Florence	35630
Lawrence	Moulton	35650
Lee	Opelika	36801
Limestone	Athens	35611
Lowndes	Hayneville	36040
Macon	Tuskegee	36083
Madison	Huntsville	35801-12
Marengo	Linden	36748
Marion	Hamilton	35570
Marshall	Guntersville	35976
Mobile	Mobile	36601-19
Monroe	Monroeville	36460
Montgomery	Montgomery	36101-15
Morgan	Decatur	35601
Perry	Marion	36756
Pickens	Carrollton	35447
Pike	Troy	36081
Randolph	Wedowee	36278
Russell	Phenix City	36867
St. Clair	Ashville	35953
Shelby	Columbiana	35051
Sumter	Livingston	35470
Talladega	Talladega	35160
Tallapoosa	Dadeville	36853
Tuscaloosa	Tuscaloosa	35401
Walker	Jasper	35501
Washington	Chatom	36518
Wilcox	Camden	36726
Winston	Double Springs	35553

ALASKA *

County	County Seat	Zip Code
Bristol Bay	Naknek	99633
Fairbanks North Star	Fairbanks	99701
Greater Anchorage Area	Anchorage	99501-41
Greater Sitka	Sitka	99835

*Alaska abolished county governments; former counties and county seats are listed here.

County	County Seat	Zip Code
Haines	Haines	99827
Juneau	Juneau	99801
Kenai		
Peninsula	Soldotna	99669
Kodiak		
Island	Kodiak	99615
Matanuska-		
Susitna	Palmer	99645

Census Divisions**

Aleutian Islands
Anchorage
Angoon
Barrow-North Slope
Bethel
Bristol Bay Borough
Bristol Bay
Cordova-McCarthy
Fairbanks
Haines
Juneau
Kenai-Cook Inlet
Ketchikan
Kobuk
Kodiak
Kuskokwim
Matanuska-Susitna
Nome
Outer Ketchikan
Prince of Wales
Seward
Sitka
Skagway-Yakuta
Southeast Fairbanks
Upper Yukon
Valdez-Chitina-Whittier
Wade Hampton
Wrangell-Petersburg
Yukon-Koyukuk

ARIZONA

County	County Seat	Zip Code
Apache	St. Johns	85936
Cochise	Bisbee	85603
Coconino	Flagstaff	86001
Gila	Globe	85501
Graham	Safford	85546
Greenlee	Clifton	85533
Maricopa	Phoenix	85001-41
Mohave	Kingman	86401
Navajo	Holbrook	86025
Pima	Tucson	85701-24
Pinal	Florence	85232
Santa Cruz	Nogales	85621
Yavapai	Prescott	86301
Yuma	Yuma	85364

ARKANSAS

County	County Seat	Zip Code
Arkansas	De Witt	72042
	and	
	Stuttgart	72160
Ashley	Hamburg	71646
Baxter	Mountain Home	72653
Benton	Bentonville	72712
Boone	Harrison	72601
Bradley	Warren	71671
Calhoun	Hampton	71744
Carroll	Berryville	72616
	and	
	Eureka Springs	72632
Chicot	Lake Village	71653
Clark	Arkadelphia	71923
Clay	Corning	72422
	and	
	Piggott	72454
Cleburne	Heber Springs	72543
Cleveland	Rison	71665
Columbia	Magnolia	71753
Conway	Morrilton	72110

**The State of Alaska and the U.S. Bureau of the Census have established Census Divisions for use in compiling statistics for the State.

County	County Seat	Zip Code	County	County Seat	Zip Code
Craighead	Jonesboro *and*	72401	Montgomery	Mount Ida	71957
			Nevada	Prescott	71857
	Lake City	72437	Newton	Jasper	72641
Crawford	Van Buren	72956	Ouachita	Camden	71701
Crittenden	Marion	72364	Perry	Perryville	72126
Cross	Wynne	72396	Phillips	Helena	72342
Dallas	Fordyce	71742	Pike	Murfreesboro	71958
Desha	Arkansas City	71630	Poinsett	Harrisburg	72432
Drew	Monticello	71655	Polk	Mena	71953
Faulkner	Conway	72032	Pope	Russellville	72801
Franklin	Charleston *and*	72933	Prairie	Des Arc *and*	72040
	Ozark	72949		De Valls Bluff	72041
Fulton	Salem	72576	Pulaski	Little Rock	72201-09
Garland	Hot Springs	71901	Randolph	Pocohontas	72455
Grant	Sheridan	72150	St. Francis	Forrest City	72335
Greene	Paragould	72450	Saline	Benton	72015
Hempstead	Hope	71801	Scott	Waldron	72958
Hot Spring	Malvern	72104	Searcy	Marshall	72650
Howard	Nashville	71852	Sebastian	Fort Smith *and*	72901
Independence	Batesville	72501		Greenwood	72936
Izard	Melbourne	72556	Sevier	De Queen	71832
Jackson	Newport	72112	Sharp	Ash Flat	72513
Jefferson	Pine Bluff	71601	Stone	Mountain View	72560
Johnson	Clarksville	72830	Union	El Dorado	71730
Lafayette	Lewisville	71845	Van Buren	Clinton	72031
Lawrence	Walnut Ridge	72476	Washington	Fayetteville	72701
Lee	Marianna	72360	White	Searcy	72143
Lincoln	Star City	71667	Woodruff	Augusta	72006
Little River	Ashdown	71822	Yell	Danville *and*	72833
Logan	Booneville *and*	72927		Dardanelle	72834
	Paris	72855			
Lonoke	Lonoke	72086			
Madison	Huntsville	72740			

CALIFORNIA

County	County Seat	Zip Code
Marion	Yellville	72687
Miller	Texarkana	75501
Mississippi	Blytheville *and*	72315
	Osceola	72370
Monroe	Clarendon	72029
Alameda	Oakland	94601-27
Alpine	Markleeville	96120
Amador	Jackson	95642
Butte	Oroville	95965
Calaveras	San Andreas	95249
Colusa	Colusa	95932

County	County Seat	Zip Code
Contra Costa	Martinez	94553
Del Norte	Crescent City	95531
El Dorado	Placerville	95667
Fresno	Fresno	93701-66
Glenn	Willows	95988
Humboldt	Eureka	95501
Imperial	El Centro	92243
Inyo	Independence	93526
Kern	Bakersfield	93301-09
Kings	Hanford	93230
Lake	Lakeport	95453
Lassen	Susanville	96130
Los Angeles	Los Angeles	90001-80
Madera	Madera	93637
Marin	San Rafael	94901-04
Mariposa	Mariposa	95338
Mendocino	Ukiah	95482
Merced	Merced	95340
Modoc	Alturas	96101
Mono	Bridgeport	93517
Monterey	Salinas	93901
Napa	Napa	94558
Nevada	Nevada City	95959
Orange	Santa Ana	92666-69
Placer	Auburn	95603
Plumas	Quincy	95971
Riverside	Riverside	92501-09
Sacramento	Sacramento	95801-60
San Benito	Hollister	95023
San Bernard-ino	San Bernard-ino	92401-10
San Diego	San Diego	92101-57
San Fran-cisco	San Fran-cisco	94101-40
San Joaquin	Stockton	95201-07
San Luis Obispo	San Luis Obispo	93401
San Mateo	Redwood City	94061-65
Santa Bar-bara	Santa Bar-bara	93101-07
Santa Clara	San Jose	95101-50
Santa Cruz	Santa Cruz	95060

County	County Seat	Zip Code
Shasta	Redding	96001
Sierra	Downieville	95936
Siskiyou	Yreka	96097
Solano	Fairfield	94533
Sonoma	Santa Rosa	95401-06
Stanislaus	Modesto	95350-54
Sutter	Yuba City	95991
Tehama	Red Bluff	96080
Trinity	Weaverville	96093
Tulare	Visalia	93277
Tuolumne	Sonora	95370
Ventura	Ventura	93001-03
Yolo	Woodland	95695
Yuba	Marysville	95901

COLORADO

County	County Seat	Zip Code
Adams	Brighton	80601
Alamosa	Alamosa	81101
Arapahoe	Littleton	80120-21
Archuleta	Pagosa Springs	81147
Baca	Springfield	81073
Bent	Las Animas	81054
Boulder	Boulder	80301-03
Chaffee	Salida	81201
Cheyenne	Cheyenne Wells	80810
Clear Creek	Georgetown	80444
Conejos	Conejos	81129
Costilla	San Luis	81152
Crowley	Ordway	81063
Custer	Westcliffe	81252
Delta	Delta	81416
Denver	Denver	80201-40
Dolores	Dove Creek	81324
Douglas	Castle Rock	80104
Eagle	Eagle	81631
Elbert	Kiowa	80117
El Paso	Colorado Springs	80901-17
Fremont	Canon City	81212
Garfield	Glenwood Springs	81601

County	County Seat	Zip Code
Gilpin	Central City	80427
Grand	Hot Sulphur Springs	80451
Gunnison	Gunnison	81230
Hinsdale	Lake City	81235
Huerfano	Walsenburg	81089
Jackson	Walden	80480
Jefferson	Golden	80401
Kiowa	Eads	81036
Kit Carson	Burlington	80807
Lake	Leadville	80461
La Plata	Durango	81301
Larimer	Fort Collins	80521
Las Animas	Trinidad	81082
Lincoln	Hugo	80821
Logan	Sterling	80751
Mesa	Grand Junction	81501
Mineral	Creede	81130
Moffat	Craig	81625
Montezuma	Cortez	81321
Montrose	Montrose	81401
Morgan	Fort Morgan	80701
Otero	La Junta	81050
Ouray	Ouray	81427
Park	Fairplay	80440
Phillips	Holyoke	80734
Pitkin	Aspen	81611
Prowers	Lamar	81052
Pueblo	Pueblo	81001-08
Rio Blanco	Meeker	81641
Rio Grande	Del Norte	81132
Routt	Steamboat Springs	80477
Saguache	Saguache	81149
San Juan	Silverton	81433
San Miguel	Telluride	81435
Sedgwick	Julesburg	80737
Summit	Breckenridge	80424
Teller	Cripple Creek	80813
Washington	Akron	80720

County	County Seat	Zip Code
Weld	Greeley	80631
Yuma	Wray	80758

CONNECTICUT*

County	County Seat	Zip Code
Fairfield	Bridgeport	06601-12
Hartford	Hartford	06101-20
Litchfield	Torrington	06790
Middlesex	Middletown	06457
New Haven	New Haven	06473
	and	
	Waterbury	06701-20
New London	New London	06320
	and	
	Norwich	06360
Tolland	Mansfield Center	06250
Windham	Willimantic	06226

DELAWARE

County	County Seat	Zip Code
Kent	Dover	19901
New Castle	Wilmington	19801-99
Sussex	Georgetown	19947

DISTRICT OF COLUMBIA**

Washington, D.C.		20001-59

FLORIDA

County	County Seat	Zip Code
Alachua	Gainesville	32601
Baker	Macclenny	32063
Bay	Panama City	32401
Bradford	Starke	32091
Brevard	Titusville	32780
Broward	Fort Lauderdale	33301-16
Calhoun	Blountstown	32424
Charlotte	Punta Gorda	33950

*Connecticut abolished county governments in 1960; former counties and county seats are listed here.

**The District of Columbia is a Federal district of the United States and is coextensive with the city of Washington.

County	County Seat	Zip Code	County	County Seat	Zip Code
Citrus	Inverness	32650	Osceola	Kissimmee	32741
Clay	Green Cove		Palm Beach	West Palm	
	Springs	32043		Beach	33401-08
Collier	East Naples	33940	Pasco	Dade City	33525
Columbia	Lake City	32055	Pinellas	Clearwater	33515-18
Dade	Miami	33101-69	Polk	Bartow	33830
De Soto	Arcadia	33821	Putnam	Palatka	32077
Dixie	Cross City	32628	St. Johns	St. Augustine	32084
Duval	Jacksonville	32201-67	St. Lucie	Fort Pierce	33450
Escambia	Pensacola	32501-12	Santa Rosa	Milton	32570
Flagler	Bunnell	32010	Sarasota	Sarasota	33577-81
Franklin	Apalachicola	32320	Seminole	Sanford	32771
Gadsden	Quincy	32351	Sumter	Bushnell	33513
Gilchrist	Trenton	32693	Suwannee	Live Oak	32060
Glades	Moore Haven	33471	Taylor	Perry	32347
Gulf	Wewahitchka	32465	Union	Lake Butler	32054
Hamilton	Jasper	32052	Volusia	De Land	32720
Hardee	Wauchula	33873	Wakulla	Crawfordville	32327
Hendry	La Belle	33935	Walton	De Funiak	
Hernando	Brooksville	32512		Springs	32433
Highlands	Sebring	33870	Washington	Chipley	32428
Hillsborough	Tampa	33601-22			
Holmes	Bonifay	32425			
Indian River	Vero Beach	32960			

GEORGIA

County	County Seat	Zip Code
Jackson	Marianna	32446	Appling	Baxley	31513
Jefferson	Monticello	32344	Atkinson	Pearson	31642
Lafayette	Mayo	32066	Bacon	Alma	31510
Lake	Tavares	32778	Baker	Newton	31770
Lee	Fort Myers	33901-05	Baldwin	Milledgeville	31061
Leon	Tallahassee	32301-11	Banks	Homer	30547
Levy	Bronson	32621	Barrow	Winder	30680
Liberty	Bristol	32321	Bartow	Cartersville	30120
Madison	Madison	32340	Ben Hill	Fitzgerald	31750
Manatee	Bradenton	33500	Berrien	Nashville	31639
Marion	Ocala	32670	Bibb	Macon	31201-08
Martin	Stuart	33494	Bleckley	Cochran	31014
Monroe	Key West	33040	Brantley	Nahunta	31553
Nassau	Fernandina		Brooks	Quitman	31643
	Beach	32034	Bryan	Pembroke	31321
Okaloosa	Crestview	32536	Bulloch	Statesboro	30458
Okeechobee	Okeechobee	33472	Burke	Waynesboro	30830
Orange	Orlando	32801-99	Butts	Jackson	30233

County	County Seat	Zip Code	County	County Seat	Zip Code
Calhoun	Morgan	31766	Franklin	Carnesville	30521
Camden	Woodbine	31569	Fulton	Atlanta	30301-96
Candler	Metter	30439	Gilmer	Eliljay	30540
Carroll	Carrollton	30117	Glascock	Gibson	30810
Catoosa	Ringgold	30736	Glynn	Brunswick	31520
Charlton	Folkston	31537	Gordon	Calhoun	30701
Chatham	Savannah	31401-09	Grady	Cairo	31728
Chatta-			Greene	Greensboro	30642
hoochee	Cusseta	31805	Gwinnett	Lawrenceville	30245
Chattooga	Summerville	30707	Habersham	Clarkesville	30523
Cherokee	Canton	30114	Hall	Gainesville	30501
Clarke	Athens	30601	Hancock	Sparta	31087
Clay	Fort Gaines	31751	Haralson	Buchanan	30113
Clayton	Jonesboro	30236	Harris	Hamilton	31811
Clinch	Homerville	31634	Hart	Hartwell	30643
Cobb	Marietta	30060	Heard	Franklin	30217
Coffee	Douglas	31533	Henry	McDonough	30253
Colquitt	Moultrie	31768	Houston	Perry	31069
Columbia	Appling	30802	Irwin	Ocilla	31774
Columbus	Columbus	31901-07	Jackson	Jefferson	30549
Cook	Adel	31620	Jasper	Monticello	31064
Coweta	Newnan	30263	Jeff Davis	Hazlehurst	31539
Crawford	Knoxville	31050	Jefferson	Louisville	30434
Crisp	Cordele	31015	Jenkins	Millen	30442
Dade	Trenton	30752	Johnson	Wrightsville	31096
Dawson	Dawsonville	30534	Jones	Gray	31032
Decatur	Bainbridge	31717	Lamar	Barnesville	30204
De Kalb	Decatur	30030-34	Lanier	Lakeland	31635
Dodge	Eastman	31023	Laurens	Dublin	31021
Dooly	Vienna	31092	Lee	Leesburg	31763
Dougherty	Albany	31701-05	Liberty	Hinesville	31313
Douglas	Douglasville	30134	Lincoln	Lincolnton	30817
Early	Blakely	31723	Long	Ludowici	31316
Echols	Statenville	31648	Lowndes	Valdosta	31601
Effingham	Springfield	31329	Lumpkin	Dahlonega	30533
Elbert	Elberton	30635	McDuffie	Thomson	30824
Emanuel	Swainsboro	30401	McIntosh	Darien	31305
Evans	Claxton	30417	Macon	Oglethorpe	31068
Fannin	Blue Ridge	30513	Madison	Danielsville	30633
Fayette	Fayetteville	30214	Marion	Buena Vista	31803
Floyd	Rome	30161	Meriwether	Greenville	30222
Forsyth	Cumming	30130	Miller	Colquitt	31737

County	County Seat	Zip Code	County	County Seat	Zip Code
Mitchell	Camilla	31730	Troup	La Grange	30240
Monroe	Forsyth	31029	Turner	Ashburn	31714
Montgomery	Mount Vernon	30445	Twiggs	Jeffersonville	31044
Morgan	Madison	30650	Union	Blairsville	30512
Murray	Chatsworth	30705	Upson	Thomaston	30286
Muscogee*			Walker	La Fayette	30728
Newton	Covington	30209	Walton	Monroe	30655
Oconee	Watkinsville	30677	Ware	Waycross	31501
Oglethorpe	Lexington	30648	Warren	Warrenton	30828
Paulding	Dallas	30132	Washington	Sandersville	31082
Peach	Fort Valley	31030	Wayne	Jesup	31545
Pickens	Jasper	30143	Webster	Preston	31824
Pierce	Blackshear	31516	Wheeler	Alamo	30411
Pike	Zebulon	30295	White	Cleveland	30528
Polk	Cedartown	30125	Whitfield	Dalton	30720
Pulaski	Hawkinsville	31036	Wilcox	Abbeville	31001
Putnam	Eatonton	31024	Wilkes	Washington	30673
Quitman	Georgetown	31754	Wilkinson	Irwinton	31042
Rabun	Clayton	30525	Worth	Sylvester	31791
Randolph	Cuthbert	31740			
Richmond	Augusta	30901-08			
Rockdale	Conyers	30207		**HAWAII**	
Schley	Ellaville	31806			
Screven	Sylvania	30467	Hawaii	Hilo	96720
Seminole	Donalsonville	31745	Honolulu	Honolulu	96801-25
Spalding	Griffin	30223	Kauai	Lihue	96766
Stephens	Toccoa	30577	Maui	Wailuku	96793
Stewart	Lumpkin	31815			
Sumter	Americus	31709		**IDAHO**	
Talbot	Talbotton	31827			
Taliaferro	Crawfordville	30631	Ada	Boise	83701-07
Tattnall	Reidsville	30453	Adams	Council	83612
Taylor	Butler	31006	Bannock	Pocatello	83201
Telfair	McRae	31055	Bear Lake	Paris	83261
Terrell	Dawson	31742	Benewah	St. Maries	83861
Thomas	Thomasville	31792	Bingham	Blackfoot	83221
Tift	Tifton	31794	Blaine	Hailey	83333
Toombs	Lyons	'30436	Boise	Idaho City	83631
Towns	Hiawassee	30546	Bonner	Sandpoint	83864
Treutlen	Soperton	30457	Bonneville	Idaho Falls	83401
			Boundary	Bonners Ferry	83805

*Muscogee County was replaced by a consolidated government area called Columbus.

County	County Seat	Zip Code
Butte	Arco	83213
Camas	Fairfield	83327
Canyon	Caldwell	83605
Caribou	Soda Springs	83276
Cassia	Burley	83318
Clark	Dubois	83423
Clearwater	Orofino	83544
Custer	Challis	83226
Elmore	Mountain Home	83647
Franklin	Preston	83263
Fremont	St. Anthony	83445
Gem	Emmett	83617
Gooding	Gooding	83330
Idaho	Grangeville	83530
Jefferson	Rigby	83442
Jerome	Jerome	83338
Kootenai	Coeur d'Alene	83814
Latah	Moscow	83843
Lemhi	Salmon	83467
Lewis	Nezperce	83543
Lincoln	Shoshone	83352
Madison	Rexburg	83440
Minidoka	Rupert	83350
Nez Perce	Lewiston	83501
Oneida	Malad City	83252
Owyhee	Murphy	83650
Payette	Payette	83661
Power	American Falls	83211
Shoshone	Wallace	83873
Teton	Driggs	83422
Twin Falls	Twin Falls	83301
Valley	Cascade	83611
Washington	Weiser	83672

ILLINOIS

County	County Seat	Zip Code
Adams	Quincy	62301
Alexander	Cairo	62914
Bond	Greenville	62246
Boone	Belvidere	61008
Brown	Mount Sterling	62353
Bureau	Princeton	61356
Calhoun	Hardin	62047
Carroll	Mount Carroll	61053
Cass	Virginia	62691
Champaign	Urbana	61801
Christian	Taylorville	62568
Clark	Marshall	62441
Clay	Louisville	62858
Clinton	Carlyle	62231
Coles	Charleston	61920
Cook	Chicago	60601-99
Crawford	Robinson	62454
Cumberland	Toledo	62468
De Kalb	Sycamore	60178
De Witt	Clinton	61727
Douglas	Tuscola	61953
Du Page	Wheaton	60187
Edgar	Paris	61944
Edwards	Albion	62806
Effingham	Effingham	62401
Fayette	Vandalia	62471
Ford	Paxton	60957
Franklin	Benton	62812
Fulton	Lewistown	61542
Gallatin	Shawneetown	62984
Greene	Carrollton	62016
Grundy	Morris	60450
Hamilton	McLeansboro	62859
Hancock	Carthage	62321
Hardin	Elizabethtown	62931
Henderson	Oquawka	61469
Henry	Cambridge	61238
Iroquois	Watseka	60970
Jackson	Murphysboro	62966
Jasper	Newton	62448
Jefferson	Mount Vernon	62864
Jersey	Jerseyville	62052
Jo Daviess	Galena	61036
Johnson	Vienna	62995
Kane	Geneva	60134
Kankakee	Kankakee	60901
Kendall	Yorkville	60560
Knox	Galesburg	61401

County	County Seat	Zip Code
Lake	Waukegan	60085
La Salle	Ottawa	61350
Lawrence	Lawrenceville	62439
Lee	Dixon	61021
Livingston	Pontiac	61764
Logan	Lincoln	62656
McDonough	Macomb	61455
McHenry	Woodstock	60098
McLean	Bloomington	61701
Macon	Decatur	62521-26
Macoupin	Carlinville	62626
Madison	Edwardsville	62025
Marion	Salem	62881
Marshall	Lacon	61540
Mason	Havana	62644
Massac	Metropolis	62960
Menard	Petersburg	62675
Mercer	Aledo	61231
Monroe	Waterloo	62298
Montgomery	Hillsboro	62049
Morgan	Jacksonville	62650
Moultrie	Sullivan	61951
Ogle	Oregon	61061
Peoria	Peoria	61601-14
Perry	Pinckneyville	62274
Piatt	Monticello	61856
Pike	Pittsfield	62363
Pope	Golconda	62938
Pulaski	Mound City	62963
Putnam	Hennepin	61327
Randolph	Chester	62233
Richland	Olney	62450
Rock Island	Rock Island	61201
St. Clair	Belleville	62220-25
Saline	Harrisburg	62946
Sangamon	Springfield	62701-08
Schuyler	Rushville	62681
Scott	Winchester	62694
Shelby	Shelbyville	62565
Stark	Toulon	61483
Stephenson	Freeport	61032
Tazewell	Pekin	61554

County	County Seat	Zip Code
Union	Jonesboro	62952
Vermilion	Danville	61832
Wabash	Mount Carmel	62863
Warren	Monmouth	61462
Washington	Nashville	62263
Wayne	Fairfield	62837
White	Carmi	62821
Whiteside	Morrison	61270
Will	Joliet	60431-36
Williamson	Marion	62959
Winnebago	Rockford	61101-11
Woodford	Eureka	61530

INDIANA

County	County Seat	Zip Code
Adams	Decatur	46733
Allen	Fort Wayne	46801-19
Bartholo-mew	Columbus	47201
Benton	Fowler	47944
Blackford	Hartford City	47348
Boone	Lebanon	46052
Brown	Nashville	47448
Carroll	Delphi	46923
Cass	Logansport	46947
Clark	Jeffersonville	47130
Clay	Brazil	47834
Clinton	Frankfort	46041
Crawford	English	47118
Daviess	Washington	47501
Dearborn	Lawrenceburg	47025
Decatur	Greensburg	47240
De Kalb	Auburn	46706
Delaware	Muncie	47302-06
Dubois	Jasper	47546
Elkhart	Goshen	46526
Fayette	Connersville	47331
Floyd	New Albany	47150
Fountain	Covington	47932
Franklin	Brookville	47012
Fulton	Rochester	46975
Gibson	Princeton	47670

County	County Seat	Zip Code	County	County Seat	Zip Code
Grant	Marion	46952	Ripley	Versailles	47042
Greene	Bloomfield	47424	Rush	Rushville	46173
Hamilton	Noblesville	46060	St. Joseph	South Bend	46601-37
Hancock	Greenfield	46140	Scott	Scottsburg	47170
Harrison	Corydon	47112	Shelby	Shelbyville	46176
Hendricks	Danville	46122	Spencer	Rockport	47635
Henry	New Castle	47362	Starke	Knox	46534
Howard	Kokomo	46901	Steuben	Angola	46703
Huntington	Huntington	46750	Sullivan	Sullivan	47882
Jackson	Brownstown	47220	Switzerland	Vevay	47043
Jasper	Rensselaer	47978	Tippecanoe	Lafayette	47901-07
Jay	Portland	47371	Tipton	Tipton	46072
Jefferson	Madison	47250	Union	Liberty	47353
Jennings	Vernon	47282	Vanderburgh	Evansville	47701-27
Johnson	Franklin	46131	Vermillion	Newport	47966
Knox	Vincennes	47591	Vigo	Terre Haute	47801-09
Kosciusko	Warsaw	46580	Wabash	Wabash	46992
Lagrange	Lagrange	46761	Warren	Williamsport	47993
Lake	Crown Point	46301	Warrick	Boonville	47601
La Porte	La Porte	46350	Washington	Salem	47167
Lawrence	Bedford	47421	Wayne	Richmond	47374
Madison	Anderson	46011-17	Wells	Bluffton	46714
Marion	Indianapolis	46201-90	White	Monticello	47960
Marshall	Plymouth	46563	Whitley	Columbia City	46725
Martin	Shoals	47581			
Miami	Peru	46970			
Monroe	Bloomington	47401		**IOWA**	
Montgomery	Crawfordsville	47933			
Morgan	Martinsville	46151	Adair	Greenfield	50849
Newton	Kentland	47951	Adams	Corning	50841
Noble	Albion	46701	Allamakee	Waukon	52172
Ohio	Rising Sun	47040	Appanoose	Centerville	52544
Orange	Paoli	47454	Audubon	Audubon	50025
Owen	Spencer	47460	Benton	Vinton	52349
Parke	Rockville	47872	Black Hawk	Waterloo	50701-07
Perry	Cannelton	47520	Boone	Boone	50036
Pike	Petersburg	47567	Bremer	Waverly	50677
Porter	Valparaiso	46383	Buchanan	Independence	50644
Posey	Mount Vernon	47620	Buena Vista	Storm Lake	50588
Pulaski	Winamac	46996	Butler	Allison	50602
Putnam	Greencastle	46135	Calhoun	Rockwell City	50579
Randolph	Winchester	47394	Carroll	Carroll	51401
			Cass	Atlantic	50022

County	County Seat	Zip Code	County	County Seat	Zip Code
Cedar	Tipton	52772	Louisa	Wapello	52653
Cerro Gordo	Mason City	50401	Lucas	Chariton	50049
Cherokee	Cherokee	51012	Lyon	Rock Rapids	51246
Chickasaw	New Hampton	50659	Madison	Winterset	50273
Clarke	Osceola	50213	Mahaska	Oskaloosa	52577
Clay	Spencer	51301	Marion	Knoxville	50138
Clayton	Elkader	52043	Marshall	Marshalltown	50158
Clinton	Clinton	52732	Mills	Glenwood	50534
Crawford	Denison	51442	Mitchell	Osage	50461
Dallas	Adel	50003	Monona	Onawa	51040
Davis	Bloomfield	52537	Monroe	Albia	52531
Decatur	Leon	50144	Montgomery	Red Oak	51566
Delaware	Manchester	52057	Muscatine	Muscatine	52761
Des Moines	Burlington	52601	O'Brien	Primghar	51245
Dickinson	Spirit Lake	51360	Osceola	Sibley	51249
Dubuque	Dubuque	52001	Page	Clarinda	51632
Emmet	Estherville	51334	Palo Alto	Emmetsburg	50536
Fayette	West Union	52175	Plymouth	Le Mars	51031
Floyd	Charles City	50616	Pocahontas	Pocahontas	50574
Franklin	Hampton	50441	Polk	Des Moines	50301-33
Fremont	Sidney	51652	Pottawat-		
Greene	Jefferson	50129	tamie	Council Bluffs	51501
Grundy	Grundy Center	50642	Poweshiek	Montezuma	50171
Guthrie	Guthrie Center	50115	Ringgold	Mount Ayr	50854
Hamilton	Webster City	50595	Sac	Sac City	50583
Hancock	Garner	50438	Scott	Davenport	52801-08
Hardin	Eldora	50627	Shelby	Harlan	51537
Harrison	Logan	51546	Sioux	Orange City	51041
Henry	Mount Pleasant	52641	Story	Nevada	50201
Howard	Cresco	52136	Tama	Toledo	52342
Humboldt	Dakota City	50529	Taylor	Bedford	50833
Ida	Ida Grove	51445	Union	Creston	50801
Iowa	Marengo	52301	Van Buren	Keosauqua	52565
Jackson	Maquoketa	52060	Wapello	Ottumwa	52501
Jasper	Newton	50208	Warren	Indianola	50125
Jefferson	Fairfield	52556	Washington	Washington	52353
Johnson	Iowa City	52240	Wayne	Corydon	50060
Jones	Anamosa	52205	Webster	Fort Dodge	50501
Keokuk	Sigourney	52591	Winnebago	Forest City	50436
Koosuth	Algona	50511	Winneshiek	Decorah	52101
Lee	Fort Madison	52627	Woodbury	Sioux City	51101-11
Linn	Cedar Rapids	52401-07	Worth	Northwood	50459

County	County Seat	Zip Code	County	County Seat	Zip Code
Wright	Clarion	50525	Harper	Anthony	67003
			Harvey	Newton	67114
			Haskell	Sublette	67877
			Hodgeman	Jetmore	67854

KANSAS

County	County Seat	Zip Code	County	County Seat	Zip Code
Allen	Iola	66749	Jackson	Holton	66436
Anderson	Garnett	66032	Jefferson	Oskaloosa	66066
Atchison	Atchison	66002	Jewell	Mankato	66956
Barber	Medicine Lodge	67104	Johnson	Olathe	66061
Barton	Great Bend	67530	Kearny	Lakin	67860
Bourbon	Fort Scott	66701	Kingman	Kingman	67068
Brown	Hiawatha	66434	Kiowa	Greensburg	67054
Butler	El Dorado	67042	Labette	Oswego	67356
Chase	Cottonwood Falls	66845	Lane	Dighton	67839
Chautauqua	Sedan	67361	Leavenworth	Leavenworth	66048
Cherokee	Columbus	66725	Lincoln	Lincoln	67455
Cheyenne	St. Francis	67756	Linn	Mound City	66056
Clark	Ashland	67831	Logan	Oakley	67748
Clay	Clay Center	67432	Lyon	Emporia	66801
Cloud	Concordia	66901	McPherson	McPherson	67460
Coffey	Burlington	66839	Marion	Marion	66861
Comanche	Coldwater	67029	Marshall	Marysville	66508
Cowley	Winfield	67156	Meade	Meade	67864
Crawford	Girard	66743	Miami	Paola	66071
Decatur	Oberlin	67749	Mitchell	Beloit	67420
Dickinson	Abilene	67410	Montgomery	Independence	67301
Doniphan	Troy	66087	Morris	Council Grove	66846
Douglas	Lawrence	66044	Morton	Elkhart	67950
Edwards	Kinsley	67547	Nemaha	Seneca	66538
Elk	Howard	67349	Neosho	Erie	66733
Ellis	Hays	67601	Ness	Ness City	67560
Ellsworth	Ellsworth	67439	Norton	Norton	67654
Finney	Garden City	67846	Osage	Lyndon	66451
Ford	Dodge City	67801	Osborne	Osborne	67473
Franklin	Ottawa	66067	Ottawa	Minneapolis	67467
Geary	Junction City	66441	Pawnee	Larned	67550
Gove	Gove	67736	Phillips	Phillipsburg	67661
Graham	Hill City	67642	Pottawa-		
Grant	Ulysses	67880	tomie	Westmoreland	66549
Gray	Cimarron	67835	Pratt	Pratt	67124
Greeley	Tribune	67879	Rawlins	Atwood	67730
Greenwood	Eureka	67045	Reno	Hutchinson	67501
Hamilton	Syracuse	67878	Republic	Belleville	66935

County	County Seat	Zip Code	County	County Seat	Zip Code
Rice	Lyons	67554	Breckinridge	Hardinsburg	40143
Riley	Manhattan	66502	Bullitt	Shepherdsville	40165
Rooks	Stockton	67669	Butler	Morgantown	42261
Rush	La Crosse	67548	Caldwell	Princeton	42445
Russell	Russell	67665	Calloway	Murray	42071
Saline	Salina	67401	Campbell	Alexandria	41001
Scott	Scott City	67871	Carlisle	Bardwell	42023
Sedgwick	Wichita	67201-38	Carroll	Carrollton	41008
Seward	Liberal	67901	Carter	Grayson	41143
Shawnee	Topeka	66601-22	Casey	Liberty	42539
Sheridan	Hoxie	67740	Christian	Hopkinsville	42240
Sherman	Goodland	67735	Clark	Winchester	40391
Smith	Smith Center	66967	Clay	Manchester	40962
Stafford	St. John	67576	Clinton	Albany	42602
Stanton	Johnson	67855	Crittenden	Marion	42064
Stevens	Hugoton	67951	Cumberland	Burkesville	42717
Sumner	Wellington	67152	Daviess	Owensboro	42301
Thomas	Colby	67701	Edmonson	Brownsville	42210
Trego	Wakeeney	67672	Elliott	Sandy Hook	41171
Wabaunsee	Alma	66401	Estill	Irvine	40336
Wallace	Sharon Springs	67758	Fayette	Lexington	40501-11
Washington	Washington	66968	Fleming	Flemingsburg	41041
Wichita	Leoti	67861	Floyd	Prestonsburg	41653
Wilson	Fredonia	66736	Franklin	Frankfort	40601
Woodson	Yates Center	66783	Fulton	Hickman	42050
Wyandotte	Kansas City	66101-19	Gallatin	Warsaw	41095
			Garrard	Lancaster	40444

KENTUCKY

County	County Seat	Zip Code
			Grant	Williamstown	41097
			Graves	Mayfield	42066
Adair	Columbia	42728	Grayson	Leitchfield	42754
Allen	Scottsville	42164	Green	Greensburg	42743
Anderson	Lawrenceburg	40342	Greenup	Greenup	41144
Ballard	Wickliffe	42087	Hancock	Hawesville	42348
Barren	Glasgow	42141	Hardin	Elizabethtown	42701
Bath	Owingsville	40360	Harlan	Harlan	40831
Bell	Pineville	40977	Harrison	Cynthiana	41031
Boone	Burlington	41005	Hart	Munfordville	42765
Bourbon	Paris	40361	Henderson	Henderson	42420
Boyd	Catlettsburg	41129	Henry	New Castle	40050
Boyle	Danville	40422	Hickman	Clinton	42031
Bracken	Brooksville	41004	Hopkins	Madisonville	42431
Breathitt	Jackson	41339	Jackson	McKee	40447

County	County Seat	Zip Code	County	County Seat	Zip Code
Jefferson	Louisville	40201-99	Pike	Pikeville	41501
Jessamine	Nicholasville	40356	Powell	Stanton	40380
Johnson	Paintsville	.41240	Pulaski	Somerset	42501
Kenton	Independence	41051	Robertson	Mount Olivet	41064
Knott	Hindman	41822	Rockcastle	Mount Vernon	40456
Knox	Barbourville	40906	Rowan	Morehead	40351
Larue	Hodgenville	42748	Russell	Jamestown	42629
Laurel	London	40741	Scott	Georgetown	40324
Lawrence	Louisa	41230	Shelby	Shelbyville	40065
Lee	Beattyville	41311	Simpson	Franklin	42134
Leslie	Hyden	41749	Spencer	Taylorsville	40071
Letcher	Whitesburg	41858	Taylor	Campbellsville	42718
Lewis	Vanceburg	41179	Todd	Elkton	42220
Lincoln	Stanford	40484	Trigg	Cadiz	42211
Livingston	Smithland	42081	Trimble	Bedford	40006
Logan	Russellville	42276	Union	Morganfield	42437
Lyon	Eddyville	42038	Warren	Bowling Green	42101
McCracken	Paducah	42001	Washington	Springfield	40069
McCreary	Whitely City	42653	Wayne	Monticello	42633
McLean	Calhoun	42327	Webster	Dixon	42409
Madison	Richmond	40475	Whitley	Williamsburg	40769
Magoffin	Salyersville	41465	Wolfe	Campton	41301
Marion	Lebanon	40033	Woodford	Versailles	40383
Marshall	Benton	42025			
Martin	Inez	41224			

LOUISIANA *

Mason	Maysville	41056	Parish	Parish Seat	Zip Code
Meade	Brandenburg	40108	Acadia	Crowley	70526
Menifee	Frenchburg	40322	Allen	Oberlin	71463
Mercer	Harrodsburg	40330	Ascension	Donaldsonville	70346
Metcalfe	Edmonton	42129	Assumption	Napoleonville	70390
Monroe	Tompkinsville	42167	Avoyelles	Marksville	71351
Montgomery	Mount Sterling	40353	Beauregard	De Ridder	70634
Morgan	West Liberty	41472	Bienville	Arcadia	71001
Muhlenberg	Greenville	42345	Bossier	Benton	71006
Nelson	Bardstown	40004	Caddo	Shreveport	71101-10
Nicholas	Carlisle	40311	Calcasieu	Lake Charles	70601
Ohio	Hartford	42347	Caldwell	Columbia	71418
Oldham	La Grange	40031	Cameron	Cameron	70631
Owen	Owenton	40359	Catahoula	Harrisonburg	71340
Owsley	Booneville	41314	Claiborne	Homer	71040
Pendleton	Falmouth	41040	Concordia	Vidalia	71373
Perry	Hazard	41701			

*Louisiana is divided into parishes rather than counties.

Parish	Parish Seat	Zip Code
De Soto	Mansfield	71052
East Baton Rouge	Baton Rouge	70801-21
East Carroll	Lake Providence	71254
East Felici-ana	Clinton	70722
Evangeline	Ville Platte	70586
Franklin	Winnsboro	71295
Grant	Colfax	71417
Iberia	New Iberia	70560
Iberville	Plaquemine	70764
Jackson	Jonesboro	71251
Jefferson	Gretna	70053
Jefferson Davis	Jennings	70546
Lafayette	Lafayette	70501
Lafourche	Thibodaux	70301
La Salle	Jena	71342
Lincoln	Ruston	71270
Livingston	Livingston	70754
Madison	Tallulah	71282
Morehouse	Bastrop	71220
Natchitoches	Natchitoches	71457
Orleans	New Orleans	70101-60
Ouachita	Monroe	71202
Plaquemines	Pointe a la Hache	70082
Pointe Coupee	New Roads	70760
Rapides	Alexandria	71301
Red River	Coushatta	71019
Richland	Rayville	71269
Sabine	Many	71449
St. Bernard	Chalmette	70043
St. Charles	Hahnville	70057
St. Helena	Greensburg	70441
St. James	Convent	70723
St. John the Baptist	Edgard	70049
St. Landry	Opelousas	70570
St. Martin	St. Martinville	70582
St. Mary	Franklin	70538
St. Tammany	Covington	70433

Parish	Parish Seat	Zip Code
Tangipahoa	Amite	70422
Tensas	St. Joseph	71366
Terrebonne	Houma	70360
Union	Farmerville	71241
Vermilion	Abbeville	70510
Vernon	Leesville	71446
Washington	Franklinton	70438
Webster	Minden	71055
West Baton Rouge	Port Allen	70767
West Carroll	Oak Grove	71263
West Felici-ana	St. Francis-ville	70775
Winn	Winnfield	71483

MAINE

County	County Seat	Zip Code
Andros-coggin	Auburn	04210
Aroostook	Houlton	04730
Cumberland	Portland	04101-12
Franklin	Farmington	04938
Hancock	Ellsworth	04605
Kennebec	Augusta	04330
Knox	Rockland	04841
Lincoln	Wiscasset	04578
Oxford	South Paris	04281
Penobscot	Bangor	04401
Piscataquis	Dover-Foxcroft	04426
Sagadahoc	Bath	04530
Somerset	Skowhegan	04976
Waldo	Belfast	04915
Washington	Machias	04654
York	Alfred	04002

MARYLAND

Allegany	Cumberland	21502
Anne Arun-del	Annapolis	21401-12
Baltimore	Towson	21204

County	County Seat	Zip Code
Baltimore (Independent City)*		21201-41
Calvert	Prince Frederick	20678
Caroline	Denton	21629
Carroll	Westminster	21157
Cecil	Elkton	21921
Charles	La Plata	20646
Dorchester	Cambridge	21613
Frederick	Frederick	21701
Garrett	Oakland	21550
Hartford	Bel Air	21014
Howard	Ellicott City	21043
Kent	Chestertown	21620
Montgomery	Rockville	20850-55
Prince Georges	Upper Marlboro	20870
Queen Annes	Centreville	21617
St. Marys	Leonardtown	20650
Somerset	Princess Anne	21853
Talbot	Easton	21601
Washington	Hagerstown	21740
Wicomico	Salisbury	21801
Worcester	Snow Hill	21863

MASSACHUSETTS

County	County Seat	Zip Code
Barnstable	Barnstable	02630
Berkshire	Pittsfield	01201
Bristol	Taunton	02780
Dukes	Edgartown	02539
Essex	Salem	01970
Franklin	Greenfield	01301
Hampden	Springfield	01101-29
Hampshire	Northampton	01060
Middlesex	Cambridge	02138
Nantucket	Nantucket	02554
Norfolk	Dedham	02026
Plymouth	Plymouth	02360-64

*An Independent City has the same status as a county.

County	County Seat	Zip Code
Suffolk	Boston	02101-215
Worcester	Worcester	01601-13

MICHIGAN

County	County Seat	Zip Code
Alcona	Harrisville	48740
Alger	Munising	49862
Allegan	Allegan	49010
Alpena	Alpena	49707
Antrim	Bellaire	49615
Arenac	Standish	48658
Baraga	L'Anse	49946
Barry	Hastings	49058
Bay	Bay City	48706
Benzie	Beulah	49617
Berrien	St. Joseph	49085
Branch	Coldwater	49036
Calhoun	Marshall	49068
Cass	Cassopolis	49031
Charlevoix	Charlevoix	49720
Cheboygan	Cheboygan	49721
Chippewa	Sault Ste. Marie	49783
Clare	Harrison	48625
Clinton	St. Johns	48879
Crawford	Grayling	49738
Delta	Escanaba	49829
Dickinson	Iron Mountain	49801
Eaton	Charlotte	48813
Emmet	Petoskey	49770
Genesee	Flint	48501-59
Gladwin	Gladwin	48624
Gogebic	Bessemer	49911
Grand Traverse	Traverse City	49684
Gratiot	Ithaca	48847
Hillsdale	Hillsdale	49242
Houghton	Houghton	49931
Huron	Bad Axe	48413
Ingham	Mason	48854
Ionia	Ionia	48846
Iosco	Tawas City	48763
Iron	Crystal Falls	49920

County	County Seat	Zip Code
Isabella	Mount Pleasant	48858
Jackson	Jackson	49201-04
Kalamazoo	Kalamazoo	49001-07
Kalkaska	Kalkaska	49646
Kent	Grand Rapids	49501-11
Keweenaw	Eagle River	49924
Lake	Baldwin	49304
Lapeer	Lapeer	48446
Leelanau	Leland	49654
Lenawee	Adrian	49221
Livingston	Howell	48843
Luce	Newberry	49868
Mackinac	St. Ignace	49781
Macomb	Mount Clemens	48043
Manistee	Manistee	49660
Marquette	Marquette	49855
Mason	Ludington	49431
Mecosta	Big Rapids	49307
Menominee	Menominee	49858
Midland	Midland	48640
Missaukee	Lake City	49651
Monroe	Monroe	48161
Montcalm	Stanton	48888
Mont-morency	Atlanta	49709
Muskegon	Muskegon	49440-45
Newaygo	White Cloud	49349
Oakland	Pontiac	48053-59
Oceana	Hart	49420
Ogemaw	West Branch	48661
Ontonagon	Ontonagon	49953
Osceola	Reed City	49677
Oscoda	Mio	48647
Otsego	Gaylord	49735
Ottawa	Grand Haven	49417
Presque Isle	Rogers City	49779
Roscommon	Roscommon	48653
Saginaw	Saginaw	48601-07
St. Clair	Port Huron	48060
St. Joseph	Centreville	49032
Sanilac	Sandusky	48471
Schoolcraft	Manistique	49854

County	County Seat	Zip Code
Shiawassee	Corunna	48817
Tuscola	Caro	48723
Van Buren	Paw Paw	49079
Washtenaw	Ann Arbor	48103-08
Wayne	Detroit	48201-42
Wexford	Cadillac	49601

MINNESOTA

County	County Seat	Zip Code
Aitkin	Aitkin	56431
Anoka	Anoka	55303
Becker	Detroit Lakes	56501
Beltrami	Bemidji	56601
Benton	Foley	56329
Big Stone	Ortonville	56278
Blue Earth	Mankato	56001
Brown	New Ulm	56073
Carlton	Carlton	55718
Carver	Chaska	55318
Cass	Walker	56484
Chippewa	Montevideo	56265
Chisago	Center City	55012
Clay	Moorhead	56560
Clearwater	Bagley	56621
Cook	Grand Marais	55604
Cottonwood	Windom	56101
Crow Wing	Brainerd	56401
Dakota	Hastings	55033
Dodge	Mantorville	55955
Douglas	Alexandria	56308
Faribault	Blue Earth	56013
Fillmore	Preston	55965
Freeborn	Albert Lea	56007
Goodhue	Red Wing	55066
Grant	Elbow Lake	56531
Hennepin	Minneapolis	55401-80
Houston	Caledonia	55921
Hubbard	Park Rapids	56470
Isanti	Cambridge	55008
Itasca	Grand Rapids	55744
Jackson	Jackson	56143
Kanabec	Mora	55051

County	County Seat	Zip Code
Kandiyohi	Willmar	56201
Kittson	Hallock	56728
Koochiching	International Falls	56649
Lac qui Parle	Madison	56256
Lake	Two Harbors	55616
Lake of the Woods	Baudette	56623
Le Sueur	Le Center	56057
Lincoln	Ivanhoe	56142
Lyon	Marshall	56258
McLeod	Glencoe	55336
Mahnomen	Mahnomen	56557
Marshall	Warren	56762
Martin	Fairmont	56031
Meeker	Litchfield	55355
Mille Lacs	Milaca	56353
Morrison	Little Falls	56345
Mower	Austin	55912
Murray	Slayton	56172
Nicollet	St. Peter	56082
Nobles	Worthington	56187
Norman	Ada	56510
Olmsted	Rochester	55901
Otter Tail	Fergus Falls	56537
Pennington	Thief River Falls	56701
Pine	Pine City	55063
Pipestone	Pipestone	56164
Polk	Crookston	56716
Pope	Glenwood	56334
Ramsey	St. Paul	55101-77
Red Lake	Red Lake Falls	56750
Redwood	Redwood Falls	56283
Renville	Olivia	56277
Rice	Faribault	55021
Rock	Luverne	56156
Roseau	Roseau	56751
St. Louis	Duluth	55801-14
Scott	Shakopee	55379
Sherburne	Elk River	55330
Sibley	Gaylord	55334
Stearns	St. Cloud	56301

County	County Seat	Zip Code
Steele	Owatonna	55060
Stevens	Morris	56267
Swift	Benson	56215
Todd	Long Prairie	56347
Traverse	Wheaton	56296
Wabasha	Wabasha	55981
Wadena	Wadena	56482
Waseca	Waseca	56093
Washington	Stillwater	55082
Watonwan	St. James	56081
Wilkin	Breckenridge	56520
Winona	Winona	55987
Wright	Buffalo	55313
Yellow Medicine	Granite Falls	56241

MISSISSIPPI

County	County Seat	Zip Code
Adams	Natchez	39120
Alcorn	Corinth	38834
Amite	Liberty	39645
Attala	Kosciusko	39090
Benton	Ashland	38603
Bolivar	Cleveland	38732
Calhoun	Pittsboro	38951
Carroll	Vaiden and Carrollton	39176 38917
Chickasaw	Houston and Okolona	38851 38860
Choctaw	Ackerman	39735
Claiborne	Port Gibson	39150
Clarke	Quitman	39355
Clay	West Point	39733
Coahoma	Clarksdale	38614
Copiah	Hazlehurst	39083
Covington	Collins	39428
De Soto	Hernando	38632
Forrest	Hattiesburg	39401
Franklin	Meadville	39653
George	Lucedale	39452

County	County Seat	Zip Code	County	County Seat	Zip Code
Greene	Leakesville	39451	Panola	Sardis	38666
Grenada	Grenada	38901		and	
Hancock	Bay St. Louis	39520		Batesville	38606
Harrison	Gulfport	39501	Pearl River	Poplarville	39470
	and		Perry	New Augusta	39462
	Biloxi	39530-34	Pike	Magnolia	39652
Hinds	Jackson	39201-18	Pontotoc	Pontotoc	38863
	and		Prentiss	Booneville	38829
	Raymond	39154	Quitman	Marks	38646
Holmes	Lexington	39095	Rankin	Brandon	39042
Humphreys	Belzoni	39038	Scott	Forest	39074
Issaquena	Mayersville	39113	Sharkey	Rolling Fork	39159
Itawamba	Fulton	38843	Simpson	Mendenhall	39114
Jackson	Pascagoula	39567	Smith	Raleigh	39153
Jasper	Bay Springs	39422	Stone	Wiggins	39577
	and		Sunflower	Indianola	38751
	Paulding	39348	Tallahatchie	Charleston	38921
Jefferson	Fayette	39069		and	
Jefferson				Sumner	38957
Davis	Prentiss	39474	Tate	Senatobia	38668
Jones	Ellisville	39437	Tippah	Ripley	38663
	and		Tishomingo	Iuka	38852
	Laurel	39440	Tunica	Tunica	38676
Kemper	De Kalb	39328	Union	New Albany	38652
Lafayette	Oxford	38655	Walthall	Tylertown	39667
Lamar	Purvis	39475	Warren	Vicksburg	39180
Lauderdale	Meridian	39301	Washington	Greenville	38701
Lawrence	Monticello	39654	Wayne	Waynesboro	39367
Leake	Carthage	39051	Webster	Walthall	39771
Lee	Tupelo	38801	Wilkinson	Woodville	39669
Leflore	Greenwood	39830	Winston	Louisville	39339
Lincoln	Brookhaven	39601	Yalobusha	Coffeeville	38922
Lowndes	Columbus	39701		and	
Madison	Canton	39046		Water Valley	38965
Marion	Columbia	39429	Yazoo	Yazoo City	39194
Marshall	Holly Springs	38635			
Monroe	Aberdeen	39730			
Montgomery	Winona	38967			

MISSOURI

County	County Seat	Zip Code
Neshoba	Philadelphia	39350
Newton	Decatur	39327	Adair	Kirksville	63501
Noxubee	Macon	39341	Andrew	Savannah	64485
Oktibbeha	Starkville	39759	Atchison	Rockport	64482
			Audrain	Mexico	65265

County	County Seat	Zip Code	County	County Seat	Zip Code
Barry	Cassville	65625	Howell	West Plains	65775
Barton	Lamar	64759	Iron	Ironton	63650
Bates	Butler	64730	Jackson	Independence	64050-54
Benton	Warsaw	65355	Jasper	Carthage	64836
Bollinger	Marble Hill	63764	Jefferson	Hillsboro	63050
Boone	Columbia	65201	Johnson	Warrensburg	64093
Buchanan	St. Joseph	64501-08	Knox	Edina	63537
Butler	Poplar Bluff	63901	Laclede	Lebanon	65536
Caldwell	Kingston	64650	Lafayette	Lexington	64067
Callaway	Fulton	65251	Lawrence	Mount Vernon	65712
Camden	Camdenton	65020	Lewis	Monticello	63457
Cape			Lincoln	Troy	63379
Girardeau	Jackson	63755	Linn	Linneus	64653
Carroll	Carrollton	64633	Livingston	Chillicothe	64601
Carter	Van Buren	63965	McDonald	Pineville	64856
Cass	Harrisonville	64701	Macon	Macon	63552
Cedar	Stockton	65785	Madison	Fredericktown	63645
Chariton	Keytesville	65261	Maries	Vienna	65582
Christian	Ozark	65721	Marion	Palmyra	63461
Clark	Kahoka	63445	Mercer	Princeton	64673
Clay	Liberty	64068	Miller	Tuscumbia	65082
Clinton	Plattsburg	64477	Mississippi	Charleston	63834
Cole	Jefferson City	65101	Moniteau	California	65018
Cooper	Boonville	65233	Monroe	Paris	65275
Crawford	Steelville	65565	Montgomery	Montgomery	
Dade	Greenfield	65661		City	63361
Dallas	Buffalo	65622	Morgan	Versailles	65084
Daviess	Gallatin	64640	New Madrid	New Madrid	63869
De Kalb	Maysville	64469	Newton	Neosho	64850
Dent	Salem	65560	Nodaway	Maryville	64468
Douglas	Ava	65608	Oregon	Alton	65606
Dunklin	Kennett	63857	Osage	Linn	65051
Franklin	Union	63084	Ozark	Gainesville	65655
Gasconade	Hermann	65041	Pemiscot	Caruthersville	63830
Gentry	Albany	64402	Perry	Perryville	63775
Greene	Springfield	65801-06	Pettis	Sedalia	65301
Grundy	Trenton	64683	Phelps	Rolla	65401
Harrison	Bethany	64424	Pike	Bowling Green	63334
Henry	Clinton	64735	Platte	Platte City	64079
Hickory	Hermitage	65668	Polk	Bolivar	65613
Holt	Oregon	64473	Pulaski	Waynesville	65583
Howard	Fayette	65248	Putnam	Unionville	63565

County	County Seat	Zip Code
Ralls	New London	63459
Randolph	Huntsville	65259
Ray	Richmond	64085
Reynolds	Centerville	63633
Ripley	Doniphan	63935
St. Charles	St. Charles	63301
St. Clair	Osceola	64776
St. Francois	Farmington	63640
St. Louis	Clayton	63105
St. Louis (Independent City)*		63101-99
Ste. Genevieve	Ste. Genevieve	63670
Saline	Marshall	65340
Schuyler	Lancaster	63548
Scotland	Memphis	63555
Scott	Benton	63736
Shannon	Eminence	65466
Shelby	Shelbyville	63469
Stoddard	Bloomfield	63825
Stone	Galena	65656
Sullivan	Milan	63556
Taney	Forsyth	65653
Texas	Houston	65483
Vernon	Nevada	64772
Warren	Warrenton	63383
Washington	Potosi	63664
Wayne	Greenville	63944
Webster	Marshfield	65706
Worth	Grant City	64456
Wright	Hartville	65667

MONTANA

County	County Seat	Zip Code
Beaverhead	Dillon	59725
Big Horn	Hardin	59034
Blaine	Chinook	59523
Broadwater	Townsend	59644
Carbon	Red Lodge	59068

County	County Seat	Zip Code
Carter	Ekalaka	59324
Cascade	Great Falls	59401-05
Chouteau	Fort Benton	59442
Custer	Miles City	59301
Daniels	Scobey	59263
Dawson	Glendive	59330
Deer Lodge	Anaconda	59711
Fallon	Baker	59313
Fergus	Lewistown	59457
Flathead	Kalispell	59901
Gallatin	Bozeman	59715
Garfield	Jordan	59337
Glacier	Cut Bank	59427
Golden Valley	Ryegate	59074
Granite	Philipsburg	59858
Hill	Havre	59501
Jefferson	Boulder	59632
Judith Basin	Stanford	59479
Lake	Polson	59860
Lewis and Clark	Helena	59601
Liberty	Chester	59522
Lincoln	Libby	59923
McCone	Circle	59215
Madison	Virginia City	59755
Meagher	White Sulphur Springs	59645
Mineral	Superior	59872
Missoula	Missoula	59801
Musselshell	Roundup	59072
Park	Livingston	59047
Petroleum	Winnett	59087
Phillips	Malta	59538
Pondera	Conrad	59425
Powder River	Broadus	59317
Powell	Deer Lodge	59722
Prairie	Terry	59349
Ravalli	Hamilton	59840
Richland	Sidney	59270
Roosevelt	Wolf Point	59201

*An Independent City has the same status as a county.

County	County Seat	Zip Code
Rosebud	Forsyth	59327
Sanders	Thompson Falls	59873
Sheridan	Plentywood	59254
Silver Bow	Butte	59701
Stillwater	Columbus	59019
Sweet Grass	Big Timber	59011
Teton	Choteau	59422
Toole	Shelby	59474
Treasure	Hysham	59038
Valley	Glasgow	59230
Wheatland	Harlowton	59036
Wibaux	Wibaux	59353
Yellowstone	Billings	59101-03

NEBRASKA

County	County Seat	Zip Code
Adams	Hastings	68901
Antelope	Neligh	68756
Arthur	Arthur	69121
Banner	Harrisburg	69345
Blaine	Brewster	68821
Boone	Albion	68620
Box Butte	Alliance	69301
Boyd	Butte	68722
Brown	Ainsworth	69210
Buffalo	Kearney	68847
Burt	Tekamah	68061
Butler	David City	68632
Cass	Plattsmouth	68048
Cedar	Hartington	68739
Chase	Imperial	69033
Cherry	Valentine	69201
Cheyenne	Sidney	69162
Clay	Clay Center	68933
Colfax	Schuyler	68661
Cuming	West Point	68788
Custer	Broken Bow	68822
Dakota	Dakota City	68731
Dawes	Chadron	69337
Dawson	Lexington	68850
Deuel	Chappell	69129
Dixon	Ponca	68770

County	County Seat	Zip Code
Dodge	Fremont	68025
Douglas	Omaha	68101-64
Dundy	Benkelman	69021
Fillmore	Geneva	68361
Franklin	Franklin	68939
Frontier	Stockville	69042
Furnas	Beaver City	68926
Gage	Beatrice	68310
Garden	Oshkosh	69154
Garfield	Burwell	68823
Gosper	Elwood	68937
Grant	Hyannis	69350
Greeley	Greeley Center	68842
Hall	Grand Island	68801
Hamilton	Aurora	68818
Harlan	Alma	68920
Hayes	Hayes Center	69032
Hitchcock	Trenton	69044
Holt	O'Neill	68763
Hooker	Mullen	69152
Howard	St. Paul	68873
Jefferson	Fairbury	68352
Johnson	Tecumseh	68450
Kearney	Minden	68959
Keith	Ogallala	69153
Keya Paha	Springview	68778
Kimball	Kimball	69145
Knox	Center	68724
Lancaster	Lincoln	68501-32
Lincoln	North Platte	69101
Logan	Stapleton	69163
Loup	Taylor	68879
McPherson	Tryon	69167
Madison	Madison	68748
Merrick	Central City	68826
Morrill	Bridgeport	69336
Nance	Fullerton	68638
Nemaha	Auburn	68305
Nuckolls	Nelson	68961
Otoe	Nebraska City	68410
Pawnee	Pawnee City	68420
Perkins	Grant	69140

County	County Seat	Zip Code	County	County Seat	Zip Code
Phelps	Holdrege	68949	Lyon	Yerington	89447
Pierce	Pierce	68767	Mineral	Hawthorne	89415
Platte	Columbus	68601	Nye	Tonopah	89049
Polk	Osceola	68651	Pershing	Lovelock	89419
Red Willow	McCook	69001	Storey	Virginia City	89440
Richardson	Falls City	68355	Washoe	Reno	89501-10
Rock	Bassett	68714	White Pine	Ely	89301
Saline	Wilber	68465			
Sarpy	Papillion	68046			
Saunders	Wahoo	68066			
Scotts Bluff	Gering	69341			
Seward	Seward	68434			
Sheridan	Rushville	69360			
Sherman	Loup City	68853			
Sioux	Harrison	69346			
Stanton	Stanton	68779			
Thayer	Hebron	68370			
Thomas	Thedford	69166			
Thurston	Pender	68047			
Valley	Ord	68862			
Washington	Blair	68008			
Wayne	Wayne	68787			
Webster	Red Cloud	68970			
Wheeler	Bartlett	68622			
York	York	68467			

NEW HAMPSHIRE

County	County Seat	Zip Code
Belknap	Laconia	03246
Carroll	Ossipee	03864
Cheshire	Keene	03431
Coos	Lancaster	03584
Grafton	Woodsville	03785
Hillsborough	Nashua	03060
Merrimack	Concord	03301
Rockingham	Exeter	03833
Strafford	Dover	03820
Sullivan	Newport	03773

NEVADA

County	County Seat	Zip Code
Carson City (Independent City)*		89701
Churchill	Fallon	89406
Clark	Las Vegas	89101-14
Douglas	Minden	89423
Elko	Elko	89801
Esmeralda	Goldfield	89013
Eureka	Eureka	89316
Humboldt	Winnemucca	89445
Lander	Austin	89310
Lincoln	Pioche	89043

*An Independent City has the same status as a county.

NEW JERSEY

County	County Seat	Zip Code
Atlantic	Mays Landing	08330
Bergen	Hackensack	07601-08
Burlington	Mount Holly	08060
Camden	Camden	08101-10
Cape May	Cape May Court House	08204
Cumberland	Bridgeton	08302
Essex	Newark	07101-14
Gloucester	Woodbury	08096
Hudson	Jersey City	07301-08
Hunterdon	Flemington	08822
Mercer	Trenton	08601-91
Middlesex	New Brunswick	08901-04
Monmouth	Freehold	07728
Morris	Morristown	07960
Ocean	Toms River	08753
Passaic	Paterson	07501-24

County	County Seat	Zip Code
Salem	Salem	08079
Somerset	Somerville	08876
Sussex	Newton	07860
Union	Elizabeth	07201-08
Warren	Belvidere	07823

NEW MEXICO

County	County Seat	Zip Code
Bernalillo	Albuquerque	87101-23
Catron	Reserve	87830
Chaves	Roswell	88201
Colfax	Raton	87740
Curry	Clovis	88101
De Baca	Fort Sumner	88119
Dona Ana	Las Cruces	88001
Eddy	Carlsbad	88220
Grant	Silver City	88061
Guadalupe	Santa Rosa	88435
Harding	Mosquero	87733
Hidalgo	Lordsburg	88045
Lea	Lovington	88260
Lincoln	Carrizozo	88301
Los Alamos	Los Alamos	87544
Luna	Deming	88030
McKinley	Gallup	87301
Mora	Mora	87732
Otero	Alamogordo	88310
Quay	Tucumcari	88401
Rio Arriba	Tierra Amarilla	87575
Roosevelt	Portales	88130
Sandoval	Bernalillo	87004
San Juan	Aztec	87410
San Miguel	Las Vegas	87701
Santa Fe	Santa Fe	87501
Sierra	Truth or Consequences	87901
Socorro	Socorro	87801
Taos	Taos	87571
Torrance	Estancia	87016
Union	Clayton	88415
Valencia	Los Lunas	87031

County	County Seat	Zip Code

NEW YORK

County	County Seat	Zip Code
Albany	Albany	12201-26
Allegany	Belmont	14813
Bronx	Bronx	10541
Broome	Binghamton	13901-05
Cattaraugus	Little Valley	14755
Cayuga	Auburn	13021
Chautauqua	Mayville	14757
Chemung	Elmira	14901-05
Chenango	Norwich	13815
Clinton	Plattsburg	12901
Columbia	Hudson	12534
Cortland	Cortland	13045
Delaware	Delhi	13753
Dutchess	Poughkeepsie	12601-03
Erie	Buffalo	14201-40
Essex	Elizabethtown	12932
Franklin	Malone	12953
Fulton	Johnstown	12095
Genesee	Batavia	14020
Greene	Catskill	12414
Hamilton	Lake Pleasant	12108
Herkimer	Herkimer	13350
Jefferson	Watertown	13601
Kings	Brooklyn	11201
Lewis	Lowville	13367
Livingston	Geneseo	14454
Madison	Wampsville	13163
Monroe	Rochester	14601-55
Montgomery	Fonda	12068
Nassau	Mineola	11501
New York	New York	10001-99
Niagara	Lockport	14094
Oneida	Utica	13501-03
Onondaga	Syracuse	13201-25
Ontario	Canandaigua	14424
Orange	Goshen	10924
Orleans	Albion	14411
Oswego	Oswego	13126
Otsego	Cooperstown	13326
Putnam	Carmel	10512

County	County Seat	Zip Code
Queens	Jamaica	11431
Rensselaer	Troy	12180-83
Richmond	Staten Island	10301
Rockland	New City	10956
St. Lawrence	Canton	13617
Saratoga	Ballston Spa	12020
Schenectady	Schenectady	12301-09
Schoharie	Schoharie	12157
Schuyler	Watkins Glen	14891
Seneca	Waterloo	13165
Steuben	Bath	14810
Suffolk	Riverhead	11901
Sullivan	Monticello	12701
Tioga	Owego	13827
Tompkins	Ithaca	14850
Ulster	Kingston	12401
Warren	Lake George	12845
Washington	Hudson Falls	12839
Wayne	Lyons	14489
Westchester	White Plains	10601-07
Wyoming	Warsaw	14569
Yates	Penn Yan	14527

NORTH CAROLINA

County	County Seat	Zip Code
Alamance	Graham	27253
Alexander	Taylorsville	28681
Alleghany	Sparta	28675
Anson	Wadesboro	28170
Ashe	Jefferson	28640
Avery	Newland	28657
Beaufort	Washington	27889
Bertie	Windsor	27983
Bladen	Elizabethtown	28337
Brunswick	Southport	28461
Buncombe	Asheville	28801-07
Burke	Morganton	28655
Cabarrus	Concord	28025
Caldwell	Lenoir	28645
Camden	Camden	27921
Carteret	Beaufort	28516
Caswell	Yanceyville	27379

County	County Seat	Zip Code
Catawba	Newton	28658
Chatham	Pittsboro	27312
Cherokee	Murphy	28906
Chowan	Edenton	27932
Clay	Hayesville	28904
Cleveland	Shelby	28150
Columbus	Whiteville	28472
Craven	New Bern	28560
Cumberland	Fayetteville	28301-08
Currituck	Currituck	27929
Dare	Manteo	27954
Davidson	Lexington	27292
Davie	Mocksville	27028
Duplin	Kenansville	28349
Durham	Durham	27701-09
Edgecombe	Tarboro	27886
Forsyth	Winston-Salem	27101-09
Franklin	Louisburg	27549
Gaston	Gastonia	28052
Gates	Gatesville	27938
Graham	Robbinville	28771
Granville	Oxford	27565
Greene	Snow Hill	28580
Guilford	Greensboro	27401-20
Halifax	Halifax	27839
Harnett	Lillington	27546
Haywood	Waynesville	28786
Henderson	Hendersonville	28739
Hertford	Winton	27986
Hoke	Raeford	28376
Hyde	Swanquarter	27885
Iredell	Statesville	28677
Jackson	Sylva	28779
Johnston	Smithfield	27577
Jones	Trenton	28585
Lee	Sanford	27330
Lenoir	Kinston	28501
Lincoln	Lincolnton	28092
McDowell	Marion	28752
Macon	Franklin	28734
Madison	Marshall	28753

County	County Seat	Zip Code
Martin	Williamston	27892
Mecklenburg	Charlotte	28201-17
Mitchell	Bakersville	28705
Montgomery	Troy	27371
Moore	Carthage	28327
Nash	Nashville	27856
New Hanover	Wilmington	28401
Northampton	Jackson	27845
Onslow	Jacksonville	28540
Orange	Hillsboro	27278
Pamlico	Bayboro	28515
Pasquotank	Elizabeth City	27909
Pender	Burgaw	28425
Perquimans	Hertford	27944
Person	Roxboro	27573
Pitt	Greenville	27834
Polk	Columbus	28722
Randolph	Asheboro	27203
Richmond	Rockingham	28379
Robeson	Lumberton	28358
Rockingham	Wentworth	27375
Rowan	Salisbury	28144
Rutherford	Rutherfordton	28139
Sampson	Clinton	28328
Scotland	Laurinburg	28352
Stanly	Albemarle	28001
Stokes	Danbury	27016
Surry	Dobson	27017
Swain	Bryson City	28713
Transylvania	Brevard	28712
Tyrrell	Columbia	27925
Union	Monroe	28110
Vance	Henderson	27536
Wake	Raleigh	27601-11
Warren	Warrenton	27589
Washington	Plymouth	27962
Watauga	Boone	28607
Wayne	Goldsboro	27530
Wilkes	Wilkesboro	28697
Wilson	Wilson	27893
Yadkin	Yadkinville	27055

County	County Seat	Zip Code
Yancey	Burnsville	28714

NORTH DAKOTA

County	County Seat	Zip Code
Adams	Hettinger	58639
Barnes	Valley City	58072
Benson	Minnewaukan	58351
Billings	Medora	58645
Bottineau	Bottineau	58318
Bowman	Bowman	58623
Burke	Bowbells	58721
Burleigh	Bismarck	58501
Cass	Fargo	58102
Cavalier	Langdon	58249
Dickey	Ellendale	58436
Divide	Crosby	58730
Dunn	Manning	58642
Eddy	New Rockford	58356
Emmons	Linton	58552
Foster	Carrington	58421
Golden Valley	Beach	58621
Grand Forks	Grand Forks	58201
Grant	Carson	58529
Griggs	Cooperstown	58425
Hettinger	Mott	58646
Kidder	Steele	58482
La Moure	La Moure	58458
Logan	Napoleon	58561
McHenry	Towner	58788
McIntosh	Ashley	58413
McKenzie	Watford City	58854
McLean	Washburn	58577
Mercer	Stanton	58571
Morton	Mandan	58554
Mountrail	Stanley	58784
Nelson	Lakota	58344
Oliver	Center	58530
Pembina	Cavalier	58220
Pierce	Rugby	58368
Ramsey	Devils Lake	58301
Ransom	Lisbon	58054

County	County Seat	Zip Code	County	County Seat	Zip Code
Renville	Mohall	58761	Fayette	Washington Court House	43160
Richland	Wahpeton	58075	Franklin	Columbus	43201-30
Rolette	Rolla	58367	Fulton	Wauseon	43567
Sargent	Forman	58032	Gallia	Gallipolis	45631
Sheridan	McClusky	58463	Geauga	Chardon	44024
Sioux	Fort Yates	58538	Greene	Xenia	45385
Slope	Amidon	58620	Guernsey	Cambridge	43725
Stark	Dickinson	58601	Hamilton	Cincinnati	45201-99
Steele	Finley	58230	Hancock	Findlay	45840
Stutsman	Jamestown	58401	Hardin	Kenton	43326
Towner	Cando	58324	Harrison	Cadiz	43907
Traill	Hillsboro	58045	Henry	Napoleon	43545
Walsh	Grafton	58237	Highland	Hillsboro	45133
Ward	Minot	58701	Hocking	Logan	43138
Wells	Fessenden	58438	Holmes	Millersburg	44654
Williams	Williston	58801	Huron	Norwalk	44857
			Jackson	Jackson	45640
			Jefferson	Steubenville	43952

OHIO

County	County Seat	Zip Code
			Knox	Mount Vernon	43050

County	County Seat	Zip Code	County	County Seat	Zip Code
Adams	West Union	45693	Lake	Painesville	44077
Allen	Lima	45801-09	Lawrence	Ironton	45638
Ashland	Ashland	44805	Licking	Newark	43055
Ashtabula	Jefferson	44047	Logan	Bellefontaine	43311
Athens	Athens	45701	Lorain	Elyria	44035-39
Auglaize	Wapakoneta	45895	Lucas	Toledo	43601-24
Belmont	St. Clairsville	43950	Madison	London	43140
Brown	Georgetown	45121	Mahoning	Youngstown	44501-15
Butler	Hamilton	45011-15	Marion	Marion	43302
Carroll	Carrollton	44615	Medina	Medina	44256
Champaign	Urbana	43078	Meigs	Pomeroy	45769
Clark	Springfield	45501-06	Mercer	Celina	45822
Clermont	Batavia	45103	Miami	Troy	45373
Clinton	Wilmington	45177	Monroe	Woodsfield	43793
Columbiana	Lisbon	44432	Montgomery	Dayton	45400
Coshocton	Coshocton	43812	Morgan	McConnelsville	43756
Crawford	Bucyrus	44820	Morrow	Mount Gilead	43338
Cuyahoga	Cleveland	44101-99	Muskingum	Zanesville	43701
Darke	Greenville	45331	Noble	Caldwell	43724
Defiance	Defiance	43512	Ottawa	Port Clinton	43452
Delaware	Delaware	43015	Paulding	Paulding	45879
Erie	Sandusky	44870	Perry	New Lexington	43764
Fairfield	Lancaster	43130			

County	County Seat	Zip Code	County	County Seat	Zip Code
Pickaway	Circleville	43113	Comanche	Lawton	73501
Pike	Waverly	45690	Cotton	Walters	73572
Portage	Ravenna	44266	Craig	Vinita	74301
Preble	Easton	45320	Creek	Sapulpa	74066
Putnam	Ottawa	45875	Custer	Arapaho	73620
Richland	Mansfield	44901-07	Delaware	Jay	74346
Ross	Chillicothe	45601	Dewey	Taloga	73667
Sandusky	Fremont	43420	Ellis	Arnett	73823
Scioto	Portsmouth	45662	Garfield	Enid	73701
Seneca	Tiffin	44883	Garvin	Pauls Valley	73075
Shelby	Sidney	45365	Grady	Chickasha	73018
Stark	Canton	44701-30	Grant	Medford	73759
Summit	Akron	44301-21	Greer	Mangum	73554
Trumbull	Warren	44481-85	Harmon	Hollis	73550
Tuscarawas	New Philadelphia	44663	Harper	Buffalo	73834
Union	Marysville	43040	Haskell	Stigler	74462
Van Wert	Van Wert	45891	Hughes	Holdenville	74848
Vinton	McArthur	45651	Jackson	Altus	73521
Warren	Lebanon	45036	Jefferson	Waurika	73573
Washington	Marietta	45750	Johnston	Tishomingo	73460
Wayne	Wooster	44691	Kay	Newkirk	74647
Williams	Bryan	43506	Kingfisher	Kingfisher	73750
Wood	Bowling Green	43402	Kiowa	Hobart	73651
Wyandot	Upper Sandusky	43351	Latimer	Wilburton	74578
			Le Flore	Poteau	74953

OKLAHOMA

County	County Seat	Zip Code	County	County Seat	Zip Code
			Lincoln	Chandler	74834
			Logan	Guthrie	73044
Adair	Stilwell	74960	Love	Marietta	73448
Alfalfa	Cherokee	73728	McClain	Purcell	73080
Atoka	Atoka	74525	McCurtain	Idabel	74745
Beaver	Beaver	73932	McIntosh	Eufaula	74432
Beckham	Sayre	73662	Major	Fairview	73737
Blaine	Watonga	73772	Marshall	Madill	73446
Bryan	Durant	74701	Mayes	Pryor Creek	74361
Caddo	Anadarko	73005	Murray	Sulphur	73086
Canadian	El Reno	73036	Muskogee	Muskogee	74401
Carter	Ardmore	73401	Noble	Perry	73077
Cherokee	Tahlequah	74464	Nowata	Nowata	74048
Choctaw	Hugo	74743	Okfuskee	Okemah	74859
Cimarron	Boise City	73933	Oklahoma	Oklahoma	
Cleveland	Norman	73069		City	73101-81
Coal	Coalgate	74538	Okmulgee	Okmulgee	74447

County	County Seat	Zip Code
Osage	Pawhuska	74056
Ottawa	Miami	74354
Pawnee	Pawnee	74058
Payne	Stillwater	74074
Pittsburg	McAlester	74501
Pontotoc	Ada	74820
Pottawat-omie	Shawnee	74801
Pushmataha	Antlers	74523
Roger Mills	Cheyenne	73628
Rogers	Claremore	74017
Seminole	Wewoka	74884
Sequoyah	Sallisaw	74955
Stephens	Duncan	73533
Texas	Guymon	73942
Tillman	Frederick	73542
Tulsa	Tulsa	74101-56
Wagoner	Wagoner	74467
Washington	Bartlesville	74003
Washita	Cordell	73632
Woods	Alva	73717
Woodward	Woodward	73801

OREGON

County	County Seat	Zip Code
Baker	Baker	97814
Benton	Corvallis	97330
Clackamas	Oregon City	97045
Clatsop	Astoria	97103
Columbia	St. Helens	97051
Coos	Coquille	97423
Crook	Prineville	97754
Curry	Gold Beach	97444
Deschutes	Bend	97701
Douglas	Roseburg	97470
Gilliam	Condon	97823
Grant	Canyon City	97820
Harney	Burns	97720
Hood River	Hood River	97031
Jackson	Medford	97501
Jefferson	Madras	97741
Josephine	Grants Pass	97526

County	County Seat	Zip Code
Klamath	Klamath Falls	97601
Lake	Lakeview	97630
Lane	Eugene	97401-05
Lincoln	Newport	97365
Linn	Albany	97321
Malheur	Vale	97918
Marion	Salem	97301-10
Morrow	Heppner	97836
Multnomah	Portland	97201-68
Polk	Dallas	97338
Sherman	Moro	97039
Tillamook	Tillamook	97141
Umatilla	Pendleton	97801
Union	La Grande	97850
Wallowa	Enterprise	97828
Wasco	The Dalles	97058
Washington	Hillsboro	97123
Wheeler	Fossil	97830
Yamhill	McMinnville	97128

PENNSYLVANIA

County	County Seat	Zip Code
Adams	Gettysburg	17325
Allegheny	Pittsburgh	15201-44
Armstrong	Kittanning	16201
Beaver	Beaver	15009
Bedford	Bedford	15522
Berks	Reading	19601-10
Blair	Hollidaysburg	16648
Bradford	Towanda	18848
Bucks	Doylestown	18901
Butler	Butler	16001
Cambria	Ebensburg	15931
Cameron	Emporium	15834
Carbon	Jim Thorpe	18229
Centre	Bellefonte	16823
Chester	West Chester	19380
Clarion	Clarion	16214
Clearfield	Clearfield	16830
Clinton	Lock Haven	17745
Columbia	Bloomsburg	17815
Crawford	Meadville	16335

County	County Seat	Zip Code
Cumberland	Carlisle	17013
Dauphin	Harrisburg	17101-28
Delaware	Media	19063-65
Elk	Ridgway	15853
Erie	Erie	16501-12
Fayette	Uniontown	15401
Forest	Tionesta	16353
Franklin	Chambersburg	17201
Fulton	McConnellsburg	17233
Greene	Waynesburg	15370
Huntingdon	Huntingdon	16652
Indiana	Indiana	15701
Jefferson	Brookville	15825
Juniata	Mifflintown	17059
Lackawanna	Scranton	18501-19
Lancaster	Lancaster	17601-04
Lawrence	New Castle	16101-05
Lebanon	Lebanon	17042
Lehigh	Allentown	18101-06
Luzerne	Wilkes-Barre	18701-10
Lycoming	Williamsport	17701
McKean	Smethport	16749
Mercer	Mercer	16137
Mifflin	Lewistown	17044
Monroe	Stroudsburg	18360
Montgomery	Norristown	19401-09
Montour	Danville	17821
Northampton	Easton	18042
Northum- berland	Sunbury	17801
Perry	New Bloomfield	17068
Philadelphia	Philadelphia	19101-55
Pike	Milford	18337
Potter	Coudersport	16915
Schuylkill	Pottsville	17901
Snyder	Middleburg	17842
Somerset	Somerset	15501
Sullivan	Laporte	18626
Susquehanna	Montrose	18801
Tioga	Wellsboro	16901
Union	Lewisburg	17837
Venango	Franklin	16323

County	County Seat	Zip Code
Warren	Warren	16365
Washington	Washington	15301
Wayne	Honesdale	18431
Westmore- land	Greensburg	15601
Wyoming	Tunkhannock	18657
York	York	17401-07

RHODE ISLAND

Bristol	Bristol	02809
Kent	East Greenwich	02818
Newport	Newport	02840
Providence	Providence	02901-20
Washington	West Kingston	02892

SOUTH CAROLINA

Abbeville	Abbeville	29620
Aiken	Aiken	29803
Allendale	Allendale	29810
Anderson	Anderson	29621
Bamberg	Bamberg	29003
Barnwell	Barnwell	29812
Beaufort	Beaufort	29902
Berkeley	Moncks Corner	29461
Calhoun	St. Matthews	29135
Charleston	Charleston	29401-12
Cherokee	Gaffney	29340
Chester	Chester	29706
Chesterfield	Chesterfield	29709
Clarendon	Manning	29102
Colleton	Walterboro	29488
Darlington	Darlington	29532
Dillon	Dillon	29536
Dorchester	St. George	29477
Edgefield	Edgefield	29824
Fairfield	Winnsboro	29180
Florence	Florence	29501
Georgetown	Georgetown	29440
Greenville	Greenville	29601-14
Greenwood	Greenwood	29646

County	County Seat	Zip Code	County	County Seat	Zip Code
Hampton	Hampton	29924	Davison	Mitchell	57301
Horry	Conway	29526	Day	Webster	57274
Jasper	Ridgeland	29936	Deuel	Clear Lake	57226
Kershaw	Camden	29020	Dewey	Timber Lake	57656
Lancaster	Lancaster	29720	Douglas	Armour	57313
Laurens	Laurens	29360	Edmunds	Ipswich	57451
Lee	Bishopville	29010	Fall River	Hot Springs	57747
Lexington	Lexington	29072	Faulk	Faulkton	57438
McCormick	McCormick	29835	Grant	Milbank	57252
Marion	Marion	29571	Gregory	Burke	57523
Marlboro	Bennettsville	29512	Haakon	Philip	57567
Newberry	Newberry	29108	Hamlin	Hayti	57241
Oconee	Walhalla	29691	Hand	Miller	57362
Orangeburg	Orangeburg	29115	Hanson	Alexandria	57311
Pickens	Pickens	29671	Harding	Buffalo	57720
Richland	Columbia	29201-11	Hughes	Pierre	57501
Saluda	Saluda	29138	Hutchinson	Olivet	57052
Spartanburg	Spartanburg	29301-03	Hyde	Highmore	57345
Sumter	Sumter	29150	Jackson	Kadoka	57543
Union	Union	29379	Jerauld	Wessington Springs	57382
Williams- burg	Kingstree	29556	Jones	Murdo	57559
York	York	29745	Kingsbury	De Smet	57231
			Lake	Madison	57042

SOUTH DAKOTA

County	County Seat	Zip Code
	Lawrence	Deadwood	57732
	Lincoln	Canton	57013
Aurora	Plankinton	57368
Beadle	Huron	57350
Bennett	Martin	57551
Bon Homme	Tyndall	57066
Brookings	Brookings	57006
Brown	Aberdeen	57401
Brule	Chamberlain	57325
Buffalo	Gannvalley	57341
Butte	Belle Fourche	57717
Campbell	Mound City	57646
Charles Mix	Lake Andes	57356
Clark	Clark	57225
Clay	Vermillion	57609
Codington	Watertown	57201
Corson	McIntosh	57641
Custer	Custer	57730

Lawrence	Deadwood	57732
Lincoln	Canton	57013
Lyman	Kennebec	57544
McCook	Salem	57058
McPherson	Leola	57456
Marshall	Britton	57430
Meade	Sturgis	57785
Mellette	White River	57579
Miner	Howard	57349
Minnehaha	Sioux Falls	57101-07
Moody	Flandreau	57028
Pennington	Rapid City	57701
Perkins	Bison	57620
Potter	Gettysburg	57442
Roberts	Sisseton	57262
Sanborn	Woonsocket	57385
Shannon	Hot Springs	57747
Spink	Redfield	57469

County	County Seat	Zip Code
Stanley	Fort Pierre	57532
Sully	Onida	57564
Todd	Winner	57580
Tripp	Winner	57580
Turner	Parker	57053
Union	Elk Point	57025
Walworth	Selby	57472
Washabaugh	Kadoka	57543
Yankton	Yankton	57078
Ziebach	Dupree	57623

TENNESSEE

County	County Seat	Zip Code
Anderson	Clinton	37716
Bedford	Shelbyville	37160
Benton	Camden	38320
Bledsoe	Pikeville	37367
Blount	Maryville	37801
Bradley	Cleveland	37311
Campbell	Jacksboro	37757
Cannon	Woodbury	37190
Carroll	Huntingdon	38344
Carter	Elizabethton	37643
Cheatham	Ashland City	37015
Chester	Henderson	38340
Claiborne	Tazewell	37879
Clay	Celina	38551
Cocke	Newport	37821
Coffee	Manchester	37355
Crockett	Alamo	38001
Cumberland	Crossville	38555
Davidson	Nashville	37201-21
Decatur	Decaturville	38329
De Kalb	Smithville	37166
Dickson	Charlotte	37036
Dyer	Dyersburg	38024
Fayette	Somerville	38068
Fentress	Jamestown	38556
Franklin	Winchester	37398
Gibson	Trenton	38382
Giles	Pulaski	38478
Grainger	Rutledge	37861

County	County Seat	Zip Code
Greene	Greeneville	37743
Grundy	Altamont	37301
Hamblen	Morristown	37814
Hamilton	Chattanooga	37401-21
Hancock	Sneedville	37869
Hardeman	Bolivar	38008
Hardin	Savannah	38372
Hawkins	Rogersville	37857
Haywood	Brownsville	38012
Henderson	Lexington	38351
Henry	Paris	38242
Hickman	Centerville	37033
Houston	Erin	37061
Humphreys	Waverly	37185
Jackson	Gainesboro	38562
Jefferson	Dandridge	37725
Johnson	Mountain City	37683
Knox	Knoxville	37901-21
Lake	Tiptonville	38079
Lauderdale	Ripley	38063
Lawrence	Lawrenceburg	38464
Lewis	Hohenwald	38462
Lincoln	Fayetteville	37334
Loudon	Loudon	37774
McMinn	Athens	37303
McNairy	Selmer	38375
Macon	Lafayette	37083
Madison	Jackson	38301
Marion	Jasper	37347
Marshall	Lewisburg	37091
Maury	Columbia	38401
Meigs	Decatur	37322
Monroe	Madisonville	37354
Montgomery	Clarksville	37040
Moore	Lynchburg	37352
Morgan	Wartburg	37887
Obion	Union City	38261
Overton	Livingston	38570
Perry	Linden	37096
Pickett	Byrdstown	38549
Polk	Benton	37307
Putnam	Cookeville	38501

County	County Seat	Zip Code	County	County Seat	Zip Code
Rhea	Dayton	37321	Blanco	Johnson City	78636
Roane	Kingston	37763	Borden	Gail	79738
Robertson	Springfield	37172	Bosque	Meridian	76665
Rutherford	Murfreesboro	37130	Bowie	Boston	75557
Scott	Huntsville	37756	Brazoria	Angleton	77515
Sequatchie	Dunlap	37327	Brazos	Bryan	77801
Sevier	Sevierville	37862	Brewster	Alpine	79830
Shelby	Memphis	38101-34	Briscoe	Silverton	79257
Smith	Carthage	37030	Brooks	Falfurrias	78355
Stewart	Dover	37058	Brown	Brownwood	76801
Sullivan	Blountville	37660	Burleson	Caldwell	77836
Sumner	Gallatin	37066	Burnet	Burnet	78611
Tipton	Covington	38019	Caldwell	Lockhart	78644
Trousdale	Hartsville	37074	Calhoun	Port Lavaca	77979
Unicoi	Erwin	37650	Callahan	Baird	79504
Union	Maynardville	37807	Cameron	Brownsville	78520
Van Buren	Spencer	38585	Camp	Pittsburg	75686
Warren	McMinnville	37110	Carson	Panhandle	79068
Washington	Jonesboro	37659	Cass	Linden	75563
Wayne	Waynesboro	38485	Castro	Dimmitt	79027
Weakley	Dresden	38225	Chambers	Anahuac	77514
White	Sparta	38583	Cherokee	Rusk	75785
Williamson	Franklin	37064	Childress	Childress	79201
Wilson	Lebanon	37087	Clay	Henrietta	76365
			Cochran	Morton	79346
TEXAS			Coke	Robert Lee	76945
			Coleman	Coleman	76834
Anderson	Palestine	75801	Collin	McKinney	75069
Andrews	Andrews	79714	Collings-		
Angelina	Lufkin	75901	worth	Wellington	79095
Aransas	Rockport	78382	Colorado	Columbus	78934
Archer	Archer City	76351	Comal	New Braunfels	78130
Armstrong	Claude	79019	Comanche	Comanche	76442
Atascosa	Jourdanton	78026	Concho	Paint Rock	76866
Austin	Bellville	77418	Cooke	Gainesville	76240
Bailey	Muleshoe	79347	Coryell	Gatesville	76528
Bandera	Bandera	78003	Cottle	Paducah	79248
Bastrop	Bastrop	78602	Crane	Crane	79731
Baylor	Seymour	76380	Crockett	Ozona	76943
Bee	Beeville	78102	Crosby	Crosbyton	79322
Bell	Belton	76513	Culberson	Van Horn	79855
Bexar	San Antonio	78201-46	Dallam	Dalhart	79022

County	County Seat	Zip Code	County	County Seat	Zip Code
Dallas	Dallas	75201-99	Hardeman	Quanah	79252
Dawson	Lamesa	79331	Hardin	Kountze	77625
Deaf Smith	Hereford	79045	Harris	Houston	77001-92
Delta	Cooper	75432	Harrison	Marshall	75670
Denton	Denton	76201	Hartley	Channing	79018
De Witt	Cuero	77954	Haskell	Haskell	79521
Dickens	Dickens	79229	Hays	San Marcos	78666
Dimmit	Carrizo Springs	78834	Hamphill	Canadian	79014
Donley	Clarendon	79226	Henderson	Athens	75751
Duval	San Diego	78384	Hidalgo	Edinburg	78539
Eastland	Eastland	76448	Hill	Hillsboro	76645
Ector	Odessa	79760	Hockley	Levelland	79336
Edwards	Rocksprings	78880	Hood	Granbury	76048
Ellis	Waxahachie	75165	Hopkins	Sulphur Springs	75482
El Paso	El Paso	79901-99	Houston	Crockett	75835
Erath	Stephenville	76401	Howard	Big Spring	79720
Falls	Marlin	76661	Hudspeth	Sierra Blanca	79851
Fannin	Bonham	75418	Hunt	Greenville	75401
Fayette	La Grange	78945	Hutchinson	Stinnett	79083
Fisher	Roby	79543	Irion	Mertzon	76941
Floyd	Floydada	79235	Jack	Jacksboro	76056
Foard	Crowell	79227	Jackson	Edna	77957
Fort Bend	Richmond	77469	Jasper	Jasper	75951
Franklin	Mount Vernon	75457	Jeff Davis	Fort Davis	79734
Freestone	Fairfield	75840	Jefferson	Beaumont	77701-09
Frio	Pearsall	78061	Jim Hogg	Hebbronville	78361
Gaines	Seminole	79360	Jim Wells	Alice	78332
Galveston	Galveston	77550	Johnson	Cleburne	76031
Garza	Post	79356	Jones	Anson	79501
Gillespie	Fredericksburg	78624	Karnes	Karnes City	78118
Glasscock	Garden City	79739	Kaufman	Kaufman	75142
Goliad	Goliad	77963	Kendall	Boerne	78006
Gonzales	Gonzales	78629	Kenedy	Sarita	78385
Gray	Pampa	79065	Kent	Jayton	79528
Grayson	Sherman	75090	Kerr	Kerrville	78028
Gregg	Longview	75601	Kimble	Junction	76849
Grimes	Anderson	77830	King	Guthrie	79236
Guadalupe	Seguin	78155	Kinney	Brackettville	78832
Hale	Plainview	79072	Kleberg	Kingsville	78363
Hall	Memphis	79245	Knox	Benjamin	79505
Hamilton	Hamilton	76531	Lamar	Paris	75460
Hansford	Spearman	79081	Lamb	Littlefield	79339

County	County Seat	Zip Code	County	County Seat	Zip Code
Lampasas	Lampasas	76550	Palo Pinto	Palo Pinto	76072
La Salle	Cotulla	78014	Panola	Carthage	75633
Lavaca	Hallettsville	77964	Parker	Weatherford	76086
Lee	Giddings	78942	Parmer	Farwell	79325
Leon	Centerville	75833	Pecos	Fort Stockton	79735
Liberty	Liberty	77575	Polk	Livingston	77351
Limestone	Groesbeck	76642	Potter	Amarillo	79101-10
Lipscomb	Lipscomb	79056	Presidio	Marfa	79843
Live Oak	George West	78022	Rains	Emory	75440
Llano	Llano	78643	Randall	Canyon	79015
Loving	Mentone	79754	Reagan	Big Lake	76932
Lubbock	Lubbock	79401-17	Real	Leakey	78873
Lynn	Tahoka	79373	Red River	Clarksville	75426
McCulloch	Brady	76825	Reeves	Pecos	79772
McLennan	Waco	76701-11	Refugio	Refugio	78377
McMullen	Tilden	78072	Roberts	Miami	79059
Madison	Madisonville	77864	Robertson	Franklin	77856
Marion	Jefferson	75657	Rockwall	Rockwall	75087
Martin	Stanton	79782	Runnels	Ballinger	76821
Mason	Mason	76856	Rusk	Henderson	75652
Matagorda	Bay City	77414	Sabine	Hemphill	75948
Maverick	Eagle Pass	78852	San Augustine	San Augustine	75972
Medina	Hondo	78861	San Jacinto	Coldspring	77331
Menard	Menard	76859	San Patricio	Sinton	78387
Midland	Midland	79701	San Saba	San Saba	76877
Milam	Cameron	76520	Schleicher	Eldorado	76936
Mills	Goldthwaite	76844	Scurry	Snyder	79549
Mitchell	Colorado City	79512	Shackelford	Albany	76430
Montague	Montague	76251	Shelby	Center	75935
Montgomery	Conroe	77301	Sherman	Stratford	79084
Moore	Dumas	79029	Smith	Tyler	75701
Morris	Daingerfield	75638	Somervell	Glen Rose	76043
Motley	Matador	79244	Starr	Rio Grande City	78582
Nacogdoches	Nacogdoches	75961	Stephens	Breckenridge	76024
Navarro	Corsicana	75110	Sterling	Sterling City	76951
Newton	Newton	75966	Stonewall	Aspermont	79502
Nolan	Sweetwater	79556	Sutton	Sonora	76950
Nueces	Corpus Christi	78401-19	Swisher	Tulia	79088
Ochiltree	Perryton	79070	Tarrant	Fort Worth	76101-79
Oldham	Vega	79092	Taylor	Abilene	79601-07
Orange	Orange	77630	Terrell	Sanderson	79848

County	County Seat	Zip Code	County	County Seat	Zip Code
Terry	Brownfield	79316	Duchesne	Duchesne	84021
Throck-morton	Throckmorton	76083	Emery	Castle Dale	84513
Titus	Mount Pleasant	75455	Garfield	Panguitch	84759
Tom Green	San Angelo	76901	Grand	Moab	84532
Travis	Austin	78701-67	Iron	Parowan	84761
Trinity	Groveton	75845	Juab	Nephi	84648
Tyler	Woodville	75979	Kane	Kanab	84741
Upshur	Gilmer	75644	Millard	Fillmore	84631
Upton	Rankin	79778	Morgan	Morgan	84050
Uvalde	Uvalde	78801	Piute	Junction	84740
Val Verde	Del Rio	78840	Rich	Randolph	84064
Van Zandt	Canton	75103	Salt Lake	Salt Lake City	84101-21
Victoria	Victoria	77901	San Juan	Monticello	84535
Walker	Huntsville	77340	Sanpete	Manti	84642
Waller	Hempstead	77445	Sevier	Richfield	84701
Ward	Monahans	79756	Summit	Coalville	84017
Washington	Brenham	77833	Tooele	Tooele	84074
Webb	Laredo	78040	Uintah	Vernal	84078
Wharton	Wharton	77488	Utah	Provo	84601
Wheeler	Wheeler	79096	Wasatch	Heber City	84032
Wichita	Wichita Falls	76301-11	Washington	St. George	84770
Wilbarger	Vernon	76384	Wayne	Loa	84747
Willacy	Raymondville	78580	Weber	Ogden	84401-06
Williamson	Georgetown	78626			
Wilson	Floresville	78114			

VERMONT

County	County Seat	Zip Code
Winkler	Kermit	79745
Wise	Decatur	76234
Wood	Quitman	75783
Yoakum	Plains	79355
Young	Graham	76374
Zapata	Zapata	78076
Zavala	Crystal City	78839

County	County Seat	Zip Code
Addison	Middlebury	05753
Bennington	Bennington *and*	05201
	Manchester	05254
Caledonia	St. Johnsbury	05819
Chittenden	Burlington	05401
Essex	Guildhall	05905
Franklin	St. Albans	05478
Grand Isle	North Hero	05474
Lamoille	Hyde Park	05655
Orange	Chelsea	05038
Orleans	Newport	05855
Rutland	Rutland	05701
Washington	Montpelier	05602
Windham	Newfane	05345
Windsor	Woodstock	05091

UTAH

County	County Seat	Zip Code
Beaver	Beaver	84713
Box Elder	Brigham City	84302
Cache	Logan	84321
Carbon	Price	84501
Daggett	Manila	84046
Davis	Farmington	84025

County	County Seat	Zip Code	County	County Seat	Zip Code

VIRGINIA

County	County Seat	Zip Code
Accomac	Accomac	23301
Albemarle	Charlottes-ville	22901-05
Alleghany	Covington*	24426
Amelia	Amelia Courthouse	23002
Amherst	Amherst	24521
Appomattox	Appomattox	24522
Arlington	Arlington	22201-16
Augusta	Staunton*	24401
Bath	Warm Springs	24484
Bedford	Bedford*	24523
Bland	Bland	24315
Botetourt	Fincastle	24090
Brunswick	Lawrenceville	23868
Buchanan	Grundy	24614
Buckingham	Buckingham	23921
Campbell	Rustburg	24588
Caroline	Bowling Green	22427
Carroll	Hillsville	24343
Charles City	Charles City	23030
Charlotte	Charlotte Courthouse	23923
Chesterfield	Chesterfield	23832
Clarke	Berryville	22611
Craig	New Castle	24127
Culpeper	Culpeper	22701
Cumberland	Cumberland	23040
Dickenson	Clintwood	24228
Dinwiddie	Dinwiddie	23841
Essex	Tappahannock	22560
Fairfax	Fairfax*	22030
Fauquier	Warrenton	22186
Floyd	Floyd	24091
Fluvanna	Palmyra	22963
Franklin	Rocky Mount	24151
Frederick	Winchester*	22601
Giles	Pearisburg	24134
Gloucester	Gloucester	23061
Goochland	Goochland	23063
Grayson	Independence	24348
Greene	Standardsville	22973
Greensville	Emporia*	23847
Halifax	Halifax	24558
Hanover	Hanover	23069
Henrico	Richmond*	24141
Henry	Martinsville*	24112
Highland	Monterey	24465
Isle of Wight	Isle of Wight	23397
James City	Williamsburg*	23185
King and Queen	King and Queen Courthouse	23085
King George	King George	22485
King William	King William	23086
Lancaster	Lancaster	22503
Lee	Jonesville	24263
Loudoun	Leesburg	22075
Louisa	Louisa	23093
Lunenburg	Lunenburg	23952
Madison	Madison	22727
Mathews	Mathews	23109
Mecklenburg	Boydton	23917
Middlesex	Saluda	23149
Montgomery	Christianburg	24073
Nelson	Lovingston	22949
New Kent	New Kent	23124
Northampton	Eastville	23347
Northumberland	Heathsville	22473
Nottoway	Nottoway	23955
Orange	Orange	22960
Page	Luray	22835
Patrick	Stuart	24171
Pittsylvania	Chatham	24531
Powhatan	Powhatan	23139

*Independent Cities that serve as county seats but are administratively independent of the county.

County	County Seat	Zip Code
Prince Edward	Farmville	23901
Prince George	Prince George	23875
Prince William	Manassas	22110
Pulaski	Pulaski	24301
Rappa- hannock	Washington	22747
Richmond	Warsaw	22572
Roanoke	Salem*	24153
Rockbridge	Lexington*	24450
Rockingham	Harrisonburg*	22801
Russell	Lebanon	24266
Scott	Gate City	24251
Shenandoah	Woodstock	22664
Smyth	Marion	24354
Southampton	Courtland	23837
Spotsylvania	Spotsylvania	22553
Stafford	Stafford	22554
Surry	Surry	23883
Sussex	Sussex	23884
Tazewell	Tazewell	24651
Warren	Front Royal	22642
Washington	Abingdon	24210
Westmore- land	Montross	22520
Wise	Wise	24293
Wythe	Wytheville	24382
York	Yorktown	23490

Independent Cities*	Zip Code
Alexandria	22301-14
Bedford	24523
Bristol	24201
Buena Vista	24416
Charlottesville	22901-05
Chesapeake	23320-25
Clifton Forge	24422

*These 38 Independent Cities have the status of counties.

Independent Cities	Zip Code
Colonial Heights	23834
Covington	24426
Danville	24541
Emporia	23847
Fairfax	22030
Falls Church	22040-46
Franklin	23851
Fredericksburg	22401
Galax	24333
Hampton	23360-69
Harrisonburg	22801
Hopewell	23860
Lexington	24450
Lynchburg	24501-05
Martinsville	24112
Newport News	23601-07
Norfolk	23501-23
Norton	24273
Petersburg	23803
Portsmouth	23701-10
Radford	24141
Richmond	23201-40
Roanoke	24001-20
Salem	24153
South Boston	24592
Staunton	24401
Suffolk	23434
Virginia Beach	23450-62
Waynesboro	22980
Williamsburg	23185
Winchester	22601

WASHINGTON

County	County Seat	Zip Code
Adams	Ritzville	99169
Asotin	Asotin	99402
Benton	Prosser	99350
Chelan	Wenatchee	98801
Clallam	Port Angeles	98362
Clark	Vancouver	98660-65

County	County Seat	Zip Code	County	County Seat	Zip Code
Columbia	Dayton	99328	Cabell	Huntington	25701-25
Cowlitz	Kelso	98626	Calhoun	Grantsville	26147
Douglas	Waterville	98858	Clay	Clay	25043
Ferry	Republic	99166	Doddridge	West Union	26456
Franklin	Pasco	99301	Fayette	Fayetteville	25840
Garfield	Pomeroy	99347	Gilmer	Glenville	26351
Grant	Ephrata	98823	Grant	Petersburg	26847
Grays			Greenbrier	Lewisburg	24901
Harbor	Montesano	98563	Hampshire	Romney	26757
Island	Coupeville	98239	Hancock	New Cumberland	26047
Jefferson	Port Townsend	98368	Hardy	Moorefield	26836
King	Seattle	98101-99	Harrison	Clarksburg	26301
Kitsap	Port Orchard	98366	Jackson	Ripley	25271
Kittitas	Ellensburg	98926	Jefferson	Charles Town	25414
Klickitat	Goldendale	98620	Kanawha	Charlestown	25301-32
Lewis	Chehalis	98532	Lewis	Weston	26452
Lincoln	Davenport	99122	Lincoln	Hamlin	25523
Mason	Shelton	98584	Logan	Logan	25601
Okanogan	Okanogan	98840	McDowell	Welch	24801
Pacific	South Bend	98586	Marion	Fairmont	26554
Pend Oreille	Newport	99156	Marshall	Moundsville	26041
Pierce	Tacoma	98401-99	Mason	Point Pleasant	25550
San Juan	Friday Harbor	98250	Mercer	Princeton	24740
Skagit	Mount Vernon	98273	Mineral	Keyser	26726
Skamania	Stevenson	98648	Mingo	Williamson	25661
Snohomish	Everett	98201-03	Monongalia	Morgantown	26505
Spokane	Spokane	99201-20	Monroe	Union	24983
Stevens	Colville	99114	Morgan	Berkeley Springs	25411
Thurston	Olympia	98501-03	Nicholas	Summersville	26651
Wahkiakum	Cathlamet	98612	Ohio	Wheeling	26003
Walla Walla	Walla Walla	99362	Pendleton	Franklin	26807
Whatcom	Bellingham	98225	Pleasants	St. Marys	26170
Whitman	Colfax	99111	Pocahontas	Marlinton	24954
Yakima	Yakima	98901-06	Preston	Kingwood	26537
			Putnam	Winfield	25213

WEST VIRGINIA

County	County Seat	Zip Code
		Raleigh	Beckley	25801
		Randolph	Elkins	26241
Barbour	Philippi	26416
Berkeley	Martinsburg	25401
Boone	Madison	25130
Braxton	Sutton	26601
Brooke	Wellsburg	26070

County	County Seat	Zip Code
Raleigh	Beckley	25801
Randolph	Elkins	26241
Ritchie	Harrisville	26362
Roane	Spencer	25276
Summers	Hinton	25951
Taylor	Grafton	26354

County	County Seat	Zip Code
Tucker	Parsons	26287
Tyler	Middlebourne	26149
Upshur	Buckhannon	26201
Wayne	Wayne	25570
Webster	Webster Springs	26288
Wetzel	New Martinsville	26155
Wirt	Elizabeth	26143
Wood	Parkersburg	26101
Wyoming	Pineville	24874

WISCONSIN

County	County Seat	Zip Code
Adams	Friendship	53934
Ashland	Ashland	54806
Barron	Barron	54812
Bayfield	Washburn	54891
Brown	Green Bay	54301-06
Buffalo	Alma	54610
Burnett	Grantsburg	54840
Calumet	Chilton	53014
Chippewa	Chippewa Falls	54729
Clark	Neillsville	54456
Columbia	Portage	53901
Crawford	Prairie du Chien	53821
Dane	Madison	53701-19
Dodge	Juneau	53039
Door	Sturgeon Bay	54235
Douglas	Superior	54880
Dunn	Menomonie	54751
Eau Claire	Eau Claire	54701
Florence	Florence	54121
Fond du Lac	Fond du Lac	54935
Forest	Crandon	54520
Grant	Lancaster	53813
Green	Monroe	53566
Green Lake	Green Lake	54941
Iowa	Dodgeville	53533
Iron	Hurley	54534
Jackson	Black River Falls	54615
Jefferson	Jefferson	53549
Juneau	Mauston	53948
Kenosha	Kenosha	53140

County	County Seat	Zip Code
Kewaunee	Kewaunee	54216
La Crosse	La Crosse	54601
Lafayette	Darlington	53530
Langlade	Antigo	54409
Lincoln	Merrill	54452
Manitowoc	Manitowoc	54220
Marathon	Wausau	54401
Marinette	Marinette	54143
Marquette	Montello	53949
Menominee	Keshena	54135
Milwaukee	Milwaukee	53201-46
Monroe	Sparta	54656
Oconto	Oconto	54153
Oneida	Rhinelander	54501
Outagamie	Appleton	54911
Ozaukee	Port Washington	53074
Pepin	Durand	54736
Pierce	Ellsworth	54011
Polk	Balsam Lake	54810
Portage	Stevens Point	54481
Price	Phillips	54555
Racine	Racine	53401-06
Richland	Richland Center	53581
Rock	Janesville	53545
Rusk	Ladysmith	54848
St. Croix	Hudson	54016
Sauk	Baraboo	53913
Sawyer	Hayward	54843
Shawano	Shawano	54166
Sheboygan	Sheboygan	53081
Taylor	Medford	54451
Trempealeau	Whitehall	54773
Vernon	Viroqua	54665
Vilas	Eagle River	54521
Walworth	Elkhorn	53121
Washburn	Shell Lake	54871
Washington	West Bend	53095
Waukesha	Waukesha	53186
Waupaca	Waupaca	54981
Waushara	Wautoma	54982
Winnebago	Oshkosh	54901
Wood	Wisconsin Rapids	54494

WYOMING

County	County Seat	Zip Code	County	County Seat	Zip Code
			Lincoln	Kemmerer	83101
			Natrona	Casper	82601
Albany	Laramie	82070	Niobrara	Lusk	82225
Big Horn	Basin	82410	Park	Cody	82414
Campbell	Gillette	82716	Platte	Wheatland	82201
Carbon	Rawlins	82301	Sheridan	Sheridan	82801
Converse	Douglas	82633	Sublette	Pinedale	82941
Crook	Sundance	82729	Sweetwater	Green River	82935
Fremont	Lander	82520	Teton	Jackson	83001
Goshen	Torrington	82240	Uinta	Evanston	82930
Hot Springs	Thermopolis	82443	Washakie	Worland	82401
Johnson	Buffalo	82834	Weston	Newcastle	82701
Laramie	Cheyenne	82001			

DIRECTORY OF U.S. EMBASSIES
AND CONSULATES

Afghanistan

U. S. Embassy
Wazir Akbar Khan Mina
Kabul, Afghanistan

Algeria

U. S. Embassy
4 Chemin Cheikh Bachir Brahimi
    (ex Baurepaire)
Algiers, Algeria

Angola

U. S. Consulate General
Avenida Paulo Dias de Novais No 42
(13th and 14th floors)
Luanda, Angola

Argentina

U. S. Embassy
Sarmiento 663
Buenos Aires, Argentina

Australia

U. S. Embassy
Moonah Place
Yarralumla
Australian Capital Territory
Canberra, Australia

U. S. Consulate General
37–40 Pitt Street
Sydney, Australia

U. S. Consulate
24 Albert Road
Melbourne, Australia

U. S. Consulate
264 St. George's Terrace
Perth, Australia

U. S. Consulate
141 Queen Street
Brisbane 4000
Brisbane, Australia

Austria

U. S. Embassy
1x Boltzmanngasse 16
A-1091
Vienna, Austria

U. S. Consulate
One Franz Josefs Kai (Room 302)
Salzburg, Austria

Bahamas

U. S. Embassy
Mosmar Building
Queens Street
Nassau, Bahamas

Bahrain

U. S. Embassy
POB 431
Manama, Bahrain

Bangladesh

U. S. Embassy
Adamjee Court Building
Montijheel Area
Dacca, Bangladesh

Barbados

U. S. Embassy
POB 302
Bridgetown, Barbados

Belgium

U. S. Embassy
27 Boulevard du Régent
Brussels, Belgium

U. S. Consulate General
64-68 Frankrijklei
Antwerp, Belgium

U. S. Mission to the European
    Communities
40 Boulevard du Régent
Brussels, Belgium

U. S. Mission to the North Atlantic
    Treaty Organization
Autoroute de Zaventem Brussels
Brussels, Belgium

Belize

U. S. Consulate
Gabourel Lane and Hutson Street
Belize City, Belize

Benin

U. S. Embassy
Rue Caporal Anani Bernard
Boîte Postale 2012
Cotonou, Benin

Bermuda

U. S. Consulate General
Vallis Building
Front Street
Hamilton, Bermuda

Bolivia

U. S. Embassy
Banco Popular del Peru Building
Corner of Callas Mercado y Colón
La Paz, Bolivia

Botswana

U. S. Embassy
Koh-I-Nor House
POB 90
Gaborone, Botswana

Brazil

U. S. Embassy
Lote No. 3 Avenida das Nações
Brasilia, Brazil

U. S. Consulate General
Avenida Presidente Wilson 147
Rio de Janeiro, Brazil

U. S. Consulate General
Edificio Conjunto Nacional
Rua Padre João Manuel 20 São Paulo
São Paulo, Brazil

U. S. Consulate
Rua Uruguai 155 (11th floor)
Porto Alegre, Brazil

U. S. Consulate
Avenida Oswaldo Cruz 165
Belém, Brazil

U. S. Consulate
Rua Gonçalves Maia 163
Recife, Brazil

U. S. Consulate
Edificio Fundação Politécnica,
    Bloco A (4th floor)
Avenida Sete de Setembro 73/79
Salvador, Brazil

Bulgaria

U. S. Embassy
One Alexander Stamboliski Boulevard
Sofia, Bulgaria

Burma

U. S. Embassy
581 Merchant Street
Rangoon, Burma

Burundi

U. S. Embassy
Chaussée Prince Louis Rwagasore
Boîte Postale 1720
Bujumbura, Burundi

Cameroon

U. S. Embassy
Rue Nachtigal
Boîte Postale 817
Yaoundé, Cameroon

U. S. Consulate
Avenue de Général LeClerc
Boîte Postale 4006
Douala, Cameroon

Canada

U. S. Embassy
100 Wellington Street
Ottawa, Ontario
Canada

U. S. Consulate General
615 Macleod Trail, S.E.
(Room 1050)
Calgary, Alberta
Canada

U. S. Consulate General
360 University Avenue
Toronto, Ontario
Canada

U. S. Consulate General
6 Donald Street
Winnipeg, Manitoba
Canada

U. S. Consulate General
POB 65
Postal Station Desjardins
Montreal, Quebec
Canada

U. S. Consulate General
Cogswell Tower (Suite 910)
Scotia Square
Halifax, Nova Scotia
Canada

U. S. Consulate General
1199 West Hastings
Vancouver, British Columbia
Canada

U. S. Consulate
One Avenue Ste. Geneviève
Quebec, Quebec
Canada

Central African Republic

U. S. Embassy
Place de la République Centrafricaine
Bangui, Central African Republic

Chad

U. S. Embassy
Rue du Lt. Colonel Colonna
    D'oranano
Boîte Postale 413
N'Djamena, Chad

Chile

U. S. Embassy
Codina Building
1343 Augustinas
Santiago, Chile

China, People's Republic of

U. S. Liaison Office
Kuang Hua Lu
Peking, China

China, Republic of
(Taiwan)

U. S. Embassy
2 Chung Hsiao West Road
Second Section
Taipei, China

Colombia

U. S. Embassy
Calle 37 8–40
Bogotá, Colombia

U. S. Consulate
Edificio Santa Helena
Avenida Primero de Mayo
Medellín, Colombia

U. S. Consulate
Edificio Seguros Tequendama
Calle 34 No. 44-63
Barranquilla, Colombia

U. S. Consulate
Edificio Pielroja
Carrera 3 11-55
Cali, Colombia

Congo, Republic of the
U. S. Embassy
Avenue du 28 Août 1940
Brazzaville, Republic of the Congo

Costa Rica
U. S. Embassy
Avenida 3 and Calle 1
San José, Costa Rica

Cyprus
U. S. Embassy
Therissos Street and Dositheos Street
Nicosia, Cyprus

Czechoslovakia
U. S. Embassy
Trziste 15 - 12548
Prague, Czechoslovakia

Denmark
U. S. Embassy
Dag Hammarskjölds Alle 24
Copenhagen, Denmark

Dominican Republic
U. S. Embassy
Corner of Calle César Nicholas Pensen
 and Calle Leopoldo Navarro
Santo Domingo, Dominican Republic

Ecuador
U. S. Embassy
120 Avenida Patria
Quito, Ecuador

U. S. Consulate General
Casilla X
Guayaquil, Ecuador

Egypt
U. S. Embassy
5 Sharia Latin America
Box 10
Cairo, Arab Republic of Egypt

U. S. Consulate General
110 Avenue Horreya
Alexandria, Arab Republic of Egypt

U. S. Consulate
8 Sharia Aby El Feda Matarch
 El Baher (Apt. 4)
Port Said, Arab Republic of Egypt

El Salvador
U. S. Embassy
1230 25 Avenida Norte
San Salvador, El Salvador

England
U. S. Embassy
24/31 Grosvenor Square, W. 1
London, England

Equatorial Guinea
U. S. Embassy
Armengol Coll and Asturias Streets
Malabo, Equatorial Guinea

Ethiopia
U. S. Embassy
Entoto Street
POB 1014
Addis Ababa, Ethiopia

U. S. Consulate General
32 Franklin D. Roosevelt Street
POB 885
Asmara, Ethiopia

Fiji

U. S. Embassy
Ratu Sukuna House
MacArthur Street
Suva, Fiji

Finland

U. S. Embassy
Itainen Puistotie 14a
Helsinki, Finland

France

U. S. Embassy
2 Avenue Gabriel 75382
Paris, France

U. S. Consulate General
9 Rue Armeny
Marseilles, France

U. S. Consulate General
15 Avenue d'Alsace
Strasbourg, France

U. S. Consulate General
4 Rue Esprit des Lois
Bordeaux, France

U. S. Consulate General
7 Quai Général Sarrail
Lyons, France

U. S. Consulate
3 Rue Dr. Barety
Nice, France

French West Indies

U. S. Consulate
14 Rue Blenac
Boîte Postale 561
Fort-de-France 97206
Martinique, French West Indies

Gabon

U. S. Embassy
Boulevard de la Mer
Boîte Postale 4000
Libreville, Gabon

Gambia

U. S. Embassy
16 Buckle Street
Banjul, The Gambia

Federal Republic of Germany (West Germany)

U. S. Embassy
Mahlemer Avenue 5300
Bonn-Bad Godesberg
Bonn, Federal Republic of Germany

U. S. Consulate General
Koeniginstrasse 5
8000 Muenchen 22
Munich, Federal Republic of
Germany

U. S. Consulate General
Urbanstrasse 7
7000 Stuttgart
Stuttgart, Federal Republic of
Germany

U. S. Consulate General
Alsterufer 27/28
2000 Hamburg 36
Box 2
Hamburg, Federal Republic of
Germany

U. S. Consulate General
Cecilienallee 5
4000 Düsseldorf
30 Germany
Box 515
Düsseldorf, Federal Republic of
Germany

U. S. Consulate General
President Kennedy Platz
Box 1
Bremen, Federal Republic of
    Germany

U. S. Consulate General
Siemayerstrasse 21
Frankfurt am Main, Federal Republic
    of Germany

U. S. Mission
Clayallee 170
One Berlin 33
West Berlin, Federal Republic of
    Germany

German Democratic Republic (East Germany)

U. S. Embassy
108 Berlin
Schadowstrasse 6
East Berlin, German Democratic
    Republic

Ghana

U. S. Embassy
Liberia and Kinbu Roads
POB 194
Accra, Ghana

Greece

U. S. Embassy
91 Vasilissis Sophias Boulevard
Athens, Greece

U. S. Consulate General
59 Vasileos Constantinou Street
Thessaloniki, Greece

Guatemala

U. S. Embassy
7–01 Avenida de la Reforma
Zone 10
Guatemala

Guinea

U. S. Embassy
Second Boulevard and Ninth Avenue
Boîte Postale 603
Conakry, Guinea

Guinea-Bissau

U. S. Embassy
Avenida Domingo Ramos
CP 297
Bissau, Guinea-Bissau

Guyana

U. S. Embassy
31 Main Street
Georgetown, Guyana

Haiti

U. S. Embassy
Harry Truman Boulevard
Port-au-Prince, Haiti

Honduras

U. S. Embassy
Avenida La Paz
Tegucigalpa, Honduras

Hong Kong

U. S. Consulate General
26 Garden Road
Hong Kong

Hungary

U. S. Embassy
V. Szabadsag Ter 12
Budapest, Hungary

Iceland

U. S. Embassy
Laufasvegur 21
Reykjavik, Iceland

India

U. S. Embassy
Shanti Path
Chanakyapuri 21
New Delhi, India

U. S. Consulate General
5/1 Ho Chi Minh Sarani
Calcutta, India

U. S. Consulate General
Lincoln House
78 Bhulabhai Desai Road
Bombay, India

U. S. Consulate General
Mount Road 6
Madras, India

Indonesia

U. S. Embassy
Medan Merdeka
Selaton 5
Jakarta, Indonesia

U. S. Consulate
Djalan Imam Bodjol 13
Medan, Indonesia

U. S. Consulate
Djalan Roya Drive
Sutomo 33
Surabaya, Indonesia

Iran

U. S. Embassy
260 Avenue Takti Jamshid
Tehran, Iran

U. S. Consulate
Pahlavi and Chahar Bagh Boulevards
Isfahan, Iran

U. S. Consulate
Charkhabi Building
Bagh Eram Avenue (near Eram Garden)
POB 500
Shiraz, Iran

U. S. Consulate
Shahnaz Avenue
Tabriz, Iran

Republic of Ireland

U. S. Embassy
42 Elgin Road
Ballsbridge
Dublin, Ireland

Northern Ireland

U. S. Consulate General
Queen's House
14 Queen Street
Belfast, Northern Ireland

Israel

U. S. Embassy
71 Hayarkon Street
Tel Aviv, Israel

U. S. Consulate General
18/223491 Agron Road 24491
Jerusalem, Israel

Italy

U. S. Embassy
Via V. Veneto 119
Rome, Italy

U. S. Consulate General
Banco d'America e d'Italia Building
Piazza Portello 6
Box G
Genoa, Italy

U. S. Consulate General
Piazza della Republic
80122 Naples
Box 18
Naples, Italy

U. S. Consulate General
Piazza Della Republica 32
Milan, Italy

U. S. Consulate General
Vaccarini 1
Palermo, Italy

U. S. Consulate
Via Alfieri 17
Box T
Turin, Italy

U. S. Consulate
38 Lungarno Amerigo Vespucci
Florence, Italy

U. S. Consulate
Via Valdirivo 19 (4th floor)
Trieste, Italy

Ivory Coast

U. S. Embassy
5 Rue Jesse Owens
Boîte Postale 1712
Abidjan, Ivory Coast

Jamaica

U. S. Embassy
43 Duke Street
Kingston, Jamaica

Japan

U. S. Embassy
13-go, No 14
Akasaka 1-chome
Minato-Ku
Tokyo, Japan

U. S. Consulate General
Sankei Building 27 (9th floor)
Umeda-cho Kita-Ku Osaka (530)
Osaka, Japan

U. S. Consulate General
10 Kano-sho 6-chome
Ikuta-ku Kobe (650)
Kobe, Japan

U. S. Consulate
N. One W. 13
Sapporo, Japan

U. S. Consulate
5–26 Ohari 2-chome
Chua-ku Fukuoka-shi 810
Box 10
Fukuoka, Japan

Jordan

U. S. Embassy
Jebel Amman
Amman, Jordan

Kenya

U. S. Embassy
Cotts House
Wabera Street
POB 30137
Nairobi, Kenya

Korea

U. S. Embassy
Sejong-Ro
Seoul, Korea

Kuwait

U. S. Embassy
c/o POB 77
Kuwait

Laos

U. S. Embassy
Rue Bartholonie
Boîte Postale 114
Vientiane, Laos

Lebanon

U. S. Embassy
Corniche at Rue Ain Mreisseh
Beirut, Lebanon

Lesotho

U. S. Embassy
Kingsway
POB 333
Maseru, Lesotho

Liberia

U. S. Embassy
United Nations Drive
Monrovia, Liberia

Libya

U. S. Embassy
Garden City Shari al Nasr
Tripoli, Libya

Luxembourg

U. S. Embassy
22 Boulevard Emmanuel Servais
Luxembourg, Luxembourg

Madagascar

U. S. Embassy
14 and 16 Rue Rainitovo
Antsahavola
Boîte Postale 620
Tananarive, Madagascar

Malawi

U. S. Embassy
POB 30016
Lilongwe, Malawi

Malaysia

U. S. Embassy
A I A Building
Jalan Ampang
POB 35
Kuala Lumpur, Malaysia

Mali

U. S. Embassy
Rue Testard and Rue Mohamed V
Bamako, Mali

Malta

U. S. Embassy
Development House (2nd floor)
Saint Anne Street
Floriana Malta
Valletta, Malta

Mauritania

U. S. Embassy
Nouakchott, Mauritania

Mauritius

U. S. Embassy
Anglo-Mauritius House
Intendance Street (6th floor)
Port Louis, Mauritius

Mexico

U. S. Embassy
Paseo de la Reforma 305
Colonia Cuauhtémoc
Mexico City, Mexico

U. S. Consulate General
Issstenson Building (3rd floor)
Miguel Hidalgo y Costilla 15
Hermosillo, Mexico

U. S. Consulate General
2286 Avenida 16 de Septiembre
Ciudad Juárez, Mexico

U. S. Consulate General
Avenida Consitución
411 Poniente
Monterrey, Mexico

U. S. Consulate General
Progreso 175
Guadalajara, Mexico

U. S. Consulate General
Topachula 96
Tijuana, Mexico

U. S. Consulate
Avenida Allende 3330
Colonia Jardín
Nuevo Laredo, Mexico

U. S. Consulate
Paseo Montejo 453
Apartado Postal 1301
Mérida, Mexico

U. S. Consulate
6 Circunvalación No. 6 at Venustiana
    Carranza
Mazatlán, Mexico

U. S. Consulate
Avenida Primera No. 232
Matamoros, Mexico

Morocco

U. S. Embassy
2 Avenue de Marrakech
Box 99
Rabat, Morocco

U. S. Consulate General
8 Building Moulary Youssef
Casablanca, Morocco

U. S. Consulate General
Chemin des Amoureux
Tangier, Morocco

Mozambique

U. S. Embassy
35 Rua Salayar (2nd floor)
Maputo, Mozambique

Nepal

U. S. Embassy
Panipokhari
Katmandu, Nepal

Netherlands

U. S. Embassy
102 Longe Voorhout
The Hague, Netherlands

U. S. Consulate General
Vlasmarkt 1
Rotterdam, Netherlands

U. S. Consulate General
Museumplein 19
Amsterdam, Netherlands

Netherlands Antilles

U. S. Consulate General
St. Anna Boulevard 19
POB 158
Vice John B. Gorsirawea 1
Curaçao, Netherlands Antilles

New Zealand

U. S. Embassy
IBM Center 155–157 Terrace
POB 1190
Wellington, New Zealand

U. S. Consulate General
AMP Building (6th floor)
Queen Street and Victoria Street East
POB 470
Auckland, New Zealand

Nicaragua

U. S. Embassy
Km 4–1
2 South Highway
Managua, Nicaragua

Niger

U. S. Embassy
Boîte Postale 201
Niamey, Niger

Nigeria

U. S. Embassy
One King's College Road
Lagos, Nigeria

U. S. Consulate
Barclay's Bank Building PMB 5221
Ibadan, Nigeria

U. S. Consulate
Ahmadu Bello Way
Kaduna, Nigeria

Norway

U. S. Embassy
Drammensveien 18
Oslo, Norway

Oman

U. S. Embassy
POB 966
Muscat, Oman

Okinawa

U. S. Consulate General
2129 Gusukuma Urasoe City
Naha, Okinawa

Pakistan

U. S. Embassy
Diplomatic Enclave Ramna 4
Islamabad, Pakistan

U. S. Consulate General
8 Abdullah Haroon Road
Karachi, Pakistan

U. S. Consulate
50 Zafar Ali Road
Lahore, Pakistan

U. S. Consulate
11 Hosp Road
Peshawar, Pakistan

Panama

U. S. Embassy
Avenida Balboa at 38th Street
Panama City, Panama

Papua New Guinea

U. S. Embassy
Armit Street
POB 3492
Port Moresby, Papua New Guinea

Paraguay

U. S. Embassy
1776 Mariscal López Avenue
Asunción, Paraguay

Peru

U. S. Embassy
Corner Avenidas Inca Garcilaso de la
    Vega and España
POB 1995
Lima, Peru

Philippines

U. S. Embassy
1201 Roxas Boulevard
Manila, Philippines

U. S. Consulate General
Philippine America Life Insurance
    Building (3rd floor)
Jones Avenue
Cebu, Philippines

Poland

U. S. Embassy
Aleje Ujazdowskie 29/31
American Embassy Warsaw
c/o American Congen
Warsaw, Poland

U. S. Consulate
Ulica Stolarka 9
31043 Kraków American Consul
    Kraków
c/o American Congen
Kraków, Poland

U. S. Consulate
Ulica Chopino 4
c/o American Congen
Poznań, Poland

Portugal

U. S. Embassy
Avenida Duque de Loulé, 39
Lisbon, Portugal

U. S. Consulate
Apartado 88
Rua Julio Dinis 826–30
Oporto, Portugal

U. S. Consulate
Avenida D. Henrique
Ponta Delgada São Miguel
Azores, Portugal

Qatar

U. S. Embassy
Farig Bin Omran
POB 2399
Doha, Qatar

Romania

U. S. Embassy
Strada Tudor Argezhi 9
American Embassy Box Buch
c/o American Congen
Bucharest, Rumania

Rwanda

U. S. Embassy
Boulevard Central
Kigali, Rwanda

Saudi Arabia

U. S. Embassy
Palestine Road Ruwais
Jidda, Saudi Arabia

U. S. Consulate General
Dhahran, Saudi Arabia

Scotland

U. S. Consulate General
3 Regent Terrace
Edinburgh, Scotland

Senegal

U. S. Embassy
Boîte Postale 49
BIAO Building
Place de l'Indépendance
Dakar, Senegal

Seychelles

U. S. Embassy
Box 148
Victoria, Seychelles

Sierra Leone

U. S. Embassy
Corner Walpole and Siaka Stevens
    Streets
Freetown, Sierra Leone

Singapore

U. S. Embassy
30 Hill Street
Singapore

Somalia

U. S. Embassy
Corso Primo Luglio
Mogadishu, Somalia

South Africa, Republic of

U. S. Embassy
Thibault House
225 Pretorius Street
Pretoria, Republic of South Africa

U. S. Consulate General
Durban Bay House (29th floor)
333 Smith Street
Durban, Republic of South Africa

U. S. Consulate General
Broadway Industries Center
Heerengracht, Foreshore
Cape Town, Republic of South Africa

U. S. Consulate General
Kine Center (11th floor)
Commissioner and Kruis Streets
POB 2155
Johannesburg, Republic of South
    Africa

Spain

U. S. Embassy
Serrano 75
Madrid, Spain

U. S. Consulate General
Via Layetana 33
Barcelona, Spain

U. S. Consulate General
Paseo de las Delicias 7
Seville, Spain

U. S. Consulate
Plaza de las Alfereces Provisionales
   2–40
Bilbao, Spain

Sri Lanka

U. S. Embassy
44 Galle Road Colpetty
Colombo, Sri Lanka

Sudan

U. S. Embassy
Gamhouria Avenue
POB 699
Khartoum, Sudan

Surinam

U. S. Embassy
Dr. Sophie Redmondstraat 13
Paramaribo, Surinam

Swaziland

U. S. Embassy
Embassy House
Allister Miller Street
POB 199
Mbabane, Swaziland

Sweden

U. S. Embassy
Strandvagen 101
Stockholm, Sweden

U. S. Consulate
Sodra Hamngatan 53
Göteborg, Sweden

Switzerland

U. S. Embassy
93/95 Jubilaumsstrasse
Bern, Switzerland

U. S. Embassy (Branch Office)
80 Rue du Lausanné
Geneva, Switzerland

U. S. Consulate General
Zollikerstrasse 141
Zurich, Switzerland

Syria

U. S. Embassy
Abu Rumaneh Al Mansur Street 2
POB 29
Damascus, Syria

Tanzania

U. S. Embassy
National Bank of Commerce Building
City Drive
POB 9123
Dar es Salaam, Tanzania

U. S. Consulate
83A Tuzungumzeni Square
POB 4
Zanzibar, Tanzania

Thailand

U. S. Embassy
95 Wireless Road
Bangkok, Thailand

U. S. Consulate
35/6 Supakitjanya Road
WBO 96237
Udorn, Thailand

U. S. Consulate
9 Sadao Road
Songkhla, Thailand

U. S. Consulate
Vidhayanond Road
Chiang Mai, Thailand

Togo

U. S. Embassy
Rue Pelletier Caventou and
    Rue Vouban
BP 852
Lomé, Togo

Trinidad

U. S. Embassy
15 Queen's Park West
Port-of-Spain, Trinidad

Tunisia

U. S. Embassy
144 Avenue de la Liberté
Tunis, Tunisia

Turkey

U. S. Embassy
110 Ataturk Boulevard
Ankara, Turkey

U. S. Consulate
386 Ataturk Caddesi
Izmir, Turkey

U. S. Consulate
104–108 Mesrutiyet Caddesi
    Tepebasi
Istanbul, Turkey

U. S. Consulate
Ataturk Caddesi
Adana, Turkey

Uganda

U. S. Embassy
9–11 Parliament Avenue
POB 7007
Embassy House
Kampala, Uganda

Union of Soviet Socialist Republics

U. S. Embassy
Ulitsa Chaykoyskogo 19/21/23
Moscow, Union of Soviet Socialist
    Republics

U. S. Consulate General
UL Petra Lavrova Street 15
Box L
Leningrad, Union of Soviet Socialist
    Republics

United Arab Emirates

U. S. Embassy
Sh Khalid Building
Corniche Road
Abu Dhabi, United Arab Emirates

Upper Volta

U. S. Embassy
Boite Postale 35
Ouagadougou, Upper Volta

Uruguay

U. S. Embassy
Calle Lauro Muller 1776
Montevideo, Uruguay

Venezuela

U. S. Embassy
Avenida Francisco de Miranda and
    Avenida Principal de la Floresta
Caracas, Venezuela

U. S. Consulate
Edificio Matema
Avenida 15 Calle 78
Maracaibo, Venezuela

Yemen Arab Republic

U. S. Embassy
Box 33
Sana, Yemen Arab Republic

Yugoslavia

U. S. Embassy
Kneza Milosa 50
Belgrade, Yugoslavia

U. S. Consulate
Zrinjevac 13
Zagreb, Yugoslavia

Zaire

U. S. Embassy
310 Avenue des Aviateurs
Kinshasa, Zaire

U. S. Consulate
1029 Boulevard de l'Ueac
Boîte Postale 1196
Lubumbashi, Zaire

U. S. Consulate
Boîte Postale 3037
Avenue Mobutu
Bukavu, Zaire

Zambia

U. S. Embassy
POB 1617
Lusaka, Zambia

FORMS OF ADDRESS

Forms of address do not always follow set guidelines; the type of salutation is often determined by the relationship between correspondents or by the purpose and content of the letter. However, a general style applies to most occasions. In formal salutations, when the addressee is a woman, "Madam" should be substituted for "Sir." When the salutation is informal, "Mrs." or "Miss" or "Ms." should be substituted for "Mr." If a woman addressee has previously stated a preference for a particular form of address this form should be used.

	Form of Address	Salutation
Academics		
assistant professor, college or university	Dr. (*or* Mr.) Joseph Stone Assistant Professor Department of ____	Dear Professor Stone:
associate professor, college or university	Dr. (*or* Mr.) Joseph Stone Associate Professor Department of ____	Dear Professor Stone:
chancellor, university	Chancellor Joseph Stone	Dear Chancellor Stone:
dean, college or university	Dean Joseph Stone *or* Dr. (*or* Mr.) Joseph Stone Dean, School of ____	Dear Dean Stone: Dear Dr. (*or* Mr.) Stone:
president, college or university	President Joseph Stone *or* Dr. (*or* Mr.) Joseph Stone President, ____	Dear President Stone: Dear Dr. (*or* Mr.) Stone:

professor, college or university	Professor Joseph Stone *or* Dr. (*or* Mr.) Joseph Stone Department of ___	Dear Professor Stone: Dear Dr. (*or* Mr.) Stone:

Clerical and Religious Orders

abbot, Roman Catholic	The Right Reverend Joseph Stone, O.S.B. Abbot of ___	Right Reverend Abbot:
archbishop, Armenian Church	His Eminence the Archbishop of ___	Your Eminence: *or* Your Excellency:
archbishop, Greek Orthodox	His Eminence Archbishop Joseph Stone	Your Eminence:
archbishop, Roman Catholic	The Most Reverend Joseph Stone Archbishop of ___	Your Excellency:
archbishop, Russian Orthodox	His Eminence the Archbishop of ___ *or* The Most Reverend Archbishop of ___	Your Grace: Right Reverend Joseph:
archdeacon, Episcopal	The Venerable Joseph Stone, Archdeacon of ___	Venerable Sir: Dear Archdeacon Stone: Dear Father Stone:
archimandrite, Russian Orthodox	Very Reverend Father Joseph Stone	Very Reverend Father: Very Reverend Father Stone:
archpriest, Russian Orthodox	Very Reverend Father Joseph Stone	Very Reverend Father: Very Reverend Father Stone:

Clerical and Religious Orders	Form of Address	Salutation
bishop, Episcopal	The Right Reverend Joseph Stone Bishop of _____	Right Reverend Sir: Dear Bishop Stone:
bishop, Greek Orthodox	The Right Reverend Joseph Stone	Your Grace:
bishop, Methodist	Bishop Joseph Stone	Dear Bishop Stone:
bishop, Roman Catholic	The Most Reverend Joseph Stone Bishop of _____	Your Excellency:
brotherhood, Roman Catholic, member of	Brother Joseph Stone, C.F.C.	Dear Brother: Dear Brother Joseph:
canon, Episcopal	The Reverend Canon Joseph Stone	Dear Canon Stone:
cantor	Cantor Joseph Stone	Dear Cantor Stone:
cardinal	His Eminence Joseph Cardinal Stone	Your Eminence:
clergyman, Protestant	The Reverend Joseph Stone or The Reverend Joseph Stone, D.D.	Dear Mr. (or Dr.) Stone:
elder, Presbyterian	Elder Joseph Stone	Dear Elder Stone:
dean of a cathedral, Episcopal	The Very Reverend Joseph Stone Dean of _____	Very Reverend Sir: Dear Dean Stone:

metropolitan, Russian Orthodox	His Eminence the Metropolitan of ___ *or* The Most Reverend Metropolitan of ___	Your Grace: Right Reverend Joseph:
monsignor, Roman Catholic	Reverend Monsignor Joseph Stone	Reverend Monsignor: Dear Monsignor: Dear Monsignor Stone:
patriarch, Armenian Church	His Beatitude the Patriarch of ___	Your Beatitude:
patriarch, Greek Orthodox	His All Holiness Patriarch Demetrios	Your All Holiness:
patriarch, Russian Orthodox	His Beatitude the Patriarch of ___	Your Beatitude:
pope	His Holiness Pope John XXIII *or* His Holiness the Pope	Your Holiness:
president, Mormon Church	President Joseph Stone Church of Jesus Christ of Latter-day Saints	Dear President Stone:
priest, Greek Orthodox	Reverend Father Joseph Stone	Dear Reverend Stone: Dear Reverend Father:
priest, Roman Catholic	The Reverend Joseph Stone, S.J.	Dear Reverend Father: Dear Father: Dear Father Stone:
priest, Russian Orthodox	The Reverend Joseph Stone	Reverend Father: Reverend Father Stone:
protopresbyter, Russian Orthodox	Very Reverend Father Joseph Stone	Very Reverend Father: Very Reverend Father Stone:

	Form of Address	Salutation
Clerical and Religious Orders		
rabbi	Rabbi Joseph Stone *or* Joseph Stone, D.D.	Dear Rabbi (*or* Dr.) Stone:
sisterhood, Roman Catholic, member of	Sister Mary Stone, C.S.J.	Dear Sister: Dear Sister Mary:
supreme patriarch, Armenian Church	His Holiness the Supreme Patriarch and Catholicos of all Armenians	Your Holiness:
Diplomats		
ambassador, U.S.	The Honorable Joseph Stone The Ambassador of the United States	Sir: Dear Mr. Ambassador:
ambassador to the U.S.	His Excellency Joseph Stone The Ambassador of ⸺	Excellency: Dear Mr. Ambassador:
chargé d'affaires, U.S.	Joseph Stone, Esq. American Chargé d'Affaires	Dear Sir:
chargé d'affaires to the U.S.	Joseph Stone, Esq. Chargé d'Affaires of ⸺	Dear Sir:
consul, U.S.	Mr. Joseph Stone American Consul	Sir: Dear Mr. Consul:
minister, U.S.	The Honorable Joseph Stone The Minister of the United States	Sir: Dear Mr. Minister:

minister to the U.S.	The Honorable Joseph Stone The Minister of ____	Sir: Dear Mr. Minister:
secretary general, United Nations	His Excellency Joseph Stone Secretary General of the United Nations	Excellency: Dear Mr. Secretary General:
U.S. representative to the United Nations	The Honorable Joseph Stone United States Representative to the United Nations	Sir: Dear Mr. Stone:
Federal, state, and local officials (government)		
alderman	The Honorable Joseph Stone	Dear Mr. Stone:
assistant to the President	The Honorable Joseph Stone Assistant to the President The White House	Dear Mr. Stone:
Attorney General, U.S.	The Honorable Joseph Stone Attorney General of the United States	Dear Mr. Attorney General:
attorney general, state	The Honorable Joseph Stone Attorney General State of ____	Dear Mr. Attorney General:
assemblyman, state	The Honorable Joseph Stone ____ Assembly State Capitol	Dear Mr. Stone:
cabinet member	The Honorable Joseph Stone Secretary of ____	Dear Mr. Secretary:

Federal, state, and local officials (government)	Form of Address	Salutation
assistant secretary of a department	The Honorable Joseph Stone Assistant Secretary of ___	Dear Mr. Stone:
undersecretary of a department	The Honorable Joseph Stone Undersecretary of ___	Dear Mr. Stone:
deputy secretary of a department	The Honorable Joseph Stone Deputy Secretary of ___	Dear Mr. Stone:
chairman, House Committee	The Honorable Joseph Stone Chairman, Committee on ___ United States House of Representatives	Dear Mr. Chairman:
chairman, joint committee of Congress	The Honorable Joseph Stone Chairman, Joint Committee on ___ Congress of the United States	Dear Mr. Chairman:
chairman, Senate Committee	The Honorable Joseph Stone Chairman, Committee on ___ United States Senate	Dear Mr. Chairman:
chief justice, U.S. Supreme Court	The Chief Justice of the United States The Supreme Court of the United States	Dear Mr. Chief Justice:
associate justice, U.S. Supreme Court	Mr. Justice Stone The Supreme Court of the United States	Dear Mr. Justice:
commissioner (federal, state, or local)	The Honorable Joseph Stone	Dear Mr. Stone:

delegate, state	The Honorable Joseph Stone House of Delegates —— State Capitol	Dear Mr. Stone:
governor	The Honorable Joseph Stone Governor of ——	Dear Governor Stone:
judge, federal	The Honorable Joseph Stone Judge of the United States Tax Court	Dear Judge Stone:
judge, state or local	The Honorable Joseph Stone Judge of the Superior Court of ——	Dear Judge Stone:
lieutenant governor	The Honorable Joseph Stone Lieutenant Governor of ——	Dear Mr. Stone:
mayor	The Honorable Joseph Stone Mayor of ——	Dear Mayor Stone:
Postmaster General	The Honorable Joseph Stone Postmaster General of the United States	Dear Mr. Postmaster General:
President, U.S.	The President The White House	Dear Mr. President:
former President, U.S.	The Honorable Joseph Stone	Dear Mr. Stone:
representative, state	The Honorable Joseph Stone House of Representatives State Capitol	Dear Mr. Stone:
representative, U.S.	The Honorable Joseph Stone United States House of Representatives	Dear Mr. Stone:
secretary of state, state	The Honorable Joseph Stone Secretary of State State Capitol	Dear Mr. Secretary:

	Form of Address	Salutation
Federal, state, and local officials (government)		
senator, state	The Honorable Joseph Stone The State Senate State Capitol	Dear Senator Stone:
senator, U.S.	The Honorable Joseph Stone United States Senate	Dear Senator Stone:
Speaker, U.S. House of Representatives	The Honorable Joseph Stone Speaker of the House of Representatives	Dear Mr. Speaker:
Vice President, U.S.	The Vice President United States Senate	Dear Mr. Vice President:
Professions		
attorney	Mr. Joseph Stone Attorney at Law *or* Joseph Stone, Esq.	Dear Mr. Stone:
chiropractor	Joseph Stone, D.C. (office) *or* Dr. Joseph Stone (residence)	Dear Dr. Stone:
dentist	Joseph Stone, D.D.S. (office) *or* Dr. Joseph Stone (residence)	Dear Dr. Stone:

physician	Joseph Stone, M.D. (office) *or* Dr. Joseph Stone (residence)	Dear Dr. Stone:
veterinarian	Joseph Stone, D.V.M. (office) *or* Dr. Joseph Stone (residence)	Dear Dr. Stone:

Military

admiral vice admiral rear admiral	Full rank, full name, abbreviation of service branch	Dear Admiral Stone:
airman first class airman airman basic	Full rank. full name, abbreviation of service branch	Dear Airman Stone:
cadet (air force, army)	Cadet Joseph Stone United States Air Force Academy United States Military Academy	Dear Cadet Stone: *or* Dear Mr. Stone:
captain, (air force, army, coast guard, marine corps, navy)	Full rank, full name, abbreviation of service branch	Dear Captain Stone:
chief petty officer (coast guard, navy)	Full rank, full name, abbreviation of service branch	Dear Mr. Stone: *or* Dear Chief Stone:

Military	Form of Address	Salutation
chief warrant officer, warrant officer (air force, army, marine corps, navy)	Full rank, full name, abbreviation of service branch	Dear Mr. Stone:
colonel, lieutenant colonel (air force, army, marine corps)	Full rank, full name, abbreviation of service branch	Dear Colonel Stone:
commander (coast guard, navy)	Full rank, full name, abbreviation of service branch	Dear Commander Stone:
commodore (navy)	Full rank, full name, abbreviation of service branch	Dear Commodore Stone:
corporal (army), lance corporal (marine corps)	Full rank, full name, abbreviation of service branch	Dear Corporal Stone:
ensign (coast guard, navy)	Full rank, full name, abbreviation of service branch	Dear Mr. Stone: *or* Dear Ensign Stone:
first lieutenant, second lieutenant (air force, army, marine corps)	Full rank, full name, abbreviation of service branch	Dear Lieutenant Stone:
general, lieutenant general, major general, brigadier general (air force, army, marine corps)	Full rank, full name, abbreviation of service branch	Dear General Stone:

Rank	Envelope form	Salutation
lieutenant commander, lieutenant, lieutenant (jg) (coast guard, navy)	Full rank, full name, abbreviation of service branch	Dear Mr. Stone: *or* Dear Lieutenant Stone:
major (air force, army, marine corps)	Full rank, full name, abbreviation of service branch	Dear Major Stone:
midshipman	Midshipman Joseph Stone United States Coast Guard Academy United States Naval Academy	Dear Midshipman Stone:
petty officer (coast guard, navy)	Full rank, full name, abbreviation of service branch	Dear Mr. Stone:
private first class, private (air force, army, marine corps)	Full rank, full name, abbreviation of service branch	Dear Private Stone:
seaman, seaman apprentice, seaman recruit (coast guard, navy)	Full rank, full name, abbreviation of service branch	Dear Seaman Stone:
master sergeant (air force, army, marine corps)	Full rank, full name, abbreviation of service branch	Dear Sergeant Stone:

Note: Other compound titles in enlisted ranks are not shown here. They all follow forms indicated for this example.

| specialist (army) | Full rank, full name, abbreviation of service branch | Dear Specialist Stone: |

PROOFREADERS' MARKS

Instruction	Mark in Margin	Mark in Type	Corrected Type
Delete	ℯ	the ~~good~~ word	the word
Insert indicated material	good	the‿word	the good word
Let it stand	stet	the good word	the good word
Make capital	cap	the word	the Word
Make lower case	lc	The Word	the Word
Set in small capitals	sc	See word.	See WORD.
Set in italic type	ital	The word is word.	The word is *word*.
Set in roman type	rom	the word	the word
Set in boldface type	bf	the entry word	the entry **word**
Set in lightface type	lf	the entry word	the entry word
Transpose	tr	the word good	the good word
Close up space	⌒	the wo rd	the word
Delete and close up space	⌒ℯ	the woord	the word
Spell out	sp	2 words	two words
Insert: space	#	theword	the word
period	⊙	This is the word	This is the word.
comma	⌃	words words, words	words, words, words
hyphen	⌃=⌃/⌃=⌃	word for word test	word-for-word test
colon	⊙	The following words	The following words:
semicolon	⌃	Scan the words skim the words.	Scan the words; skim the words.
apostrophe	⌄	Johns words	John's words
quotation marks	⌄/⌄/	the word word	the word "word"
parentheses	(/)/	The word word is in parentheses.	The word (word) is in parentheses.
brackets	[/]/	He read from the Word the Bible.	He read from the Word [the Bible].
en dash	1/N	1964 1972	1964–1972
em dash	1/M/1/M/	The dictionary how often it is needed belongs in every home.	The dictionary—how often it is needed—belongs in every home.
superior type	⌄	$2 = 4$	$2^2 = 4$
inferior type	⌃	HO	H_2O
asterisk	⌄	word	word*
dagger	†	a word	a word†
double dagger	‡	words and words	words and words‡
section symbol	§	Book Reviews	§Book Reviews
virgule	/	either or	either/or
Start paragraph	¶	"Where is it?" "It's on the shelf."	"Where is it?" "It's on the shelf."

Instruction	Mark in Margin	Mark in Type	Corrected Type
Run in	*run in*	The entry word is printed in boldface. The pronunciation follows.	The entry word is printed in boldface. The pronunciation follows.
Turn right side up	ꝰ	the word	the word
Move left	⊏	⊏ the word	the word
Move right	⊐	the word	the word
Move up	⊓	the word	the word
Move down	⊔	the word	the word
Align	‖	the word the word the word	the word the word the word
Straighten line	=	the word	the word
Wrong font	*wf*	the word	the word
Broken type	×	the word	the word

ROMAN NUMERALS

Roman numerals are often used to list topics in outlines and legal memoranda, pagination of the front matter in books, in copyright dates, documents, and dates on monuments. The Roman numeral system is made up of seven symbols: I(1), V(5), X(10), L(50), C(100), D(500), and M(1000). Zero is not used in the system. The following table lists Roman numerals that are used frequently.

I	1	XCVIII	98
II	2	IC	99
III	3	C	100
IV	4	CI	101
V	5	CL	150
VI	6	CC	200
VII	7	CCL	250
VIII	8	CCC	300
IX	9	CCCL	350
X	10	CD	400
XI	11	CDL	450
XII	12	D	500
XIII	13	DL	550
XIV	14	DC	600
XV	15	DCL	650
XVI	16	DCC	700
XVII	17	DCCL	750
XVIII	18	DCCC	800
XIX	19	DCCCL	850
XX	20	CM	900
XXI	21	CML	950
XXIX	29	M	1000
XXX	30	MDCLXVI	1666
XL	40	MCMLXX	1970
XLVIII	48	MCMLXXVI	1976
IL	49	MCMLXXVII	1977
L	50	MCMLXXVIII	1978
LX	60	MCMLXXIX	1979
LXX	70	MCMLXXX	1980
LXXX	80	MCMXC	1990
XC	90	MM	2000

PERPETUAL CALENDAR

Our present calendar — the Gregorian calendar — was calculated by Pope Gregory XIII in 1582. Great Britain and her colonies did not adopt the Gregorian calendar until 1752. Eleven of the months in this calendar have 30 or 31 days. The month of February has 28 days except every fourth year, or leap year, when its days "leap" to 29. However, century years that cannot by divided by 400, such as 1700, 1800, and 1900, are not leap years and February will have 28 days. The century year 2000 will be a leap year. This is necessary so that calendar and solar years will remain the same.

Directions: Pick desired year from chart below. The number shown with each year indicates what calendar to use for that year.

1776... 9	1806... 4	1836...13	1866... 2	1896...11	1926... 6	1956... 8	1986... 4	2016...13	2046... 2
1777... 4	1807... 5	1837... 1	1867... 3	1897... 6	1927... 7	1957... 3	1987... 5	2017... 1	2047... 3
1778... 5	1808...13	1838... 2	1868...11	1898... 7	1928... 8	1958... 4	1988...13	2018... 2	2048...11
1779... 6	1809... 1	1839... 3	1869... 6	1899... 1	1929... 3	1959... 5	1989... 1	2019... 3	2049... 6
1780...14	1810... 2	1840...11	1870... 7	1900... 2	1930... 4	1960...13	1990... 2	2020...11	2050... 7
1781... 2	1811... 3	1841... 6	1871... 1	1901... 3	1931... 5	1961... 1	1991... 3	2021... 6	2051... 1
1782... 3	1812...11	1842... 7	1872... 9	1902... 4	1932...13	1962... 2	1992...11	2022... 7	2052... 9
1783... 4	1813... 6	1843... 1	1873... 4	1903... 5	1933... 1	1963... 3	1993... 6	2023... 1	2053... 4
1784...12	1814... 7	1844... 9	1874... 5	1904...13	1934... 2	1964...11	1994... 7	2024... 9	2054... 5
1785... 7	1815... 1	1845... 4	1875... 6	1905... 1	1935... 3	1965... 6	1995... 1	2025... 4	2055... 6
1786... 1	1816... 9	1846... 5	1876...14	1906... 2	1936...11	1966... 7	1996... 9	2026... 5	2056...14
1787... 2	1817... 4	1847... 6	1877... 2	1907... 3	1937... 6	1967... 1	1997... 4	2027... 6	2057... 2
1788...10	1818... 5	1848...14	1878... 3	1908...11	1938... 7	1968... 9	1998... 5	2028...14	2058... 3
1789... 5	1819... 6	1849... 2	1879... 4	1909... 6	1939... 1	1969... 4	1999... 6	2029... 2	2059... 4
1790... 6	1820...14	1850... 3	1880...12	1910... 7	1940... 9	1970... 5	2000...14	2030... 3	2060...12
1791... 7	1821... 2	1851... 4	1881... 7	1911... 1	1941... 4	1971... 6	2001... 2	2031... 4	2061... 7
1792... 8	1822... 3	1852...12	1882... 1	1912... 9	1942... 5	1972...14	2002... 3	2032...12	2062... 1
1793... 3	1823... 4	1853... 7	1883... 2	1913... 4	1943... 6	1973... 2	2003... 4	2033... 7	2063... 2
1794... 4	1824...12	1854... 1	1884...10	1914... 5	1944...14	1974... 3	2004...12	2034... 1	2064...10
1795... 5	1825... 7	1855... 2	1885... 5	1915... 6	1945... 2	1975... 4	2005... 7	2035... 2	2065... 5
1796...13	1826... 1	1856...10	1886... 6	1916...14	1946... 3	1976...12	2006... 1	2036...10	2066... 6
1797... 1	1827... 2	1857... 5	1887... 7	1917... 2	1947... 4	1977... 7	2007... 2	2037... 5	2067... 7
1798... 2	1828...10	1858... 6	1888... 8	1918... 3	1948...12	1978... 1	2008...10	2038... 6	2068... 8
1799... 3	1829... 5	1859... 7	1889... 3	1919... 4	1949... 7	1979... 2	2009... 5	2039... 7	2069... 3
1800... 4	1830... 6	1860... 8	1890... 4	1920...12	1950... 1	1980...10	2010... 6	2040... 8	2070... 4
1801... 5	1831... 7	1861... 3	1891... 5	1921... 7	1951... 2	1981... 5	2011... 7	2041... 3	2071... 5
1802... 6	1832... 8	1862... 4	1892...13	1922... 1	1952...10	1982... 6	2012... 8	2042... 4	2072...13
1803... 7	1833... 3	1863... 5	1893... 1	1923... 2	1953... 5	1983... 7	2013... 3	2043... 5	2073... 1
1804... 8	1834... 4	1864...13	1894... 2	1924...10	1954... 6	1984... 8	2014... 4	2044...13	2074... 2
1805... 3	1835... 5	1865... 1	1895... 3	1925... 5	1955... 7	1985... 3	2015... 5	2045... 1	2075... 3

1   1978

JANUARY
S M T W T F S
1 2 3 4 5 6 7
8 9 10 11 12 13 14
15 16 17 18 19 20 21
22 23 24 25 26 27 28
29 30 31

FEBRUARY
S M T W T F S
1 2 3 4
5 6 7 8 9 10 11
12 13 14 15 16 17 18
19 20 21 22 23 24 25
26 27 28

MARCH
S M T W T F S
1 2 3 4
5 6 7 8 9 10 11
12 13 14 15 16 17 18
19 20 21 22 23 24 25
26 27 28 29 30 31

APRIL
S M T W T F S
1
2 3 4 5 6 7 8
9 10 11 12 13 14 15
16 17 18 19 20 21 22
23 24 25 26 27 28 29
30

MAY
S M T W T F S
1 2 3 4 5 6
7 8 9 10 11 12 13
14 15 16 17 18 19 20
21 22 23 24 25 26 27
28 29 30 31

JUNE
S M T W T F S
1 2 3
4 5 6 7 8 9 10
11 12 13 14 15 16 17
18 19 20 21 22 23 24
25 26 27 28 29 30

JULY
S M T W T F S
1
2 3 4 5 6 7 8
9 10 11 12 13 14 15
16 17 18 19 20 21 22
23 24 25 26 27 28 29
30 31

AUGUST
S M T W T F S
1 2 3 4 5
6 7 8 9 10 11 12
13 14 15 16 17 18 19
20 21 22 23 24 25 26
27 28 29 30 31

SEPTEMBER
S M T W T F S
1 2
3 4 5 6 7 8 9
10 11 12 13 14 15 16
17 18 19 20 21 22 23
24 25 26 27 28 29 30

OCTOBER
S M T W T F S
1 2 3 4 5 6 7
8 9 10 11 12 13 14
15 16 17 18 19 20 21
22 23 24 25 26 27 28
29 30 31

NOVEMBER
S M T W T F S
1 2 3 4
5 6 7 8 9 10 11
12 13 14 15 16 17 18
19 20 21 22 23 24 25
26 27 28 29 30

DECEMBER
S M T W T F S
1 2
3 4 5 6 7 8 9
10 11 12 13 14 15 16
17 18 19 20 21 22 23
24 25 26 27 28 29 30
31

2   1979

JANUARY
S M T W T F S
1 2 3 4 5 6
7 8 9 10 11 12 13
14 15 16 17 18 19 20
21 22 23 24 25 26 27
28 29 30 31

FEBRUARY
S M T W T F S
1 2 3
4 5 6 7 8 9 10
11 12 13 14 15 16 17
18 19 20 21 22 23 24
25 26 27 28

MARCH
S M T W T F S
1 2 3
4 5 6 7 8 9 10
11 12 13 14 15 16 17
18 19 20 21 22 23 24
25 26 27 28 29 30 31

APRIL
S M T W T F S
1 2 3 4 5 6 7
8 9 10 11 12 13 14
15 16 17 18 19 20 21
22 23 24 25 26 27 28
29 30

MAY
S M T W T F S
1 2 3 4 5
6 7 8 9 10 11 12
13 14 15 16 17 18 19
20 21 22 23 24 25 26
27 28 29 30 31

JUNE
S M T W T F S
1 2
3 4 5 6 7 8 9
10 11 12 13 14 15 16
17 18 19 20 21 22 23
24 25 26 27 28 29 30

JULY
S M T W T F S
1 2 3 4 5 6 7
8 9 10 11 12 13 14
15 16 17 18 19 20 21
22 23 24 25 26 27 28
29 30 31

AUGUST
S M T W T F S
1 2 3 4
5 6 7 8 9 10 11
12 13 14 15 16 17 18
19 20 21 22 23 24 25
26 27 28 29 30 31

SEPTEMBER
S M T W T F S
1
2 3 4 5 6 7 8
9 10 11 12 13 14 15
16 17 18 19 20 21 22
23 24 25 26 27 28 29
30

OCTOBER
S M T W T F S
1 2 3 4 5 6
7 8 9 10 11 12 13
14 15 16 17 18 19 20
21 22 23 24 25 26 27
28 29 30 31

NOVEMBER
S M T W T F S
1 2 3
4 5 6 7 8 9 10
11 12 13 14 15 16 17
18 19 20 21 22 23 24
25 26 27 28 29 30

DECEMBER
S M T W T F S
1
2 3 4 5 6 7 8
9 10 11 12 13 14 15
16 17 18 19 20 21 22
23 24 25 26 27 28 29
30 31

3

JANUARY
```
S  M  T  W  T  F  S
         1  2  3  4  5
6  7  8  9 10 11 12
13 14 15 16 17 18 19
20 21 22 23 24 25 26
27 28 29 30 31
```

FEBRUARY
```
S  M  T  W  T  F  S
               1  2
3  4  5  6  7  8  9
10 11 12 13 14 15 16
17 18 19 20 21 22 23
24 25 26 27 28
```

MARCH
```
S  M  T  W  T  F  S
               1  2
3  4  5  6  7  8  9
10 11 12 13 14 15 16
17 18 19 20 21 22 23
24 25 26 27 28 29 30
31
```

APRIL
```
S  M  T  W  T  F  S
   1  2  3  4  5  6
7  8  9 10 11 12 13
14 15 16 17 18 19 20
21 22 23 24 25 26 27
28 29 30
```

MAY
```
S  M  T  W  T  F  S
      1  2  3  4
5  6  7  8  9 10 11
12 13 14 15 16 17 18
19 20 21 22 23 24 25
26 27 28 29 30 31
```

JUNE
```
S  M  T  W  T  F  S
                  1
2  3  4  5  6  7  8
9 10 11 12 13 14 15
16 17 18 19 20 21 22
23 24 25 26 27 28 29
30
```

JULY
```
S  M  T  W  T  F  S
   1  2  3  4  5  6
7  8  9 10 11 12 13
14 15 16 17 18 19 20
21 22 23 24 25 26 27
28 29 30 31
```

AUGUST
```
S  M  T  W  T  F  S
         1  2  3
4  5  6  7  8  9 10
11 12 13 14 15 16 17
18 19 20 21 22 23 24
25 26 27 28 29 30 31
```

SEPTEMBER
```
S  M  T  W  T  F  S
1  2  3  4  5  6  7
8  9 10 11 12 13 14
15 16 17 18 19 20 21
22 23 24 25 26 27 28
29 30
```

OCTOBER
```
S  M  T  W  T  F  S
      1  2  3  4  5
6  7  8  9 10 11 12
13 14 15 16 17 18 19
20 21 22 23 24 25 26
27 28 29 30 31
```

NOVEMBER
```
S  M  T  W  T  F  S
               1  2
3  4  5  6  7  8  9
10 11 12 13 14 15 16
17 18 19 20 21 22 23
24 25 26 27 28 29 30
```

DECEMBER
```
S  M  T  W  T  F  S
1  2  3  4  5  6  7
8  9 10 11 12 13 14
15 16 17 18 19 20 21
22 23 24 25 26 27 28
29 30 31
```

4

JANUARY
```
S  M  T  W  T  F  S
      1  2  3  4
5  6  7  8  9 10 11
12 13 14 15 16 17 18
19 20 21 22 23 24 25
26 27 28 29 30 31
```

FEBRUARY
```
S  M  T  W  T  F  S
                  1
2  3  4  5  6  7  8
9 10 11 12 13 14 15
16 17 18 19 20 21 22
23 24 25 26 27 28
```

MARCH
```
S  M  T  W  T  F  S
                  1
2  3  4  5  6  7  8
9 10 11 12 13 14 15
16 17 18 19 20 21 22
23 24 25 26 27 28 29
30 31
```

APRIL
```
S  M  T  W  T  F  S
      1  2  3  4  5
6  7  8  9 10 11 12
13 14 15 16 17 18 19
20 21 22 23 24 25 26
27 28 29 30
```

MAY
```
S  M  T  W  T  F  S
               1  2  3
4  5  6  7  8  9 10
11 12 13 14 15 16 17
18 19 20 21 22 23 24
25 26 27 28 29 30 31
```

JUNE
```
S  M  T  W  T  F  S
1  2  3  4  5  6  7
8  9 10 11 12 13 14
15 16 17 18 19 20 21
22 23 24 25 26 27 28
29 30
```

JULY
```
S  M  T  W  T  F  S
      1  2  3  4  5
6  7  8  9 10 11 12
13 14 15 16 17 18 19
20 21 22 23 24 25 26
27 28 29 30 31
```

AUGUST
```
S  M  T  W  T  F  S
               1  2
3  4  5  6  7  8  9
10 11 12 13 14 15 16
17 18 19 20 21 22 23
24 25 26 27 28 29 30
31
```

SEPTEMBER
```
S  M  T  W  T  F  S
   1  2  3  4  5  6
7  8  9 10 11 12 13
14 15 16 17 18 19 20
21 22 23 24 25 26 27
28 29 30
```

OCTOBER
```
S  M  T  W  T  F  S
         1  2  3  4
5  6  7  8  9 10 11
12 13 14 15 16 17 18
19 20 21 22 23 24 25
26 27 28 29 30 31
```

NOVEMBER
```
S  M  T  W  T  F  S
                  1
2  3  4  5  6  7  8
9 10 11 12 13 14 15
16 17 18 19 20 21 22
23 24 25 26 27 28 29
30
```

DECEMBER
```
S  M  T  W  T  F  S
   1  2  3  4  5  6
7  8  9 10 11 12 13
14 15 16 17 18 19 20
21 22 23 24 25 26 27
28 29 30 31
```

5

JANUARY
```
S  M  T  W  T  F  S
               1  2  3
4  5  6  7  8  9 10
11 12 13 14 15 16 17
18 19 20 21 22 23 24
25 26 27 28 29 30 31
```

FEBRUARY
```
S  M  T  W  T  F  S
1  2  3  4  5  6  7
8  9 10 11 12 13 14
15 16 17 18 19 20 21
22 23 24 25 26 27 28
```

MARCH
```
S  M  T  W  T  F  S
1  2  3  4  5  6  7
8  9 10 11 12 13 14
15 16 17 18 19 20 21
22 23 24 25 26 27 28
29 30 31
```

APRIL
```
S  M  T  W  T  F  S
         1  2  3  4
5  6  7  8  9 10 11
12 13 14 15 16 17 18
19 20 21 22 23 24 25
26 27 28 29 30
```

MAY
```
S  M  T  W  T  F  S
               1  2
3  4  5  6  7  8  9
10 11 12 13 14 15 16
17 18 19 20 21 22 23
24 25 26 27 28 29 30
31
```

JUNE
```
S  M  T  W  T  F  S
   1  2  3  4  5  6
7  8  9 10 11 12 13
14 15 16 17 18 19 20
21 22 23 24 25 26 27
28 29 30
```

JULY
```
S  M  T  W  T  F  S
         1  2  3  4
5  6  7  8  9 10 11
12 13 14 15 16 17 18
19 20 21 22 23 24 25
26 27 28 29 30 31
```

AUGUST
```
S  M  T  W  T  F  S
                  1
2  3  4  5  6  7  8
9 10 11 12 13 14 15
16 17 18 19 20 21 22
23 24 25 26 27 28 29
30 31
```

SEPTEMBER
```
S  M  T  W  T  F  S
      1  2  3  4  5
6  7  8  9 10 11 12
13 14 15 16 17 18 19
20 21 22 23 24 25 26
27 28 29 30
```

OCTOBER
```
S  M  T  W  T  F  S
               1  2  3
4  5  6  7  8  9 10
11 12 13 14 15 16 17
18 19 20 21 22 23 24
25 26 27 28 29 30 31
```

NOVEMBER
```
S  M  T  W  T  F  S
1  2  3  4  5  6  7
8  9 10 11 12 13 14
15 16 17 18 19 20 21
22 23 24 25 26 27 28
29 30
```

DECEMBER
```
S  M  T  W  T  F  S
      1  2  3  4  5
6  7  8  9 10 11 12
13 14 15 16 17 18 19
20 21 22 23 24 25 26
27 28 29 30 31
```

6

JANUARY
```
S  M  T  W  T  F  S
               1  2
3  4  5  6  7  8  9
10 11 12 13 14 15 16
17 18 19 20 21 22 23
24 25 26 27 28 29 30
31
```

FEBRUARY
```
S  M  T  W  T  F  S
   1  2  3  4  5  6
7  8  9 10 11 12 13
14 15 16 17 18 19 20
21 22 23 24 25 26 27
28
```

MARCH
```
S  M  T  W  T  F  S
   1  2  3  4  5  6
7  8  9 10 11 12 13
14 15 16 17 18 19 20
21 22 23 24 25 26 27
28 29 30 31
```

APRIL
```
S  M  T  W  T  F  S
         1  2  3
4  5  6  7  8  9 10
11 12 13 14 15 16 17
18 19 20 21 22 23 24
25 26 27 28 29 30
```

MAY
```
S  M  T  W  T  F  S
                  1
2  3  4  5  6  7  8
9 10 11 12 13 14 15
16 17 18 19 20 21 22
23 24 25 26 27 28 29
30 31
```

JUNE
```
S  M  T  W  T  F  S
      1  2  3  4  5
6  7  8  9 10 11 12
13 14 15 16 17 18 19
20 21 22 23 24 25 26
27 28 29 30
```

JULY
```
S  M  T  W  T  F  S
         1  2  3
4  5  6  7  8  9 10
11 12 13 14 15 16 17
18 19 20 21 22 23 24
25 26 27 28 29 30 31
```

AUGUST
```
S  M  T  W  T  F  S
1  2  3  4  5  6  7
8  9 10 11 12 13 14
15 16 17 18 19 20 21
22 23 24 25 26 27 28
29 30 31
```

SEPTEMBER
```
S  M  T  W  T  F  S
         1  2  3  4
5  6  7  8  9 10 11
12 13 14 15 16 17 18
19 20 21 22 23 24 25
26 27 28 29 30
```

OCTOBER
```
S  M  T  W  T  F  S
               1  2
3  4  5  6  7  8  9
10 11 12 13 14 15 16
17 18 19 20 21 22 23
24 25 26 27 28 29 30
31
```

NOVEMBER
```
S  M  T  W  T  F  S
   1  2  3  4  5  6
7  8  9 10 11 12 13
14 15 16 17 18 19 20
21 22 23 24 25 26 27
28 29 30
```

DECEMBER
```
S  M  T  W  T  F  S
         1  2  3  4
5  6  7  8  9 10 11
12 13 14 15 16 17 18
19 20 21 22 23 24 25
26 27 28 29 30 31
```

7 — 1977

JANUARY
S M T W T F S
              1
2 3 4 5 6 7 8
9 10 11 12 13 14 15
16 17 18 19 20 21 22
23 24 25 26 27 28 29
30 31

FEBRUARY
S M T W T F S
    1 2 3 4 5
6 7 8 9 10 11 12
13 14 15 16 17 18 19
20 21 22 23 24 25 26
27 28

MARCH
S M T W T F S
    1 2 3 4 5
6 7 8 9 10 11 12
13 14 15 16 17 18 19
20 21 22 23 24 25 26
27 28 29 30 31

APRIL
S M T W T F S
          1 2
3 4 5 6 7 8 9
10 11 12 13 14 15 16
17 18 19 20 21 22 23
24 25 26 27 28 29 30

MAY
S M T W T F S
1 2 3 4 5 6 7
8 9 10 11 12 13 14
15 16 17 18 19 20 21
22 23 24 25 26 27 28
29 30 31

JUNE
S M T W T F S
      1 2 3 4
5 6 7 8 9 10 11
12 13 14 15 16 17 18
19 20 21 22 23 24 25
26 27 28 29 30

JULY
S M T W T F S
        1 2
3 4 5 6 7 8 9
10 11 12 13 14 15 16
17 18 19 20 21 22 23
24 25 26 27 28 29 30
31

AUGUST
S M T W T F S
 1 2 3 4 5 6
7 8 9 10 11 12 13
14 15 16 17 18 19 20
21 22 23 24 25 26 27
28 29 30 31

SEPTEMBER
S M T W T F S
      1 2 3
4 5 6 7 8 9 10
11 12 13 14 15 16 17
18 19 20 21 22 23 24
25 26 27 28 29 30

OCTOBER
S M T W T F S
              1
2 3 4 5 6 7 8
9 10 11 12 13 14 15
16 17 18 19 20 21 22
23 24 25 26 27 28 29
30 31

NOVEMBER
S M T W T F S
  1 2 3 4 5
6 7 8 9 10 11 12
13 14 15 16 17 18 19
20 21 22 23 24 25 26
27 28 29 30

DECEMBER
S M T W T F S
      1 2 3
4 5 6 7 8 9 10
11 12 13 14 15 16 17
18 19 20 21 22 23 24
25 26 27 28 29 30 31

8

JANUARY
S M T W T F S
1 2 3 4 5 6 7
8 9 10 11 12 13 14
15 16 17 18 19 20 21
22 23 24 25 26 27 28
29 30 31

FEBRUARY
S M T W T F S
    1 2 3 4
5 6 7 8 9 10 11
12 13 14 15 16 17 18
19 20 21 22 23 24 25
26 27 28 29

MARCH
S M T W T F S
        1 2 3
4 5 6 7 8 9 10
11 12 13 14 15 16 17
18 19 20 21 22 23 24
25 26 27 28 29 30 31

APRIL
S M T W T F S
1 2 3 4 5 6 7
8 9 10 11 12 13 14
15 16 17 18 19 20 21
22 23 24 25 26 27 28
29 30

MAY
S M T W T F S
 1 2 3 4 5 6
7 8 9 10 11 12 13
14 15 16 17 18 19 20
21 22 23 24 25 26 27
28 29 30 31

JUNE
S M T W T F S
          1 2
3 4 5 6 7 8 9
10 11 12 13 14 15 16
17 18 19 20 21 22 23
24 25 26 27 28 29 30

JULY
S M T W T F S
1 2 3 4 5 6 7
8 9 10 11 12 13 14
15 16 17 18 19 20 21
22 23 24 25 26 27 28
29 30 31

AUGUST
S M T W T F S
    1 2 3 4
5 6 7 8 9 10 11
12 13 14 15 16 17 18
19 20 21 22 23 24 25
26 27 28 29 30 31

SEPTEMBER
S M T W T F S
2 3 4 5 6 7 8
9 10 11 12 13 14 15
16 17 18 19 20 21 22
23 24 25 26 27 28 29
30

OCTOBER
S M T W T F S
 1 2 3 4 5 6
7 8 9 10 11 12 13
14 15 16 17 18 19 20
21 22 23 24 25 26 27
28 29 30 31

NOVEMBER
S M T W T F S
      1 2 3
4 5 6 7 8 9 10
11 12 13 14 15 16 17
18 19 20 21 22 23 24
25 26 27 28 29 30

DECEMBER
S M T W T F S
            1
2 3 4 5 6 7 8
9 10 11 12 13 14 15
16 17 18 19 20 21 22
23 24 25 26 27 28 29
30 31

9

JANUARY
S M T W T F S
1 2 3 4 5 6
7 8 9 10 11 12 13
14 15 16 17 18 19 20
21 22 23 24 25 26 27
28 29 30 31

FEBRUARY
S M T W T F S
      1 2 3
4 5 6 7 8 9 10
11 12 13 14 15 16 17
18 19 20 21 22 23 24
25 26 27 28 29

MARCH
S M T W T F S
          1 2
3 4 5 6 7 8 9
10 11 12 13 14 15 16
17 18 19 20 21 22 23
24 25 26 27 28 29 30
31

APRIL
S M T W T F S
 1 2 3 4 5 6
7 8 9 10 11 12 13
14 15 16 17 18 19 20
21 22 23 24 25 26 27
28 29 30

MAY
S M T W T F S
    1 2 3 4
5 6 7 8 9 10 11
12 13 14 15 16 17 18
19 20 21 22 23 24 25
26 27 28 29 30 31

JUNE
S M T W T F S
              1
2 3 4 5 6 7 8
9 10 11 12 13 14 15
16 17 18 19 20 21 22
23 24 25 26 27 28 29
30

JULY
S M T W T F S
1 2 3 4 5
7 8 9 10 11 12 13
14 15 16 17 18 19 20
21 22 23 24 25 26 27
28 29 30 31

AUGUST
S M T W T F S
      1 2 3
4 5 6 7 8 9 10
11 12 13 14 15 16 17
18 19 20 21 22 23 24
25 26 27 28 29 30 31

SEPTEMBER
S M T W T F S
1 2 3 4 5 6 7
8 9 10 11 12 13 14
15 16 17 18 19 20 21
22 23 24 25 26 27 28
29 30

OCTOBER
S M T W T F S
    1 2 3 4 5
6 7 8 9 10 11 12
13 14 15 16 17 18 19
20 21 22 23 24 25 26
27 28 29 30 31

NOVEMBER
S M T W T F S
         1 2
3 4 5 6 7 8 9
10 11 12 13 14 15 16
17 18 19 20 21 22 23
24 25 26 27 28 29 30

DECEMBER
S M T W T F S
1 2 3 4 5 6 7
8 9 10 11 12 13 14
15 16 17 18 19 20 21
22 23 24 25 26 27 28
29 30 31

10

JANUARY
S M T W T F S
    1 2 3 4 5
6 7 8 9 10 11 12
13 14 15 16 17 18 19
20 21 22 23 24 25 26
27 28 29 30 31

FEBRUARY
S M T W T F S
        1 2
3 4 5 6 7 8 9
10 11 12 13 14 15 16
17 18 19 20 21 22 23
24 25 26 27 28 29

MARCH
S M T W T F S
              1
2 3 4 5 6 7 8
9 10 11 12 13 14 15
16 17 18 19 20 21 22
23 24 25 26 27 28 29
30 31

APRIL
S M T W T F S
    1 2 3 4 5
6 7 8 9 10 11 12
13 14 15 16 17 18 19
20 21 22 23 24 25 26
27 28 29 30

MAY
S M T W T F S
        1 2 3
4 5 6 7 8 9 10
11 12 13 14 15 16 17
18 19 20 21 22 23 24
25 26 27 28 29 30 31

JUNE
S M T W T F S
1 2 3 4 5 6 7
8 9 10 11 12 13 14
15 16 17 18 19 20 21
22 23 24 25 26 27 28
29 30

JULY
S M T W T F S
    1 2 3 4 5
6 7 8 9 10 11 12
13 14 15 16 17 18 19
20 21 22 23 24 25 26
27 28 29 30 31

AUGUST
S M T W T F S
          1 2
3 4 5 6 7 8 9
10 11 12 13 14 15 16
17 18 19 20 21 22 23
24 25 26 27 28 29 30
31

SEPTEMBER
S M T W T F S
 1 2 3 4 5 6
7 8 9 10 11 12 13
14 15 16 17 18 19 20
21 22 23 24 25 26 27
28 29 30

OCTOBER
S M T W T F S
        1 2 3 4
5 6 7 8 9 10 11
12 13 14 15 16 17 18
19 20 21 22 23 24 25
26 27 28 29 30 31

NOVEMBER
S M T W T F S
  1 2 3 4 5
6 7 8 9 10 11 12
13 14 15 16 17 18 19
20 21 22 23 24 25 26
27 28 29 30

DECEMBER
S M T W T F S
1 2 3 4 5 6
7 8 9 10 11 12 13
14 15 16 17 18 19 20
21 22 23 24 25 26 27
28 29 30 31

11

```
     JANUARY              FEBRUARY               MARCH
S  M  T  W  T  F  S   S  M  T  W  T  F  S   S  M  T  W  T  F  S
         1  2  3  4                   1   1  2  3  4  5  6  7
 5  6  7  8  9 10 11   2  3  4  5  6  7  8   8  9 10 11 12 13 14
12 13 14 15 16 17 18   9 10 11 12 13 14 15  15 16 17 18 19 20 21
19 20 21 22 23 24 25  16 17 18 19 20 21 22  22 23 24 25 26 27 28
26 27 28 29 30 31     23 24 25 26 27 28 29  29 30 31

      APRIL                  MAY                   JUNE
S  M  T  W  T  F  S   S  M  T  W  T  F  S   S  M  T  W  T  F  S
         1  2  3  4                   1  2      1  2  3  4  5  6
 5  6  7  8  9 10 11   3  4  5  6  7  8  9   7  8  9 10 11 12 13
12 13 14 15 16 17 18  10 11 12 13 14 15 16  14 15 16 17 18 19 20
19 20 21 22 23 24 25  17 18 19 20 21 22 23  21 22 23 24 25 26 27
26 27 28 29 30        24 25 26 27 28 29 30  28 29 30
                      31

       JULY                AUGUST              SEPTEMBER
S  M  T  W  T  F  S   S  M  T  W  T  F  S   S  M  T  W  T  F  S
         1  2  3  4                      1         1  2  3  4  5
 5  6  7  8  9 10 11   2  3  4  5  6  7  8   6  7  8  9 10 11 12
12 13 14 15 16 17 18   9 10 11 12 13 14 15  13 14 15 16 17 18 19
19 20 21 22 23 24 25  16 17 18 19 20 21 22  20 21 22 23 24 25 26
26 27 28 29 30 31     23 24 25 26 27 28 29  27 28 29 30
                      30 31

     OCTOBER              NOVEMBER              DECEMBER
S  M  T  W  T  F  S   S  M  T  W  T  F  S   S  M  T  W  T  F  S
            1  2  3   1  2  3  4  5  6  7         1  2  3  4  5
 4  5  6  7  8  9 10   8  9 10 11 12 13 14   6  7  8  9 10 11 12
11 12 13 14 15 16 17  15 16 17 18 19 20 21  13 14 15 16 17 18 19
18 19 20 21 22 23 24  22 23 24 25 26 27 28  20 21 22 23 24 25 26
25 26 27 28 29 30 31  29 30                 27 28 29 30 31
```

12

```
     JANUARY              FEBRUARY               MARCH
S  M  T  W  T  F  S   S  M  T  W  T  F  S   S  M  T  W  T  F  S
            1  2  3   1  2  3  4  5  6  7   1  2  3  4  5  6
 4  5  6  7  8  9 10   8  9 10 11 12 13 14   7  8  9 10 11 12 13
11 12 13 14 15 16 17  15 16 17 18 19 20 21  14 15 16 17 18 19 20
18 19 20 21 22 23 24  22 23 24 25 26 27 28  21 22 23 24 25 26 27
25 26 27 28 29 30 31  29                    28 29 30 31

      APRIL                  MAY                   JUNE
S  M  T  W  T  F  S   S  M  T  W  T  F  S   S  M  T  W  T  F  S
         1  2  3                      1         1  2  3  4  5
 4  5  6  7  8  9 10   2  3  4  5  6  7  8   6  7  8  9 10 11 12
11 12 13 14 15 16 17   9 10 11 12 13 14 15  13 14 15 16 17 18 19
18 19 20 21 22 23 24  16 17 18 19 20 21 22  20 21 22 23 24 25 26
25 26 27 28 29 30     23 24 25 26 27 28 29  27 28 29 30
                      30 31

       JULY                AUGUST              SEPTEMBER
S  M  T  W  T  F  S   S  M  T  W  T  F  S   S  M  T  W  T  F  S
            1  2  3   1  2  3  4  5  6  7            1  2  3  4
 4  5  6  7  8  9 10   8  9 10 11 12 13 14   5  6  7  8  9 10 11
11 12 13 14 15 16 17  15 16 17 18 19 20 21  12 13 14 15 16 17 18
18 19 20 21 22 23 24  22 23 24 25 26 27 28  19 20 21 22 23 24 25
25 26 27 28 29 30 31  29 30 31              26 27 28 29 30

     OCTOBER              NOVEMBER              DECEMBER
S  M  T  W  T  F  S   S  M  T  W  T  F  S   S  M  T  W  T  F  S
            1  2         1  2  3  4  5  6            1  2  3  4
 3  4  5  6  7  8  9   7  8  9 10 11 12 13   5  6  7  8  9 10 11
10 11 12 13 14 15 16  14 15 16 17 18 19 20  12 13 14 15 16 17 18
17 18 19 20 21 22 23  21 22 23 24 25 26 27  19 20 21 22 23 24 25
24 25 26 27 28 29 30  28 29 30              26 27 28 29 30 31
31
```

13

```
     JANUARY              FEBRUARY               MARCH
S  M  T  W  T  F  S   S  M  T  W  T  F  S   S  M  T  W  T  F  S
                1  2      1  2  3  4  5  6      1  2  3  4  5
 3  4  5  6  7  8  9   7  8  9 10 11 12 13   6  7  8  9 10 11 12
10 11 12 13 14 15 16  14 15 16 17 18 19 20  13 14 15 16 17 18 19
17 18 19 20 21 22 23  21 22 23 24 25 26 27  20 21 22 23 24 25 26
24 25 26 27 28 29 30  28 29                 27 28 29 30 31
31

      APRIL                  MAY                   JUNE
S  M  T  W  T  F  S   S  M  T  W  T  F  S   S  M  T  W  T  F  S
                1  2   1  2  3  4  5  6  7            1  2  3  4
 3  4  5  6  7  8  9   8  9 10 11 12 13 14   5  6  7  8  9 10 11
10 11 12 13 14 15 16  15 16 17 18 19 20 21  12 13 14 15 16 17 18
17 18 19 20 21 22 23  22 23 24 25 26 27 28  19 20 21 22 23 24 25
24 25 26 27 28 29 30  29 30 31              26 27 28 29 30

       JULY                AUGUST              SEPTEMBER
S  M  T  W  T  F  S   S  M  T  W  T  F  S   S  M  T  W  T  F  S
                1  2      1  2  3  4  5  6            1  2  3
 3  4  5  6  7  8  9   7  8  9 10 11 12 13   4  5  6  7  8  9 10
10 11 12 13 14 15 16  14 15 16 17 18 19 20  11 12 13 14 15 16 17
17 18 19 20 21 22 23  21 22 23 24 25 26 27  18 19 20 21 22 23 24
24 25 26 27 28 29 30  28 29 30 31           25 26 27 28 29 30
31

     OCTOBER              NOVEMBER              DECEMBER
S  M  T  W  T  F  S   S  M  T  W  T  F  S   S  M  T  W  T  F  S
                1         1  2  3  4  5            1  2  3
 2  3  4  5  6  7  8   6  7  8  9 10 11 12   4  5  6  7  8  9 10
 9 10 11 12 13 14 15  13 14 15 16 17 18 19  11 12 13 14 15 16 17
16 17 18 19 20 21 22  20 21 22 23 24 25 26  18 19 20 21 22 23 24
23 24 25 26 27 28 29  27 28 29 30           25 26 27 28 29 30 31
30 31
```

14

```
     JANUARY              FEBRUARY               MARCH
S  M  T  W  T  F  S   S  M  T  W  T  F  S   S  M  T  W  T  F  S
                1         1  2  3  4  5            1  2  3  4
 2  3  4  5  6  7  8   6  7  8  9 10 11 12   5  6  7  8  9 10 11
 9 10 11 12 13 14 15  13 14 15 16 17 18 19  12 13 14 15 16 17 18
16 17 18 19 20 21 22  20 21 22 23 24 25 26  19 20 21 22 23 24 25
23 24 25 26 27 28 29  27 28 29              26 27 28 29 30 31
30 31

      APRIL                  MAY                   JUNE
S  M  T  W  T  F  S   S  M  T  W  T  F  S   S  M  T  W  T  F  S
                1         1  2  3  4  5  6            1  2  3
 2  3  4  5  6  7  8   7  8  9 10 11 12 13   4  5  6  7  8  9 10
 9 10 11 12 13 14 15  14 15 16 17 18 19 20  11 12 13 14 15 16 17
16 17 18 19 20 21 22  21 22 23 24 25 26 27  18 19 20 21 22 23 24
23 24 25 26 27 28 29  28 29 30 31           25 26 27 28 29 30
30

       JULY                AUGUST              SEPTEMBER
S  M  T  W  T  F  S   S  M  T  W  T  F  S   S  M  T  W  T  F  S
                1         1  2  3  4  5            1  2
 2  3  4  5  6  7  8   6  7  8  9 10 11 12   3  4  5  6  7  8  9
 9 10 11 12 13 14 15  13 14 15 16 17 18 19  10 11 12 13 14 15 16
16 17 18 19 20 21 22  20 21 22 23 24 25 26  17 18 19 20 21 22 23
23 24 25 26 27 28 29  27 28 29 30 31        24 25 26 27 28 29 30
30 31

     OCTOBER              NOVEMBER              DECEMBER
S  M  T  W  T  F  S   S  M  T  W  T  F  S   S  M  T  W  T  F  S
 1  2  3  4  5  6  7            1  2  3  4            1  2
 8  9 10 11 12 13 14   5  6  7  8  9 10 11   3  4  5  6  7  8  9
15 16 17 18 19 20 21  12 13 14 15 16 17 18  10 11 12 13 14 15 16
22 23 24 25 26 27 28  19 20 21 22 23 24 25  17 18 19 20 21 22 23
29 30 31              26 27 28 29 30        24 25 26 27 28 29 30
                                            31
```

POSTAL ABBREVIATIONS

Alabama	AL	Maine	ME	Pennsylvania	PA
Alaska	AK	Maryland	MD	Rhode Island	RI
Arizona	AZ	Massachusetts	MA	South Carolina	SC
Arkansas	AR	Michigan	MI	South Dakota	SD
California	CA	Minnesota	MN	Tennessee	TN
Colorado	CO	Mississippi	MS	Texas	TX
Connecticut	CT	Missouri	MO	Utah	UT
Delaware	DE	Montana	MT	Vermont	VT
District of Columbia	DC	Nebraska	NE	Virginia	VA
Florida	FL	Nevada	NV	Washington	WA
Georgia	GA	New Hampshire	NH	West Virginia	WV
Hawaii	HI	New Jersey	NJ	Wisconsin	WI
Idaho	ID	New Mexico	NM	Wyoming	WY
Illinois	IL	New York	NY		
Indiana	IN	North Carolina	NC		
Iowa	IA	North Dakota	ND		
Kansas	KS	Ohio	OH	Guam	GU
Kentucky	KY	Oklahoma	OK	Puerto Rico	PR
Louisiana	LA	Oregon	OR	Virgin Islands	VI

TELEPHONE AREA CODES

Place	Area Code	Place	Area Code	Place	Area Code

ALABAMA
All points   205

ALASKA
All points   907

ARIZONA
All points   602

ARKANSAS
All points   501

CALIFORNIA

Place	Area Code
Alameda	415
Alhambra	213
Altadena	213
Anaheim	714
Arcadia	213
Azusa	213
Bakersfield	805
Baldwin Park	213
Bell Gardens	213
Bellflower	213
Belmont	415
Berkeley	415
Beverly Hills	213
Burbank	213
Burlingame	415
Buena Pk.	714
Campbell	408
Carmichael	916
Carson	213
Castro Valley	415
Chula Vista	714
Claremont	714
Compton	213
Concord	415
Corona	714
Costa Mesa	714
Covina	213
Culver City	213
Cypress	714
Daly City	415
Davis	916
Downey	213
East Los Angeles	213
El Cerrito	415

CALIFORNIA (Cont'd)

Place	Area Code
El Monte	213
Escondido	714
Eureka	707
Fairfield	707
Fountain Valley	714
Fremont	415
Fresno	209
Fullerton	714
Gardena	213
Garden Grove	714
Glendale	213
Glendora	213
Hacienda Heights	213
Hawthorne	213
Hollywood	213
Huntington Beach	714
Huntington Park	213
Inglewood	213
La Habra	213
Lakewood	213
La Mesa	714
La Mirada	714
Lancaster	805
La Puente	213
Lawndale	213
Livermore	415
Lodi	209
Lompoc	805
Long Beach	213
Los Altos	415
Los Angeles	213
Los Gatos	408
Lynwood	213
Manhattan Beach	213
Menlo Park	415
Merced	209
Milpitas	408
Modesto	209
Monrovia	213
Montclair	714
Montebello	213
Monterey	408
Monterey Park	213
Mountain View	415
Napa	707
National City	714
Newark	415

CALIFORNIA (Cont'd)

Place	Area Code
Newport Beach	714
North Highlands	916
Norwalk	213
Novato	415
Oakland	415
Oceanside	714
Ontario	714
Orange	714
Oxnard	805
Pacifica	415
Palo Alto	415
Palos Verdes	213
Paramount	213
Pasadena	213
Petaluma	707
Pico Rivera	213
Pleasant Hill	415
Rancho Cordova	916
Redlands	714
Redondo Beach	213
Redwood City	415
Rialto	714
Richmond	415
Riverside	714
Rosemead	213
Sacramento	916
Salinas	408
San Bernardino	714
San Bruno	415
San Carlos	415
San Diego	714
San Francisco	415
San Gabriel	213
San Jose	408
San Leandro	415
San Lorenzo	415
San Luis Obispo	805
San Rafael	415
Santa Ana	714
Santa Barbara	805
Santa Clara	408
Santa Cruz	408
Santa Maria	805
Santa Monica	213
Santa Rosa	707
Seal Beach	213
Seaside	408

Place	Area Code	Place	Area Code	Place	Area Code

CALIFORNIA (Cont'd)

Place	Area Code
Simi Valley	805
South Gate	213
South Pasadena	213
South San Francisco	415
South Whittier	213
Spring Valley	714
Stockton	209
Sunnyvale	408
Temple City	213
Thousand Oaks	805
Torrance	213
Upland	714
Vallejo	707
Ventura	805
Visalia	209
Vista	714
Walnut Creek	415
West Covina	213
West Hollywood	213
Westminster	714
Whittier	213

COLORADO

Place	Area Code
All points	303

CONNECTICUT

Place	Area Code
All points	203

DELAWARE

Place	Area Code
All points	302

DISTRICT OF COLUMBIA

Place	Area Code
Washington	202

FLORIDA

Place	Area Code
Boca Raton	305
Carol City	305
Clearwater	813
Coral Gables	305
Daytona Beach	904
Fort Lauderdale	305
Fort Myers	813
Fort Pierce	305
Gainesville	904

FLORIDA (Cont'd)

Place	Area Code
Hallandale	305
Hialeah	305
Jacksonville	904
Kendall	305
Key West	305
Lakeland	813
Lake Worth	305
Melbourne	305
Merritt Island	305
Miami	305
Miami Beach	305
Miramar	305
North Miami	305
North Miami Beach	305
Ocala	904
Orlando	305
Panama City	904
Pensacola	904
Plantation	305
Pompano Beach	305
St. Petersburg	813
Sarasota	813
Tallahassee	904
Tampa	813
Titusville	305
West Palm Beach	305

GEORGIA

Place	Area Code
Albany	912
Athens	404
Atlanta	404
Augusta	404
Columbus	404
East Point	404
Fort Benning	404
Gainesville	404
Griffin	404
La Grange	404
Macon	912
Marietta	404
Rome	404
Savannah	912
Valdosta	912
Warner Robins	912

HAWAII

Place	Area Code
All points	808

IDAHO

Place	Area Code
All points	208

ILLINOIS

Place	Area Code
Addison	312
Alton	618
Arlington Heights	312
Aurora	312
Belleville	618
Berwyn	312
Bloomington	309
Blue Island	312
Calumet City	312
Carbondale	618
Carpentersville	312
Champaign	217
Chicago	312
Chicago Heights	312
Cicero	312
Danville	217
Decatur	217
De Kalb	815
Des Plaines	312
Dolton	312
Downers Grove	312
East St. Louis	618
Elgin	312
Elk Grove Village	312
Elmhurst	312
Elmwood Park	309
Evanston	312
Evergreen Park	312
Freeport	815
Galesburg	309
Granite City	618
Harvey	312
Highland Park	312
Hinsdale	312
Hoffman Estates	312
Joliet	815
Kankakee	815
La Grange	312
Lansing	312
Lombard	312
Maywood	312
Melrose Park	312
Moline	309
Morton Grove	312
Mount Prospect	312
Naperville	312

Place	Area Code	Place	Area Code	Place	Area Code
ILLINOIS		**IOWA**		**LOUISIANA**	
(Cont'd)		Ames	515	(Cont'd)	
Niles	312	Burlington	319	Kenner	504
Normal	309	Cedar Falls	319	Lafayette	318
Northbrook	312	Cedar Rapids	319	Lake Charles	318
North Chicago	312	Clinton	319	Marrero	504
Oak Lawn	312	Council Bluffs	712	Metairie	504
Oak Park	312	Davenport	319	Monroe	318
Palatine	312	Des Moines	515	New Iberia	318
Park Forest	312	Dubuque	319	New Orleans	504
Park Ridge	312	Fort Dodge	515	Scotlandville	504
Pekin	309	Iowa City	319	Shreveport	318
Peoria	309	Marshalltown	515		
Rantoul	217	Ottumwa	515	**MAINE**	
Rockford	815	Sioux City	712	All points	207
Rock Island	309	Waterloo	319		
Schaumburg	312			**MARYLAND**	
Skokie	312	**KANSAS**		All points	301
South Holland	312	Emporia	316		
Springfield	217	Hutchinson	316	**MASSACHUSETTS**	
Urbana	217	Kansas City	913	Amherst	413
Villa Park	312	Lawrence	913	Andover	617
Waukegan	312	Leavenworth	913	Arlington	617
Wheaton	312	Manhattan	913	Attleboro	617
Wilmette	312	Overland Park	913	Barnstable	617
		Salina	913	Belmont	617
INDIANA		Topeka	913	Beverly	617
Anderson	317	Wichita	316	Billerica	617
Bloomington	812			Boston	617
Columbus	812	**KENTUCKY**		Braintree	617
East Chicago	219	Ashland	606	Brockton	617
Elkhart	219	Bowling Green	502	Brookline	617
Evansville	812	Covington	606	Cambridge	617
Fort Wayne	219	Fort Knox	502	Chelmsford	617
Gary	219	Frankfort	502	Chelsea	617
Hammond	219	Henderson	502	Chicopee	413
Highland	219	Lexington	606	Danvers	617
Indianapolis	317	Louisville	502	Dedham	617
Kokomo	317	Newport	606	Everett	617
Lafayette	317	Owensboro	502	Fall River	617
Marion	317	Paducah	502	Fitchburg	617
Merrillville	219	Pleasure Ridge Park	502	Framingham	617
Michigan City	219	Valley Station	502	Gardner	617
Mishawaka	219			Gloucester	617
Muncie	317	**LOUISIANA**		Greenfield	413
New Albany	812	Alexandria	318	Haverhill	617
Richmond	317	Baton Rouge	504	Holyoke	413
South Bend	219	Bossier City	318	Lawrence	617
Terre Haute	812	Gretna	504	Leominster	617
		Houma	504	Lexington	617

Place	Area Code	Place	Area Code	Place	Area Code

MASSACHUSETTS (Cont'd)

Longmeadow	413
Lowell	617
Lynn	617
Malden	617
Marblehead	617
Marlboro	617
Medford	617
Melrose	617
Methuen	617
Milton	617
Natick	617
Needham	617
New Bedford	617
Newton	617
North Adams	413
Northampton	413
Norwood	617
Peabody	617
Pittsfield	413
Quincy	617
Randolph	617
Reading	617
Revere	617
Roxbury	617
Saugus	617
Salem	617
Somerville	617
Springfield	413
Stoughton	617
Taunton	617
Tewksbury	617
Wakefield	617
Waltham	617
Watertown	617
Wellesley	617
Westfield	413
West Springfield	413
Weymouth	617
Woburn	617
Worcester	617

MICHIGAN

Allen Park	313
Ann Arbor	313
Battle Creek	616
Bay City	517
Benton Harbor	616
Birmingham	313

MICHIGAN (Cont'd)

Dearborn	313
Detroit	313
East Detroit	313
East Lansing	517
Ferndale	313
Flint	313
Garden City	313
Grand Rapids	616
Hamtramck	313
Hazel Park	313
Highland Park	313
Holland	616
Inkster	313
Jackson	517
Kalamazoo	616
Lansing	517
Livonia	313
Madison Heights	313
Marquette	906
Midland	517
Monroe	313
Muskegon	616
Niles	616
Oak Park	313
Pontiac	313
Portage	616
Port Huron	313
Roseville	313
Royal Oak	313
Saginaw	517
St. Clair Shores	313
St. Joseph	616
Southfield	313
Southgate	313
Sterling Heights	313
Taylor	313
Trenton	313
Troy	313
Warren	313
Westland	313
Wyandotte	313
Wyoming	616
Ypsilanti	313

MINNESOTA

Austin	507
Bloomington	612
Brooklyn Center	612

MINNESOTA (Cont'd)

Columbia Heights	612
Coon Rapids	612
Crystal	612
Duluth	218
Edina	612
Fridley	612
Mankato	507
Minneapolis	612
Minnetonka	612
Moorhead	218
New Hope	612
Rochester	507
Roseville	612
St. Cloud	612
St. Louis Park	612
St. Paul	612
White Bear Lake	612
Winona	507

MISSISSIPPI

All points	601

MISSOURI

Affton	314
Cape Girardeau	314
Columbia	314
Ferguson	314
Florissant	314
Fort Leonard Wood	314
Gladstone	816
Independence	816
Jefferson City	314
Joplin	417
Kansas City	816
Kirkwood	314
Lemay	314
Overland	314
Raytown	816
Sedalia	816
Springfield	417
St. Charles	314
St. Joseph	816
St. Louis	314
University City	314
Webster Groves	314

MONTANA

All points	406

Place	Area Code	Place	Area Code	Place	Area Code

NEBRASKA

Fremont	402
Grand Island	308
Hastings	402
Lincoln	402
North Platte	308
Omaha	402

NEVADA

All points	702

NEW HAMPSHIRE

All points	603

NEW JERSEY

Asbury Park	201
Atlantic City	609
Barnegat	609
Bayonne	201
Belleville	201
Bellmawr	609
Bergenfield	201
Bloomfield	201
Bound Brook	201
Bridgeton	609
Burlington	609
Camden	609
Carteret	201
Cliffside Park	201
Clifton	201
Collingswood	609
Dover	201
Dumont	201
East Orange	201
East Paterson	201
Eatontown	201
Elizabeth	201
Englewood	201
Ewing	609
Fair Lawn	201
Flemington	201
Fort Dix	609
Fort Lee	201
Garfield	201
Glassboro	609
Glen Ridge	201
Gloucester	609
Hackensack	201
Haddonfield	609
Hasbrouck Heights	201

NEW JERSEY (Cont'd)

Hawthorne	201
Hoboken	201
Irvington	201
Jersey City	201
Kearny	201
Lakewood	201
Linden	201
Long Branch	201
Madison	201
Maplewood	201
Mendham	201
Metuchen	201
Middlesex	201
Millburn	201
Millville	609
Montclair	201
Morristown	201
Mount Holly	609
Newark	201
New Brunswick	201
New Milford	201
North Arlington	201
North Plainfield	201
Nutley	201
Old Bridge	201
Orange	201
Paramus	201
Passaic	201
Paterson	201
Perth Amboy	201
Phillipsburg	201
Plainfield	201
Pleasantville	609
Point Pleasant	201
Pompton Lakes	201
Princeton	609
Rahway	201
Red Bank	201
Ridgefield	201
Ridgewood	201
Roselle	201
Rutherford	201
Sayreville	201
Somerville	201
South Amboy	201
South Orange	201
South Plainfield	201

NEW JERSEY (Cont'd)

South River	201
Summit	201
Teaneck	201
Trenton	609
Union City	201
Verona	201
Vineland	609
Weehawken	201
Westfield	201
West New York	201
West Orange	201
Wildwood	609
Woodbridge	201
Woodbury	609
Wyckoff	201

NEW MEXICO

All points	505

NEW YORK

Albany & Suburbs	518
Amagansett	516
Amityville	516
Amsterdam	518
Armonk Village	914
Auburn	315
Babylon	516
Baldwin	516
Batavia	716
Bay Shore	516
Bedford Village	914
Bellmore	516
Bethpage	516
Binghamton	607
Brentwood	516
Brewster	914
Bridgehampton	516
Bronx	212
Bronxville	914
Brooklyn	212
Brookville	516
Buffalo & Suburbs	716
Callicoon	914
Carmel	914
Center Moriches	516
Central Islip	516
Chappaqua	914

Place	Area Code	Place	Area Code	Place	Area Code
NEW YORK (Cont'd)		**NEW YORK** (Cont'd)		**NEW YORK** (Cont'd)	
Cohoes	518	Hicksville	516	New Rochelle	914
Cold Spring	914	Hudson	518	New York City	212
Commack	516	Huntington	516	Niagara	716
Congers	914	Huntington Station	516	North Babylon	516
Copiague	516	Hurleyville	914	North Bellmore	516
Corning	607	Irvington	914	North Massapequa	516
Cortland	607	Islip	516	North Tonawanda	716
Croton-on-Hudson	914	Ithaca	607	Norwich	607
Deer Park	516	Jamestown	716	Nyack	914
Depew	716	Jeffersonville	914	Oceanside	516
Dobbs Ferry	914	Johnson City	607	Olean	716
Dunkirk	716	Kenmore	716	Oneida	315
Eastchester	914	Kerhonkson	914	Oneonta	607
East Hampton	516	Kiamesha	914	Ossining	914
East Massapequa	516	Kingston	914	Oswego	315
East Meadow	516	Lackawanna	716	Oyster Bay	516
Eastport	516	Lake Huntington	914	Patchogue	516
Ellenville	914	Lakeland	914	Pearl River	914
Elmira	607	Lake Success	516	Peekskill	914
Elmsford	914	Larchmont	914	Pelham	914
Elwood	516	Levittown	516	Piermont	914
Endicott	607	Liberty	914	Plainview	516
Endwell	607	Lindenhurst	516	Plattsburgh	518
Fairmount	315	Livingston Manor	914	Pleasantville	914
Fallsburg	914	Lockport	716	Port Chester	914
Farmingdale	516	Long Beach	516	Port Jefferson	516
Fire Island	516	Long Island	516	Port Washington	516
Fishers Island	516	Lynbrook	516	Potsdam	315
Floral Park	516	Mahopac	914	Poughkeepsie	914
Franklin Square	516	Mamaroneck	914	Queens County	212
Freeport	516	Manhasset	516	Riverhead	516
Fulton	315	Manhattan	212	Rochester	716
Garden City	516	Massapequa	516	Rockville Centre	516
Garrison	914	Massapequa Park	516	Roosevelt	516
Geneva	315	Massena	315	Rome	315
Glen Cove	516	Merrick	516	Ronkonkoma	516
Glens Falls	518	Middletown	914	Roscoe	607
Gloversville	518	Mineola	516	Roslyn	516
Grahamsville	914	Montauk Point	516	Rye	914
Great Neck	516	Monticello	914	Sag Harbor	516
Grossinger	914	Mount Kisco	914	Saratoga Springs	518
Hamilton	315	Mount Vernon	914	Sayville	516
Hampton Bays	516	Nanuet	914	Scarsdale	914
Harrison	914	Narrowsburg	914	Schenectady	518
Hastings-on-Hudson	914	Newark	315	Seaford	516
Haverstraw	914	Newburgh	914	Shelter Island	516
Hempstead	516	New City	914	Sloatsburg	914

Place	Area Code	Place	Area Code	Place	Area Code

NEW YORK
(Cont'd)

Smithtown	516
Southampton	516
Spring Valley	914
Staten Island	212
Stony Point	914
Suffern	914
Syracuse & Suburbs	315
Tarrytown	914
Ticonderoga	518
Tonawanda	716
Troy	518
Tuckahoe	914
Uniondale	516
Utica & Suburbs	315
Valley Stream	516
Wantagh	516
Watertown	315
Westbury	516
Westchester Co.	914
Westhampton	516
West Hempstead	516
West Islip	516
Wheatley Hills	516
White Lake	914
White Plains	914
Woodbourne	914
Woodmere	516
Woodridge	914
Woodstock	914
Wyandanch	516
Yonkers	914
Yorktown Heights	914

NORTH CAROLINA

Asheville	704
Burlington	919
Camp Le Jeune	919
Chapel Hill	919
Charlotte	704
Durham	919
Fayetteville	919
Fort Bragg	919
Gastonia	704
Goldsboro	919
Greensboro	919
Greenville	919
High Point	919

NORTH CAROLINA
(Cont'd)

Kannapolis	704
Kinston	919
Lexington	704
Raleigh	919
Rocky Mount	919
Salisbury	704
Wilmington	919
Wilson	919
Winston-Salem	919

NORTH DAKOTA

All points	701

OHIO

Akron	216
Alliance	216
Ashtabula	216
Athens	614
Austintown	216
Barberton	216
Boardman	216
Brook Park	216
Canton	216
Chillicothe	614
Cincinnati	513
Cleveland	216
Columbus	614
Cuyahoga Falls	216
Dayton	513
East Cleveland	216
East Liverpool	216
Elyria	216
Euclid	216
Fairborn	513
Findlay	419
Garfield Heights	216
Hamilton	513
Kent	216
Kettering	513
Lakewood	216
Lancaster	614
Lima	419
Lorain	216
Mansfield	419
Maple Heights	216
Marion	614
Massillon	216
Mentor	216

OHIO
(Cont'd)

Middletown	513
Newark	614
North Olmsted	216
Norwood	513
Parma	216
Parma Heights	216
Portsmouth	614
Rocky River	216
Sandusky	419
Shaker Heights	216
South Euclid	216
Springfield	513
Steubenville	614
Toledo	419
Upper Arlington	614
Warren	216
Whitehall	614
Xenia	513
Youngstown	216
Zanesville	614

OKLAHOMA

Altus	405
Bartlesville	918
Bethany	405
Dill City	405
Enid	405
Lawton	405
Midwest City	405
Muskogee	918
Oklahoma City	405
Ponca City	405
Shawnee	405
Stillwater	405
Tulsa	918

OREGON

All points	503

PENNSYLVANIA

Allentown	215
Altoona	814
Beaver Falls	412
Bellefonte	814
Bethel Park	412
Bethlehem	215
Bloomsburg	717
Bradford	814

Place	Area Code	Place	Area Code	Place	Area Code
PENNSYLVANIA (Cont'd)		**TENNESSEE**		**TEXAS** (Cont'd)	
		Chattanooga	615		
		Clarksville	615	Paris	214
Chambersburg	717	Jackson	901	Pasadena	713
Chester	215	Johnson City	615	Port Arthur	713
Columbia	717	Kingsport	615	Richardson	214
DuBois	814	Knoxville	615	San Angelo	915
Easton	215	Memphis	901	San Antonio	512
Erie	814	Murfreesboro	615	Sherman	214
Greensburg	412	Nashville	615	Temple	817
Harrisburg	717	Oak Ridge	615	Texarkana	214
Hazelton	717			Texas City	713
Indiana	412	**TEXAS**		Tyler	214
Johnstown	814	Abilene	915	Victoria	512
Lancaster	717	Amarillo	806	Waco	817
Lebanon	717	Arlington	817	Wharton	713
Levittown	215	Austin	512	Wichita Falls	817
Lock Haven	717	Baytown	713		
McKeesport	412	Beaumont	713	**UTAH**	
Monroeville	412	Big Spring	915	All points	801
New Castle	412	Brownsville	512		
Norristown	215	Bryan	713	**VERMONT**	
Philadelphia	215	Corpus Christi	512	All points	802
Pittsburgh	412	Dallas	214		
Pottstown	215	Denison	214	**VIRGINIA**	
Reading	212	Denton	817	Alexandria	703
Scranton	717	El Paso	915	Annandale	703
Sharon	412	Farmers Branch	214	Arlington	703
State College	814	Fort Hood	817	Charlottesville	804
Stroudsburg	717	Fort Worth	817	Chesapeake	804
Sunbury	717	Galveston	713	Covington	703
Uniontown	814	Garland	214	Danville	804
Warren	814	Grand Prairie	214	Hampton	804
Washington	412	Harlingen	512	Hopewell	804
Wayne	215	Houston	713	Jefferson	804
West Chester	215	Hurst	817	Lynchburg	804
West Mifflin	412	Irving	214	Newport News	804
Wilkes Barre	717	Killeen	817	Norfolk	804
Wilkinsburg	412	Kingsville	512	Petersburg	804
Williamsport	717	Laredo	512	Portsmouth	804
York	717	Longview	214	Richmond	804
		Lubbock	806	Roanoke	703
RHODE ISLAND		Lufkin	713	Staunton	703
All points	401	Marshall	214	Virginia Beach	804
		McAllen	512	Woodbridge	703
SOUTH CAROLINA		Mesquite	214		
All points	803	Midland	915	**WASHINGTON**	
		Nacogdoches	713	Bellevue	206
SOUTH DAKOTA		Odessa	915	Bellingham	206
All points	605	Orange	713	Bremerton	206

Place	Area Code	Place	Area Code	Place	Area Code

WASHINGTON (Cont'd)

Edmonds	206
Everett	206
Fort Lewis	206
Longview	206
Olympia	206
Renton	206
Richland	509
Seattle	206
Spokane	509
Tacoma	206
Vancouver	206
Walla Walla	509
Yakima	509

WEST VIRGINIA

All points	304

WISCONSIN

Appleton	414
Beloit	608
Brookfield	414
Eau Claire	715
Fond Du Lac	414
Green Bay	414
Greenfield	414
Janesville	608
Kenosha	414
La Crosse	608
Madison	608
Manitowoc	414
Menomonee Falls	414
Milwaukee	414
Neenah	414
New Berlin	414
Oshkosh	414

WISCONSIN (Cont'd)

Racine	414
Sheboygan	414
South Milwaukee	414
Stevens Point	715
Superior	715
Waukesha	414
Wausau	715
Wauwatosa	414
West Allis	414

WYOMING

All points	307

WIDE AREA TELEPHONE SERVICE

All points	800

CANADIAN PROVINCES

ALBERTA

All points	403

BRITISH COLUMBIA

All points	604

MANITOBA

All points	204

NEW BRUNSWICK

All points	506

NEWFOUNDLAND

All points	709

NOVA SCOTIA

All points	902

ONTARIO

Fort William	807
London	519
North Bay	705
Ottawa	613
Toronto	416

PRINCE EDWARD ISLAND

All points	902

QUEBEC

Montreal	514
Quebec	418
Sherbrooke	819

SASKATCHEWAN

All points	306

MEXICO

Las Palomas	903
Mexicali	903
Mexico City	905
Tijuana	903

BERMUDA

All points	809

PUERTO RICO

All points	809

VIRGIN ISLANDS

All points	809